Confronting Memories of World War II

CONFRONTING MEMORIES OF WORLD WAR II

EUROPEAN AND ASIAN LEGACIES

*

Edited by

Daniel Chirot, Gi-Wook Shin, and Daniel Sneider

*

UNIVERSITY OF WASHINGTON PRESS

Seattle and London

© 2014 by the University of Washington Press
Printed and bound in the United States
Composed in Minion Pro, a typeface designed by Robert Slimbach
18 17 16 15 14   5 4 3 2 1

Publication of this book was made possible in part by subventions from the Walter H. Shorenstein Asia-Pacific Research Center at Stanford University, the Job and Gertrud Tamaki Professorship in International Studies at the University of Washington, and the Herbert J. Ellison Professorship of Russian and Eurasian Studies at the University of Washington.

All rights reserved. No part of this publication may be reproduced or transmitted in any form or by any means, electronic or mechanical, including photocopy, recording, or any information storage or retrieval system, without permission in writing from the publisher.

University of Washington Press
PO Box 50096, Seattle, WA 98145, USA
www.washington.edu/uwpress

Library of Congress Cataloging-in-Publication Data
Confronting memories of World War II : European and Asian legacies / edited by Daniel Chirot, Gi-Wook Shin, and Daniel Sneider.
    pages cm
Includes bibliographical references and index.
ISBN 978-0-295-99345-4 (hardback : alkaline paper) —
ISBN 978-0-295-99346-1 (paperback : alkaline paper)
1. World War, 1939–1945—Social aspects—Europe. 2. World War, 1939–1945—Social aspects—Asia. 3. World War, 1939–1945—Influence. 4. Collective memory—Europe. 5. Collective memory—Asia. 6. World War, 1939–1945—Psychological aspects. 7. Psychic trauma—Social aspects. 8. Reconciliation—Political aspects. 9. Europe—Politics and government—1945- 10. Asia—Politics and government—1945- I. Chirot, Daniel. II. Shin, Gi-Wook. III. Sneider, Daniel C.
D744.7.E8C66 2014
940.53'1—dc23   2013045010

The paper used in this publication is acid-free and meets the minimum requirements of American National Standard for Information Sciences—Permanence of Paper for Printed Library Materials, ANSI Z39.48-1984.∞

To Dong-gun Shin (1920–1994), Hélène Chirot (1920–2008),
and the millions of Asians and Europeans who lived through
the horrors of terrible wars but were fortunate enough to
survive and rebuild their lives

Contents

Acknowledgments
ix

Introduction
Daniel Chirot, Gi-Wook Shin, and Daniel Sneider
3

I. THE DEBATE OVER REMEMBRANCES OF WORLD WAR II

1. Admitting Guilt Is Neither Common Nor Easy: Comparing World War II Memories in Europe and East Asia   *Daniel Chirot*
13

2. Interrupted Memories: The Debate over Wartime Memory in Northeast Asia   *Daniel Sneider*
45

II. DIVIDED MEMORIES ABOUT COLLABORATION AND RESISTANCE

3. Different Strokes: Historical Realism and the Politics of History in Europe and Asia   *Thomas Berger*
79

4. Divided Memories of World War II in the Netherlands and the Dutch East Indies: Sukarno and Anne Frank as Icons of Dutch Historical Imagination   *Frances Gouda*
105

5. France and the Memory of Occupation   *Julian Jackson*
135

III. PATHS TO RECONCILIATION

6. Historical Reconciliation in Northeast Asia:
Past Efforts, Future Steps, and the U.S. Role   *Gi-Wook Shin*
157

7. Israelis and Germany after the
Second World War: Is Reconciliation Possible?
Can Universal Lessons Be Drawn?   *Fania Oz-Salzberger*
186

IV. THE PAST AS PRESENT AND THE PSYCHOLOGICAL RESPONSE TO DIFFERENT KINDS OF MEMORY

8. Historical Memories and International
Relations in Northeast Asia   *Gilbert Rozman*
211

9. Divisive Historical Memories:
Russia and Eastern Europe   *Igor Torbakov*
234

10. Guilt, Shame, Balts, Jews   *Roger Petersen*
258

Bibliography
283

Contributors
315

Index
318

Acknowledgments

A workshop of a small group of the best analysts of the contentious twentieth century in both Europe and East Asia was convened at Stanford University on June 16–17, 2011, to deepen the comparative scholarship of how historical memory of the wartime past has been formed and how that legacy continues to shape current history in both regions. Each panel focused on a key question and paired specialists from Asian and European studies to address that same question.

This book is based on papers presented at the conference as well as on the multiyear project of Stanford's Walter H. Shorenstein Asia-Pacific Research Center (APARC), "Divided Memories and Reconciliation." Divided Memories began as a comparative study of the formation of elite and popular historical consciousness of the Sino-Japanese War and Pacific War periods in China, Japan, Korea, Taiwan, and the United States, with the aim of promoting understanding and reconciliation. The project enjoyed the generous support of the Northeast Asia History Foundation in Korea and the United States–Japan Foundation. With the essays in this book, that project has expanded its reach into Europe to better understand the complexities of World War II memories, which, after all, have so deeply affected and continue to shape attitudes in much of the world.

We are grateful to the Shorenstein APARC for its support of the conference and the preparation of this book. We also appreciate comments and suggestions made by discussants at the conference: Roland Hsu, Chiho Sawada, Yumi Moon, Franziska Seraphim, and Yinan He. At Stanford, Debbie Warren provided valuable support in organizing the conference, and Joyce Lee greatly helped prepare this book for publication. At the University of Washington, Rebecca Dadlani's work was important, and both the Job and Gertrud Tamaki and Herbert J. Ellison Endowments also contributed to this project. We should also thank the excellent editors at the University of Washington Press, and the great work done by our copy editor, Jane Lichty.

Confronting Memories of World War II

Introduction

In 2013, hardly a day went by without some mention in many leading news media throughout the world of the dispute between China and Japan over a set of tiny islands variously called Senkaku by Japan, which owns them, and Diaoyu by China, which claims them. Typical is the story in the *New York Times* on February 28, 2013, that mentions not only the increasing tension between the two countries but also the fact that Japan's prime minister, Shinzo Abe, had supposedly compared the situation to the Falkland Islands dispute between Argentina, which called these Atlantic islands Malvinas, and their owner, the United Kingdom, in 1982.[1]

The year 1982 was when Argentina's vicious military dictators whipped up ultranationalist passions to cover up their incompetence and cruelty by making an issue over some trivial islands seven hundred kilometers from southern Argentina settled by British fishermen 150 years earlier. Argentina invaded, there was a short war, and hundreds of soldiers on both sides died. Argentina suffered a humiliating defeat, but, as a result, its military dictatorship collapsed.

There are some similarities in both cases but also alarming differences, because a war between China and Japan over a few uninhabited rocks in the Pacific could turn into a major disaster. In both cases, however, reawakened old histories brought up by regimes seeking to bolster their legitimacy, wounded pride about the past, and memories of colonial annexations by a formerly great power, now in reduced circumstances, played key roles. In East Asia in 2013, however, there is a more recent historical memory that has been brought into play—that is, World War II.

This East Asian confrontation, which has been heating up for several years, is all the more meaningful because it is hardly the only one to involve memories of past outrages, wounded honor, and national pride in this region. As several of the essays in our book point out, there is also an almost equally bitter dispute between South Korea and Japan over some islands in the sea between them and the meaning of Japanese imperialism in the first half of the twentieth century when it colonized Korea. These are the Dokdo (in Korean) or Takeshima (in Japanese) islands. Though strategically far less dangerous than the Chinese-Japanese conflict, the dispute between South Korea and Japan also brings up historical memories and nationalist outrage in both countries.

How could it be that history and memory play such an important role? Even if there are contemporary economic and strategic reasons for such territorial issues, all of them, including various Japanese claims to some northern islands now controlled by Russia and Chinese claims to a vast part of the South China Sea, could be negotiated peacefully but are far more serious because they have been linked to contested historical interpretations of late nineteenth- to mid-twentieth-century wars.

This situation is all the more surprising because in most (though not all) parts of Europe, as we shall see, memories of the great and hugely destructive wars of the twentieth century, and especially World War II when Germany occupied most of Europe, slaughtering millions and causing almost unfathomable ruin, are no longer highly contested. Nor are there any territorial issues between Germany and its neighbors, though there well could have been. Why is it that in Europe there is a widespread perception that "justice," however that may be defined, has been more or less done, and reconciliation between previously bitter enemies has been possible, while in East Asia, historical memories are reaching a critical point not really seen before? Why is it that in Asia angry memories have been reawakened so strongly, whereas in Europe the opposite would seem to be the case?

Such questions are relevant for many parts of the world, and the general issue of how history is interpreted, how it is used and manipulated, and how nationalist versions can play a very emotional role is a huge one.

In this book we will look at these kinds of controversies as they pertain to what was the bloodiest war in history, at least in terms of absolute numbers of deaths, World War II. We will explain why there is such a perceived contrast between European and Asian memories, but also why close attention to detail shows that the contrast is not quite as great as superficial generalizations would suggest.

The Pacific part of the war is sometimes said to have begun as early as 1931, when Japan conquered Manchuria, and if not then, in 1937 when it invaded the rest of China, but Japan's imperial expansion and seizure of territories began well before then, in the Sino-Japanese War of 1894–95 and the subjugation of Korea in 1905. These come up in the revived historical memories and bitterness that now afflict the region. In Europe, World War

II began in 1939, but if there were anything like the anger China and Korea direct at Japan, there is no doubt that some Western European nationalists, particularly the French, would be associating this terrible war with German aggression in 1914 and even Prussia's invasion of France in 1870.

Yet, even as China makes claims against Japan based on Japan's past aggression, and both South Korea and China demand further Japanese apologies, it seems completely impossible that there could be any territorial dispute between France and Germany today. While memories of World War II continue to produce countless histories, films, personal accounts, and works of fiction even as the last survivors are quickly dying of old age, nasty conflicts over what actually happened, who was responsible, and what should now be done occur only rarely and do not get connected to major issues of international relations. Germany is not making any claims to regain the substantial territories it lost as result of its twentieth-century wars, and none of its neighbors have claims against it. In fact, in Europe it is only in the Balkans and the former Soviet Union that there are boundary issues tied to historical memories, and these have little to do with Germany's role in history. Why, then, do such matters come up in East Asia, with Japan as a focus for anger and recrimination?

There are some pat explanations. Germany—at least West Germany (but not Communist East Germany, which existed from 1949 to 1990)—apologized for Nazi crimes. Japan never really made such an admission, or so it is widely believed. Upon closer examination, this turns out to be a vast simplification and leaves out the fact that the Germans could never have killed so many, and especially could not have carried out the genocide of Jews, if it had not been helped by collaborators all over the territories it occupied or with which it was allied during World War II. It also neglects the fact that Japanese leaders have apologized, as both Gi-Wook Shin's and Daniel Sneider's essays in this book show. But somehow, it is felt, with good reason, as these two essays and Thomas Berger's demonstrate, that Japan's apologies have not been considered to be heartfelt.

Another obvious complication in the nice, simple story about a deeply remorseful Germany and an arrogant, unrepentant Japan is that Germany's change of heart was hardly immediate, and as both Daniel Chirot's and Julian Jackson's chapters explain, it was not matched for a long time by any repentance on the part of those who collaborated with the Germans, including very notably the French state, which took a half century to come to grips with how its officials worked with the Germans and barely resisted occupation from 1940 to 1943, when, belatedly, resistance grew as it became ever more apparent that Germany was going to lose the war. Nor, as Berger rather acidly highlights, has Austria, willingly and (mostly) happily annexed by Nazi Germany in 1938, been willing to face up to its people's role in Nazi crimes. In light of this, Japanese reactions begin to seem normal, and Germany's unusual. So why did Germany undergo a moral transformation, while Japan on the whole did not, even if the notion of a solidly right-wing, unrepentant Japan is itself significantly exaggerated?

The situation becomes even more complicated once we begin to look at the diversity of occupation stories and legacies of colonialism. Frances Gouda's essay about the Netherlands is eye-opening. The death rate among Dutch Jews was on par with the rate of those murdered in some of the worst-hit parts of Eastern Europe and considerably higher than in France. The Netherlands had a young Jewish girl who became the symbol of the Holocaust, Anne Frank, whose memory has become perhaps the best-known story of all those terrible years because of her almost unbelievably sensitive and tragic diary, but the country as a whole was somewhat reluctant to recognize that too many of its people acquiesced to what was going on during Nazi rule. Also, the Dutch never fully made the connection between the way they were occupied and the cruelty they had imposed on their colony in the East Indies, today's Indonesia. This continued in the nasty war they pursued after World War II when they tried to reconquer that lucrative territory following its three-year period of Japanese occupation. As the Dutch see it, the Germans were bad, and the Dutch were good, so when they fought their colonial war from 1945 to 1949 to block Indonesian independence, they interpreted Indonesian nationalists as nothing more than Fascist, that is, Japanese collaborators who had turned Communist.

Eastern Europe presents another kind of problem. As explained in Daniel Chirot's, Igor Torbakov's, and Roger Petersen's chapters, Communist rule imposed by Soviet armies and Joseph Stalin's regime after 1945 denied much of what had happened, particularly the disproportionate suffering of the Jews. The overwhelming majority of European Jews who died in the Holocaust lived in these regions, and the Communist regimes that followed the war effectively whitewashed their own people's anti-Semitism and collaboration with the Nazis. Yet, not only did much of East and Central Europe suffer immensely from German occupation, but it continued afterward to be oppressed by the Soviets, who imprisoned, exiled, and killed many, so that today, memories of the long decades of Communist rule overshadow the shorter and more distant time of German domination.

As for the Soviet Union, its dissolution in 1991 following the collapse of Communism in East-Central Europe in 1989 has led to another kind of memory and bitterness. Russians today, as Torbakov shows, are still justifiably proud of the role they played in defeating Adolf Hitler during World War II and angrily denounce former Communist lands where Soviet domination is equated with Nazi rule, or even considered worse. Petersen's essay, which uses Lithuania as an instructive example of different levels of shame or guilt over past histories makes it clear that for most Lithuanians what happened to them when they were forcibly annexed to the Soviet Union until 1991 was worse than what had happened to their Jews during World War II. This is not so much a question of what is commonly called "Holocaust denial" as it is of saying that for today's Lithuanians, Jews were "others" who are no longer present, and trying to shame Lithuania into making amends for the collaboration of some Lithuanians in this Holocaust is not likely to resonate very widely with their population.

What about the Jews themselves? In what may be the most astonishing of all accounts in this book, Fania Oz-Salzberger shows that on the whole young Israelis no longer resent Germany and even find it to be one of the most congenial of European countries. How could this be when so many Israelis are among either the diminishing number of aged survivors of the Holocaust or the far more numerous descendants of such people? Not only that, but as any visitor to Israel who has been to its spectacular Yad Vashem genocide museum and research center knows, memories of the Holocaust, or Shoah as it called in Hebrew, are absolutely central to the historical vision that Israel has of itself. In the various crises it has had, and continues to have with some of its neighbors, the memory of this tragedy is emphasized, and Israel's citizens are reminded, as if they needed to be, that Jews remain endangered by genocidal anti-Semitism. But Germany is no longer the main target of these worries.

Even in this complex case, however, reality is not quite so simple. Oz-Salzberger's essay shows that until 1960, the Holocaust itself was somewhat downplayed in Israel, partly because there remained a lingering suspicion that if Europe's Jews had been like prewar Zionist settlers to Palestine, they would have fought back much harder. Only with the Adolf Eichmann trial in 1961 did Israeli opinion come to grips with the full nature of what had happened under Nazi occupation.

So, with such diversity of reactions, with so complex a mixture of admission and evasion of the horrors of World War II in Europe itself, of colonialism's cruelties, and of various kinds of criminality and collaboration, the nature of historical controversies over Japan's failure to fully address its past no longer seems so unique. But knowing this does not explain why today the issue has become so contentious, almost seventy years after the end of World War II.

Certainly, this is partly Japan's fault. In December 2012, Japan elected Shinzo Abe as its prime minister. He has had a long history of sympathizing with Japan's right-wing nationalists who deny any guilt for what Japan did during World War II or its period of colonial rule in parts of East Asia. These nationalists adamantly oppose any expression of apology. Instead, they claim that Japan fought to liberate Asia from European colonial rule, that it was provoked into war by the United States, that it committed no crimes, and that it was victimized by criminal American fire bombings of Japanese cities and the use of nuclear weapons in 1945. Shin, Sneider, and Berger all cover the complicated and actually varied Japanese opinions about their country's role in World War II, and they cite some of the work they have done in other volumes on this subject.

Japanese and German schoolbooks' interpretations of World War II are a particularly sensitive matter. Shin and Sneider have published a book on this topic.[2] So have other scholars. They all agree that the most heated controversies have been over Japanese school history books. Do they or do they not cover the subject fairly, the way German schoolbooks are generally deemed to do? A recent comparative book by Julian Dierkes broadly agrees with the arguments made in our book. After the war, there was a lively debate in Japan about the war and Japan's guilt and how to teach it, but over time, this discussion has so diminished that today few Japanese are fully aware of Japanese cruelty and responsibility. The opposite holds for Germany, where at first the Nazi period was barely covered in schoolbooks, but over time, it came to be done much more thoroughly, so that in recent decades Germans have been very well educated about the nature of Nazi crimes and Germany's responsibility.[3]

A British Broadcasting Company (BBC) piece by Mariko Oi in 2013 highlights the complaints that China and Korea have about Japanese interpretations of the war and the way it is taught in schools. It is not so much a matter of denial as of neglect and failure to cover what happened. At the same time, right-wing nationalist politicians and leaders, including Prime

Minister Abe, are even now talking about taking back the limited apologies made in the past such as the Kono Statement of 1993.⁴

We should be perfectly clear. The possibility that a German chancellor, or Austrian president, or the leader of any state that was allied or collaborated with Germany during World War II would take a position like Abe's over the meaning of World War II is completely unthinkable. On the other hand, in all fairness, it has to be said that Russia's president, Vladimir Putin, and his political allies, including the highly nationalist Russian Orthodox Church, have made former tyrant Joseph Stalin once more a nationalist hero.⁵

But despite Japan's culpability, or that of many of its conservatives who have whitewashed Japan's imperial and aggressive record, is this really the cause of the growing conflict over some East Asian islands? Some would say that it is, but the chapters of this book raise doubts by showing that, first of all, these kinds of historical controversies have not been constant and in this particular case have only heated up relatively recently. Second, the pessimistic but convincing chapter by Gilbert Rozman puts the entire matter in a very different light. His contention is that Chinese official historians since about 1990 have been systematically rewriting Asian and even world history to legitimize growing Chinese big power claims. As he shows, in topics ranging from the ancient kingdom of Koguryo, claimed by the Koreans as one of their ancestral realms but now said by Chinese historians to have been Chinese, to claims that China's domination over East Asia was always peaceful and benign unlike European and Japanese imperialism, to interpretations of World War II, and to contemporary international issues, China is portrayed in such a way as to suggest that the world will be a better place when China becomes the leading, kindly power. This assertion is hardly better than Japan's claims that its empire was only meant to free Asia from European rule or Hitler's claim that Germany was defending European civilization against an Asian (by which he meant Russian-Jewish) menace. Rozman suggests that we ought to be more alarmed by China's assertions than by Japanese excuses for what they did during World War II. If many Japanese are guilty of not confronting the enormity of their aggression and crimes in the past, it is most unlikely that Japan will ever again invade its neighbors or that it will be in a position to do so. But China?

In conclusion, then, this volume does not mean to suggest that history is inevitable fate and that past aggression, if not followed by profuse apologies, necessarily leads to new conflicts. After all, what nation has a completely clean past? What it does suggest, however, is that honest appraisal of the past rather than nationalist distortion can help reconciliation. There will always be some controversies about what happened in the past, but there are also realities that cannot be negated. Germany did start World War II and commit monstrous crimes. Japan was an aggressive and cruel imperial power. So recognition of these facts, and teaching reality to students, is a necessary first step toward creating a more peaceful environment. This hardly means that in the United States there should not be an examination of the moral and ethical difficulties of deciding to incinerate enemy civilians as part of a war effort or that France should go back to ignoring its official complicity in rounding up Jews to deliver to the Germans while occupied by Germany. All honest examination of the past leads to better understanding.

At the same time, we should be aware of the fact that systematic distortion of history that privileges nationalist narratives and belittles others, be they domestic minorities or external nations, is dangerous. Exactly such mythologized narratives predominated in Europe from the nineteenth century well into the twentieth. They were official dogma in Japan during its period of imperial expansion. They have existed everywhere, and their presence has often prefigured aggressive wars.

Just because Japan was guilty of atrocities during World War II hardly justifies ultranationalist historical distortion by China today, and the spread of such ideas is not a reassuring sign. Nor can such stories simply be passed off as harmless exaggerations in any nation.

With this volume, we hope we have contributed to some important clarifications about crucial historical issues and in at least a small way helped to show that unbiased, balanced scholarship can be a force for better understanding, greater tolerance, and some measure of reconciliation.

1 Buckley, "China Accuses Japan of Escalating Tensions."
2 Shin and Sneider, eds., *History Textbooks and the Wars in Asia*.
3 Dierkes, *Postwar History Education*.
4 Oi, "What Japanese History Lessons Leave Out."
5 Gutterman, "Dead Sixty Years, Stalin's Influence Lingers."

PART 1

THE DEBATE OVER REMEMBRANCES OF WORLD WAR II

Chapter 1

Admitting Guilt Is Neither Common Nor Easy

*Comparing World War II Memories in
Europe and East Asia*

DANIEL CHIROT

If we are to discuss remembrances, expressions of guilt, and the possibilities of reconciliation for past wartime and colonial wrongs, we need to cast a wide net, because there are few if any states and nations so free of wrongdoing that they are entitled to propose for themselves perfectly pure appraisals of their histories. Good-faith efforts to obtain as honest as possible a perspective on history not only allows us to better understand important degrees of difference between past wars and occupations but also encourages greater openness among even those who have a greater burden of guilt to bear. Naturally, recovering the meaning of the past is no easy task, and even the most honest appraisals will not settle all conflicts that originated in prior invasions and conflicts; but doing so in as true a way as possible is a good start in that direction. Sometimes, grand historical narratives are the key to better understanding, but at the same time looking at relatively small, more personally affecting examples of the moral complexities of past conflicts may also allow us to better understand how difficult it can really be to make honest appraisals. Take, for example, the following story.

On December 9, 2011, exactly sixty-four years after Dutch troops had shot 430 boys and men in an Indonesian village during that country's war of independence against Dutch colonial rule (1945–49), "the Dutch Ambassador, Tjeerd de Zwaan, made [an] apology before hundreds of villagers in Rawagede." Dutch troops had come to the village looking for a resistance leader and "when the villagers said they did not know where he was, the soldiers rounded up nearly all the men and took them to a field, where, squatting in rows with both hands placed on the backs of their heads, they were shot one by one." The apology, however, came only after a Dutch court had declared in September 2011 that the Dutch state was responsible for the massacre.[1]

Frances Gouda's chapter in this volume eloquently explains the contradictions in Dutch memories of World War II. The virtual canonization of Anne Frank was accompanied for a long time by an unwillingness to face up to the fact that a good many Dutch had collaborated with the German occupiers during World War II and the even greater reluctance to admit to the wrongness of the Dutch government's attempt to regain control of its Indonesian (the former Dutch East Indies) colony after it was liberated from Japanese occupation in 1945. To this day, as Gouda points out, Sukarno and most of his leading associates are still portrayed as fascist collaborators because they willingly cooperated with the Japanese occupiers in the hopes of obtaining independence from the Netherlands.

Telling this story is not to claim that the atrocities perpetrated by the Dutch in their last colonial war approached the scale of the genocidal behavior of the Germans during World War II or even the enslavement and slaughter of millions by the Japanese in East and Southeast Asia during the wars they conducted from 1931 to 1945, but of course, for the village of Rawagede, the events of December 9, 1947, and for other Indonesians victims of this war, the results were terrible enough.

This *New York Times* story reminded me of something far more personal. I was born in a French village called Bélâbre in November 1942 in a house on the corner of avenue Jean Jaurès and a little side street now named rue du 10 Juillet 1944. Jean Jaurès (1859–1914) was the great French socialist leader murdered at the start of World War I by a nationalist extremist who (quite wrongly) thought that the French socialist party might try to block France's entry into the war against Germany, and the village of Bélâbre happened to be a mostly socialist village that honored his memory. As for the other street, what happened on July 10, 1944?

During World War II, Vichy France was theoretically independent but actually subservient to Germany, and what little formal autonomy it had after France surrendered to Germany in 1940 was badly eroded when German troops occupied it directly in November 1942 and prompted my father, uncles, and grandfather to flee two weeks before my birth, leaving my grandmother and very pregnant mother in the village. Julian Jackson's chapter and many of his well-known books discuss the longtime unwillingness of the French to face up to how much of the French establishment and population collaborated quite willingly with the German occupiers and made their rounding up of Jews possible. Socialist Bélâbre, however, was mostly unsympathetic to the Vichy regime, and the mayor of its roughly fifteen hundred people during the war, a man named Anatole Ferrant (1886–1972), helped the resistance. He also protected my grandmother, my mother, and me by providing false papers and ration coupons and making sure we were warned whenever local *milices* (right-wing militias) or police might come through the village looking for Jews or anti-German resisters, particularly as the resistance movement increased in 1943 and more effectively in early 1944. (From 1948 to 1955, Ferrant was an elected senator in the national parliament, largely in recognition of his war service, because the region as a whole generally voted for more conservative candidates.)

On July 10, 1944, the village was being occupied by parts of the German SS division "Das Reich" that had one month earlier committed the atrocity of Oradour, a village to our south, where 642 inhabitants, including women and children, had been put in the village church and then burned to death. By July, the Germans were in full retreat from this part of France to escape being trapped by the Allied advance that was threatening to break out from Normandy. A battle broke out between the Germans and some resistance fighters near Bélâbre, which the heavily armed Germans easily won on that day, and afterward they immediately executed forty-six prisoners, telling the villagers to bury them. The men in the village, including boys as young as fourteen, were lined up on the village square in front of the church and threatened with execution. Ultimately, the village was spared, though the Germans committed a substantial number of murders, including of civilians, in surrounding villages and towns as they continued to retreat. In Maillé, to the north of my village, for example, they slaughtered 124 inhabitants, mostly women and children, in August.[2] Why Bélâbre was spared this fate I do not know. The SS Das Reich division had earlier served on the eastern front, where they had committed far more atrocities. As they left Bélâbre, elements of the division were strafed and bombed by the British Royal Air Force, and many were killed. The villagers went out and pillaged what was left, and my mother made a little shirt for me out of German parachute silk, which turned out to be a very durable kind of cloth.

What the Germans did in France was relatively mild compared to the far, far more extensive killing they conducted in what Timothy Snyder aptly labeled in his book with that title, the "bloodlands" of Eastern Europe and the western Soviet Union, not only in the death camps they operated in those regions but in the massacres of millions of civilians and prisoners of war and of course vast numbers of Jews who were killed on the spot, as in Babi Yar, Ukraine, without ever being shipped off to camps or even herded into ghettos, where hundreds of thousands more died of starvation and disease. Cases such as Oradour or Maillé were relatively rare in France. But again, for those French villagers killed, it hardly mattered that their country as a whole received a "gentler" treatment than did Poland, Belorussia, or Ukraine.[3]

Here we get to a moral as well as what some would see as a kind of a legal, definitional problem. What happened in my village of Bélâbre and the region as a whole, or for that matter in the Indonesian village of Rawagede, is extremely common in war. Wars have never been, and are not now, fought in nice, orderly ways in which only uniformed combatants line up in neat ranks to kill each other, and after a while, one side decides it has been beaten and surrenders. Civilians always get killed, whether on purpose or as what is now called "collateral damage."

When an enemy army occupies territory inhabited by populations that do not want to be occupied, some sort of resistance is likely, and if that is conducted by irregular forces, they will be viewed as "terrorists" or in some sense illegal combatants by the occupying army. If these irregular or guerrilla forces are largely inferior in armaments, they will conduct asymmetrical warfare and hide among, or at least be supported by, local civilians. This will lead to reprisals, torture, and the killing of innocents in order to elicit information about the guerrillas and to choke off their sources of supply. Furthermore, some locals will collaborate with the occupiers and be targeted for retribution by the resisters. Colonial wars have almost all been fought in this way as stronger powers tried to conquer and control weaker ones but met stiff guerrilla resistance.

The United States, for example, conducted exactly this kind of warfare aimed at civilians in order to subdue the Philippines from 1899 to 1902. The U.S. commander, General Franklin Bell, used widespread terror and intimidation of the local population. He wrote that "to combat such a population it is necessary to make a state of war as insupportable as possible ... by keeping the minds of the people in such a state of anxiety and apprehension that living under such conditions will soon become unbearable." Men, women, and children were slaughtered in large numbers along with captured prisoners. Between one hundred thousand and two hundred thousand were killed.[4] An excellent recent history of genocides lists many other examples of this kind of ruthless, sometimes even genocidal, campaign conducted by colonial powers from the Roman Empire to the more recent Europeans colonies in Africa, the Americas, and Australia.[5]

In the wars in which Americans were involved after World War II in Korea and Vietnam large numbers of noncombatants were also killed. In both cases Communist and anti-Communist forces, local or American, were often ruthless, though of course each side emphasized the killings perpetrated by the other side while underplaying their own actions. The Indonesian war of independence against the Dutch was hardly unique, and it would take far too long to try to catalog recent similar examples from France's Algerian war to India's suppression of dissent in Kashmir to Russia's Chechen war.

It is not just that resistors in occupied territories are part of the local population, but in any war supplies are critically important to maintain a fighting force, so even if there is no guerrilla war, both sides will try to deprive each other of resources while attempting to paralyze civilian production and resistance, which inevitably means that some civilians will be targeted. Whether this involves aerial bombing or large-scale burning and destruction of rear areas as in General William Tecumseh Sherman's march through the Confederate South during the American Civil War, the results are neither neat nor pretty. American Southerners long held a grudge against Sherman, and of course the Japanese can point to the massive destruction of their cities, up to and most dramatically including the dropping of the atomic bombs on Hiroshima and Nagasaki, to justify their claim that they were victims of a cruel and vindictive United States.

So why should apologies be offered for what is, after all is said and done, just common warfare practiced by all warring states? That is a question that can be and is often asked by those of whom apologies are demanded. A major example is the case, supported by overwhelming evidence, that the Ottoman Empire conducted a genocide against Armenians in 1915. But the Turkish government to this day continues to say that the killings were part of a war between Armenian nationalists and the Turkish Ottoman authorities, that both sides suffered great casualties, and that therefore, regrettable as this loss may be, there is no reason for the Turks to be apologetic. Needless to say, Armenians furiously reject this argument and say that what happened was criminal genocide, pure and simple.[6]

Broaching the question of genocide, we begin to see some of what needs to be answered when questions of guilt, apology, and perhaps reconciliation are raised. Here, we need to simplify the dubiously complex ways in which genocide has been interpreted by the United Nations (UN) and the major powers since a genocide convention was introduced as part of international law in 1948 (though the United States only ratified its participation in the convention in 1988 under President Ronald Reagan). Genocide is the deliberate attempt to exterminate any group of people identified by religion, ethnicity, nationality, region inhabited, economic class, or political ideology. (Class and ideology were deliberately excluded from the original 1948 convention because Joseph Stalin's Soviet Union did not want them included, as it had murdered millions on those grounds.) Properly defined, genocide implies that all those in this group—men, women, children, noncombatants, those who resist as well as those who do not—should be eliminated. It goes beyond just defeating an identified enemy, but implies wiping out a whole designated group of people.[7]

We will see below that Germany's recognition that what it did went beyond ordinary war crimes and was genocidal made it both easier and more necessary for Germans to face what had happened, though that took some time after 1945. The Jews hunted down by the Nazis were almost all powerless noncombatants (though eventually, in the East, there was some resistance). Indeed, it was for this reason that the term and notion of *genocide* was first applied, though it was recognized from the start that in retrospect the Armenian case was also genocide.[8]

Unfortunately, in the very large majority of cases where apologies are called for, it is not so simple. If the killing of men captured fighting the Germans near Bélâbre on July 10, 1944, was at most a war crime (prisoners of war are not supposed to be executed), what about the killing of women and children in Oradour? That was not genocide in the sense that the Germans were not intent on exterminating all the French, but in that village they did. And what about the Dutch case in Indonesia when only noncombatant males, including some young boys, were targeted? That was a war crime, and though it came sixty-four years late, the Dutch government was surely right to apologize. But should all colonial powers now apologize to those they colonized by force? Do they owe reparations?

The question can be asked as well of those who fought against outside forces. Should the Vietnamese Communist Party apologize for the massacres it conducted during its war against the Americans and the South Vietnamese government, most notably but certainly not only in Hué, where thousands of civilians, many of them uninvolved with either side, were brutally slaughtered in 1968?[9] Much depends on a different question, one that no legal code or carefully wrought definition of what is right and what is wrong in warfare can ever clarify. Was a particular war morally justified? There is a rich and ancient literature on this question as well, but it comes down to passing judgment on the motives and means with which various parties conduct wars.

Now we enter into the realm of national pride and historical memory, something ably discussed in many of the chapters in this volume, particularly those by Roger Petersen and Igor Torbakov. At the time Western powers conquered their colonies, especially when the liberal governments of France and England extended their empires in the nineteenth century, they typically felt morally justified in their actions because they claimed to be more civilized and acting in the long-term interests of those they were subjugating.[10] The Turkish government claimed that it was justified in what it did to the Armenians because that action was necessary to save the Turkish Muslim population from being destroyed.[11] The government of the United States justified, and still justifies, the use of atomic bombs by saying that they shortened the war and saved countless American and even more Japanese lives.[12] Formerly colonized people, Armenians, and most Japanese do not buy these arguments. Lithuanians, as Petersen's chapter argues, view Soviet brutality against their people as worse than what Adolf Hitler's Germans did to them, but Russians, as Torbakov points out, deeply resent having Soviet Russia's actions equated with Nazi Germany's or, even more, as something worse.

In order to begin to explain why Germany, or at least West Germany, so profoundly apologized for its World War II actions while Japan's official apologies have seemed halfhearted, we need to keep in mind the complexities of each country's changing political contexts. As Daniel Sneider's, Gi-Wook Shin's, and Thomas Berger's chapters demonstrate, it is not that all Japanese refuse to acknowledge what they did during their war, or even that there have been no official apologies, but that many, probably most, Japanese do not really see their country as having been that much more wrong than other powers. On the other hand, most Koreans and Chinese feel that they were terribly wronged by a particularly vicious Japan.

The other side of this comparison is that while Germany's full admission that it was morally and legally culpable of genocide opened the way for reconciliation in Europe, it also allowed the rest of Europe to evade for a long time, and in many cases to this day, responsibility in sustaining German crimes by providing large numbers of collaborators and allies, while in East Asia China and Korea have not had to face their own record of partial collaboration.

THE HISTORICAL CONTEXT: GERMANY AND EUROPE COMPARED TO JAPAN AND ASIA

A few years ago Germany introduced a new schoolbook about the Holocaust for thirteen- and fourteen-year-olds. It is a "comic" (or better, a graphic) book, that is, a series of illustrations in which the characters speak in "bubbles." The topic is hardly comic, as it features the life of a German Jewish girl saved from death when a kindly policeman intercepts her as she is about to return from school. He tells her that her parents have been arrested and that she should flee. She never sees her parents again and survives Nazism to tell her grandchildren what happened. This book is meant to encourage children to identify with the complexities of moral choice and personal responsibility when faced by the nightmarish regime that ruled their country from 1933 to 1945.[13] It is hard to imagine a Japanese school assigning a book that would be so emotionally troubling to children of that age or one that would call for so much open discussion about a terrible episode in their country's history.

It is not that there are no Japanese eager to face their brutal World War II record, particularly among those on the left and in the Japanese Teachers Union. Yet it is still possible for right-wing nationalist Japanese, including members of its parliament, to force the banning of a film about the Yasukuni Shrine, which commemorates Japanese war dead, including some from World War II who were convicted of war crimes. Right-wing threats can also force the cancellation of a Teachers Union's meeting by a hotel where it was scheduled to take place.[14] On February 22, 2012, Takashi Kawamure, mayor of Nagoya, the "sister" Japanese city of Nanjing, where a horrible massacre of hundreds of thousands of Chinese civilians by the Japanese army had occurred in late 1937, told a visiting delegation from Nanjing that he doubted any such event had taken place. Nanjing promptly broke off its "sister" relations with Nagoya.[15] Clearly, if there were no tolerance for this kind of attitude, and for the sometime intimidation by Japan's leaders and by public opinion of those who do recognize Japan's murderous behavior during the war, it would not occur. Germany also has right-wing extremists, but they are considered marginal, and such kinds of publicly repressive occurrences are completely unthinkable in today's Germany. The idea that a German mayor of a leading city could somehow deny the Holocaust, and not be immediately forced to resign, is inconceivable.

To be sure, in Italy defending Benito Mussolini is not all that unusual on the far right, and when former prime minister Silvio Berlusconi did it in a speech supposed to commemorate the Holocaust on January 27, 2013, it was not the first time. On the other hand, Berlusconi quickly apologized and said that he had been misunderstood, whereas when Japanese prime minister Shinzo Abe has publicly sided with right-wing ultranationalists who want to glorify Japan's wartime behavior and reject "apology diplomacy," he has not felt the need to soft-pedal his views. How far Abe will be able to push his right-wing nationalism remains a question, but the mere fact that it has not damaged his popularity or caused him to publicly backtrack is telling.[16]

It is well known that in the case of Germany, the Holocaust has been widely taught in schools for a long time and that the public airing of films and television shows over at least the past three to four decades has deeply marked German thinking. The introduction of more personal, child-oriented graphic textbooks is meant to make children think yet more deeply about how they would react, not to soften or evade German guilt, though it does show that at least some Germans during wartime did not approve of what was being done to Jews, even if there were not enough of them willing to act to have any effect on their government's policies. West Germans eventually recognized their guilt after World War II, promised to never repeat such crimes, taught their children about the horrors of the Holocaust, and made heroes of those few Germans who resisted Hitler. Germans have therefore been largely accepted as reformed, good Europeans. This fact is reflected in (the now unified) Germany's schoolbooks that downplay nationalism in favor of appreciation of a "more globalized and diversified world."[17] Germany's attitude has contributed greatly to European unity, and this relationship is unlikely to change very much despite the reawakening of some anti-German sentiments during the euro fiscal crisis of the 2010s.

Japan, on the other hand, has generally been evasive about its brutality and is now still being accused by the countries it victimized, particularly Korea and, most stridently, China.[18] It is not that Japanese schoolbooks tell lies but rather that the subject of the war has not been strongly taught, and this shortcoming has produced a public that generally denies Japan's guilt.[19] Such a position makes it possible for many Japanese, probably a substantial majority, to believe that the war their country conducted was a noble effort to free Asia of European colonialism and that in the end they were victimized rather than having been the victimizers. South Korea, China, Japan, and Southeast Asia may be increasingly economically interdependent, but in some ways the acrimony over war memories seems to be undiminished.

While some Germans have sought to portray themselves as victims rather than perpetrators of the war, or as defenders of European Civilization against "Asian" (by which they really mean Russian!) barbarism, this view has not gained wide acceptance in Germany. This issue was fought out in a very public way in what was called the "historians' conflict" (*Historikerstreit*) in the 1980s.[20] In the end there has been no revival of any major effort to exonerate the Nazis, least of all at the elite level. Even the racist skinheads who sometimes use Nazi symbols are no more than marginalized, angry, anti-immigrant, lower-class youths with virtually no major political or intellectual support.[21]

As Fania Oz-Salzberger's chapter in this volume points out, perhaps even more astonishing is that ultimately in Israel there has been an acceptance of German repentance. Today, Israel's historical self-image is strongly connected to the Holocaust, as exemplified by the spectacular museum of Yad Vashem in Jerusalem, but young Israelis seem to no longer bear a grudge against Germans as a people.

The situation is not, however, as clear-cut as it would seem to be. The widely read and cited comparative book on the subject, Ian Buruma's *The Wages of Guilt*, is much too sophisticated and subtle to fall into the trap of presenting so simpleminded a contrast.[22] It shows how complicated a story both German and Japanese postwar behavior and attitudes really have been and how, in both cases, they have hardly remained frozen. There have been many strands of opinion in both cases, and some attitudes have changed over time. Furthermore, once the entire story of World War II in Europe is examined, the problem becomes far more complex, and far less dichotomized, because in Europe, too, it has taken many decades for reality to be faced, and that process is far from complete to this day.

Looking in more detail at German memories of the war as a single trajectory toward repentance and admission of wrongdoing runs into several problems. The first of these is that the German story is very much embedded in all of Europe's interpretation of what happened. For a long time, until some ten to twenty years ago, depending on which European country we are talking about, this was the most troubling aspect of how the world war was remembered. The countries occupied by Germany in Western Europe, without exception, constructed stories that blamed everything bad on Germans and a fairly small number of virtually criminal and deviant collaborators. It was more complicated in Central Europe and the Balkans, where the Germans had various allied states (Hungary, Croatia, Slovakia, Romania, Bulgaria, along with Italy, which occupied parts of the Balkans) and also deliberately exacerbated ethnic tensions in mixed areas, but there, also, similar stories were put forward. Where the Soviet Union set up Communist regimes in the East after the war, not only Nazi Germany but also the local "reactionary bourgeoisie" and upper classes were blamed. In all cases, however, the guilty were said to be either outsiders or a relatively small number of treacherous locals who were quickly disposed of after the war. There was therefore no perceived need for any general national self-examination, much less repentance for wrongdoing, in either Western or Eastern Europe, except among Germans.

This story, that the Germans and small numbers of domestic collaborators were the only ones responsible, is mostly a postwar fabrication. It neglects not only that there were in fact many violent, large-scale reprisals after the war against those suspected of collaborating with Germans but also that in many cases once that was settled, the much larger number of collaborators and fascist sympathizers who survived faded into the background and how much help the Germans really had received was forgotten.[23]

The most important country occupied by the Germans in Western Europe was France. France abjectly surrendered in 1940 when it could have continued to fight from its protected colonial holdings in North Africa. Then, the collaborationist, pro-German Vichy government of Marshal Philippe Pétain was both popular and almost wholly supported by the French civil service, police, and military, as Jackson's chapter in this volume shows. The now famous speech transmitted from London via the BBC by General Charles de Gaulle after the French surrender in 1940, urging France to fight on, was heard by almost no one at the time, and only tiny numbers of French officials, either from France itself or from the unoccupied colonies spread throughout the world, rallied to his cause. The only important colonial governor to join de Gaulle's Free French movement was also the only black Caribbean French high civil servant, Félix Éboué, governor of Chad, whose dislike of racist ideologies convinced him to abandon Vichy. The only two generals to join de Gaulle from the colonial forces were immediately pushed out of their positions.[24] De Gaulle himself was at the time a fairly obscure brigadier general who had been quickly brought into the last wartime cabinet as a junior minister because he seemed to be the sole French high officer to understand the importance of tank warfare. Today, his BBC speech of 1940 is widely memorialized as the start of a resistance movement, but in fact there was no resistance until a year later when the French Communists turned against Germany at the time Hitler broke his treaty with Stalin and invaded the Soviet Union in June 1941. Even then, the resistance did not gain much strength until 1943, when, after German defeats in North Africa and at Stalingrad and after the United States began to actively fight in North Africa and then Italy, it became evident that Germany was going to lose the war. In fact, after France's surrender in 1940, French industrial production, largely for the benefit of the German war effort, actually increased.[25]

The situation varied from country to country, but generally local authorities and elites worked with Germans quite cooperatively except in cases such as Poland and the Soviet Union, where the population was automatically condemned to eventual enslavement by Nazi racial policies and where officials, intellectuals, and potential leaders were specifically targeted for annihilation.[26] Germany never had enough soldiers or police in most of the countries it occupied to effectively control them alone. Most occupied European countries, and even supposedly neutral Spain, contributed volunteer soldiers to fight with the Germans on the eastern front against the Soviets.[27] On top of this, Germany's allies—Italy, Finland (which did not participate in the Holocaust and was involved only because it had earlier been invaded by the Soviet Union), Hungary, Romania, Bulgaria, and the puppet states of Croatia and Slovakia—were mostly cooperative, and only Croatia (as part of the larger Yugoslav Communist forces) produced an early resistance of any sort. Though the Communists throughout Eastern and Central Europe later publicized stories of partisan resistance to pro-German governments, most accounts were largely myths except in Poland, Yugoslavia, and occupied parts of the Soviet Union. In Bulgaria, for example, a meaningful partisan movement sprang up only a few months before the arrival of the Soviet army in the summer of 1944, and the same was true for Hungary, while in Romania it was King Michael who overthrew the pro-German dictator Ion Antonescu in August 1944 and turned the country over to the invading Soviet army just as it was entering Romania.[28] Austria, which managed to have itself defined after the war as the first victim of German aggression because it was annexed by Germany in 1938, was actually mostly pro-Nazi.[29] In occupied Greece, the small and rather ineffective resistance was bitterly split between Communists and anti-Communists, while collaborators helped the Germans and Italians keep control. At the end of the war, as Greece was liberated by the British, a civil war broke out between the Greek Communist Party and conservatives, so that ultimately most of the former collaborators were enlisted in the anti-Communist cause. To this day, Greeks have not integrated into their national consciousness a realistic appraisal of what happened.[30]

The Communist version of what had happened during the war was also taught in East Germany, so that blame was assigned to West Germany, where the old order had supposedly survived. East Germany felt that it had no need to confront Nazism, leaving its people unprepared for the new world in which they found themselves after reunification in 1990.[31] The same story of Communist partisan activity was put forward by Communists in Western Europe, especially in Italy and France, where there were very large Communist parties after the war.

Communists did play an important role in the resistances in these countries, but as we have seen, in France that was not significant until 1943, and by then Communists were far from being the only participants. The same happened in Italy. It was only after Mussolini's overthrow in 1943, followed immediately by the seizure of most of Italy by German troops, that resistance began.[32] In other words, as in most of Europe where there were either governments allied to Germany or puppet regimes beholden to the Germans, it was only the decisive turn of events against Germany that unleashed major resistance.

For decades after World War II, Germans' acceptance of their guilt allowed the rest of Europe to evade this truth, namely, that they had been mostly quite willing to help the Nazis and close their eyes to gruesome German brutality as long as it seemed that Germany was winning. In official histories and books, what were often minor acts of resistance, or tardy ones that became effective only from 1943 on, were played up; collaboration by broad swaths of officialdom was overlooked; and the need for any kind of remorse or apology to the many victims, including, of course, Jews and Roma (or Gypsies), was not part of remembrance.

The second, somewhat related, problem with the simple contrast between Europeans' and Asians' memories of the war is that most of the Central and Eastern European countries, where the worst abuses and the most killing took place, evaded responsibility even more than Western Europe. In part this evasion was because of the Communist interpretation of fascism and Nazism as a class phenomenon, the last gasp of a historically condemned bourgeois order. Thus the ultranationalism and ethnic hatreds that had so troubled this part of Europe even before World War I and only grew worse between 1918 and 1939, were brushed off as yet another manifestation of the evils of the corrupt old order, now replaced by healthy socialism. The problems of ethnonationalist conflict were swept under the rug, even though that had been part of the background cause of the rise of fascism and the early success of the Nazi occupations throughout almost the entire region.

By the time Communists took power in Eastern Europe after the war, many ethnic problems actually had been settled by the Nazis (through the extermination of most of the Jewish minorities in Central and Eastern Europe), by the movement of borders after 1945 and mass exchanges of population, or by the largest example of ethnic cleansing in European history when ethnic Germans were expelled from Poland and Czechoslovakia or internally displaced in the Soviet Union. Some 11.5 million Germans whose ancestors had been living in these regions for centuries were forced out. Though the numbers are (naturally) contested, it is likely that well over a million died in the process.[33]

Little of this violent history was incorporated into the official record. In Poland, the bulk of the genuinely large resistance had actually been anti-Communist and nationalist. This position was denied by the Communists. At the same time, the suffering of the Jews during the war, Poland's long-standing anti-Semitism well before 1939, and the continuing violent anti-Semitism after the war were also played down to the point of being practically ignored.[34]

One of the most unfortunate aspects of these fabrications was that even in the case where there was the most genuine, strong, Communist resistance movement, Yugoslavia, the story was overused and eventually lost its power as Communism's legitimacy faded. Tito, the leader of the Communist partisans during the war and Yugoslavia's dictator until his death in

1980, based much of his reputation and his party's legitimacy on the partisan myth that all good Yugoslavs had joined together to fight the bourgeois, treacherous domestic fascists and foreign invaders. Here we have a perfect example of why schoolbooks are not necessarily effective if they tell a story that loses credibility. In fact, the Yugoslav war from 1941 to 1945 was a complex combination of a struggle against German and Italian occupiers as well as a very nasty, multisided civil war between the country's various ethnic nationalists. It is true that Tito's Communists worked hard to overcome ethnic divisions, but the partisan story repeated endlessly in classrooms and in state propaganda did not make people forget the bitter ethnic divisions that had also existed. By emphasizing the myth of class unity over ethnic division, Tito's state failed to explain the troubling past. Already by the time of Tito's death, ethnic strains were evident, and in the 1980s they grew out of control. In the 1990s, they exploded into a tragic war that killed hundreds of thousands and broke the country apart into its various ethnonationalist groups.[35]

The third problem with the easy dichotomy contrasting "good" Germany and a reconciled, harmonious Europe to "bad" Japan and a troubled East Asia has to do with what was brought up earlier, the question of genocide and morality raised by the Holocaust. Acceptance in Germany was far from immediate, and though for well over a decade and perhaps as many as two it was accepted elsewhere but not made central to World War II memories, it is now very widely recognized in Europe that Nazi Germany's genocidal policy toward Jews was a totally inexcusable crime for which it is impossible to find any justification, unless one admits to being an anti-Semite who approves of the eradication of Jews in the world.

Yehuda Bauer, probably Israel's most prominent analyst of the Holocaust, or the Shoah as it is now generally called in Israel, has emphasized the complete lack of rational realism that lay behind it.[36] How many Jews were there in Germany in 1933 when Hitler came to power? How much of a threat were they? In 1933, Jews made up some 0.8 percent of the German population, or just over 500,000 out of 66 million, and most of these considered themselves German patriots. Three hundred seventy-five thousand were left by 1938 before *Kristallnacht* (the first systematic organized pogrom against Jews in Germany, though already many anti-Semitic laws had been approved and actions occurred). Though Austria's annexation had added another 185,000 (out of a total population of 6.8 million, or 2.7 percent of the Austrian total), many of these quickly fled. In any case, by then, German Jews had already been excluded from public life, from most professions, and had had much of their property taken away, so this small minority could not, by any rational calculation, have been considered seriously threatening.[37] Yet the persecution intensified and turned into genocide by 1941.

We could go into the fantasies of Jewish control of finance or the press or any of the other anti-Semitic demons conjured up in Europe and elsewhere, but the astonishing fact is how little substance these had in Germany itself or in any of the major Western European countries with Jewish communities. Jews were 0.7 percent of the British population and 0.4 percent of France's. Only in some of the East-Central European countries, Poland, Latvia, Lithuania, Hungary, and Romania, were they more than 4 percent of the total. In the Soviet Union, there were 3 million Jews, about 1.6 percent of the total, and even in the Ukraine, where most lived, they were only 2.8 percent of the population.[38] Aside from the Soviet Union, none of these eastern countries could have been considered a threat to Germany. Poland, with the largest concentration of Jews in Europe, was anti-Semitic itself and hardly run by Jews. It was, in any case, quickly defeated and conquered in 1939. Hungary and Romania became German allies. As for the Soviet Union, Hitler in 1940 said that the invasion of the Soviet Union would be "child's play" because Slavs were subhuman inferiors, so no matter how many Jews there were in the East, he could not have felt that their presence was in any sense an immediate threat to German power.[39] There is, of course, the persistence of myths about how this tiny minority secretly ran the affairs of the major powers. The Nazis as well as anti-Semites throughout the world believed, and still believe, in the *Protocols of the Elders of Zion*, and new editions are still being printed. Édouard Drumont's 1886 best-selling French book, *La France juive* was an earlier version of the same myths. There have been so many refutations of the lies in these works that it is hardly worth going over them. The point is that if someone believes in these stories, then indeed the Jews are a deadly menace, no matter what objective evidence there is to disprove them.

Once the gruesome consequences of this kind of exterminationist anti-Semitism became generally known, and eventually very widely publicized, it became almost impossible for Germans to come up with convincing justifications of the war and genocide that they had begun. It is precisely because of the Shoah that efforts by right-wing German historians to excuse Nazism as a reaction to outside (mostly Soviet) threats fell flat.[40]

Cruel as the Japanese were in territories they occupied, and murderous as they were in the many massacres they perpetrated, there is no single, clear-cut program of genocide that can be ascribed to them. Theirs was in some ways an exceptionally brutal colonial war, and even Nanjing, far from being part of a plan to exterminate all Chinese, was in a sense a very large-scale version of many such episodes in many wars of occupation. This is not to excuse Japan's actions by any means but to point out that it is easier to evade responsibility for such an act by claiming that it was part of a war than it is to try to justify or somehow overlook the Shoah. So, in the end, even though many more non-Jews than Jews died in Europe during World War II, it was the Jewish question that gradually became a central part of the historical memory of German guilt.

In Europe the Jewish problem was for the first two postwar decades relegated to obscurity, even denial, and in some cases this lasted well into the 1990s. This was true at first even in Germany, where, according to Buruma, the full extent of the nightmare was not quite recognized by the general public until the showing of an American television drama on the Holocaust in Germany in 1979. *Der Spiegel*, a leading West German newspaper, commented at the time: "An American television series, made in a trivial style, produced more for commercial than for moral reasons, more for entertainment than for enlightenment, accomplished what hundreds of [German] books, plays, films, and television programs have failed to do in the more than three decades since the end of the war: to inform the Germans about crimes against Jews committed in their name, so that millions were emotionally touched and moved."[41] Aside from being well produced, the American television show featured an assimilated middle-class family that was not obviously Jewish in any way, and perhaps this is what so startled the Germans.

As a French Jewish baby who was protected with his mother and grandmother during the war in a small village, and as a professional social scientist, I recall thinking in 1979 that this show was too smooth and not nearly horrible enough. But that may have been the secret of its success in the United States and especially in Germany. It was easier to identify with the family portrayed than with the skeletal, dying concentration camp prisoners one sees in documentaries and pictures. In any case, after this series aired, West German (but not East German) textbooks placed increased emphasis on Nazi crimes that killed some 6 million Jews. Furthermore, the number of monuments and museums featuring the persecution of Jews under Nazi rule has proliferated, so that now German guilt is very solidly established, and new generations come out of school aware of how xenophobic ultranationalism and racist theories resulted in such a catastrophe.

What most of the rest of Europe failed to do for a long time, however, was to admit that the Germans could never have killed so many Jews without the help of the countries they had occupied and to which they were allied. In the few cases where local authorities resisted German demands, very few Jews were caught and killed. So, for example, Bulgarian public and church opinion protected Bulgarian Jews in Bulgaria proper but not in the parts of Greece and Yugoslavia occupied by the Bulgarians during the war. There, Jews were turned over to the Germans.[42] The same was true of Hungary, where the administration of Admiral Miklós Horthy protected its own Jews, particularly those in Budapest, but turned over the ones in the parts of Transylvania it occupied. Elie Wiesel, probably the most famous of all Holocaust survivor writers, was from that Transylvanian Jewish community, almost all of whom perished in the Nazi camps. Only after Horthy was overthrown by the Germans in 1944 for trying to start negotiations for a separate peace with the Allies, and a Hungarian extremist anti-Semitic party was put in power, were Budapest's Jews arrested and sent to concentration camps in large numbers.[43]

Romania's pro-German wartime dictator, Marshal Antonescu, had no qualms about slaughtering Jews in Bessarabia (today's Republic of Moldova) and in Romanian Moldova, where local anti-Semitic feelings were high, but those farther south, and particularly in Bucharest, were more protected because they were thought to be economically useful, and there most survived.[44]

Yet to this day the full extent of these countries' complicity in the Holocaust and, in cases such as Romania and Hungary, the nature of their particularly vicious native fascist movement remain poorly known and not widely taught in schools. What remains part of the general perception is the help they gave to some selected portions of their Jewish populations, not what happened to the majority of Jews.

In Romania recognition of what had happened to the Jews was partially exposed right after the war but then erased from public discourse. By the time the Communist regime was overthrown at the end of 1989, few Romanians had much of a sense of how increasingly racist, xenophobic, and stridently anti-Semitic the atmosphere had been in the 1920s and 1930s and how viciously cruel the Antonescu regime had been from 1940 to 1944, when it was replaced to try to mollify the invading Soviet army. There was almost no serious Romanian scholarship on that period until the 1990s. On the contrary, by the late Communist period the regime had begun rehabilitating Antonescu, portraying him as a dedicated, honest, and reform-minded nationalist rather than as a member of the anti-Semitic Iron Guard. It even provided material support for an American scholar, Larry Watts, to spread this story. After the fall of Communism, Watts continued to receive ample help from the Romanian military, which was intent on proving that Antonescu had been a hero.[45] Indeed, when the proceedings of the Communist-led trial of Antonescu that led to his execution in 1946 were published in Romania in 1996, he was again made out to be a noble, heroic figure.[46] Only more recently has some Romanian scholarship exposed the deep roots of the nasty ideologies espoused by much of Romania's intellectual and political elite in the pre–World War II period and during the war itself, and of course by Antonescu.[47]

Despite this long period of denial, in Romania, as elsewhere in some of the former Communist parts of East-Central Europe, this perception did start to change in the early 2000s. Largely this reform was in order to gain acceptance into the European Union, where recognition of the extent of widespread guilt had already been under way for at least a decade or more.[48] In Romania a special commission was set up in 2003 to examine the record. Wiesel was made its chairman. The report spelled out the extent of the Antonescu regime's decisive role in committing atrocities against Jews and how much of this was done by the Romanians themselves. These findings reversed the previous perception that the Holocaust was something done by Germans and of minor importance in Romania. Today, at least in universities, this history is taught along with that of the atrocities committed by the postwar Communist regime. It has not eliminated right-wing insistence that Antonescu was a nationalist hero, but it has at least somewhat, if not yet decisively, altered the perception of younger Romanians.[49] Changing the general perception of what really happened, in Romania and elsewhere in the region, will take much longer.

The admission of how much of a role Eastern and Central European xenophobia, anti-Semitism, and general racism contributed to the Nazi Holocaust has had something to do with the fact that a disproportionate number of the Communist cadres right after World War II were Jewish. This was partly because Communist parties were originally very small except in Czechoslovakia and Yugoslavia, their leaders consisted largely of marginalized minorities, and Stalin recognized that Jews could be trusted as loyal, subservient henchmen because they were unlikely to be able rely on domestic forces to back them since locals were generally anti-Semitic. Later, these Jewish Communists became some of the main victims of the purges in Eastern Europe as Stalin set out to destroy what was left of Jewish life in the Soviet Empire. These factors contributed first to a systematic downplaying of the Holocaust, and then resulted in a lasting anti-Semitism that in many cases still blames Jews for their countries' misfortunes.[50] It will take a long time for such popular misconceptions to go away.

Nowhere is this situation more evident than in Poland, where Jan Gross's best-selling 2001 book, *Neighbors*, caused a sensational debate to break out. Gross, a Polish American historian at Princeton, documented how in 1941 in a Polish town that was half Jewish and half Christian, the Christians turned on their sixteen hundred Jewish neighbors and slaughtered almost all of them—beating them to death, herding them into buildings and burning them, or hunting them down in the fields as they tried to escape, all without any prompting by the Germans who were occupying the area but not that particular town. Only seven Jews survived. Poland had generally portrayed itself solely as a victim of the Germans and therefore free of any possible guilt. Indeed, Poles were deemed part of an inferior race by the Nazis, their intellectuals and leaders were killed in large numbers, and every effort was made to wipe out Polish culture. Poles, along with Yugoslavs, proportionately suffered the highest casualties in Europe during the war; yet Poland was also one of the most anti-Semitic countries in Europe, and some Poles helped the Germans round up Jews. Some other Poles did hide Jews or help them, but most did not, and in some cases, as in the town Gross studied, they took the initiative in killing Jews. Gross's book woke the country up to what had really happened, but it was also bitterly attacked by Polish nationalists and by many parts of the Catholic Church, which is particularly powerful in Poland. Even Lech Wałęsa, Poland's heroic anti-Communist leader and its first post-Communist president, accused Gross of just being another greedy Jew spreading lies to make money. Still, the book finally led to an official apology by the Polish government and a new monument erected to commemorate the massacre described by Gross. Subsequently, in 2006, Gross published a new book, *Fear*, in which he described how some of the few surviving Jews (over 85 percent of the roughly 3 million Polish Jews were killed) who returned to their homes after World War II were set upon by Christian

Poles and massacred. This account produced another burst of nationalist outrage in Poland, where the debate about the whole issue remains bitterly divisive. It is not just in East Asia where descriptions of massacres that took place more than seventy years ago are still contentious and subject to nationalist distortions.[51]

In Lithuania, once home to a Jewish community of some 160,000 (7.6 percent of the population, the second-largest percentage after Poland) some two-thirds were wiped out. As Petersen's chapter in this volume points out, though Lithuania had traditionally had much anti-Semitism, it had not been as bad before the war as in neighboring Poland. On the other hand, Lithuania was traumatized by a very brutal Soviet occupation from 1939 to 1941, during the period when the Nazi-Soviet treaty of 1939 had divided up Eastern Europe between Hitler and Stalin. So, when the Germans broke the treaty by invading in 1941, they were seen as liberators by the Lithuanians, many of whom blamed Jews for the Soviet occupation. Many Lithuanian collaborators helped the Nazis between 1941 and 1944. During the time from World War II until 1991 when Lithuania was under Soviet Communist rule, collaboration with the Germans was officially deemed to have been a "bourgeois nationalist" phenomenon, though the killing of Jews itself was downplayed. It is no surprise, then, that the period since independence in 1991 has seen a confused conflict between various political factions over what happened. This situation is complicated, as elsewhere in Eastern Europe, by the fact that Jews are often blamed for having worked with the Communists, whose murderous repressions and mass deportations initiated a new Soviet occupation that lasted until 1991. The myth that confounded "Jews" with "Communists" made it difficult to come to grips with what had happened during the German occupation. It is only now that some efforts are being made to clarify the historical record, but it will take a long time before this becomes absorbed into school teaching or general public perception.[52]

In Austria, also, the fact that in 1938 the population and state officials rallied to the Nazi cause and instituted large-scale expulsion and killing of the substantial Jewish population was for a long time largely overlooked except by a few scholars. Austria's former president Kurt Waldheim, who had previously served as the UN's secretary-general before returning to Austria to run for president, was exposed as a significant participant in Nazi war crimes in the Balkans during the war, against Greek Jews and Yugoslavs. Both the U.S. and the Soviet intelligence services knew of his record before he became UN secretary-general, but both countries had backed him for this post, perhaps because they felt that he could easily be blackmailed and would therefore be more compliant. The deceitfulness of his public biography was openly revealed only after his UN term, while he was running for Austria's presidency. The revelation, however, had little impact. The Austrians still chose him as their president.[53] Berger's chapter in this volume actually makes a convincing case that Japan's and Austria's evasions about their records during World War II long had many common elements. In Austria, however, starting in the 1990s there have been changes, including the erection of monuments commemorating the tragedy of the Holocaust and admissions that Austrians were willing participants. Recently, in January 2013, the Vienna Philharmonic promised at last to open its archives that reveal how sympathetic its musicians were to the Nazi cause.[54] Almost seventy years of evasion had to pass before this admission occurred, but that is not so different from what has happened elsewhere in Europe, except in Germany.

In the Soviet Union, official anti-Semitism blocked out most of the story of the persecution and destruction of Jews. After the war, Stalin became increasingly anti-Semitic, and this attitude remained part of a policy of discrimination until the fall of Communism in 1991. Even now, however, Russian anti-Semitism is too omnipresent to produce much official acknowledgment of the massive suffering of Jews during the German occupation, and schoolbooks that are not even willing to admit anything close to the full extent of Stalin's own crimes are hardly likely to dwell on the unfortunate situation of the Jews during and after World War II. Though Hitler's crimes are taught in Russian schools, what happened to the Jews is not.[55]

Nor has this kind of evasiveness been limited to the Soviet Union or Central or Eastern Europe. Few French Jews would have been sent to concentration camps without the cooperation of the French police and denunciations by French citizens. To be sure, about three-quarters of French Jews survived, a higher number than in countries farther east, and a much higher proportion than in the Netherlands. Their survival was partly because France is a relatively large country, and the Germans had few occupying troops to devote to running it. At the same time, this very fact meant that it would have been easier for the French to protect all of their Jews, and in parts of France that were more left-wing, as well as in more Protestants towns and villages (Protestants are only about 3 percent of France's population but have played a disproportionately large role in the economy and politics), Jews were better protected than in right-wing areas, though this was not uniformly so. Where local authorities did not cooperate with orders from the Germans and from the Vichy government to turn in Jews, relatively few were caught.[56]

After the war, France compensated few of its Jews whose property had been looted during the war, mostly by other French citizens, and it was not until July 1995 that a French president apologized for what had happened. Now it is different, as Jackson's chapter explains. In Paris there are plaques commemorating the arrest of French Jews, as well as a new Holocaust museum in what used to be the old Jewish quarter of the city. But it took a long time for this recognition to happen.[57] France only began to include materials on the Holocaust in its schools in the late 1970s, and the way to best do so remains a subject of controversy. In February 2008, President Nicolas Sarkozy suggested that every child in school be assigned the biography of one of the French Jewish Holocaust victims, a proposal that was widely deemed excessive, though it was admitted that it was necessary to somehow revive the study of this topic to make it more relevant.[58] This treatment shows once more that it is Germany that has taken the lead in addressing the subject and that other European countries have consistently lagged behind. The controversy raised by the French president's remark shows also how much the contestation over memories now seventy years old remains alive.

The Netherlands, Buruma's home country, also had a somewhat darker record than most of its citizens were willing to acknowledge after the war when everything was blamed on the Germans and the small domestic Dutch Nazi Party. Anne Frank was probably turned in by Dutch neighbors. While the majority of the Dutch did not like the German occupation, and local Nazis were a minority, there were enough willing collaborators to run a dependent Dutch civil service. Partly because of this collaboration, but also largely because of the Netherlands' small size, over 70 percent of the 140,000 Dutch Jews were killed.[59]

Policy toward Jews was largely a secondary consideration for most Western Europeans during World War II. Though Jews had made up less than 1 percent of any West European country before the war (most European Jews lived in the East), there was generally enough anti-Semitism to make most people in the occupied countries indifferent to their fate or, in the case of many officials, to cooperate with German orders.

Compared to countries farther east, and also to Russia, Western Europe has finally admitted that it was not just Germans who committed crimes, but this acceptance has taken decades of work by historians and filmmakers and organized efforts to bring about such recognition. In all these cases, it took a new generation that came to the fore twenty-five years after the war to start the process of admission. Their elders preferred to forget as much as possible and to keep quiet, except for the Communists who distorted history to vilify their bourgeois enemies in order to better conceal Communism's own crimes. That recognition and admission is just beginning in the eastern parts of Europe, even though the overwhelming majority of Jews killed were in the East.

The contrast between Germany and to some extent (belatedly) much of Western Europe and Japan or East Asia in general, therefore, stands. But the reluctance of almost all of Europe to face its nationals' participation as well as the widespread feigned ignorance and indifference to the horrors that occurred during and right after World War II should serve to remind us that there is nothing easy about confronting such moral evil. Europe's admissions of guilt and acceptance of historical truth did not surface quickly and the process of reconciliation with the past remains problematic and has barely begun in some countries.

If we turn back to Germany itself, a fourth problem appears in the effort to explain the contrast between its behavior and Japan's. It is obviously true that West Germany's acceptance of its guilt contributed to the reconciliation with the rest of Europe, while Japan's ambiguous and in some cases blatantly evasive treatment of the issue has continued to sour relations with its neighbors despite the development of close economic links. But did West Germany really have any choice? A key difference between Germany and Japan was the international situation in which they found themselves in the years immediately following the war.[60]

France, humbled and in terrible economic shape by 1945, was, nevertheless, the most powerful country on the West European mainland (excluding island Britain), and the French wanted to see Germany dismantled and permanently crippled. The other formerly occupied West Europe countries were bitterly hostile to Germany as well and deeply embarrassed about the fact that so many of their citizens had collaborated with the Germans. The United States and the Soviet Union, however, did not want to fragment Germany into little pieces. Stalin hoped to be able to milk postwar Germany for reparations that his country desperately needed, and the United

States, along with Britain, understood that a punitive peace after World War I had set the stage for Hitler's rise and so did not want to repeat the same mistake. The creation of an occupied but economically more united Germany served their purposes better than the kind of revenge France wanted.[61]

As the Cold War developed, and especially in 1948, with strong Communist parties in France and Italy, and the final, complete subjugation of Eastern Europe by the Soviets, the Americans began to think of West Germany as a possible bulwark against Communism, while the Soviets formally set up a separate East German state in 1949. But without French and general West European acceptance of West Germany as a legitimate, trustworthy state, it would have been impossible to construct a strong, united North Atlantic Treaty Organization (NATO) and probably very difficult to bring about the kind of West European economic recovery able to dampen pro-Communist sentiment where it was already strong. It took years of difficult negotiations and the participation of some farsighted French and German diplomats to bring reconciliation about, but helped by the dire international situation and U.S. pressure, it happened. France and Germany began to take steps to cooperate economically, first in the coal and steel industries and then more broadly. Political leaders Maurice Schuman and Jean Monnet of France led the way, starting in 1950, in changing French attitudes. In West Germany, the elderly Konrad Adenauer had become head of his country. Adenauer had a history of being friendly to France and Britain in the early 1920s, when he was mayor of Cologne. Jailed several times by the Nazis, he had barely survived the war, but as the leader of the new Christian Democratic Party he was also fervently anti-Communist. He was therefore receptive to overtures from France. A patient, diplomatic, and generous United States greatly helped the process along. What was required was for West Germany to make it clear that it would not fall back into the same aggressive ultranationalism that had dominated it in the first half of the twentieth century.[62]

Franco-German friendship and mutual confidence thus grew and became the basis of united Europe, first through the Common Market and then eventually in the European Union. This alliance remains the bedrock of European unity, even after the collapse of East Germany and its reunification with West Germany in 1990.[63]

Part of the bargain was that Germany had to firmly renounce its aggressive past. Slowly, German schools changed the way they taught history, and with the rise of new postwar generations attitudes changed. Programs were set up in the 1950s and 1960s to exchange high school students between the two countries. Those who took part in these exchanges still remember them as being among the more significant events of their youth. A German friend born just after the war told me how he was sent on such an exchange program and met his first love, a French girl his age. She had to keep it a secret for fear that if her father found out she was involved with a German, he would kill both of them. To these youths, this attitude made no sense at all, but that was how some in the older generation that had actually experienced the war still felt. In France, also, the teaching of history changed, though much more slowly. Since the mid-1980s, French textbooks have gradually shifted away from a nationalist perspective toward a more pan-European and even global emphasis, whereas in Germany the process began earlier and has gone much farther.[64]

Such a process was neither necessary nor even possible in East Asia. First of all, the Americans agreed to maintain the Japanese emperor (something that would have been totally unthinkable with Hitler, had he not committed suicide) in order to better control Japan, so it became far easier for the Japanese to evade the issue of responsibility.[65] Just as importantly, the countries that had been occupied by Japan had almost no say at all in determining Japan's fate. China was embroiled in civil war until 1949, and then, especially in 1950, China became a direct enemy of the United States. Korea was weak and divided, and after the Korean War, it was in ruins.[66] In Southeast Asia the main issues were a set of anticolonial wars and the dissolution of the French, British, and Dutch empires. Influencing policy toward defeated Japan was neither possible nor particularly important.[67]

Thailand skillfully extricated itself from its wartime association with the Japanese and became pro-American. Perhaps only someone born in France still notices that the Victory Monument in Bangkok celebrates a Thai victory over the French in Laos in 1941, at a time when French Indochina was dominated by the Japanese and France itself was helpless.[68]

In short, there were no hostile Asians the Japanese needed to placate or listen to until much later when a recovered South Korea and an emergent China began to make demands for apologies. By then, the pattern of Japanese weak official apologies combined with evasion had been fixed for a long time. To be sure, Japanese leftists did seek to expose their country's brutality and aggression during the war, but they tacked this on to a strong anti-Americanism unlikely to win much sympathy from the United

States. The dominant Japanese conservatives were, at first, very much the same elites who had run Japan before and during the war, except for a few top people who were purged, and today's elite made its way in the same Japanese conservative circles that ruled in the 1950s and 1960s. So, there is little pressure for Japan to change, and since both the Japanese Left and Right can agree that they were the innocent victims of the nuclear bombings and Western aggression, the situation has not changed much.[69] This is all the more so because China and South Korea have been perfectly willing to cooperate economically with Japan, even as they complain about its refusal to make official apologies or change its textbooks. And in addition, whatever claims may be made against it, it is certainly not as completely clear that Japan committed genocide, unlike Germany. Massive killings and brutality, yes, but there is no Asian *Judenfrage* (Jewish question).

Finally, there is the question of collaboration. In Europe, as the Germans took the blame for what had happened, it was easy for a full generation to evade the fact that so many other Europeans had helped the Nazis. By the time this began to change in the 1970s and 1980s, West European unity was a solidly established fact, and few felt endangered by the gradual admission in other countries that they too may have been partially at fault. But what about in East Asia? How many Koreans worked willingly with the Japanese? To what extent have Koreans faced up to this? Undoubtedly, the fact that Park Chung Hee, the longtime military dictator of South Korea, was trained as a Japanese military officer and had once taken a Japanese name kept South Korean complaints about Japan to a minimum during his rule until his 1979 assassination and also helped South Korean economic cooperation with the Japanese.[70] There were many Chinese who also worked with the Japanese, but during Mao Zedong's rule, this was mostly blamed on bad class elements as in Communist Eastern Europe. Thus the early postwar decades put little pressure on Japan itself to apologize. As post-Mao Chinese reforms weakened the legitimacy of socialist ideology, and the Communist Party replaced this by emphasizing nationalism, however, hostility toward Japan and the cultivation of memories of Japanese atrocities came to the fore once more in the 1980s and 1990s.[71] This occurrence is something a Japanese public and its conservative politicians have had a hard time understanding or accepting because, unlike in West Germany, there was so little pressure to face the facts in the immediate postwar decades.

GUILT, SHAME, AND THE REALITY OF HUMAN FRAILTY WHEN FACED WITH EVIL

Some previous analysts have suggested that perhaps another difference between Germany and Japan, not yet mentioned here, has something to do with a difference between the two cultures, with the former being one that emphasizes "confession" while the latter stresses "guilt" and "shame." Buruma correctly dismisses this explanation as rather dubious and shallow.[72] Even if one were to try to delve more deeply into the differences between the two cultures, it would be very difficult to prove that these played a major role because there are far more obvious and convincing explanations.

On the other hand, Petersen's chapter in this book is much more perceptive in explaining the psychological difference between "guilt" and "shame." He points out that guilt attaches to specific actions, whereas shame is connected to overall character, and if this explanation is applied to a nation as a whole, the effects are quite different. Germans, in effect, were allowed to admit that they had been guilty of crimes but that compensation and certain changes in their education would expiate this guilt. It would certainly seem that as China and South Korea have since the 1980s turned to trying to shame Japan, there has been growing resistance by the Japanese, who do not want to demean their entire national culture. The difference between "guilt" and "shame" may seem subtle, but as Petersen explains, those who confess when being shamed are most likely to do so in a formalistic, emotionless way, which is exactly what Japanese officials have done. It is telling that even in the school lesson prepared for German children that was mentioned at the beginning of this chapter, it is a kindly policeman who saves the Jewish child. Many Germans were guilty, but there were also some who were not, so that it is possible to feel redemption by looking at those who behaved better.

In 2009, a Chinese film called *City of Life and Death* about the Nanjing massacre was released. While it is unsparing in portraying Japanese brutality, it was heavily criticized by many Chinese because one of the Japanese characters is actually kindly and ultimately commits suicide because he cannot bear what his army has done. Those who made such complaints wanted to shame Japan by suggesting that all Japanese are monsters. In fact, as Buruma's review of this film explains, Nanjing itself has long been discussed in Japan, though again right-wing nationalists deny the massacre took place. Still, saying that all Japanese culture is inherently evil makes it less likely that the Japanese will change their views. The Japanese army was guilty of a major moral crime, without a doubt, killing over a hundred thousand civilians (though probably not as many as the three hundred thousand Iris Chang and the Nanjing Memorial museum's "Wall of Calamity" claim); but the controversy in China and Japan about this film shows how unresolvable the issue of Japan's wartime guilt can be if no way is found to move toward a more realistic version of history.[73] Trying to shame Japan into seeing itself as a nation of monsters will not do that.

In short, West Germany has been exceptional in its admission of guilt, even if it ultimately had little choice because of the genocide the Nazis committed and because of Germany's international situation after World War II. Most European countries did have significant numbers of collaborators, and some of them had quite terrible records of ultranationalism and vicious treatment of their Jews. They were very slow to admit this guilt to themselves and to the rest of the world, while some still remain ambivalent. Seen in that light, it begins to seem that the Japanese public's reluctance to face the past, and its continuing view of Japan as a victim rather than as an instigator of morally repugnant aggression, is normal if unfortunate. That is what is to be expected, and there is nothing uniquely Japanese about it.

We should not be surprised by this conclusion. White American Southerners long evaded and, to some extent, still fail to come to grips with the fact that they fought a bloody civil war not for "states' rights" but to preserve slavery. The Russian government today is busy trying to urge Russians to forget how cruel and needlessly bloody Stalin really was. China downplays Mao's crimes, and as Gil Rozman's chapter in this volume shows, it is actively rewriting history to exonerate itself from any past wrongdoing and to portray Japan and the United States as inherently shameful. The Turkish government denies that its Ottoman predecessors conducted a genocide against Armenians, though historians have more than adequately documented what happened. The Catholic Church has spent decades trying to avoid admitting the sexual scandals that have besmirched its reputation, though when forced to do so, it has relented somewhat.

Because history is after all usually meant to serve the present rather than the past, we should be used to this. As professional scholars, however, some of us can help accelerate the process of recognition, admission, and therefore reconciliation by providing the raw material that honest intellectuals and political leaders will use when they finally come to accept the necessity of facing the past.

As a final note, I should point out that a few hundred meters from our house in Bélâbre there was a small hotel. Because the village was very close to the border between theoretically more benign Vichy France and the territory occupied directly by the Germans, refugees, some of whom were undoubtedly Jews, would walk across the poorly guarded border and, once in the village, would be directed to the hotel, where they could eat and sleep. The next morning, they would be turned over to the police, and for many, probably most, that meant prison and often death. We were never turned in because my mother and grandmother had arrived from Paris before the horror of it all had been fully felt, so people knew us and could therefore let their sympathies overcome their fears. We do not need to take a scholarly approach to understand that the closer one gets to reality, the more complex and contradictory human reactions to extreme stress really are. There are those who are purely evil, and there are saints, but both are really quite rare. Accepting this may be the first essential step that needs to be taken if historical reconciliation about war memories is ever to take place.

1 *New York Times*, "Indonesia: Dutch Apologize for 1947 Massacre."
2 Most of this information can be found through Google.fr. See also Rakotoarison, "Carnage de Maillé"; and "Ferrant, Anatole." Part of the story was told to me by my late mother, Hélène Chirot (1920-2008). For a detailed analysis of what happened in the much more famous village of Oradour, today the site of a major museum, see Farmer, *Martyred Village*.
3 Snyder, *Bloodlands*.
4 Bell quoted in Valentino, *Final Solutions*, 201-2; Jones, *Honor in the Dust*.
5 Kiernan, *Blood and Soil*.
6 Akçam, *A Shameful Act*.
7 Chirot and McCauley, *Why Not Kill Them All?*
8 Power, *A Problem from Hell*.
9 Karnow, *Vietnam: A History*, 521-31.
10 Pitts, *A Turn to Empire*.
11 On why many Turks have always perceived the Western insistence on an admission of genocide to be an example of Western hypocrisy, see Akçam, *A Shameful Act*, 368-76.
12 Miscamble, *The Most Controversial Decision*.
13 Kimmelman, "No Laughs, No Thrills."
14 McCurry, "Far Right Closes Yasukuni Screening."
15 Fackler, "Japanese Mayor's Comments."
16 Mackenzie, "Berlusconi Defends Mussolini"; *Economist*, "Back to the Future"; Lind, "The Limits on Nationalism in Japan."
17 Soysal, Bertilotti, and Mannitz in Schissler and Soysal, eds., *The Nation, Europe, and the World*, 13-34.

18 He, "Remembering and Forgetting the War"; He, *The Search for Reconciliation.*
19 Mitani in Shin and Sneider, eds., *History Textbooks and the Wars in Asia.* For more on this topic, see other chapters in Shin and Sneider.
20 Maier, *The Unmasterable Past.*
21 Craig, *Politics and Culture in Modern Germany*, 339.
22 Buruma, *The Wages of Guilt.*
23 Deák's introduction, in Deák, Gross, and Judt, eds., *The Politics of Retribution in Europe*, 3–14. In the same volume, see also Deák's chapter.
24 De Gaulle, *The Complete War Memoirs*, 86, 108.
25 Jackson, *France: The Dark Years, 1940-1944.*
26 Gross, *Polish Society under German Occupation.*
27 Payne, *Franco and Hitler.*
28 Crampton, *A Concise History of Bulgaria*, 175; Deák, Gross, and Judt, eds., *The Politics of Retribution in Europe*, 55, 67.
29 Beller, *A Concise History of Austria*, 231–48.
30 Mazower, *Inside Hitler's Greece*; Mazower in Deák, Gross, and Judt, eds., *The Politics of Retribution in Europe.*
31 Judt in Deák, Gross, and Judt, eds., *The Politics of Retribution in Europe*, 307–8.
32 Wilhelm, *The Other Italy.*
33 Naimark, *Fires of Hatred*, 14, 108–38; Snyder, *Bloodlands*, 313–37.
34 Gross, *Polish Society under German Occupation*; Gross in Deák, Gross, and Judt, eds., *The Politics of Retribution in Europe.*
35 Glenny, *The Balkans*, 570–93, 622–62.
36 Bauer, *Rethinking the Holocaust*, 266.
37 Holborn, *A History of Modern Germany*; Mitchell, *European Historical Statistics*, 3–4.
38 Gilbert, *Jewish History Atlas.*
39 Speer, *Inside the Third Reich*, 306.
40 Maier, *The Unmasterable Past.*
41 *Der Spiegel* quoted in Buruma, *The Wages of Guilt*, 88.
42 Crampton, *A Concise History of Bulgaria*, 171–73.
43 Deák, Gross, and Judt, *The Politics of Retribution in Europe*, 64–67.
44 Ioanid, *The Holocaust in Romania.*
45 Watts, *Romanian Cassandra.*
46 Ciucă, ed., *Procesul Mareșalului Antonescu.*
47 Solonari, *Purifying the Nation.*
48 Judt, *Postwar*, 803.
49 Petrescu and Petrescu in Baumgartl, ed., *Postdiktatorische Geschichtskulturen im Süden unde Osten Europas*, especially 528–30.
50 Judt in Deák, Gross, and Judt, eds., *The Politics of Retribution in Europe*, 312–13; Schöpflin, *Politics in Eastern Europe*, 42–43; Yuri Slezkine, *The Jewish Century*, 313–14.
51 Gross, *Neighbors*; Gross, *Fear*; Engel, "On Continuity and Discontinuity." See also Gilbert, *Jewish History Atlas*, 85–88.
52 Suziedelis, "The Perception of the Holocaust"; Gilbert, *Jewish History Atlas*, 85–88.
53 Mitten, *The Politics of Anti-Semitic Prejudice.*
54 Oestreich, "Orchestra to Disclose Its Nazi Past."
55 Weiner, *Making Sense of War*, 114–26; Maier in Schissler and Soysal, eds., *The Nation, Europe, and the World.*

56 Marrus and Paxton, *Vichy et les Juifs*, 191–96, 325–39.
57 *Le Monde*, "Une dette imprescriptible"; Trigano, "Que faire avec l'indemnisation des spoliations."
58 Le Bars, "Le projet de parrainage d'enfants de la Shoah contesté."
59 Romijn in Deák, Gross, and Judt, eds., *The Politics of Retribution in Europe*; Hilberg, *Perpetrators Victims Bystanders*, 209–11.
60 Dujarric, "Retour sur un Japon conquérant."
61 Giles, *The Locust Years*, 99–102; Friend, *The Linchpin*, 12–16.
62 Friend, *The Linchpin*, 16–25.
63 Ibid.; Friend, *Unequal Partners*.
64 Soysal, Bertilotti, and Mannitz in Schissler and Soysal, eds., *The Nation, Europe, and the World*, 18.
65 Buruma, *The Wages of Guilt*, 172–76. For a general comparison of how German and Japanese teachings on World War II have developed, see Dierkes, *Postwar History Education*.
66 Cumings, *Korea's Place in the Sun*, 185–298.
67 Weinberg, *A World at Arms*, 534.
68 Fineman, *A Special Relationship*, 91–94.
69 Buruma, *The Wages of Guilt*, 295–96.
70 Cumings, *Korea's Place in the Sun*, 349–56.
71 He, *The Search for Reconciliation*, chaps. 2 and 3; Chang in Lary and MacKinnon, eds., *Scars of War*, 136–60.
72 Buruma, *The Wages of Guilt*, 116.
73 Buruma, "From Tenderness to Savagery"; Chang, *The Rape of Nanking*.

Chapter 2

Interrupted Memories

The Debate over Wartime Memory in Northeast Asia

DANIEL SNEIDER

There are two obstacles to understanding how historical memory about the wartime period has been formed in Northeast Asia. The first is the existence of persistent national myths about war memory—myths created within those nations and perceptions formed from the outside and entrenched through the media and popular culture. The second obstacle is the lack of comparative context. The study of historical memory, until recently, has been focused almost entirely on Japan, without comparison to other principal actors in Asia such as China and Korea or to the United States. And while there has been some exploration of the comparison between Japan and Germany, it has been limited.

The existence of distinct historical memories is a central obstacle to the ability of Asian nations to finally reconcile their still profound tensions over the wartime past.

> Questions about what happened in the past touch upon the most sensitive issues of national identity, the formation of historical memories, and national myths that play a powerful role to this day. Whether it be Japanese atrocities in China or the US decision to drop atomic bombs on Japan, no nation is immune to the charge that it has formed a less-than-complete view of the past. All share a reluctance to fully confront the complexity of their own past actions and blame others for their historical fates.[1]

The existence of multiple and contending memories is hardly an issue for scholars alone. That reality continues to shape current international relations in Northeast Asia, even acting as a source of tension and conflict, as Gilbert Rozman forcefully argues elsewhere in this volume. Historical issues remain central to the formation of national identity in all the countries that were principal participants in war in Asia. Narratives about the wartime period are fashioned to serve the needs of regime legitimacy in China, Korea, and Japan, Rozman writes. As a result, as Thomas Berger writes in this volume, it is difficult to be sanguine about the prospect that Asia may be able to achieve even the limited progress toward reconciliation that has been achieved in Europe.

Japan remains, as it should, the focus of the discussion of wartime memory in Asia. The central question that has concerned scholars, the media, and, in recent decades, governments has been whether Japan as a nation-state and the Japanese as a people have sufficiently acknowledged, and demonstrated contrition for, their wartime aggression and the war crimes committed during the war. The common perception is that the Japanese see themselves as victims of the war, rather than the perpetrators of aggression. Even worse, Japan tolerates a significant body of opinion, embraced by its political leaders, media, and even scholars, that continues to deny responsibility for aggression and for wartime acts of brutality and criminality. In this view, Japan contrasts unfavorably with its wartime ally Germany, which has confronted its wartime responsibility and is legally and morally intolerant of the public expression of denial of its criminality.

This perception of Japan is, in certain respects, undeniable, but it is also simplistic. Japanese war memory is heavily contested ground within the country and has been so since the first days after Japan's surrender. There are competing narratives regarding the war within Japan—a conservative, or revisionist, narrative that does indeed include those who deny Japan's aggressive intent and defend its wartime record; a progressive narrative that embraces Japan's responsibility as the aggressor in both the Asian and Pacific theaters of the war, as well its record of war crimes; and a pacifist narrative that sees war itself as crime, holding both Japanese militarism and the Allied invaders responsible for the destruction wrought by the war. What all three narratives do share is a sense of Japan's victimization. The massive destruction visited upon the Japanese home islands from American air attacks, culminating in the atomic bombings, is seared into the national memory. But the narratives disagree quite passionately about who is responsible for the destruction of the nation.

The widespread perception of Japan as a nation in denial is based largely on the belief that the conservative narrative represents the predominant war memory. Given the half century of near monopoly of political power by the conservative Liberal Democratic Party (LDP), that perception is understandable. Conservative politicians have frequently voiced such views—though at the extreme, such outbursts have been followed by forced resignation. The conservative media, fed by activists and even academics, have publicized war crime denials that would be considered unacceptable in much of Europe. Conservative-authored history textbooks have received government approval, prompting protest, even street demonstrations, in China and Korea.

Yet historically the progressive narrative has been equally, if not more, prominent in Japanese discourse. In the first years after the war, the Japanese Left shaped the intellectual discussion of the war, embracing a Marxist-influenced historiography that depicted Japan as an imperialist aggressor, driven by economic depression to expansion into Asia and conflict with the West, ruled by a military-led corporatist state. The Left was, if anything, consumed by guilt over Japan's actions in Asia—and tended in later years, as it embraced an anti–United States ideology, to separate the war with the United States as a case of inter-imperialist rivalry. Japanese textbooks, if one reads the textbooks that are most widely used, still contain this historical view of the causes of the war in Asia and are unambiguous regarding Japan's responsibility for aggression, though less so regarding specific acts of criminality.

If there is a dominant narrative in Japan, however, it is the pacifist narrative. While that narrative acknowledges that Japan's aggression was the triggering event that led to the nation's destruction, it is essentially ahistorical. It sees war as the enemy and thus leads to the vague sense that no one, and perhaps no nation, can be held responsible for those events.

The failure of Japan to come to some historical consensus regarding the war is a subject of some complexity. As Franziska Seraphim has argued forcefully in her book on war memory in Japan, the contest over war memory has taken place within a framework of both organized social and political groups within Japan and, since the 1980s, within a globalized public culture.[2] This contest has been significantly shaped by the global Cold War, as Berger discusses in this volume. The United States' occupation of Japan had empowered the Japanese Left to challenge the legacy of the wartime state, including the formation of historical memory. But the decision of the United States to suppress the Left and to re-empower significant parts of the wartime regime in the service of the global struggle against Communism undermined and effectively interrupted the internal contest over wartime memory.

As Gi-Wook Shin argues elsewhere in this volume, the manner in which the United States shaped the postwar settlement and the construction of the Cold War system in Asia effectively hindered the possibilities of historical reconciliation in the region and continues to do so today. Despite that responsibility, the United States has been extremely reluctant to play any role in reconciling differences over wartime history, Shin notes.

Indeed, as Daniel Chirot has argued, such geopolitical realities also help explain the dichotomy between Japan and Germany.[3] Germany's contrition was driven by the need to rejoin a unified Western Europe and in particular the imperative to reconcile with France. Germany's readiness to confront its wartime past was the pathway to a reassertion of German leadership in the European Community (and later the European Union). The Cold War struggle against the Soviet Union provided crucial impetus to this process of reconciliation.

Japan, in contrast, faced no such imperative. Rather, Japan, at the urging of the United States, was positioned in a prolonged Cold War confrontation with its principal victim in World War II, China. Korea was divided by the same Cold War and focused on recovery from the devastating civil war. For their part, both Communist-led China and South Korea were too preoccupied with their internal struggles for legitimacy to focus on the issues of wartime memory. It was not until the 1980s that the wartime memory issue emerged as an interstate issue in Northeast Asia, not coincidentally at a time when the Cold War was easing and when the three Northeast Asian powers were being compelled by the forces of economic integration to seriously engage the need to create regional institutions.

The Cold War and its aftermath also influenced the formation of war memory in both China and South Korea. In both cases, war memory is a less contested arena. Powerful national narratives dominate the formation of war memory. But the shifting needs of national identity formation, with a changed internal and global context, have been reflected in clearly evolving narratives, which Rozman details in the case of China.

During the first decades of Communist rule in China, there was very little focus on the struggle against Japan or on Japanese war crimes. The Communist Party was preoccupied by its ongoing contest for legitimacy with the defeated Nationalists (Kuomintang, or KMT), now installed on Taiwan, and on its bid for leadership within the Communist world. The narrative about the war emphasized the civil war against the KMT, putting forward the argument that the Communists had been the true architects of resistance to the Japanese invaders. The war was presented within the standard Marxist framework as a global struggle against fascism, led by the Soviet Union. In the past three decades, the narrative has shifted significantly with the changing needs of the Chinese leadership. Now the emphasis is on national unity, though led by the Communists, against the foreign foe. The assertion of China's role as the architect of Japan's defeat is now central, along with China's victimization at the hands of a brutal and criminal invader. It is a narrative that suits the nationalist mobilization of a populace no longer motivated by neo-Communist ideology.

South Korea offers a parallel case of shifting national narratives. In the first years after liberation, there was a fierce contest over the wartime and colonial past between progressive and conservative Koreans. The former sought to shape an independent Korea that forcefully rejected the colonial past, including the role of Korean economic, political, and cultural elites who had been shaped by the Japanese colonial administration and in some cases had actively collaborated with their Japanese rulers. The American military occupation authority intervened, perhaps naively, into this struggle, relying on the Japanese-trained Koreans to create a functional administration, though it was led by the anti-Japanese exile Syngman Rhee.

The Korean War, and the establishment of authoritarian rule in the South, effectively interrupted that contest. The military-led government of Park Chung Hee, who had been trained by the Japanese military, was even less eager to tackle the difficult question of collaboration. Until the democratic overthrow of the military-led government of Chun Doo-Hwan in 1987, the dominant national narrative was one of unified national resistance to Japanese rule. That version of wartime memory is still entrenched in Korean textbooks and public narratives.

Democratization and the end of the global Cold War brought a fresh effort to reengage the interrupted discussion of collaboration and the complex impact of Japanese colonial rule on Korea's national development. In 2005, South Korea's progressive rulers created a Truth and Reconciliation Commission, aimed in part at looking at the legacy of Japanese rule, including new judgments against those deemed to have collaborated with Japan.

The formation of wartime memory thus remains an ongoing process throughout Northeast Asia. Debates over the past, interrupted by Cold

War imperatives, have resumed. Internal contests now take place in a global setting, creating an even greater level of complexity to the shaping of perceptions of the past. What follows is a glimpse of the state of those discussions in China, South Korea, and Japan.

FASHIONING A PATRIOTIC NARRATIVE IN CONTEMPORARY CHINA

In the southwest suburbs of Beijing, the granite Luguo Bridge stretches across the Yongding River, supported by hundreds of stone pillars, on each of which stands a carved lion. Built originally in the twelfth century, it was such a marvel that it drew the recorded admiration of the famous thirteenth-century Venetian traveler, Marco Polo, leading it to be known in the West as the Marco Polo Bridge.

The bridge acquired a much different significance in Chinese history on the night of July 7, 1937. Chinese and Japanese troops engaged in a brief exchange of fire at the western end of the bridge, leading to a skirmish known to Western historians as the Marco Polo Bridge Incident. The minor clash led to the eruption of full-scale war between imperial Japan and China later that month, a war that went on for more than eight years and resulted in the deaths of millions and the destruction of a nation.

The scale and brutal character of the war in China is largely invisible to Westerners who are otherwise steeped in the history of their own participation in the global conflict known as World War II. Japanese losses in the Sino-Japanese War period from 1937 to 1941 are estimated at 410,000 killed and some 920,000 wounded. Figures for Chinese suffering are less reliable, but Western historians believe that as many as 10 million Chinese soldiers were killed in the fighting, and civilian casualties were at least as high and perhaps as large as twice that number. The battles that stretched from the north of China to the jungles of Burma made tens of millions of Chinese into refugees and shattered the economic and political structure of China, literally ripping the country apart.[4]

A stone's throw from the end of the Luguo Bridge, the Chinese government erected a low-slung, stolid museum to commemorate this war, its doors opening in July 1987. A bronze sculpture, *The Awakening Lion*, meant to echo those on the nearby bridge and embody a China arisen from its slumber, sits in the center of a large plaza outside the gates to the white marble building. The ponderous name of the museum, inscribed in large gold Chinese characters above the entry doors, leaves no doubt as to the narrative message to be received within: Museum of the War of Chinese People's Resistance against Japanese Aggression.

In the entry lobby, the visitor is greeted by a massive wall sculpture of Chinese soldiers and an array of grim citizens, united in their collective resistance to the Japanese invader. The museum tells a clear and simple story of a united people, led by the Communist Party of China, engaged in heroic struggle. The war is not so much a tale of suffering as a rallying of the Chinese people against imperialist aggression, the beginning of the reversal of centuries of decline.

On a recent spring morning in 2011, the museum was almost entirely filled with groups of Chinese schoolchildren, dressed in matching shirts and jackets, with the obligatory red scarves tied around their necks, but also sporting backpacks decorated with Garfield and anime heroes. Their teachers lectured them as they passed by battle dioramas and a reproduction of a cave in Yenan where the Communist leadership huddled to plot military strategy. Another room detailed Japanese atrocities—nine hundred cities bombed, civilians murdered, prisoners of war killed, slave labor, biological and chemical warfare, "slave education," opium traffic, a plundered economy. The captions on the museum exhibits are only in Chinese—the audience for this history lesson is almost entirely internal, though museum officials say some two hundred thousand foreigners have visited since it opened in 1987, most of them Japanese.

A little over a thousand kilometers to the south, in Nanjing, the capital of Nationalist China in 1937, a modest museum commemorating the infamous Japanese atrocities committed in that city in 1937 opened it doors around the same time, in 1985. Beginning in the mid-1990s however, the Nanjing Memorial underwent major renovation and expansion, the latest completed in 2007. The new museum conveys a narrative of Chinese victimization at the hands of a depraved Japanese army, connecting this to China's history of humiliation at the hands of Western and Japanese imperialists. The museum graphically depicts the deliberate murder, sometimes by hand, of some three hundred thousand Chinese soldiers and civilians, including women and children, in the battle to conquer the Chinese capital. This public structure also bears a long but clear formal name: Memorial Hall of the Victims in Nanjing Massacre by Japanese Invaders.

In contrast to the Beijing museum, the Nanjing Memorial is clearly aimed at a global as well as a Chinese audience. Captions are translated into Japanese and English, and a gift shop offers an array of materials in foreign languages. It attracts more visitors than any other museum in China—some 5.5 million a year—without an entrance fee. On a weekday, the visitors were a mix of adults and children, including groups of military recruits.

According to the museum director, Zhu Cheng Shan, the renovation was intended to emulate, in its design and content, the emotionally wrenching Holocaust Museum in Washington, D.C., and similar memorials such as Yad Vashem in Jerusalem and Auschwitz in Poland and even the Japanese museums in Hiroshima and Nagasaki marking the victims of the atomic bombings.[5] The main hall is a modern structure, featuring a long swooping roofline, with a dizzying array of architectural elements outside and within, drawn from those and other museums around the world. On a long black marble wall in the entry plaza, the number three hundred thousand is emblazoned with explanations in multiple languages on what the museum calls the "Wall of Calamity." Inside, visitors are guided through a sophisticated series of well-designed exhibits of artifacts of the slaughter, from photographs to the preserved site of a mass grave discovered in the renovation process. The narrative skillfully weaves together the story not only of Chinese victims but also of the foreigners who played a key role in trying to protect them and in telling the story of the massacre to the world. A multistory wall of archival materials stores the recorded testimony of survivors.

The message of the Nanjing Memorial is unrelentingly clear—this is China's own holocaust. In a small corner of the courtyard in front of the museum offices, stands a bronze statue of the Chinese American writer Iris Chang, author of the 1997 book *The Rape of Nanking: The Forgotten Holocaust of World War II*. That volume is widely credited with bringing global attention to these events, and the Chinese authorities have unreservedly embraced that idea, reinforced through a steady stream of films, books, and television productions, a wave of which marked the seventieth anniversary of the event.

Both the assertion of a united national resistance and the embrace of China's suffering at the hands of foreign invaders are relatively new in revolutionary China. In its first decades in power, the Chinese Communist leadership had deliberately downplayed the anti-Japanese struggle in the early years of the People's Republic of China in favor of a historical narrative that focused on the civil war contest between the Communists and

Chinese Nationalists. The focus was mainly on the purported Communist role in leading that struggle and the Nationalist failure to fight the invader, indeed its betrayal of the united front formed to fight the Japanese for the sake of its struggle against the Communists. During the Cultural Revolution, when formal education was virtually halted, the wartime era was mainly portrayed through propagandistic films. The so-called Red classics, such as *Tunnel Warfare* and *Landmine Warfare*, depicted Communist guerrillas of the Eighth Route Army in the north and the New Fourth Army in the south successfully attacking the Japanese army.

The main battlefronts of the Sino-Japanese War, which were under the leadership of the Nationalists, were almost absent from this narrative of the war. This was a narrative shaped to serve the ongoing contest for legitimacy between the Communists and the Nationalists. In the Cold War decades when the People's Republic of China (PRC) still counted itself as part of the Communist world, albeit in competition with the Soviet Union for leadership of that world, the Chinese Communist Party (CCP) was also not eager to acknowledge a war of resistance in which China and the United States were allied.

Remembrance of the Nanjing massacre posed particular challenges for Communist historical narratives about the war. The battle in Nanjing was entirely a Nationalist affair, without any Communist involvement—and it was hardly a heroic affair. The nationalist government made initial efforts after the war to gather evidence of Japanese crimes to submit to the war crimes tribunals in Tokyo and those held in China, as well as to memorialize the event. But the civil war, and the Cold War that followed, cut off any further contacts with the wartime allies or even with Japanese seeking to illuminate the crimes of imperial Japan. "It is a great shame that commemoration of the massacre was interrupted by domestic conflict and the international situation," says museum director Zhu when I talked with him. "Political contradictions prevented these kinds of issues from being addressed."

There was also a pragmatic reason for the Chinese government to downplay the war against Japan before the 1980s. Chinese leader Deng Xiaoping was eager to normalize relations with Japan, which China did in 1972, and to open up the flow of Japanese economic aid that followed that decision. Japanese assistance was crucial to the early stages of Chinese economic recovery and growth following the disastrous years of the Cultural Revolution.

The decision to erect these two museums in the mid-1980s marked the first steps toward a changed policy on the construction of historical memory about the wartime period in Communist China. Over a period of two decades, from the early 1980s onward, the Chinese Communist Party began to downplay the civil war in favor of a national war against Japan. Faced with the shocking challenge to its leadership from Chinese youth demonstrations in the Tiananmen revolt of 1989, the Communist regime accelerated this with the launching of the Patriotic Education Campaign. Begun in 1991, the campaign was designed to provide young Chinese with a version of history that de-emphasized the Maoist-era narrative of class struggle within China in favor of the depiction of China as a victim of humiliation and brutality at the hands of foreign powers, going back to the days of the Opium Wars.[6]

External factors certainly had some impact on this shift. Nanjing Memorial director Zhu claims that the idea for the construction of his museum was prompted by the dispute that erupted with Japan in 1982 over the revision of Japanese history textbooks to remove language describing the war as an "invasion" and an act of aggression.[7] The dispute and the apparent lack of recognition of the Nanjing events in Japanese textbooks encouraged some in China who argued that there was a need to commemorate and document the Nanjing massacre.

Chinese commentators also attribute this shift to the impact of the process of reform and opening after 1979, which brought with it a greater flow of information, including access to the translations of works by Western historians. The CCP began revising its own history to some extent in the mid-1980s, says Li Datong, who led an effort at the party newspaper, *China Youth Daily*, to challenge the orthodox version of wartime history.[8]

In public, however, the wartime historical narrative changed much more slowly. The war resistance museum acknowledges the contribution of the KMT in the war, but still is careful to claim the CCP's leadership of that effort. The museum's exhibits devote considerable space to the Communist war effort, with photographs of Mao Tse-tung, Zhou Enlai, and others plotting strategy in the caves of Yenan. But the account now gives a nod to the KMT's role in fighting the Japanese, as the illustrated history of the war distributed at the museum summarizes:

> China's War of Resistance Against Japan was a nationwide war against aggression. The troops of the Kuomintang and the Communist Party

fought against Japanese invaders sometimes each on their own, while at other times in coordination. Both battlefields were important components of the Chinese people's War of Resistance. However, taking a panoramic view of the eight-year history of the War of Resistance, we must point out that the Chinese Communist Party and the people's armed forces under its leadership played the role of mainstay in the war. . . . The political influence and leading role of the Communists cannot be measured by gains from a few military campaigns.[9]

This backhanded acknowledgment of the Nationalists' role is used to build another, broader and more important assertion about the war—that Chinese resistance, overcoming more than a century of humiliation, was decisive in defeating Japan as part of the global "anti-Fascist war." China is depicted as the "first country to fight the Fascist aggressor," its contribution decisive in the outcome of the global conflict, pinning down millions of Japanese troops, allowing the West and the Soviet Union to concentrate their forces on Nazi Germany, and defeating Japanese forces in the battlefield. According to this revised historical narrative, Soviet entry into the war, once celebrated according to Marxist orthodoxy, and the American battle in the Pacific, including the use of atomic weapons, did not decide the outcome. Those two events "hastened the surrender," war resistance museum director Li Zongyuan says, "but they didn't play a decisive role."[10]

This assertion of Chinese primacy in the outcome of World War II proved to be an even more contentious issue than that of Japanese war crimes when a Harvard-organized conference of Western, Japanese, and Chinese scholars gathered in 2004 to discuss the military history of the Sino-Japanese War. "The China theater was not merely important, it was *the* critical theater in World War II," Chinese participants argued.[11] The Western scholars who edited the volume that emerged from the conference beg to differ: "The fact of the matter is that China was indeed a tertiary theater in World War II."

The debate over the cause of Japan's defeat was also contentious. Western and Japanese scholars point to the American naval war as the key to Japan's downfall, concluding: "Japan, including its forces in China, was brought to its knees not by Chinese armies but through the destruction of the Japanese homeland by aerial bombs, submarine torpedoes, and nuclear weapons."

Such judgments are not found in Chinese histories, certainly not in the textbooks and other materials that are used to shape the historical memory of Chinese youth. China's secondary school history textbooks provide a revealing window onto both the shifting nature of the historical narrative offered within China and the rather dramatic embrace of this newer, patriotic version of the past.

The standard textbook on Chinese contemporary and modern history, published by the state's Peoples Education Publishing House, was in circulation from the 1980s through the middle of the first decade of this century. Beginning in 2004, it was gradually replaced throughout the country by a new, completely revised textbook, *Chinese History*, which offered a significantly altered version of the wartime period, one more in tune with the Patriotic Education Campaign begun in the 1990s.[12]

The older volume, which featured Mao standing before a microphone to announce the formation of the Peoples Republic, still reflected the more traditional Communist narrative about this period, though with some sense of the shift already taking place in the 1980s. It divides the wartime era into two chapters. The first, "The Ten-Year Confrontation between the CCP and KMT (1927–1937)," is twenty-seven pages in length. The second, "The Anti-Japanese War of the Chinese Nation (1937–1945)," is shorter, some twenty pages.

The first chapter offers a classical account of the confrontation between the CCP and the KMT, describing the latter as increasingly becoming an accommodator of Japanese imperialists and an instrument of British and American pursuit of their own interests in China. It condemns KMT leader Chiang Kai-shek's policy of "no resistance" to Japan's takeover of Manchuria in 1931 and its advance into northeast China.

The second chapter offers a more redemptive tale of the formation of a united front, at the urging of the CCP, to resist Japan's expansion into full-scale war in 1937. Nationalist troops are credited with waging many battles against the Japanese invader, from Shanghai to the south. The Nanjing massacre is described but given relatively short shrift—it occupies only two paragraphs, with only one photograph of bodies being buried by Japanese soldiers. It is Mao's strategy of "protracted war" that is credited with drawing Japan into a quagmire of extended conflict. Students are asked to answer this question: "After the Marco Polo Bridge Incident, what were the differences and similarities between the attitudes of the CCP and the KMT in confronting the invasion by Japanese imperialism?" As the narrative moves on, the textbook describes how KMT policy "turns reactionary," sabotaging the united effort by turning its fire more toward the Communist foe. CCP members, in contrast, are depicted as the true nationalists, rallying the populace against Japan.

The end of the war is given in a brief summary: The war concludes in Europe in May 1945. The Soviet Union declares war on Japan and destroys the elite Japanese Kwantung Army in the northeast. Communist forces launch a nationwide counterattack. And on August 15, the Japanese surrender (no mention of the atomic bombing appears in this account). "Thus the Chinese People's Anti-Japanese War ultimately achieved its final victory," concludes the textbook chapter.

The revised Chinese history textbook offers some continuity with this historical narrative but also some stunning revision. The events of the civil war are dealt with separately from those of the anti-Japanese war, as part of a section on "democratic revolutions in modern China" from the mid-nineteenth century Taiping rebellion to the establishment of the PRC. The war with Japan is the second lesson in a chapter tellingly titled "World Powers' Military Aggression and Chinese Peoples' Resistance (1840–1945)," a narrative of foreign intervention and resistance from the Opium Wars to World War II.

The lesson on the anti-Japanese war is now brief—a mere three pages is devoted to the subject—and deeply imbued with the didactic themes of the Patriotic Education Campaign. The chapter begins with Japan's surrender, described as a moment of "victory after the brave eight-year fight." The war is set in the context of a Japanese imperial design to conquer China, going back to the Sino-Japanese War of 1894–95 and proceeding through the Manchurian incident of 1931 and growing tensions in Shanghai and northern China, and leading to the opening of full-scale war in 1937. "Facing the threat of Japan's invasion," the textbook tells students, "the KMT and CCP stopped their civil war and built an anti-Japanese national united front." Nothing is said about later KMT betrayal, though the CCP is given credit for leading the battle after 1941.

This new patriotic version devotes far more space to a detailed description of the Nanjing massacre including graphic accounts of atrocities there and elsewhere in China. It poses a discussion subject for students: "Japanese right-wing forces vigorously deny that the Japanese military committed the Nanjing massacre—the ultimate act of human cruelty—during its invasion of China. They consider it a type of wartime behavior. What do you think of the issue?"

Finally, while the textbook links the surrender of the Japanese to the success of "world anti-Fascist forces," it places this "victory" in a clearly nationalist framework:

> The victory in the Anti-Japanese War was at the time the first complete success that the Chinese people had achieved in fighting against foreign invaders in more than 100 years. It greatly strengthened Chinese national pride and the confidence of people throughout the nation and established a firm foundation for the victory of the democratic revolution in the whole country. China's Anti-Japanese War was an important part of the world Anti-Fascist War. The Chinese peoples' resistance against the Japanese made a great contribution to the victory of the world Anti-Fascist War. The international status of China was raised.

This textbook reflects the rise of Sino-Japanese tensions at the time, triggered in part by the decision of Prime Minister Junichiro Koizumi to conduct annual visits to the Yasukuni Shrine to Japan's war dead, beginning in 2001. Those tensions were fed by the approval in 2001 of a history textbook authored by right-wing scholars, the so-called *New History Textbook*, which offered a more unrepentant account of Japan's aggression in Asia (though very few school districts adopted the textbook for use). In the spring of 2005, the Chinese government backed a massive Internet campaign to collect signatures opposing Japan's bid for permanent membership in the United Nations Security Council. A central theme of this campaign was that Japan was unsuited for membership because of its failure to face up to its wartime past. A Japanese government decision to authorize a second edition of the right-wing textbook in April 2005 triggered a wave of protest across China. Protesters gathered at the Japanese Embassy in Beijing, throwing stones and shouting, "Be ashamed of distorting history." The protests spread to Shanghai and ultimately sent the relations between the two countries into a freeze that persisted until late 2006 when a visit by the new Japanese premier led to the formation of a joint committee to study history issues.[13]

In September 2005, Chinese leader Hu Jintao gave this new version of wartime history an official imprimatur in a speech marking the sixtieth anniversary of the end of the war. Significantly, Hu acknowledged the contributions of the Nationalists in fighting the Japanese, while at the same time continuing to assert Communist leadership. The speech was aimed in part at Taiwan, pairing a warning against pro-independence forces then in power and offering an olive branch to the KMT, which the Chinese government saw now as a force against secession on the island. Hu had invited the Taiwanese Nationalist political leaders to visit the mainland that spring, the first such visit since 1949.

While there remain tensions behind closed doors over the rendering of historical truth about the wartime period, the patriotic campaign can claim success in implanting its message, particularly among China's younger generation. Polls conducted over the previous decade exploring Chinese attitudes toward Japan show a strong association with the wartime memory issues, relatively undiminished even in the past few years when relations have markedly improved.

Since 2005, the Japanese think tank Genron NPO and *China Daily* have conducted a joint opinion poll in both countries that has explored mutual perceptions. Asked what comes to mind when they think of Japan, Chinese respondents have consistently put the Nanjing massacre in first place, closely followed by Japanese electronic goods.[14] The "history issue" is named by the vast majority of Chinese as the main obstacle to development of better relations. Even in a recent poll, released in August 2010, Chinese attribute their negative perceptions of Japan (which remain a majority) to the wartime past and a belief that Japanese "do not properly acknowledge their wartime aggression."

At various moments, the Chinese state has unleashed this new patriotism for its own policy ends. But often it finds itself having to pull back on the reins for fear that antiforeign feelings can turn inward. Indeed, in the relatively less controlled world of the Chinese Internet, "netizens" engage in often vitriolic assaults on those who are considered less than patriotic. The construction of wartime memory in China thus remains an ongoing process, entangled in the complex needs of the Chinese state and Communist Party to retain legitimacy in a rapidly changing China. Because of its need to offer a new, patriotic narrative to replace the Marxian ideology of the past, they have opened the door both to a potentially uncontrolled nationalism and to a questioning of their legitimacy. Despite the power of the state and party to enforce orthodoxy, there now exists a real and growing debate about the past in China.

CONFRONTING COLLABORATION IN KOREA

Less than an hour's train ride from the South Korean capital, outside of the city of Cheonan, the South Korean government constructed a national museum dedicated to the struggle against Japanese colonial rule. The Independence Hall of Korea is a sprawling complex of stone pavilions and modern exhibition halls, set against the backdrop of forested hills. On a snowy weekday in December 2010, the only visitors were small groups of schoolchildren and new recruits to the armed forces, marched through the exhibitions for the purposes of patriotic education.

The opening hall offers an overview of some five thousand years of Korean history, from the prehistoric period to the modern era. From there, however, the exhibit offers an excruciatingly detailed rendition of the advance of Japanese imperialism into the Korean peninsula, the reaction of Koreans to the loss of their independence, and the ongoing struggle against "attempts to distort the country's national history" by Japan and others. It is a classic tale of colonialism and resistance, with scant reference to those Koreans who supported Japan, benefited from its rule, and actively collaborated as members of the Japanese Imperial Army, the police, and even as guards in the prisoner of war camps in Southeast Asia.

The museum brushes aside the debate, now more vibrant in Korea, about the modernizing impact of colonial rule. "Japan looted Korea economically," the museum exhibit explains. "Korea was turned into a base for supply of raw materials and cheap labor to Japan." The plundering of Korea is later linked broadly to Japan's "aggressive war," but the museum otherwise does not mention the Japanese invasion of China or offer a broader context for Japanese colonial policy, including the forced mobilization of labor that was prompted by the morass in China and the tide of defeat in the Pacific.

Most of the exhibit space is devoted to a detailed rendition, often accompanied by life-size dioramas, of every aspect of Korean resistance, from the student movements and exile political groups to armed guerrilla movements (though without a nod to the Communist role in those movements). Dioramas show Japanese torturing Korean prisoners, beating them to gain information. Others display the fate of the "comfort women," the Korean women dragooned into brothels organized by the Japanese military to service its soldiers. The war's end is portrayed as the victory of

Korean dedication to independence—there is barely any mention of the U.S. war in the Pacific.

The rendition of the wartime and colonial period is closely mirrored in Korean high school history textbooks, which offer extended accounts of the colonial period, of Japanese brutality and repression, of exploitation of Korea, and of Korean resistance. But they offer almost no context for these acts. There is very little teaching about the war that shaped the intensification of Japanese brutality and forced labor—indeed, Korean students are taught almost nothing about the Japanese invasion of China or the circumstances that led to Japan's surrender. The atomic bombing of Japan, in which tens of thousands of Koreans were also killed, is not even included in the history textbook produced by the government's Ministry of Education, the main textbook in use in Korean schools.[15]

The avoidance of collaboration in the museum is not surprising. The museum was built in the 1980s under the Chun Doo-hwan regime, at a time when it was under growing revolt from within the country by students, human rights activists, and others. The museum clearly reflects the desire to wrap authoritarian rule in the mantle of nationalism. Ironically, the museum opened its doors on the anniversary of liberation, August 15, in 1987, less than two months after popular revolt forced the Chun regime to agree to free elections.

Korean democratization brought with it an effort to reopen the unhealed wounds of the Korean wartime experience. The election of two successive progressive governments, beginning in 1997 with the victory of longtime opposition leader Kim Dae Jung, led to organized efforts to delve into long-hidden sore spots, among them the role of collaborators, the massacres of Korean leftists in the south during the early years after liberation, and American killings of civilians during the Korean War. Following passage of the Act on Clearing Up Past Incidents for Truth and Reconciliation, a commission was formed in 2005 to investigate abuses under Japanese rule and the period of authoritarian government in South Korea.

Alongside, private groups formed to investigate the role of "pro-Japanese collaborators." In 2009, a three thousand-page "directory" of collaborators was published. Altogether 4,389 people have been named in the reference work, put together by the Institute for Research in Collaborationist Activities, among them former president Park Chung Hee. The publication picked up a struggle over Korean history that had been broadly suppressed during the decades of authoritarian rule. This work was cited and explained in an interview given by progressive novelist Cho Jeong Rae, a board member of the institute, who said: "The dictionary is significant as a record of the history of the collaborators. It is a disgrace and misfortune of our nation that would not resolve this issue just after liberation. We lost our national dignity and social order as a result of that failure. . . . How can we demand apology from Japan when we ourselves cannot resolve the domestic collaborator issue?"[16]

The view of the past from Korean conservatives is, as one might expect, diametrically opposed. The dictionary "was compiled by a pro-North, leftist group," asserts Cho Gab Je, a journalist and the author of numerous books on Korean contemporary history, including a twelve-volume biography of Park. "Their acts are all based on ideology and propagandistic intention. The production of the dictionary is intended to attack the people who contributed to the building of South Korea. It sensationalizes the history of pro-Japanese activities."[17]

This conflict has made its way into popular culture. The 2005 Korean film *Blue Swallow* offered a somewhat heroic portrait of Park Kyung-won, an early Korean female pilot who was trained by the Japanese. Park took part in a "friendship" flight to Japanese-occupied Manchuria, earning her the label of being a pro-Japanese collaborator. The airing of a film about a famous collaborator proved to be highly controversial in Korea.

For some Korean historians, both the dictionary and the commission are problematic efforts to deal with a complex past. Among Korean historians there is an increasingly fierce debate about the issue of "colonial modernization," the argument that Japanese colonial rule created the basis for Korea's later economic development through the building of infrastructure, the fostering of education, and the development of industry. Progressives reject that contention, responding that even if Japanese rule contributed to modernization, it was only done to facilitate its colonial rule and exploitation.

This debate has a long history in Korea. After colonial rule ended, a major task for Korean historians was to refute the Japanese justification for their colonial rule, that they had modernized a Korea hopelessly stuck in its feudal past. The new nationalist historiography portrayed Japanese rule as exploitative and argued that, in fact, Japan had destroyed the birth of capitalist modernization in Korea.

Beginning in the 1980s, however, such nationalist perspective was challenged and reexamined from both inside and outside of the Korean academic community, especially by economic historians in Korea, Japan, and the United States.[18] These scholars sought to offer more "objective" scholarly analyses that went beyond the value-laden views of both the nationalists and the defenders of colonialism.

This new scholarship focused on examining the socioeconomic changes that took place in Korea as a result of the intensive wartime industrial growth during the waning years of Japanese rule. The industrialization of this period was recast as "colonial, dependent development," not sufficient for full-scale modernization but at least substantial enough to create the foundation for Korea's postwar growth from the 1960s. Rejecting the stark dichotomy of development versus exploitation—and of collaboration versus resistance—these scholars tried to offer a more nuanced description of socioeconomic changes under Japanese rule.

While this new perspective had gained much recognition by the 1990s, it also provoked strong reaction from nationalist scholars. "Discussing the question of whether Japanese rule contributed to the modernization of Korea is like stepping into a minefield," wrote Korean scholar Chulwoo Lee.[19] "The pompous claims of Japanese colonialists that they were modernizing Korean society and the use of those claims to justify colonial rule are vivid memories for Koreans, as is the support many contemporary Westerners gave Japanese imperialism for bringing the blessings of modernity to Asia. Moreover, under the sway of modernization theory, postwar Western scholars have tended to credit Japanese rule for the material and institutional changes that occurred during the colonial period."

This struggle over the wartime past in Korea continues unabated. Ironically, these debates have become embroiled in the parallel discussions among Japanese about the same issues. There is a growing interaction between Korean and Japanese progressives and between the Korean "New Right" historians and colleagues in Japan. Thus the internal debates within Korea, as with China, have become intertwined with those in Japan.

MULTIPLE MEMORIES OF WAR IN POSTWAR JAPAN

Yasukuni Shrine, Japan's Shinto memorial to the nation's war dead, sits off a busy Tokyo boulevard, just north of the deep green waters of the moat surrounding the Imperial Palace grounds in the center of the city. Casual visitors to the shrine can easily miss its significance. A long stone pathway leads from the large steel *torii*, or gate, at the entrance to the shrine, past the statue of Omura Masujiro, the samurai-scholar who is considered the founder of Japan's modern military following the Meiji revolution of 1868. Beyond lies the main shrine, with its classical sloping tiled roofs, where Shinto priests in stiff robes move quietly within the inner courtyard. Except on holidays or in the spring when Tokyoites gather to sit below the blooming cherry trees that line the shrine pathways, Yasukuni is a quiet place, attracting few visitors.

Yet Yasukuni holds powerful significance for Japanese—and for Japan's neighbors. Since its construction in the second year of the Meiji emperor's reign, the shrine has served to honor the almost 2.5 million people who died in a series of wars from the internal struggles to create the modern nation to Japan's wars as an emergent great power, beginning with the Sino-Japanese War of 1894–95 and ending with the disastrous conflict in the Pacific. Even though the shrine's formal ties to the Japanese state were severed after the war, it remains a highly symbolic evocation of the trilogy of emperor, Shintoism, and military prowess that was the centerpiece of Japan's wartime ideology.

Yasukuni Shrine has come to embody the frictions over wartime memory between Japan and its neighbors, triggering serious tensions in the first decade of this century between Japan and China and between Japan and Korea. The memorial represents a denial of war responsibility and of aggression, exemplified by the decision to include among the enshrined war dead some fifty thousand former colonial subjects, mostly Korean and Taiwanese, who were conscripted to serve their conquerors. The shrine also honors around one hundred thousand civilians in Okinawa, many of whom were dragooned into deadly service by the imperial army, some forced to commit mass suicide to prevent their surrender to the invading American forces.[20] The most controversial expression of this denial of wartime responsibility was the decision of the shrine authorities, made in secret in 1969 in consultation with officials of the Health and Welfare Ministry, to honor by enshrinement the fourteen Japanese military and civilian leaders who were convicted as Class A war criminals, the highest level of criminal responsibility, and sentenced to death by the Allied Tokyo War Crimes Tribunal. The actual enshrinement of the high-level war criminals, among them Japan's wartime leader Tojo Hideki, was not publicly carried out until 1978.²¹ That decision prompted Emperor Hirohito, Japan's wartime emperor, to stop visiting the shrine, as he had done numerous times since the end of the war, according to a memo written in 1988 by the grand steward of the Imperial Household Agency, Tomita Tomohiko.²²

Although Yasukuni's formal ties to the Japanese state were severed by the occupation authorities, Japanese leaders began to visit the shrine at festivals to pay their respects to the war dead, beginning even before the restoration of sovereignty in 1952. The most sensitive visits were those that took place on August 15, the anniversary of Japan's surrender in 1945, a date with even greater symbolic import. To preserve the illusion that these visits had no official meaning, the prime ministers would usually declare themselves to be paying their respects, along with other prominent politicians, as "private citizens." In 1985, the nationalist conservative leader Nakasone Yasuhiro defiantly visited in his official capacity as the prime minister, triggering a storm of protest from around Asia and effectively ending that practice. But Prime Minister Koizumi revived the controversy by inaugurating a series of six annual visits, beginning in 2001, visits that triggered official protest from China, South Korea, and other Asian neighbors and sent Sino-Japanese relations into a virtual deep freeze for years.²³

The implied narrative of the shrine regarding the wartime period is not evident, especially to a casual visitor. But the message is unavoidably clear at the shrine's Yushukan war museum, tucked off to the side and, until recently, largely ignored. Yushukan was first established in 1882 to display the relics of Japan's wars, from the diaries of soldiers and samurai swords to the Zero fighter that occupies the entry of the museum. In the 1930s, as Japan embarked on war in China, the museum offered Japanese children a hands-on experience where they could sit in the cockpit of a bomber or fire an air rifle at a target. Millions of visitors, many of them students, came to the museum during those years.²⁴

The war museum and its exhibition hall were shut down as well by the occupation authorities. A limited number of exhibits reopened in the early 1960s, but the entire museum was not opened to the public until 1985, after a restoration. In a visit two years after the reopening, the museum offered a somewhat subdued though clearly unrepentant presentation of Japan's wartime past. Outside the building, a one-man human torpedo, the *kaiten*, was displayed. Inside, visitors could see Japanese weapons and models, including the *Ohka*, a rocket-propelled glider intended to be flown into enemy ships, celebrating, along with the *kaiten*, the heroism of suicide attacks carried out by a desperate Japanese military in the waning days of the war. Wandering through the dimly lit stucco building, the visitor came upon a large hall, used for the gatherings of groups of aging veterans, dominated at one end by a massive mural painting of Japanese fighter planes, the rising sun emblem on their wings glittering as they dove out of the sun at an invisible target, suggesting Pearl Harbor was below them.

Foreigners were largely ignorant of the reopened Yushukan. Most of those who happened by accident on the building could not read the Japanese captions on the exhibit cases. All that changed in 2002 when a new, expanded and more modern museum opened its doors, complete with well-lighted exhibition rooms and halls, the contents carefully explained in translated descriptions, although sometimes with sanitized language. The narrative of the war was now visible to foreign visitors, who were appalled to discover a version of history in which the enemy was virtually absent and Japanese actions, from the Sino-Japanese War to the war in the Pacific, are portrayed as acts of heroism and self-defense. This is an unabashedly revisionist view of the past, as Rozman and others have termed it.

The lobby, partly open to the outside and surrounded by glass walls, is dominated by a Type of fighter, the "Zero," the main aircraft of the Japanese Imperial Navy from the Sino-Japanese War onward, painted a shining dark green, the large red insignia emblazoned on the wings and fuselage. To the right is a Japanese locomotive of the type that ran along the rail lines between Thailand and Burma in Japanese-conquered Southeast Asia. The description offers no hint of the tens of thousands of prisoners who died building those railways. Visitors wander through a series of exhibition rooms, beginning with the "Spirit of the Samurai," moving through the early history of Meiji Japan and its internal struggles, and then on to the Sino-Japanese War of 1894–95, the Russo-Japanese War, the takeover of Manchuria in 1931, and then the "China Incident," as the start of the war in 1937 is so carefully labeled. An entire floor is dedicated to the "Greater East Asian War," the term used by the wartime regime. The final rooms are devoted to the display of "mementos of the Noble Spirits enshrined at Yasukuni Shrine," featuring the heart-rendering final messages of kamikaze pilots penned to loved ones before heading off to certain death.

Taken as one seamless narrative, Yushukan presents a history of "glorious" warfare leading up to the struggle with the United States and its allies. The museum presents the war as the inevitable product of Japan's efforts to forge a pan-Asian peace, even to liberate Asia from Western colonialism, in the face of outside encroachment. The annexation of Korea, in this version of history, was an effort to free that country from Chinese domination. As Japanese insisted at the time, Japan's war with the United States is portrayed as a justified response to the hostile assault from the West—the "ABCD Encirclement" of Japan by the United States, Britain, China, and the Netherlands—that culminated in the economic embargo imposed by the United States.[25] Even Japan's defeat is presented in this light on an exhibition placard: "When the war ended the people of Asia returned to their homes. Those whose desire for independence had been awakened were no longer the obedient servants of their [Western] colonizers. . . . One after another, the nations of Southeast Asia won their independence and their successes inspired Africa and other areas as well."[26] The Allied judgment against Japan, delivered in the Tokyo War Crimes Tribunal, is largely dismissed—the museum features instead in its final gallery a tribute to Justice Radhabinod Pal, the Indian member of the Tokyo Tribunal who offered a dissenting opinion pronouncing the Japanese innocent of war crimes and putting blame for the war on the aggression of American and British imperialism.

It is a sanitized history, comforting perhaps to some veterans and to those on the Japanese right who share this memory of the past, but disturbing to those who were the victims of Japan's colonial rule and wartime aggression, including the Japanese people themselves. "Neatly obliterated from the historical memory of Yushukan are the historical facts of Japanese war crimes, of Japanese colonialism and aggression, and of Japanese defeat," writes British historian John Breen.[27]

For many outside Japan, the Yushukan narrative is the principal, if not the dominant, narrative accepted in postwar Japan. Seen through the lens of media reportage, official statements, and even the writings of academics in the West and in much of Asia, this justifies what one scholar calls "the orthodox interpretation of Japanese war memories."[28] According to this "orthodoxy," Japan was the clear aggressor in the war, it committed numerous atrocities on a scale comparable to Nazi Germany, and both its government and people have failed to acknowledge, much less address, its war responsibility. In that rendition of the war, the only acceptable Japanese response is guilt and contrition, one compatible with the Allied narrative of a "good war" fought to defeat evil foes.

Within that neat understanding, legitimate issues of historical and political debate are put to the side. Was Japan really solely responsible for the war in Asia and the Pacific? Can Japan's crimes, horrific as they were, be compared to those of the Holocaust? Has Japan, both as a state and as a people, truly failed to show contrition for its acts? The answers to those questions are far more complex than the orthodox view of Japan's war memory would allow.

At the root of the flawed nature of this orthodoxy is the assertion that the conservative or revisionist war memory is the predominant one in Japan. This presumption is not surprising, given not only the impression formed by media and others but also the existence of largely monolithic war memory narratives in Korea and China, where at both the official and unofficial level the narrative is an undifferentiated tale of victimization by an evil invader and of heroic resistance. Scant reference is given to problems of collaboration and even support for the Japanese colonizer and invader since it does not meet the more urgent need to use the past to shape national identity.

Japan does not present any such homogeneity of war memory. Since the first days of the American occupation of Japan—and, in fact, even before that—the events of the war and how they should be recorded has been a heavily contested battleground. Undoubtedly, Yushukan faithfully represents the conservative view of the war in Japan, one that can be easily found in the pages of right-wing media and is entrenched in the ranks of the former ruling conservative LDP, with scholarly gloss provided by members of the academic and literary intelligentsia. But if anything, they see themselves as somewhat of a beleaguered minority in Japan, engaged in a decades-long war with their ideological foes on the left to reclaim a sense of Japanese pride.

Japanese progressives dominated the early attempts to define Japan's war memory, taking their cue from Japan's occupiers. Amid the ruin and rubble of occupied Japan, they embraced the narrative of wartime responsibility embodied in the Tokyo war crimes tribunals. In those early years of occupation, amid the burst of democratic fervor and the rise of the long-suppressed Japanese Left, Japanese anger was directed at the wartime regime, dominated by the military and its allies in the political elite, nominally headed by Emperor Hirohito.

The issue of war responsibility was heavily debated in the 1950s and 1960s, when progressive views held more sway. Liberal intellectuals such as Maruyama Masao argued that aspects of Japanese social structure and popular culture created fertile ground for the rise of militarism in the

1930s. In his classic work, "The Logic and Psychology of Ultranationalism" (originally published in 1946), he blamed the prewar imperial system for fostering the growth of an extreme nationalist form of Japanese fascism and a lack of personal responsibility. Filmmakers such as Kon Ichikawa explored the grim realities of the war in *Harp of Burma* (*Biruma no tategoto*; 1956) and *Fires on the Plain* (*Nobi*; 1959), which offered stark portrayals of the bleak conditions of the Japanese army in retreat. Perhaps the most powerful critique of the war was offered in Jumpei Gomikawa's *Ningen no joken* (*The Human Condition*), a trilogy of films, made from 1959 to 1961. It also appeared in novel and manga forms. These all offered a unremittingly harsh portrait of Japanese rule in northern China, including depictions of forced labor in the service of Japanese corporations, sexual slavery, and acts of brutality committed by soldiers against ordinary Chinese.

The retreat of the Japanese Left in both political and intellectual life in Japan from the 1960s onward, propelled by the tides of the Cold War and the fading attraction of the Soviet and Chinese Communist systems, was reflected in a growing revisionist voice on wartime memory issues. The counterattack focused in part on the educational system, where the Right mounted a fierce critique of the left-wing Japanese Teachers Union for allegedly carrying a Marxist narrative about the past into the classroom. The intense battles over textbooks actually began in the 1950s, as the LDP began the campaign to revise textbooks, but they gained intensity in the 1980s when textbook content became an issue of international contention between Japan and China and Korea.

The progressive narrative has lost much of its organizational power with the collapse of the Japanese Socialist Party as the principal opposition force, though the current Democratic Party of Japan still reflects that view of historical responsibility. But it remains a strong current of popular culture. To find the narrative in full form, one can visit another museum, far from Tokyo, perched on a cliff overlooking the Pacific Ocean on the southern Japanese island of Okinawa. Here, beginning in late March 1945, the war finally reached Japanese home territory in the form of the American-led invasion of Okinawa. The battle that ensued was a terrible one, fought for months in a "typhoon of steel" that altered the island's landscape and claimed the lives of upward of two hundred thousand people, more than half of them civilians.

The Okinawa Peace Memorial Museum does not celebrate a heroic resistance. The centerpiece of its narrative is Okinawa's civilians, the victims of both the American invaders and a brutal Japanese Imperial Army. Most famous among them are the young women and schoolchildren forced to commit suicide by the Japanese army rather than surrender to the Americans.

"Some were blown apart by shells, some finding themselves in a hopeless situation were driven to suicide, some died of starvation, some succumbed to malaria, while others fell victim to the retreating Japanese troops," the museum brochure tells visitors. A display inside the museum offers graphic depiction of this last situation. In a diorama, a grim Japanese soldier stands menacingly over an Okinawan family huddled in a cave, his bayonet glinting in the spotlight as the mother tries to smother the cries of her child. "At the hands of Japanese soldiers, civilians were massacred, forced to kill themselves and each other," the caption explains.

The main museum, a long curving white building, graced by a series of red-tile roofs typical of that tropical island, sits on a slight hilltop in the Peace Park in Mabuni, where the last resistance to the Americans was mounted. Below, on a bluff overlooking the sea, semicircles of zigzagging black marble walls are inscribed with the names of all who died on the island, from the Allied soldiers and their Japanese army foes to the civilians who lost their lives. Modeled on the Vietnam War memorial in Washington, D.C., the walls offer a poignant salute to the concept that Okinawa symbolizes, in the museum's own words, "the absurdity of war and atrocities it inevitably brings about."

The narrative of history offered in the Okinawa museum offers a very different view of who was responsible for this conflict. The "road to the battle of Okinawa" begins in the first exhibition room with an explanation of Japanese expansionism, which includes the annexation of Okinawa to the Japanese mainland, "aimed at making the Okinawans as faithful subjects of the Emperor." The Japanese Empire, as the museum tells visitors, set about building a strong army and invading neighboring countries, beginning with the Manchurian Incident and leading inexorably to this "last battleground." For this museum, it is not the "Greater East Asian War" but rather "the fifteen-year war," a term of reference more popular among progressive historians, encapsulating the view of the war as a relentless imperialist venture that started with the takeover of Manchuria in 1931.

The museum, which replaced a smaller, less imposing structure, was the creation of Masahide Ota, the preeminent Okinawan historian of the war, who was elected governor in 1990. Ota was conscripted as a high school student into a unit called the Blood and Iron Student Corps and sent to work with pick and shovel to build airfields and fortifications for the imperial army. When the American forces landed, the unit was sent into the battlefield without any training.

As a college student in the early 1950s, Ota wrote his first book about the Battle of Okinawa, the first of many, a powerful collection of personal accounts of his high school classmates who survived the war. Educated later in the United States, Ota dedicated himself to telling the story of the Battle of Okinawa for a general audience, initially as a journalist and popular writer. He went on to write a dozen books about the war, and after winning the governorship in 1990 he pushed to build a new museum that would reflect the Okinawan experience of war. But Ota, as a progressive, has also dedicated himself to opposing the massive American base presence that remained entrenched on Okinawa ever since the island reverted to Japanese administration in 1972.

The progressive narrative has faded somewhat in its influence, along with the organized Japanese Left. The pacifist narrative, however, remains predominant, overlapping in certain respects with both the conservative and progressive narratives. In this version of the past, war itself is the enemy, an experience of destruction of the Japanese nation, and to a lesser extent of its neighbors, that should never be repeated. It is a narrative of victimization, one that condemns the act of war and rejects the notion of a "just war."

That antiwar narrative is ubiquitous in Japanese popular culture, from novels and television to the cinema. The most visible, and visited, expression of this pacifist narrative can be found in the Peace Memorial Museum built near ground zero in the western Japanese city of Hiroshima, the site of the first use of the atomic bomb in warfare. The graceful three-building structure is set at the entrance to a large park, where every year the city holds a ceremony to mark the moment on August 6, 1945, when the bomb was detonated over the city. Up until then, Hiroshima had been spared from the horrific wave of airborne attacks on Japanese cities, including the March 9–10 firebombing of Tokyo that claimed some one hundred thousand lives.

The decision to use the atomic bomb remains a subject of intense debate among historians and military experts, not least in the United States: Was it truly necessary, to end the war and to save lives, both of Japanese and of the Allied soldiers gearing up for invasion of the Japanese mainland? Did a second bomb have to be dropped on Nagasaki? Wasn't Japan on the verge of surrender anyway? Did the bombing cause Japan to surrender, or did other factors force the decision, including the Soviet entry into the war two days later? Were there other factors, such as the desire to limit the Soviet Union's postwar role, behind the American decision?

If those questions remain hotly debated elsewhere, there is no question as to how they are answered for the millions who still visit the Hiroshima museum, by far the most visited war museum in Japan. The museum offers a brief nod to the Japanese aggression that preceded this moment. Following a renovation of the museum in 1994, new exhibits were mounted to acknowledge that Japan's aggression started the war, including the slaughter of Chinese in Nanjing in 1937. The museum authorities understood this was necessary to legitimize the message of victimization that is at the center of the museum's narrative.[29]

Visitors to the museum weave their way through several floors of exhibits, spread over two buildings, that offer an emotionally powerful tale of the enormous destructive power of the weapon. The museum takes you past artifacts of its effects, from a charred children's lunch box, bottles melted into bizarre twisted shapes, and the shadow of a victim who was sitting on some steps when the flash of heat whitened the stone around him. The terror of radiation, which claimed its victims for years afterward, is explored in detail. The bombing's death toll by the end of 1945 was estimated at over one hundred thousand, and perhaps as many more died within five years from the aftereffects of the bombing.

The historical message of the museum is unmistakable—it rejects the justification that the atomic bombing was necessary to save lives. It rather embraces the view, popular on the Japanese left and among revisionist historians in the United States, that the Americans were looking past Japan's surrender to the postwar order and the coming contest for world domination with the Soviet Union. In an exhibit devoted to the question of why the United States decided to drop the bomb, the museum offers this version of history: "After Germany's surrender, tension mounted between the United States and the Soviet Union regarding the disposition of postwar Europe. The United States began worrying about the increased influence the Soviets would obtain if they joined the war against Japan in mid-August as planned. The United States believed that if the atomic bomb ended the war, the United States would establish postwar supremacy over the Soviets."

That view leaves aside the arguments made by the Americans at the time, though certainly disputed subsequently, that the use of the atomic bomb hastened surrender and saved lives. Perhaps more importantly, it isolates the atomic bombings as a singular event, only loosely related to the decisions that set Japan upon a path of colonialism and aggression and led to the war with the United States.

The evasion of responsibility has its origins, in part, in the decisions made by the American occupation of Japan. The most important decision was made even before the occupation began when the Americans accepted the surrender of Japan with the understanding that it would allow the emperor system in Japan to continue in place. Supreme Commander General Douglas MacArthur made a fateful decision to leave Emperor Hirohito on his throne, calculating with some degree of justification that the emperor could play a valuable role in persuading the Japanese people to accept foreign occupation. MacArthur compounded the impact of his decision by taking the emperor and his wartime role out of the deliberations of the Tokyo War Crimes Tribunal.[30]

Whatever the rationale of that decision, it also allowed Japanese themselves, who had been loyal subjects of the emperor, to avoid serious examination of their own responsibility. The exigencies of the Cold War further led the occupation to suppress the Japanese Left in the late 1940s and to allow, if not encourage, the reentry into politics of key parts of the wartime establishment. Thus the question of who was responsible for Japan's war in Asia and the Pacific remained a matter of debate, unresolved to this day in Japan.

The failure to resolve this question was the driving impetus for a special project undertaken by the conservative *Yomiuri Shimbun*, the largest circulation daily in the world. The research institute of the newspaper carried out a massive historical research project aimed at answering the central issue of the war: "Who was responsible?" The results of that project, which involved documentary research, interviews, and other historical investigation, were published in the newspaper in a series of articles in 2005, tied to the sixtieth anniversary of the end of the war. It was later published as a two-volume study, including in other languages.

The study was the brainchild of Tsuneo Watanabe, the aging but still powerful publisher of the *Yomiuri*. As a young man entering university in 1945, he was drafted and stationed on the coast to await the invading Americans. Watanabe had witnessed the firebombing of Tokyo, and he saw Japan's defeat coming, even welcomed it. In the early years of the occupation, Watanabe joined the Communists out of opposition to the emperor system. Today, Watanabe is a powerful member of the conservative establishment in Japan, able to meet with the emperor and empress, and a supporter of the humanized, more democratic version of the monarchy. But even now, Watanabe does not forgive Emperor Hirohito.

Watanabe ordered the *Yomiuri* research and publication out of concern that the passing of the wartime generation would leave the successive generations of Japanese without a clear understanding of the war and what it meant for Japan.

The *Yomiuri* research team sought to "retry" the Tokyo War Crimes Tribunal to identify those most responsible for the disastrous decision to go to war and its conduct. They do not disagree with the Tokyo judgments, including the Allied decision not to prosecute the emperor and the conviction of the fourteen Class A war criminals, led by Tojo. Indeed, Watanabe has crusaded against the Yasukuni Shrine authorities for their decision to enshrine those men and joined with the editor of the liberal *Asahi Shimbun* in calling for the creation of a national war cemetery to replace Yasukuni.

But the *Yomiuri* goes beyond that, adding others to the list of those who deserve the opprobrium of responsibility for the war, among them Prime Minister Konoe Fumimaro, who held that post when the attack on Pearl Harbor was decided, and several others. The *Yomiuri* also criticizes the United States for the firebombing of Japanese cities and the dropping of the atomic bombs, while also putting blame on the Soviet Union for unilaterally revoking the neutrality pact with Japan and declaring war in early August 1945.

Ultimately, however, responsibility is decisively placed upon Japan itself and its wartime leaders. As Watanabe makes clear in the introduction to the publication of the volume on the project, without the Japanese taking responsibility, there is no hope for reconciliation: "The Yomiuri Shimbun's efforts were based on its belief that there can be no genuinely honest and friendly dialogue with those countries which suffered considerable damage and casualties in the wars with Japan, without correctly understanding Japan's past. To that end, we, the Japanese people, should follow our consciences in explaining on our own how barbaric the wars were and who should be held responsible."[31]

ASIA TODAY

In Asia today, the debates about the wartime past are not only ongoing. They also continue to influence relations among the three principal wartime actors, fueling tensions over the past that many fear could once again trigger conflict. In 2012, for example, Japanese and Chinese vessels and military aircraft buzzed each other in the waters surrounding a set of islets—the Senkakus for the Japanese, the Diaoyus for the Chinese—claimed by both countries, a legacy of a territorial dispute left unresolved at the close of the war. Japanese and South Koreans exchanged harsh words over a similar territorial dispute, one that evokes for Koreans the charged memory of the colonial era. Wartime issues such as the handling of compensation for the comfort women and the content of textbooks became the subject of official démarches and warnings about the revival of Japanese "militarism" or the rise of nationalism on all sides.

The past in Northeast Asia is thus very much a part of the present. The divided memories and clashing narratives of the war are the subject not only of historians but of journalists, politicians, diplomats, and even soldiers. Unlike Europe, Asia has barely begun to reconcile over the war.

1. Shin in Shin and Sneider, eds., *History Textbooks and the Wars in Asia*, 3–4. The Walter H. Shorenstein Asia-Pacific Research Center's Divided Memories project has engaged in a comparative study of high school history textbooks in China, Japan, South Korea, Taiwan, and the United States, as well as comparative studies of the impact of dramatic film and elite opinion on the formation of historical memory. For the textbook study, see Shin and Sneider, eds., *History Textbooks and the Wars in Asia*.
2. Seraphim, *War Memory and Social Politics in Japan*.
3. Chirot in Shin and Sneider, eds., *History Textbooks and the Wars in Asia*, 269–85.
4. Peattie, Drea, and Van de Ven, eds., *The Battle for China*, 46–47.
5. Interview, April 26, 2010.
6. Wang, "National Humiliation, History Education."
7. For a description of these events, see Sneider, "The War over Words," in Shin and Sneider, eds., *History Textbooks and the Wars in Asia*.
8. Interview, April 24, 2010.
9. Zhang and Liu, *An Illustrated History*.
10. Interview, April 22, 2010.
11. Peattie, Drea, and Van de Ven, eds., *The Battle for China*, 422.
12. The sections of those textbooks dealing with the 1931–51 wartime era were translated in full by the Divided Memories and Reconciliation project at Stanford University, directed by Gi-Wook Shin and Daniel Sneider. The material cited here and all Chinese quotations in the

discussion are drawn from the full translations prepared for that project. Shin and Sneider, eds., *History Textbooks and the Wars in Asia*, 23–97.
13 Sneider in Shin and Sneider, eds., *History Textbooks and the Wars in Asia*, 252–60.
14 Polling data are available on the Genron NPO website, at http://www.genron-npo.net.
15 Shin and Sneider, eds., *History Textbooks and the Wars in Asia*, 36.
16 Interview, Seoul, December 17, 2009.
17 Interview, Seoul, April 3, 2010.
18 See Pyongjik, *The Economic Structure of Modern Korea*; Eckert, *Offspring of Empire*; Shin and Robinson, eds., *Colonial Modernity in Korea*.
19 Lee in Shin and Robinson, eds., *Colonial Modernity in Korea*, 21.
20 Tetsuya in Breen, ed., *Yasukuni, the War Dead*.
21 *Japan Times*, "Yasukuni, State in '69 OK'd War Criminal Inclusion."
22 Tomita's memo was published by the *Nihon Keizai Shinbu* in 2006. See Takahashi in Breen, ed., *Yasukuni, the War Dead*, 108; and *Japan Times*, "Hirohito Visits to Yasukuni Stopped."
23 Seraphim, *War Memory and Social Politics in Japan*, 235–57.
24 Yoshida, "Revising the Past, Complicating the Future."
25 Western media reports on the exhibit prompted shrine authorities to slightly rewrite the captions that implied American responsibility for the start of the war, though similarly troubling depictions of the war in Asia were not redone.
26 Cited by Yoshida, "Revising the Past, Complicating the Future." Some of the exhibition panels were slightly rewritten recently in response to American complaints, particularly those that attributed the attack on Pearl Harbor as a justified response to the American pressures on Japan.
27 Breen in Breen, ed., *Yasukuni, the War Dead*, 155.
28 Seaton, *Japan's Contested War Memories*, 2–3.
29 Breen, ed., *Yasukuni, the War Dead*, 177–79.
30 The decision remains a subject of intense debate among historians, for example, in the contrasting treatment of this decision by John W. Dower in *Embracing Defeat: Japan in the Wake of World War II* and in an indictment of the emperor's direct role by Herbert P. Bix in his biography *Hirohito and the Making of Modern Japan*.
31 Yomiuri Shimbun, *Who Was Responsible?*, 9.

PART II

DIVIDED MEMORIES ABOUT COLLABORATION AND RESISTANCE

Chapter 3

Different Strokes

Historical Realism and the Politics of History in Europe and Asia

THOMAS BERGER

One of the most striking developments in international politics in recent decades has been the heightened salience of history and historical justice issues. While such questions have long been a concern on the level of domestic politics, only recently have states sought through the offer of apologies and reparations to right the wrongs that they may have committed against other states.[1] While there is general acknowledgment of the existence of this trend toward apology, uncertainty abounds regarding its causes and consequences and its varying impact on different regions of the world.[2]

In some cases, notably Western Europe, the tendency of countries to offer apologies for past misdeeds is associated with a real, even transformative, improvement in interstate relations. In other regions, however, such as in the former Soviet Union and East Asia, history is associated as much with interstate acrimony and tension as it is with a taming of conflicting dimensions of international politics. To offer a preliminary exploration of the dynamics at play a case will be made for what will be called here a *historical realist* understanding of historical justice issues.[3] Realism means recognizing that powerful forces encourage states to pursue historical justice issues around the world. In particular, the global spread of human rights norms provides legitimacy to demands for redress for past wrongs, while the increased density of economic and political ties between countries gives such demands increased leverage in the form of law suits, threats of economic sanctions, and media attention. As a result, political leaders and governments find it increasingly difficult to ignore demands for justice. To put it another way, given the realities of modern international politics, sooner or later we are all going to be sorry.

A realistic approach to tensions over historical accuracy, however, also requires an appreciation of the impact that concrete interests have on the kinds of historical narratives adopted by states as well as of the significant sociocultural hurdles that leaders have to overcome to reshape the ways their societies regard the past. As a result, the barriers to creating a historical narrative that is acceptable across national boundaries tend to be formidable and, in some instances, insurmountable.

The clash between the mounting pressures to confront historical injustices and the barriers to achieving a mutually accepted stance on the past creates a serious dilemma for policy makers. While political leaders need to address past injustices, their efforts at reconciliation with other nations must be tempered by the realization that in many instances the best that can be achieved is a management of historically rooted tensions. In short, while the dynamics giving rise to the history may be global in scale, how those dynamics unfold differs greatly from case to case. Consequently, in each instance a different political response may be required—different strokes for different folks, as it were.

After establishing a framework around which a comparison will be organized, this chapter will look at the evolution of Germany's, Austria's, and Japan's policies relating to World War II across three periods: the early Cold War (from roughly 1945 to the early 1970s), the late Cold War (from the early 1970s to 1991), and finally during the post–Cold War period (from 1991 to today).

THE DETERMINANTS AND METRICS OF APOLOGETICS

Why do countries choose or not choose to apologize for possible past misdeeds? And what are the practical consequences of their doing so? Each of these questions involves a different set of dependent and independent variables.

For the first question, the key dependent variables are government policies that relate to the past. Some analysts treat this simply as a question of whether governments offer an apology for past wrongdoings; however, such admissions are merely one component of a broader set of procedures that together constitute the "official historical narrative" of the state. There are at least four additional components beyond the type of political rhetoric employed by political leaders. A second dimension of the official narrative of states is the way in which the past is commemorated through museums, monuments, and holidays. A third aspect is how history is portrayed in textbooks and in the school curriculum. A fourth element is reparations and compensation policies—who the state defines as a victim of past abuses and what sort of financial responsibility does it assume for them. Fifth, and finally, there is the issue of how past injustices are dealt with through the criminal justice system—that is, trials, purges, and the curtailing of the civil liberties of those who would challenge the official narrative (e.g., laws against Holocaust denial or bans on neo-Nazi organizations). While there may be tensions between different components of the official narrative, by looking at the overall range of policies—as opposed to examining a single policy domain—it may be possible to gauge more accurately the degree of contrition or impenitence of the official narrative.[4]

In terms of independent variables, three broad schools of thought can be identified. The first is the "historical determinist" position, which argues that people's actual historical experiences set the parameters for the type of official narrative that can be maintained. While it is, of course, possible for the state to promote a historical narrative that is at odds with the memory of a society, it does so at a cost. This is particularly true if the official narrative is one that challenges experiences that were profoundly traumatic for the individuals or groups that continue to bear them. Official narratives that are at odds with societal memory will be perceived as illegitimate and are likely to generate political resistance, especially in democratic societies. Even if on pragmatic grounds states choose to adopt an official narrative that differs significantly from social memory, counter-narratives will continue to exist. Given the opportunity, these counter- or insurgent narratives resurface, possibly forcing a wholesale reformulation of the endorsed account.[5]

A second position, the instrumentalist approach, offers a very different perspective. Whereas the historical determinist position maintains that societal-based memories over time shape the kind of sanctioned narrative that states adopt, instrumentalists argue that the official account determines how societies remember the past. Political leaders and other influential elites create historical narratives that serve their tangible interests. The chronicle adopted by the state reflects the balance of power among influential political actors. While it may serve the interests of elites to promote a penitent story, under different circumstances they may choose an impenitent one.

A third perspective is the culturalist position, which argues that both the way the past is experienced and how political actors understand their interests are shaped by their cultural background. In the past, such arguments focused on deeply held, relatively unchanging beliefs founded on religious values and child-rearing practices (e.g., Ruth Benedict's famous discussion of "shame" versus "guilt" cultures).[6] In more recent times, such explicitly essentialist and culturalist arguments have become less popular. Instead, the trend has been toward ascribing the differences between Europe and Asia on historical justice issues to changes in a dynamic discourse on history and justice, for example, to the incomplete diffusion of human rights norms in the Asian region.

Obviously, these three positions are not mutually exclusive. Rather, they can be viewed as "ideal-typical" theories in the Weberian sense, heuristic constructions that highlight certain aspects of a phenomenon but which never exist in reality in their pure form. Determining how these different forces shape outcomes is a task for empirical investigation. This is best done by tracing the evolution of a nation's official narrative and exploring the reasons behind the decision to adopt more or less penitent stances regarding history.[7] Comparison across cases can help eliminate or control powerful background forces, such as differences in historical circumstances or cultural factors. To the extent that Germany and Austria have similar historical and cultural backgrounds, one should expect some similarity in the broad trajectory of the evolution of their historical narratives as compared to that of Japan.[8]

The second question that needs to be addressed is, to what extent does the official historical narrative shape other aspects of political behavior? Do clashing versions of events fuel domestic and international political tensions? Can states place their relations on a more stable basis by pursuing reconciliation on past transgressions? Or are the kinds of historical narratives that states pursue, symbolic tempests full of sound and fury and signifying nothing, largely irrelevant? Here there are two main positions. The first is that historical narratives are, in fact, important. Especially from a historical determinist or culturalist perspective, the emotions generated by clashing views on history can be significant drivers for political action.[9] The alternative view is that historical narratives have no effect on interstate or intergroup relations independent of other factors—such as tensions over economic issues or changes in the balance of military power. This can be taken as the default position of most international relations analysts who focus on the pursuits of power and wealth as the driving forces in interstate relations.[10]

These two positions should not be viewed as mutually exclusive. Rather, they define the far ends of a spectrum of possibilities, ranging from the complete irrelevance to the overwhelming importance of the historical narrative in shaping interstate affairs. As with the question of the determinants of the official narrative, it is an issue that has to be adjudicated on the basis of the available empirical evidence.

THE ORIGINS OF THE OFFICIAL HISTORICAL NARRATIVES IN EUROPE AND ASIA—1945–1970

In the years immediately following 1945, Austria, Germany, and Japan were placed under strict occupation regimes that implemented similar policies designed to instill a historical narrative emphasizing the moral bankruptcy of their wartime governments. The Allied efforts on this score were motivated not merely by popular demands for vengeance but were guided also by the conviction that liberal, democratic order could only be created in the former Axis powers if the policies of their previous governments were thoroughly discredited and made illegitimate. Such a rehabilitation of former adversaries was believed essential to the reconstruction of Europe and Asia and to the creation of a more peaceful and stable international order.

The primary instrument to this end was the trials of the senior German and Japanese wartime leadership held in Nuremberg and Tokyo, respectively. Here, the prosecution made considerable efforts to demonstrate that Axis leaders were guilty not only of war crimes but of even greater misdeeds against peace and humanity. The top-level trials were supplemented by thousands of trials of lesser war criminals as well as massive purges. Criminal justice measures were bolstered by efforts to reshape the public discourse on history. Strict press censorship was imposed, and a wide array of official and semiofficial organizations deemed supporters of the wartime regime were dismantled. New school textbooks were issued that detailed German and Japanese offenses. Newspapers, cinema halls, and radio stations were ordered to produce special stories and shows that detailed wartime atrocities. In addition, large sums of money and material were extracted in war reparations, especially in Germany.

There were, of course, significant differences. In the case of Austria, the Allied powers designated it as the "first victim of Nazism," and almost immediately after the occupation began, an Austrian government composed of political leaders who purportedly had opposed the regime was installed. As a result, the Austrians themselves were in charge of creating a new historical narrative—a charge that they eagerly embraced in order to distinguish themselves from their former fellow citizens of the Third Reich in Germany. In certain respects, this led to an implementation of occupation policies even more thorough than in West Germany, especially with regard to the rapid purging of former Nazis. In other areas—especially regarding the restitution of property—the Austrians trailed the Germans significantly.

In Japan, too, the implementation of Allied policies lagged behind Germany, though not as much as in Austria. This was in part the result of the greater dependence of occupation authorities on the existing Japanese bureaucracy. In addition, the Allied prosecution of war criminals was hampered by various missteps as well as a calculated decision on political grounds to not try the Japanese emperor.[11] Japanese compensation policies also differed insofar as the bulk of it came in the form of the relinquishment of Japanese property in its former colonial possessions overseas—estimated by the Pauley Commission in 1948 as being $50 billion in value.[12] Japan paid very little direct compensation to its victims overseas, and there was no large-scale program of compensating internal victims of political persecution as there was in Germany and—to a lesser extent—Austria.

Despite these differences, the overall character of the early postwar official narrative in all three countries was remarkably similar. And in all three cases, it generated generally comparable political dynamics. Despite initial widespread support for punishing those believed responsible for having led their countries into catastrophe, within a relatively short time, popular enthusiasm for pursuing the issue quickly cooled. A variety of factors contributed to this outcome. First, the mechanisms through which historical justice issues were pursued were thoroughly inadequate to the task of assessing the guilt or innocence of the tens of millions of Austrians, Germans, and Japanese who potentially had been perpetrators or accomplices in the crimes of the pre-1945 era. Inevitably, there were miscarriages of justice where some of those who were severely punished should have been given more lenient treatment, while others who had been guilty of gross misdeeds were set free (sometimes, as in the case of the doctors in charge of Japan's wartime bacteriological warfare program, with Allied complicity). The fact that it was only the crimes of the Axis countries that were pursued, while the often grotesque brutalities committed by the Allied forces were ignored, contributed to popular resentment and fed the perception that the trials were largely an exercise in "victor's justice" lacking in broader moral legitimacy.

In addition, the Allied policies imposed significant costs on societies that were still reeling from the effects of the war and faced enormous economic, social, and political challenges. Approximately 6 million Germans, 3 million Japanese, and 350,000 Austrians had been killed in the war. Millions of refugees from territories that had been annexed or liberated had to be settled in bombed cities. The economies of all three countries had largely collapsed, and even feeding their populations would have been almost impossible without massive infusions of American aid. Increasingly, the efforts to pursue historical justice issues came to be viewed as a costly distraction not only by most of the citizens and political leaders of the occupied countries but by many of the occupation authorities as well. Even before the Cold War increased pressures to speed up the rehabilitation of former elites in order to resist the threat of Communism, Allied leaders became increasingly disenchanted with the entire project of trying to reeducate the German and Japanese populations. By 1948, as the Cold War set forth in earnest, the effort to change the former Axis nations' view of their history was largely abandoned.

As a result, the collective memory that emerged on a societal level in Austria, Germany, and Japan was a largely impenitent one. Even in Germany, the main focus of popular memory was on the suffering of the German people during the war, and discussions of the suffering that Germans had inflicted on others were largely avoided.[13] The same was true, but even more so, in Austria. Relatively speaking, on a societal level there was a greater openness about discussing wartime atrocities in Japan than in either Germany or Austria, at least on the level of popular cinema and literature.[14] Yet, there as well, the primary focus was on the suffering of Japanese civilians, while the horrors inflicted on the people of Asia tended to be comparatively ignored.[15] It seemed as if in all three societies there had emerged a consensus that—in the words of German federal president Hermann Lübbe—a certain silence (*eine gewisse Stille*) was needed to recover from the trauma of the war.

In terms of the official narrative, however, there were significant differences. Of the three, the Federal Republic's official narrative was by far the most penitent. On a rhetorical level, senior German leaders, beginning with Chancellor Konrad Adenauer, openly acknowledged German responsibility for the war and strongly repudiated the crimes of the Third Reich (even as they diluted the responsibility of ordinary Germans by emphasizing that these had been committed "in Germany's name").[16] This rhetorical stance was reinforced by the continuation of trials of war criminals—albeit on a considerably reduced scale—as well as the implementation of a massive reparations program that over the course of the Cold War would pay out tens of billions in reparations to foreign victims of German atrocities. Although German education and commemorative polices tended to avoid the Nazi past during the early Cold War period, the level of contrition was considerable.

The official narratives of Austria or Japan were far less penitent in comparison. In Japan's case, all trials ceased before the occupation came to an end, and the Japanese government assiduously avoided any acknowledgment of responsibility for the war and the colonial period beyond its acceptance of the verdict of the Tokyo War Crimes Tribunal, as was required by the Peace Treaty of San Francisco. Although Japan offered considerable sums to the various countries it had invaded as part of the diplomatic normalization process, it insisted on defining these as foreign aid, not compensation. Commemorative practices focused on paying respects to the war dead, most notably at the Yasukuni Shrine where—with secret government assistance—the names of the over 2 million soldiers and sailors who had died in Japan's wars were enshrined including the names of the fourteen Class A war criminals who were executed or died in Allied confinement. Likewise, the Ministry of Education made use of its supervisory powers to clamp down on the teaching of Japanese atrocities in the classroom.

If anything, Austria outdid Japan in its impenitence. Emphasizing Allied wartime propaganda that defined Austria as the "first victim of Nazism," the Austrian government portrayed itself as a liberated nation and avoided paying virtually any compensation for loss or suffering to the hundreds of thousands of slave laborers, concentration camp survivors, and former Austrian citizens who had fled the country and were living abroad. Trials regarding war crimes continued, but only on a desultory level and resulting in few convictions. Austrian commemorative and educational policies emphatically disassociated Austria from Germany and the Third Reich, despite the fact that Adolf Hitler and a disproportionate share of the senior Nazi leadership were Austrians and that after 1938 Austria had become a fully integrated part of the Third Reich with hardly any significant opposition.

What is interesting about the Austria-Japan comparison is that it undermines some of the more simplistic historical determinist and culturalist arguments explaining Germany's penitent stance on history. Despite having a cultural background quite similar to Germany's, and despite being deeply implicated in the crimes of the Third Reich, Austria was, if anything, even less contrite than Japan. At least under the terms of the Treaty of San Francisco, which ended the war between Japan and the Western powers, the Japanese government committed itself to accepting the verdict of the Tokyo War Crimes Tribunal. In contrast, the Austria government eagerly advertised itself as being the "first victim of Nazism." Moreover, on a societal level there was a greater public discussion of wartime atrocities in Japan than in Japan. In Austria, the silence was deafening. Neither being part of Judeo-Christian civilization nor the enormity of Auschwitz prevented Austrians from being blithely unrepentant about the past.

In light of public attitudes at the time, there is good reason to think that if left to its own devices, the Federal Republic of Germany might have gone in a similar direction. Overwhelmingly, the evidence suggests that the German government adopted a repentant official account for instrumentalist reasons. German leaders were inclined to believe that unless Germany appeased its political partners on the historical issues stemming from World War II—especially in the United States and Western Europe—it would be unable to forge the close relationships it needed. Germany's extraordinarily difficult geopolitical position as a divided nation on the front lines of the Cold War, facing as many as 3 million Soviet troops inside its borders on the East German side, greatly heightened its sensitivity to external pressure. While there is also evidence to suggest that many German leaders, especially ones who had been persecuted by the Nazis, felt strong sympathy for the victims, they faced an uphill struggle in winning the support of the country as a whole.

Austria, conversely, was a small, neutral nation that made a specialty of not overly favoring either side in the East-West confrontation. Its security depended on its standing apart from the fray, while it was able to reap the benefits of European economic integration through its membership in the European Free Trade Association (EFTA). On a domestic level, winning the ex-Nazi vote became a critical element in the competition between the conservative Austrian People's Party and the Social Democrats. Ironically, the Social Democrats under a Jewish chancellor—Bruno Kreisky, several of whose family members had been killed by the Nazis—were able to take power in 1970 thanks to an electoral alliance with the far-right Freedom Party led by an ex–Waffen SS man, Friedrich Peters. Not surprisingly, the Social Democrats were unwilling to actively pursue the issue of Austria's role in the crimes of the Third Reich.

Japan paid a somewhat higher price for its impenitent attitude, in particular in the context of its relationship with Korea. For nearly a decade, from 1953 to 1962, efforts to normalize diplomatic relations with its closest neighbor were undermined by Japan's brazen attitude toward the past. Nonetheless, as an island nation more worried about the dangers of strategic entanglement than abandonment, the Japanese government had less need to cooperate with its neighbors on defense and security than Germany had and consequently was less susceptible to outside pressure on historical issues.[17] And as the by far largest economic power in Asia, Japan enjoyed the upper hand in negotiating with most of its Asian neighbors. With the exception of Korea, other Asian countries—including Taiwan and the People's Republic of China—usually found that they were able to get more out of Japan by not pushing too hard on the historical justice issue.

GETTING TO SORRY—1970–1991

As the Cold War progressed, pressures gradually mounted on all three countries to move toward a more penitent stance on the past. The first to do so was the Federal Republic. During the 1960s and the era of détente, Germany came under increased international pressure to normalize its relations with the Soviet Union and its eastern neighbors. Doing so, however, necessarily raised the question of reparations for the victims of the Third Reich living in the East. These external pressures were reinforced by developments in the German domestic scene. The coming of age of the first postwar generation of young Germans reopened the question of German guilt with a vengeance. Young student leaders used the issue of the complicity of the older generation in Hitler's crimes to launch a pointed critique of the entire postwar German system. The Social Democratic

Party under the leadership of Chancellor Willy Brandt took up the issue of history in order to appeal to the students and other reformist elements in German society, equating the increased openness about the past to being supportive of détente and consolidating Germany's postwar democracy.

The Social Democratic Party's reopening of the history issue led to renewed contrition in German political rhetoric, most notably with Brandt's grand gesture of falling to his knees before the monument to the Warsaw Ghetto in 1970.[18] Other aspects of the German official narrative, however, were slower to change, due in part to German public opinion. Data regarding the nation's attitude revealed considerable skepticism about many aspects of the official narrative being promoted by the Social Democratic government. For instance, in 1971 only 41 percent of Germans surveyed thought that the chancellor's gesture had been appropriate, while 48 percent thought that it had been "exaggerated."[19] German conservatives, concentrated in the Christian Democratic Party fought a stubborn rearguard action against the Brandt government's policies. While there was a significant new emphasis in many German schools on the crimes of the past, there was only a marginal increase in reparations offered to victims living in Eastern Europe. And fierce political battles were fought over issues such as the extension of the statute of limitations for the prosecution of the crimes of the Third Reich.

When the Christian Democrats displaced the Social Democrats in 1983, Chancellor Helmut Kohl sought to shift the national story back in a less remorseful direction, using political rhetoric that suggested that the new generation of Germans could no longer be held responsible for the sins of their parents and advocating the propagation of a more positive view of German history through museums and other important commemorative sites. The high point in this new campaign on history came in 1985, when Kohl expended enormous political capital to secure the visit of U.S. president Ronald Reagan to the German military cemetery in the town of Bitburg, where among others forty-nine members of the Waffen SS were buried.[20]

Coming during a period of heightened East-West tensions, from a conservative perspective it was very much in German national interest to promote a more healthy form of patriotism. Moreover, at the time the Kohl administration seemed solidly in control of government and enjoyed substantial public support for the Bitburg visits (polls showed between 64 and 72 percent of Germans thought that the trip had been a good thing).

Nonetheless, public views on the past had been slowly shifting on historical issues, encouraged by broader global cultural trends that can be traced back to at least the late 1970s. Whereas earlier substantial majorities of Germans had supported drawing a line through the past and disregarding the issue, an increasing number of Germans supported confronting the darker sides of German history, despite the costs and pain that might be associated with doing so.

These views were no longer restricted to the left wing of the political spectrum but now spilled over into the conservative camp as well. They were given their most eloquent expression by federal president Richard von Weizsäcker, who in a speech commemorating the fortieth anniversary of the end of World War II emphasized that the date represented a day not only of defeat for Germany but also of liberation and that while young Germans after the war might not be responsible for the past, they were responsible for its consequences. Weizsäcker's speech crystallized the mood of the country and received widespread support. Continued remembrance of the horrors of the Nazi regime was now supported by members of the political Right as well as the Left. While there continued to be debate and dissonance on the issue, a new and more genuinely contrite stance on history spread across the different domains of the official narrative, including commemoration and education.[21]

Change came more slowly in Austria, mainly because both the Left and the Right continued to court the support of the Far Right for electoral purposes. Austria's impenitent stance on history, however, became the object of increasing international and domestic political criticism. Austria's unwillingness to confront the past triggered a series of diplomatic and international media scandals beginning and culminating in 1986 when former United Nations secretary-general Kurt Waldheim was elected to the largely ceremonial office of president despite revelations that he long had covered up his role as a staff officer during the savage counterinsurgency war in the Balkans. For the next five years, Waldheim was invited to make only a single state visit, even though that was the principal function of his office.[22]

At the time, the Austrian media and public opinion rallied behind their beleaguered president. As in Germany, however, beneath the surface popular and elite attitudes were slowly shifting in the direction of greater unease with Austria's impenitent stance on history. These shifts began, as they had in Germany, on a societal level with increased coverage in the

Austrian left and center-left press of Austria's role in the Holocaust and the other horrors of the Third Reich.[23] Whereas in the 1970s less than half of all respondents favored continued remembrance, in the 1980s over 50 percent did. By the 1990s that figure would rise to over 60 percent.[24] Changes in public attitudes spilled over into changes in elite views as well. Despite support for Waldheim and a general tendency to reject foreign criticism as unjustified, increasingly the Austrian politicians, especially on the left, found themselves discomfited by their nation's Nazi past.

For the most part, these changes in elite and public attitudes had a minimal impact on the official narrative into the 1990s. While there was some greater discussion of Nazi atrocities in Austrian textbooks and some increased celebration of the fight against fascism, for the most part these were only superficial changes. Austria continued to offer no apology for its role in the Holocaust, it offered no compensation to its victims, and there was no serious effort to use the criminal justice system to pursue the issue of historical justice. However, a consensus was forming that Austria would soon have to do much more. A confidential memorandum prepared in 1987 for Austrian chancellor Franz Vranitzky strongly advocated abandoning Austria's legalistic and ungenerous stance on history, admitting co-responsibility for the crimes of the Third Reich and the payment of compensation to its victims. Such a policy, argued one of the chancellor's closest advisors, the veteran journalist Hugo Portisch, was justified in moral terms and in terms of Austria's national interest.[25]

In the later stages of the Cold War, Japan arguably went further than Austria toward adopting a penitent official narrative. As in Europe, changing Japanese popular attitudes on history paved the way for greater engagement. Beginning in the 1970s, especially after Japan's reestablishment of diplomatic relations with China, there was a new public openness to confronting the darker side of Japan's imperial past, beginning with the massive success of the best-selling travelogues by *Asahi* journalist Honda Katsuichi.[26] While Japanese public opinion remained ambiguous regarding the war and Japanese responsibility for imperial-era atrocities, survey data showed an increasing willingness to acknowledge that Japan had done things it should regret and for which it should apologize.

This shift in attitudes led to increased coverage of the darker sides of modern Japanese history in school textbooks already in the 1970s. However, the impetus for a larger shift in the official narrative came as a result of international pressure. Much like Kohl in Germany, the Japanese prime minister for much of the first half of the 1980s—Nakasone Yasuhiro—was an archconservative who believed that a restoration of national pride was a vital component for building a political consensus behind a stronger stance on defense and national security issues. His efforts to promote such a sense of patriotism through the official historical narrative, however, sparked enormous controversy, not only in Japan, but also quite unexpectedly in its two closest and most influential Asian neighbors, China and South Korea, where the emergence of strong civil society actors was making their governments increasingly sensitive to historical issues.[27]

The first shock came in 1982, when media reports surfaced of planned textbook revisions that would have whitewashed many of the more unsavory aspects of Japan's modern history. The vehemence of first Korean and then Chinese diplomatic protests took the Japanese government by surprise. Domestic public opinion was also quite critical. According to a *Mainichi* newspaper poll taken that year, only 6 percent supported the position that the "darker sides of the past should not be taught in the classroom," whereas 92 percent took the position that all aspects of the wartime past should be taught.[28] As a result, the Japanese government quickly disavowed that any changes were planned. Furthermore, the Ministry of Education produced new guidelines for school textbooks stating that they should take into account the historical sensitivities of Japan's neighbors (while written by private authors, all textbooks in Japan have to be approved by the ministry if they are to be adopted in Japanese schools).[29]

The textbook controversy was soon followed in 1985 by a second uproar over Prime Minister Nakasone's visit to the Yasukuni Shrine in Tokyo. Much like Kohl's trip to Bitburg, Nakasone linked the trip to a political agenda calling for pride in national service and a willingness to sacrifice and take risks for the sake of the country. And like Bitburg, the trip provoked a storm of international criticism. Especially significant were signals Nakasone received from senior Chinese political statesman Hu Yaobang, who warned that Nakasone's actions were provoking nationalist sentiment in China and undermining the position of those like Hu who sought to promote Sino-Japanese political cooperation. Nakasone took Hu's warnings to heart and refused to make any further trips to the shrine, despite strong conservative pressure to do so.[30] In the following year, Nakasone went further, issuing a series of official statements in which he stated that the invasion of China had been a war of aggression, and he instructed the Ministry of Education to force the revision of new textbooks produced by conservative authors who wished to downplay the Nanjing massacre and other wartime atrocities.[31] A few weeks later, when the conservative education minister Fujio Masayuki published an article in which he justified the annexation of Korea in 1910 as having been a mutually agreed-upon arrangement, Nakasone forced him to resign.[32]

While regional institutions remained relatively weak in East Asia compared to Europe, Japan was taking an increasingly active role in promoting political and economic integration. In the context of the early to mid-1980s, both China and South Korea were key allies in checking the growth of Soviet military power in the region. For the fiercely conservative Nakasone, good relations with Beijing and Seoul were critical if Japan was to take on the expanded regional security role that he was seeking. Moreover, Japanese business and political leaders were eager to take advantage of the growing East Asian market and investing heavily in creating overseas production chains that took advantage of cheap Asian land and labor in order to remain competitive in overseas markets.

As the Cold War wound down, it appeared that the official historical narrative in all three countries was moving toward increased contrition. Germany was at the forefront of this trend, driven once again by its extreme sensitivity to external forces—in this case the international pressures favoring détente—as well as the domestic political calculations of the Social Democratic Party as it sought to harness the energy of the student movement. In Austria and Japan as well, instrumental factors played an important role in shifting the official narrative toward greater contrition. In the case of Japan, growing economic and political ties to a rapidly growing Asian region increased the leverage that its former victims had over the Japanese government. As a result, even strongly nationalist leaders such as Nakasone came to believe that it was in the national interest to avoid alienating Japan's neighbors over historical issues. In the Austrian case, growing transnational sensitivity to how the country dealt with its Nazi past increased the costs of maintaining an impenitent official narrative. By the late 1980s it was becoming obvious that a far-reaching reconsideration of the nation's policies was in order.

It would be difficult, however, to tell the story of Austria's, Germany's, and Japan's evolving official narrative from an instrumental perspective alone. Despite the significant differences in their cultural, political, and geostrategic situations, in all three countries there was growing public sensitivity to the issue of historical guilt and increased acknowledgment that the crimes of the past needed to be addressed and in some form atoned for. In the case of Germany and Austria, this trend could be plausibly attributed to the development of the burgeoning global discourse on the Holocaust.[33] However, that similar dynamics were observable in Japan as well suggests that something more fundamental was going on. Increased contact with other societies was augmenting public awareness of different perspectives on the past, while the spread of the discourse on human rights suggested that the kinds of atrocities that had been committed in the past had to be identified and condemned in order to bring healing to their victims in the present and to prevent their repetition in the future. This change in attitudes increased the cost of an impenitent historical stance both domestically and internationally, encouraging what appeared to be a worldwide trend toward greater contrition.

THE GREAT DIVERGENCE—1991–2010

At first, the end of the Cold War reinforced the trend toward increased penitence. By the beginning of the twenty-first century, however, in both Europe and Asia diplomatic relations were severely strained by disagreements over the legacies of the Second World War. In Europe, on the one hand, these tensions proved relatively mild and after a brief period were largely contained. In East Asia, on the other hand, the effects were more disruptive and lasting as overheated nationalist sentiments focusing on historical issues led to a real rupture in diplomacy and created lasting feelings of resentment focused on related issues—notably territorial disputes.

In Germany, the end of the Cold War led to a renewal and intensification of efforts to pursue reconciliation with its neighbors. One of the most immediate and important changes was in the area of compensation. The collapse of the Iron Curtain and the end of East-West tensions removed many of the traditional objections to providing compensation to the victims of Nazism who lived in the East. Simultaneously, the need to integrate the countries of Eastern and Central Europe into a new regional order gave those countries and the groups of victims living in them considerable leverage and enhanced democratic legitimacy. After a period of intense negotiation, large sums in compensation were paid to the largest group of long-neglected victims, the over one million surviving slave laborers in Eastern Europe.[34] New diplomatic efforts were also made to reach out and directly pursue reconciliation through contacts with political leaders in the newly democratic countries of the East, especially in Poland and the Czech Republic. In addition, within Germany there was a massive expansion of memorial sites dedicated to commemorating the horrors of the Nazi era, especially in the newly reestablished capital of Berlin, and a very painful reevaluation was undertaken of the role that individuals at all levels of German society had played in mass killings of the 1930s and 1940s. In the process, many cherished myths, such as the belief that ordinary Wehrmacht soldiers had no role in the killings, were challenged and abandoned.[35]

In Austria, the end of the Cold War heralded a fundamental shift in the country's official historical narrative, beginning with two dramatic speeches in 1991 and then 1993, in which Austrian chancellor Vranitzky advanced the thesis that Austria as a nation shared co-responsibility (*Mitschuld*) with Germany for the Holocaust. Other senior Austrian political leaders made similar statements, and soon thereafter Austria began to compensate those who had been victimized by Nazism on Austrian soil. Textbooks took up the question of the country's willing role in the crimes of the Third Reich, and monuments commemorating the victims of Nazi persecution were erected, most famously the statue in Albertina Platz in downtown Vienna portraying the humiliation of the city's Jewish population after the Anschluss in 1938.[36] The National Assembly also revised and strengthened long moribund legal provisions prohibiting the dissemination of pro-Nazi propaganda. In short, virtually every aspect of Austria's official narrative shifted toward a more penitent direction.

In Asia, Japan too sought to pursue the goal of reconciliation with its neighbors. This shift in policy was most evident on the level of political rhetoric, as a series of prime ministers offered increasingly clear and unambiguous apologies for the policies of wartime Japan. There was some movement as well in the area of compensation policy. After being confronted with new evidence that the imperial army had in fact been involved in the forcible recruitment of women as "comfort women," the Japanese government offered an official apology and established a special, public-private fund—the Asian Women's Fund—designed to provide assistance to any surviving comfort women. However, the sums involved were paltry compared to the amounts that were paid out by both Austria and Germany. Other movements toward a more penitent stance were frustrated by continued resistance from conservative sectors of Japanese politics. Efforts at apology were frequently undercut by revisionist comments by senior politicians, while plans for a creation of a national museum dealing with modern Japanese history were watered down so that the issue of Japan's responsibility for the suffering of other Asian people was avoided altogether.[37]

Regardless of their scope or thoroughness, these Austrian, German, and Japanese efforts to pursue reconciliation on historical issues met with some success in the 1990s. German gestures toward its eastern neighbors were welcomed by the Polish and Czech governments and were reciprocated by a new willingness to acknowledge the injustices that had been inflicted on the ethnic Germans who had been driven out of Eastern Europe at the end of World War II. Austria's new stance on historical issues was a precondition for its successful accession to the greatly empowered European Union (EU).[38] For its part, Japan managed to avoid new confrontations with China, and after a highly successful visit to Japan by Korean president Kim Dae Jung in 1998, Japan and Korea appeared to be on the path to a genuine reconciliation along the lines of what Germany had achieved with its Western neighbors after 1945.[39]

In all three cases the move toward greater contrition provoked social and political backlashes and triggered severe diplomatic crises. In Austria, the far-right Freedom Party enjoyed growing electoral success under its charismatic new leader, Jörg Haider. In the 2000 elections, the Freedom Party emerged as the second-largest party in Austria and joined the new government as the junior coalition partner to the center-right Peoples Party. The prospect of Haider—who was known for his revisionist views regarding history—having a prominent role in the new government alarmed other European countries. Many leaders feared that the Freedom Party's success would further encourage the rise of similar right-wing parties in the rest of Europe. The EU placed a diplomatic blockade on Austria, suspending the operation of all EU committees in which Austria participated, and demanded that the new Austrian government recommit itself to a penitent official historical narrative. The new government soon caved to European pressure, offering an official declaration—with the approval of both members of the governing coalition, including the Freedom Party—in which it reaffirmed Austria's co-responsibility for the crimes of the Third Reich. This statement was soon followed by a series of apologies by federal president Thomas Klestil and other senior Austrian leaders. In addition, the Austrian government expanded its efforts to provide compensation to former slave laborers and people who had had their property stripped away from them by the Nazi regime. One of the more notable of these measures was an innovative new program to restore looted art treasures.[40]

In Germany, the backlash was more limited. As the Federal Republic pursued closer ties with its eastern neighbors, the issue of the suffering of German civilians during the war reemerged, driven by the lobbying of the large and well-organized groups that represented the millions of ethnic Germans and their descendants who had been expelled from Eastern Europe. Against the backdrop of renewed European concern with the mass expulsion of ethnic Croats, Serbs, Bosnians, and Albanians in former Yugoslavia, the claims of these groups gained new legitimacy.

German pressures on this issue, even if not backed by the federal government, provoked a sharply negative response in Poland and the Czech Republic. Many Czechs and Poles felt that given the enormous damage that Germany had inflicted on their countries the expulsion of the Germans had been understandable, if not totally justifiable. In addition, many feared that acknowledging the German position would open the door for the restitution of lost property to their former German owners. German relations with its two closest eastern neighbors were beset with tension for several years, especially after the 2005 election of the nationalist and rabidly anti-German Lech Kaczynski. The Kaczynski government launched a bitter campaign criticizing the German government for its stance on the expellee issue and demanding increased compensation for Poland's wartime losses. The acrimony reached its high point at the 2007 EU summit in Brussels, when the European governments met to consider a new constitution. German-Polish clashes over historical issues brought negotiations to a virtual standstill.

In the end, however, other West European countries came to Germany's aid, criticizing the Polish government for its hard-line posturing on the history issue. The Polish government subsequently backed off from its more extreme demands, and the conference ended relatively successfully.[41] Soon afterward, German-Polish diplomatic tensions largely subsided. At no point did public opinion in the two countries shift in a sharply negative direction, despite evidence that the two peoples continued to harbor fundamentally different views of their history. Throughout the crisis, attitudes toward one another remained far better than they had been immediately after the end of the Cold War, when Polish and Czech opinion surveys suggested that Germany was viewed with immense distrust and, like the former Soviet Union, was seen as a serious security threat.[42] Nearly two decades of efforts to promote reconciliation appear to have had some effect after all.

A more negative situation emerged in Asia. Tensions over historical issues simmered throughout the 1990s, especially in Sino-Japanese relations, and those tensions boiled over early in the twenty-first century as a result of two developments. The first was a campaign by a group of highly vocal and politically well-connected conservative intellectuals who produced and promoted the adoption of revisionist school textbooks.[43] The second was the decision by Prime Minister Koizumi Junichiro to honor a campaign pledge he made to visit the Yasukuni Shrine every year that he was in office.[44] Both the textbook campaign and the Yasukuni visits reflected the continued ability of conservative groups to shape important aspects of the Japanese official historical narrative despite the broader trend in the direction of greater contrition.[45] And both the textbooks and the Yasukuni visits enraged Japan's neighbors, triggering a steadily worsening crisis in regional diplomacy.[46]

After initial attempts to amend differences over historical issues, by 2002 opposition from Beijing and Seoul hardened. Direct, bilateral talks at the senior governmental level broke down and increasingly vitriolic anti-Japanese demonstrations began to poison public sentiment in all three countries. Particularly disturbing were large-scale violent protests that broke out in the spring of 2005. Over the space of several weeks, huge crowds were allowed by the authorities to gather in Beijing, Shanghai, and other major Chinese cities and voice their anger at Japan's stance on history. Japanese diplomatic facilities and Japanese-owned businesses were pelted with debris and Japanese tourists assaulted before the authorities finally stepped in to defuse the situation.

Eventually, the dispute over historical issues subsided. In 2007, Prime Minister Koizumi stepped down, and his successors assiduously sought to avoid needlessly antagonizing Japan's neighbors over historical issues. The controversies of the 2000s, however, left deep scars. Public perceptions of neighboring countries became increasingly negative, and the fear of military conflict sharpened considerably. In 2006, Japanese government data showed for instance that 78 percent of those surveyed said that there was a risk that Japan would be dragged into war, a level of threat perception far greater than even at the height of the Cold War.[47] Public opinion in China and Korea was, if anything, even more negative.[48]

Potentially even more dangerous was the escalation of tensions over territorial issues, in particular the Takeshima/Dokdo islands dispute between Japan and Korea and the Senkaku/Diaoyu islands dispute between Japan and China. While a number of different issues were involved in these disputes, including competition for national resources (oil, gas, and fish) as well as geostrategic concerns, for China and Korea in particular questions of national pride and historical justice played a central role. For Korea, Japan's historical invasion of Korea began with its annexation of the islands in 1904, and its continued claim on the islands was an effort to whitewash history and legitimate its war of aggression against Korea.[49] In addition, Japan's unwillingness to be more forthcoming on the comfort women issue was the immediate trigger for President Lee Myun Bak's very public visit to the disputed islands in August 2012.[50] Similarly, from the Chinese perspective, Japan stole the Senkaku/Diaoyu islands at the time of the Sino-Japanese War of 1894–95.[51] Reclaiming the islands is being defined as a core Chinese interest and part of its greater campaign to restore China to the preeminent position that it enjoyed in Asia prior to its "century of humiliation" at the hands of the imperial powers.[52]

To date, all sides have sought to avoid an actualized military conflict. Given the present military realities, no country—China, Korea, or Japan—can hope to resolve these disputes through military means. Given the high level of interdependence between their economies, the cost of conflict would be prohibitive. At the same time, the powerful nationalist passions stirred by the conflicts have led to a breakdown of cooperation. Worse yet, the insertion of paramilitary forces around the disputed Senkaku/Diaoyu islands, backed by regular military forces, raises the real possibility of inadvertent escalation. Disputes over history in Asia are leading to increasing and very real costs in the present.

CONCLUSIONS

The renewal of tensions over history after the Cold War in both Europe and Asia underscores the precarious nature of any apparent solution to the history problem. While states may appear to have worked out official narratives that satisfy domestic and international political pressures, changes in the international system and in domestic politics both in one's own country and in neighboring countries can create new and unexpected pressures that lead to a renewal of tensions.

In some cases, these tensions can be attributed to instrumentalist calculations of interest. For instance, Koizumi's need to win conservative support in his bid for the presidency of the Liberal Democratic Party encouraged him to make his pledge to visit Yasukuni. Likewise, the decision of Chinese and Korean leaders to promote strongly nationalist historical narratives in their countries can be understood as bids for enhanced legitimacy on the part of deeply unpopular governments.

The difficulties that leaders had in controlling these sentiments, however, also reflect the ability of cultural discourses to take on a dynamic of their own, as well as of the tenacity of groups such as the German expellee organizations to hold onto their own insurgent narratives in the face of government discouragement. Political leaders, faced with cross-cutting domestic and international pressures, and fearful of the potentially open-ended nature of any attempt to appease demands for reconciliation, are often at a loss as to an appropriate response.[53] Nowhere is this more evident than in the context of the apparently intractable disputes over territorial issues in Asia. It is precisely the complex mixture of forces that are at play that makes a historical realist understanding of the history problem necessary.

Yet, while by its very nature the history problem is protean and difficult to manage, there are certain broader conditions that can either exacerbate or dampen its toxicity. First, the ability of a political system to create a consensus and push through an integrated policy on historical issues greatly affects the manageability of the problem. One of the factors hampering Japan's ability to successfully pursue historical reconciliation with its neighbors has been the difficulties Japanese leaders face imposing their views in an unusually fractious political system. Even a prime minister like Murayama Tomiichi, who was strongly committed to changing the official narrative, was confounded time and again by his inability to prevent conservative members of his government from undermining government policy. In contrast, once Austria made the decision to shift toward a more penitent official stance on history, it was able to do so relatively swiftly and efficiently across the entire range of policies that constitute the official narrative.

Second, in addition to a capacity for political leadership, governments need a strong incentive to pursue the typically very thorny, emotional, and complicated set of issues involved in disputes over history. As can be seen from the Asian case, deepening economic integration and enhanced social contacts alone do not provide sufficient incentives to prevent serious difficulties from emerging, although they did strongly encourage regional leaders and elites (especially business elites) to try to dampen historically grounded disputes when they did emerge. In the European context, the EU has provided an important framework that has encouraged governments to pursue historical reconciliation and enabled them to better handle those disputes when they did emerge. The ability of German-Polish relations to recover relatively rapidly from the tensions arising over the expellee issue provides strong testimony to the utility of the EU in this regard. In contrast, the relatively poor state of Japanese-South Korean relations, despite many strong interests the two countries share, reflects the pernicious impact of the absence of such a structure.

Looking to the future, one can be fairly optimistic of the continued ability of countries in Western and, increasingly, in Central Europe to manage tensions over historical issues. Despite the current crisis in various aspects of the EU governance structure, the EU has strongly discouraged member states from catering to the kind of nationalist forces that might resort to using history as a tool to pursue their own agendas. Similarly, although a strong nationalist element is evident in European politics and may even grow as a result of problems associated with immigration and economic integration, so far these forces have not prevented the implementation of effective, conciliatory official historical narratives. The farther east one goes in Europe, however, the murkier the picture becomes. In particular, the relations between Russia and its former satellites are fraught with difficult historical issues that could spark serious and potentially dangerous conflicts.[54]

Likewise, it is difficult to be sanguine about East Asia. Although since 2007 political elites in Japan, China, and South Korea have largely avoided the problem, opinion data and elite discourse on history-related issues continue to reflect deep gaps between the different countries. Disturbingly, these nationalist sentiments at play in the battles over history are finding new outlets, most notably in reference to the maritime territorial disputes. Even if leaders in Japan were to come forth committed to pursuing reconciliation, the fluid nature of Japanese politics and the often incoherent character of the policy-making process as well as the absence of larger, regional institutional structures comparable to the EU suggest that they would have an uphill battle.[55] Certainly, serious reconciliation with the People's Republic of China would be difficult, given the growing number of issues on which the two countries clash, particularly in the security realm. The prospects for success are much better in the context of relations between Japan and the Republic of Korea. Such a campaign would entail returning to the gains that were made following the Kim Dae Jung–Obuchi Keizo summit of 1998, but would need to be backed up by a sustained effort by both sides—the Korean as well as the Japanese[56]—across the broader spectrum of policies that constitute the official historical narrative in the two countries. In other words, it would need to be informed by a historical realist's understanding of the nature of the problem.

1. Jon Elster begins his investigation of the issue with the ancient Greeks. See Elster, *Closing the Books*. On recent efforts to right wrongs, see Barkan, *The Guilt of Nations*; and Gary Bass, *To Stay the Hand of Vengeance*.
2. On this acknowledgment, see for instance Henry Kissinger's *Does America Need a Foreign Policy?*, chap. 7. Kissinger's appreciation of this issue may have been heightened by repeated attempts to indict him for decisions he made while in government, including supporting the overthrow of the Salvador Allende government in Chile. The old joke about a neoconservative being a liberal who has just been mugged could be reformulated in this instance as a neoliberal being a realist who has just been indicted.
3. This essay is an offshoot of my larger research project, Berger, *War, Guilt, and World Politics*.
4. The failure to compare different dimensions of a country's official narrative leads often to very different assessments. For instance, Jane W. Yamazaki and Jennifer Lind, who emphasize the official statements of Japanese leaders, come to the conclusion that Japan has been quite penitent about its past misdeeds. See Yamazaki, *Japanese Apologies for World War II*; and Lind, *Sorry States*. George Hicks, on the other hand, who heavily emphasizes compensation for the comfort women and other victim groups, sees Japan as being relatively impenitent. See Hicks, *Japan's War Memories*.
5. See for instance the discussion in David E. Lorey and William H. Beezley's introduction in Lorey and Beezley, eds., *Genocide, Collective Violence, and Popular Memory*.
6. Benedict, *The Chrysanthemum and the Sword*; Koschmann, ed., *Authority and the Individual in Japan*.
7. In the language of social scientific methodology, this task is referred to as process tracing. See George and Bennett, *Case Studies and Theory Development*.
8. On the comparative case study method, see ibid.
9. On the disruptive impact of nationalism on efforts to build Asian regional institutions, see especially Rozman, *Northeast Asia's Stunted Regionalism*; and Kamo in Yamamoto, ed., *Globalism, Regionalism, and Nationalism*. On the impact of Japanese impenitence on threat perceptions, see Christensen, "China, the U.S.-Japan Alliance, and the Security Dilemma."
10. This position is in fact quite close to that of Lind, *Sorry States*.
11. The U.S. commander in charge of the occupation of Japan, General Douglas MacArthur, wrote a dramatic telegram to Washington, warning that if the Allies did put the emperor on trial "a vendetta for revenge will thereby be initiated whose cycle may well not be complete for centuries, if ever. It is quite possible that a million troops would be required, which would have to be maintained for an indefinite number of years." Quoted in Finn, *Winners in Peace*, 73, 71–74. The United States also used the threat of putting the emperor on trial to force the reluctant Japanese cabinet to accept a draft constitution written entirely by MacArthur's legal staff.

12 Ibid., 70–71.
13 Niven, ed., *Germans as Victims*.
14 See Buchholz in Inoguchi and Jackson, eds., *Memories of War*.
15 Orr, *The Victim as Hero*.
16 In this sense, there were considerable similarities with Japan, which to the extent that it admitted any wrongdoing, tended to attribute it to the action of a "militarist clique."
17 See Tsuchiyama in Gourevitch, Inoguchi, and Purrington, eds, *United States–Japan Relations*.
18 For a recent reevaluation of the politics behind Brandt's much-celebrated trip, see Wolffsohn and Brechenmacher, *Denkmalsturz? Brants Kniefall*.
19 Data cited in *Time*, "Willy Brandt, Person of the Year."
20 For a thorough recounting of the events surrounding the Bitburg visit, see Levkov, ed., *Bitburg and Beyond*. For a recent assessment written by the former mayor of Bitburg, see Hallet, *Umstrittenen Versöhnung*.
21 For a good discussion, see Art, *The Politics of the Nazi Past*, 65–72.
22 Ibid., 111–30; Gehler in Gehler and Sickinger, *Politische Affären und Skandale in Österreich*, 614–65.
23 Bischof, "Victims? Perpetrators? 'Punching Bags'?," 7; Uhl in Lebow, Kansteiner, and Fogu, eds., *Politics and Memory in Postwar Europe*, 60–61. On the press, see especially Wassermann, *Zuviel Vergangenheit tut nicht gut!*, 294–348.
24 Wassermann, *Naziland Österreich!?*, 160. As in Germany, many commentators stressed the impact on public opinion of the mass media and in particular the broadcast of the American-made television miniseries, *Shoah*. See Bischof, "Victims? Perpetrators? 'Punching Bags'?"; Uhl in Lebow, Kansteiner, and Fogu, eds., *Politics and Memory in Postwar Europe*, 60–61; and Wassermann, *Zuviel Vergangenheit tut nicht gut!*, 294–348.
25 Pick, *Guilty Victim*, 197–99.
26 Honda, *Chūgoku no tabi*; Honda, *Chūgoku no Nihongun*.
27 See the chapter by Gi-Wook Shin in this book, as well as Reilly, *Strong Society, Smart State*.
28 Saaler, *Politics, Memory, and Public Opinion*, 131. Other polling data revealed continued ambiguity about Japanese history. See Yoshida, *Nihonjin no sensōkan*, 199.
29 Jeans, "Victims or Victimizers?," 185; Yoshimasa, "The History of the Textbook Controversy," 35–36.
30 Tanaka in Hasegawa and Togo, eds., *East Asia's Haunted Present*, 125–27. Hu's fears proved well founded, and the anti-Japanese demonstrations in 1985 contributed to Hu's eventual downfall. See He, *The Search for Reconciliation*, 212–14, 230–32.
31 Wakamiya, *The Postwar Conservative View of Asia*, 177–78.
32 Ibid., 199–201.
33 Novick, *The Holocaust and American Life*. In both Austria and Germany, the popular success of a cultural product, the American television series *Holocaust* starring Meryl Streep, played a particularly important role in changing popular attitudes.
34 For an overview of the development of the issue, see Arning, *Späte Abrechnung*. For a detailed account of the negotiations by an insider, see Eizenstat, *Imperfect Justice*, chaps. 10–13.
35 Young, *At Memory's Edge*.
36 Uhl in Lebow, Kansteiner, and Fogu, eds., *Politics and Memory in Postwar Europe*, 60–61.
37 See the chapters by Gi-Wook Shin and Daniel Sneider in this volume.
38 Bischof, "Victims? Perpetrators? 'Punching Bags'?" 26.
39 See Wakamiya, *The Postwar Conservative View of Asia*, 256–61; He, *Overcoming Shadows of the Past*, 248–49; and Green, *Japan's Reluctant Realism*, 96–98.

40 See Merlingen, Mudde, and Sedelmeier, "The Right and the Righteous?"; Gehler in Gehler, Pelinka, and Bischof, eds., *Österreich in der Europäischen Union*; and Eizenstat, *Imperfect Justice*, chap. 10.

41 *Frankfurter Allgemeine Zeitung*, "Schwierige Verhandlungen in Brüssel"; *Frankfurter Allgemeine Zeitung*, "Europa sucht neue Wurzeln."

42 See Falkowski and Popko, *The Germans about Poland*; Falkowski, *Meinungen der Polen über die deutsch-polnischen Beziehungen*, especially 3, 7, 8; and Cwiek-Karpowicz, *Public Opinion on Fears and Hopes*.

43 On general background to the 2001 textbook dispute, see Mitani and Hirota, *Rekishi kyōkasho mondai*. On some of the diplomatic consequences, see Bukh, "Japan's History Textbook Debate," 683–704.

44 For overviews of the literature, see Bukh, "Japan's History Textbook Debate"; and Tanaka in Hasegawa and Togo, eds., *East Asia's Haunted Present*.

45 Oguma and Ueno, *Iyashi nashionarizumu*.

46 Tensions in Asia were exacerbated by the emergence of discourses on history in Korea and China that heightened public awareness of past Japanese atrocities and made the two governments more sensitive to signs of Japanese revisionism. See Shin and Sneider, eds., *History Textbooks and the Wars in Asia*.

47 Japanese Cabinet Office, *Gaikō ni kan suru yoronchōsa*, table 10. At the height of the Cold War in 1982, only 53 percent of those surveyed said that there was a chance of Japanese involvement in a war, despite the fact that actual Soviet military capabilities then were far greater than those of China, South Korea, or North Korea in 2006.

48 On China, see Gries, *China's New Nationalism*; and Reilly, *Strong Society, Smart State*.

49 See for instance *Asahi*, "Kankoku daitoryo," 1, 2, 7.

50 On this point the author is particularly grateful to the comments of former ambassador Togo Kazuhiko and Professor Lee Jong Won of Waseda University.

51 *BBC News Asia*, "Japan and China Trade Barbs."

52 On the islands as a "core" Chinese interest, see Gilbert Rozman's chapter in this volume. See also Mizokami, "Sekai no kansen"; and Buckley, "China Leader Affirms Policy."

53 On how ideas and interests can combine to make it very costly for leaders to confront the past, see Torpey in Shin, Park, and Yang, eds., *Rethinking Historical Injustice and Reconciliation*, especially 181, 184, 186–87.

54 See Igor Torbakov's chapter in this volume.

55 One reflection of the fluid nature of the Japanese political system is the fact that over the past five years there have been six Japanese prime ministers.

56 As Shin argues in his chapter in this volume, the first step has to come from the Japanese side, since historically it was the victimizer. However, for reconciliation to work it is essential that the South Korean government shows that it is willing to help stage-manage the process. In the past, Korean leaders—with the important exception of Kim Dae Jung—have failed to support Japan in its efforts to apologize. As a result, a mood of "apology fatigue" has set in where many Japanese feel that no matter how hard they try, Koreans will continue to despise them. The author is grateful in particular to Professors Kitaoka Shinichi and Onuma Yasuaki and former vice minister Tanaka Hitoshi on this point.

Chapter 4

Divided Memories of World War II in the Netherlands and the Dutch East Indies

Sukarno and Anne Frank as Icons of Dutch Historical Imagination

FRANCES GOUDA

With a bit of hyperbole, one could argue that during the past fifty years, the memory of Anne Frank has served not only as an icon in World War II memories in the Netherlands but also as a foil for lingering questions about the varying degrees of Nazi collaboration among a sizable proportion of the Dutch population during the German occupation in 1940-45.[1] It is equally plausible to assert that memorial practices in the Netherlands with regard to World War II in Southeast Asia have singled out Sukarno as symbol of Indonesian Nationalists' collaboration with the Japanese enemy in the Dutch East Indies during 1942-45. As a result, the sometimes obsessive concern in the post-1945 era with Sukarno's supporting role in the Japanese occupation has served as a lightning rod among the Dutch public in general and among former European administrators and settlers of the Dutch East Indies in particular. It is as if the Dutch focus on Sukarno's aiding and abetting the enemy during World War II in the Indonesian archipelago has stifled an honest postcolonial assessment of Dutch complicity in the technologies of oppression—a veritable "state of violence"—which the Japanese easily took over in 1942 and further perfected in the course of World War II.[2] Sukarno's collusion with Japan's military occupiers not only influences Dutch historical memory of World War II in Southeast Asia; it has also encumbered postwar appraisals of the Indonesian nationalist movement and the legitimacy of its demands for independence after more than three centuries of Dutch colonial rule.

By stating the case in this manner, several issues must be interrogated. In the first instance, it requires an exploration of the intellectual maneuvers and moral judgments that have framed Anne Frank (a young girl and innocent victim of the Nazi Holocaust) and Sukarno (an adult anticolonial politician who willingly collaborated with Japanese military authorities in 1942–45) as icons of memory.[3] This concept of "icon of memory" is introduced here to highlight something historians have increasingly been concerned with, namely, the ways in which people remember, forget, and distort parts of their history.[4] Icons of memory arise due to what has been called the "scarcity principle" in cultural memory, meaning that most recollections of minor and even major historical events tend to fade, even if some are recycled in a recurrent process of "producing meaning in an ongoing way through selection, representation and interpretation."[5] Both Anne Frank and Sukarno have emerged as icons of memory in the Netherlands through paradoxical patterns of repetition and omission, making them not only sufficiently stable but also flexible enough to function in changing historical contexts.[6]

Second, thinking comparatively about Anne Frank and Sukarno as icons of World War II remembrances requires an examination of the intellectual formation of "memory work"—as some postmodern or postcolonial commentators prefer to call it—in the Netherlands since 1945 and how it might be related to postwar political developments. Iconic memory is part of an individual inclination and a communal practice grounded in fluctuating currents of affection and disaffection, of remembering and forgetting, and of cohesion versus "othering." This organic process makes it necessary to consider the ways in which national historical memory is stipulated at different historical junctures, not only to mitigate a lingering sense of national disquiet about World War II but also to boost a reconfigured postwar national character, that is, a new identity grounded in a less prominent place in the postwar international order because of the dismantling of the lucrative Dutch empire in Southeast Asia. Crucial, in this context, is cultural memory's selective nature and its intrinsic connection with what might seem its opposite but is, in fact, a necessary counterpart: forgetting. How did the icons of memory that came to be called "Anne Frank" and "Sukarno" emerge and evolve in the postwar Netherlands, and what were the urgent needs that these icons fulfilled, both in terms of memory and either amnesia or aphasia?[7] Above all, it is necessary to examine the tendency in the Netherlands to frame World War II in Europe and Asia in moral terms in an apparently compulsive need to make comparative judgments about good and evil. The ongoing debate about a narrative that presents the Nazi occupation of the Netherlands as a murky "gray past," populated by people who were neither heroes nor villains but made only self-interested decisions in chaotic times—as contrasted with a starkly delineated black-and-white portrayal filled with stories about victims and perpetrators—has flared up again in recent years, if only because dozens of the *Nebenklager* (civilian plaintiffs) in the John (Ivan) Demjanjuk trial in Munich in 2010–11 are descendants of the approximately twenty-five thousand Dutch Jews murdered in Sobibor.

Dutch memorial practices concerning World War II in colonial Indonesia, however, present a more convoluted picture. European settlers in Southeast Asia, both *totoks* (Dutch-born residents) and the 70 percent majority of Indo-Dutch inhabitants (i.e., Europeans born in the Indonesian archipelago who often possessed a biracial ancestry), were either killed or inhumanely treated as civilians in Japanese internment camps or as prisoners of war and forced laborers in projects such as building the Burma-Siam railroad. As a consequence, the moral debate about victims and perpetrators in Southeast Asia reveals a different dynamic. From a Dutch historical perspective, the Japanese enemies and their co-opted allies among Indonesian Nationalists such as Sukarno are characterized across the board as evil perpetrators, while all Europeans with white, golden, or "chocolate" complexions are portrayed as innocent victims.[8] This simple, binary perspective obviates the urgent need to come to terms with a long colonial history since the very early seventeenth century grounded in the mobilization of indigenous labor for the financial benefits of the mother country. Indonesian Nationalists' complicity in Japanese cruelty during World War II and the *bersiap* (literally "be prepared") period that came in its wake during the autumn of 1945—when radical Indonesian "freedom fighters" murdered approximately thirty-five hundred Indies- or Dutch-born Europeans recently released from Japanese internment camps, while they returned others to makeshift prison colonies—has contributed to the absence of a genuine postcolonial reckoning in the contemporary Netherlands.

DIVIDED MEMORIES: ANNE FRANK AND WORLD WAR II IN THE EUROPEAN METROPOLE

On April 3, 1946, the preeminent Dutch historian Jan Romein wrote an opinion piece titled "A Child's Voice" in the Amsterdam newspaper *Het Parool* after reading Anne Frank's not yet published diary. He suggested that the vilest of human crimes was the urge to destroy a society's "sources of culture" and that the murder of this young girl "confirmed mankind's losing battle against its own beast-like nature." At the same time, Romein noted that Anne Frank's preternaturally mature diary confirmed the "infinite possibilities of human nature, which reside in humor, compassion and love."[9] Since her death in Bergen-Belsen at age fifteen, the truncated life of Anne Frank has been transformed into a "universal symbol of the Holocaust."[10] As a "worldwide idol," her personal history evokes a reverence on a scale that has been compared to the memory of other transnational icons such as Mahatma Gandhi or Martin Luther King.[11] In recent years, she has even been transformed into a "global comic book hero." In a Mexican comic book, for instance, she has been celebrated as an embodiment of the triumph of good over evil, whereas a comic strip in the Philippines has translated her into a tragic symbol of unrequited love. A Japanese cartoon artist has heralded her as an avatar of pacifism, while in Italy her World War II experience is cartoonishly drawn into the Christian tradition of the "Lives of Saints" in which a painting of the Holy Virgin appears on the wall of the Frank family's hiding place in Amsterdam.[12]

Frank's diary was edited and published in Dutch in 1947 and soon thereafter translated in many foreign languages, including German. It first appeared in Germany during the early 1950s, the era of "cold amnesty" (*kalte Amnestie*) when prosecutions of war crimes—and the general pursuit of denazification—were temporarily shelved or even furtively dismissed as opportunistic or hypocritical American inventions.[13] During the 1950s, the democratic revival and economic reconstruction of Germany and other Western European nations within the Cold War struggle against Soviet- or Chinese-inspired Communism were imperative, whereas the memory of the Allied victory over fascism no longer seemed to demand either ardent commemoration or the active punishment of World War II criminals. The theater play written by the American writers Frances Goodrich and Alfred Hackett, however, provided a turning point and produced during the second half of the 1950s a movement among young German people who were imbued with "Anne Frank fever." The German adaptation of the play drew more than a million visitors into theaters; in 1957, a plaque was placed on the Frankfurt house where she was born: "Her Life and Her Death—Our Obligation."[14]

With the exception of the Adolf Eichmann trial in Jerusalem in 1961, little national or international attention during the 1950s and 1960s was devoted to the prosecution of war crimes, whether in Germany or in the Netherlands or other European countries occupied by the Nazis during World War II.[15] About the trial in 1966 of twelve SS members who had worked in the death camp Sobibor, the newspaper *Der Zeit* reported that few German citizens recognized the name of the camp; in fact, one of the housewives who was interviewed allegedly presumed "Sobibor to be the name of a new detergent."[16] It would not be until the 1980s and 1990s that the most spectacular trials of World War II perpetrators would take place (Klaus Barbie, 1983, 1987; Paul Touvier, 1989; and Maurice Papon, 1997—in France; Ivan [John] Demjanjuk in Israel, 1986, and repeated in Munich in 2010–11; Kurt Waldheim in Austria, 1986; and Erich Priebke in Italy, 1996).

Although controversies surrounding the wartime conduct of several prominent Dutch citizens occasioned intermittent uproar during the postwar decades, starting in the 1970s Dutch memories of World War II were mostly forged by, and beholden to, Lou de Jong's government-sponsored, multivolume series about the Kingdom of the Netherlands during the Second World War (*Het Koninkrijk der Nederlanden in de Tweede Wereldoorlog*). Between 1969 and 1988, the monumental tomes appeared like clockwork and tacitly claimed to be "the ethical compass of the nation" by erecting "a moral superstructure grounded in the binary opposites of good and evil."[17] During the first twenty or thirty years after 1945, the average survivor could easily remember his or her own ambivalent experiences of the Nazi occupation. As a consequence, the Dutch public seemed to hunger for De Jong's grand chronicle that not only celebrated unequivocal "heroic deeds" but also recounted the many "villainous acts" that had occurred beyond the average person's limited social circle and provincial range of vision.[18] In their complicated daily lives during 1940–45, many Dutch citizens had undoubtedly been confronted with either their own moral failings or the human frailties of friends and neighbors who had made both right and wrong decisions. De Jong's magnum opus, instead, transcended the mundane recollections of the Dutch public by staging the history of World War II as an epic struggle between the "devils and angels" of collaboration and resistance, between culpability and righteousness, between right and left.[19]

During the past ten years, however, a highly contested revisionist trend has emerged. In 2001, the Dutch historian Chris van der Heijden wrote a book titled *Gray Past: The Netherlands and World War II* (*Grijs verleden: Nederland en de Tweede Wereldoorlog*) in a calculated effort to move beyond a World War II historiography he challenged as being mired in a one-dimensional black-and-white attribution of either virtue or guilt. Too little is known about the murky terrain in the middle, Van der Heijden admonished, where most ordinary people made a combination of strategic adjustments and concessions in daily life, more often impelled by coincidence rather than deliberate decisions, geared toward the survival of self and of their next of kin.[20] In *Gray Past*, he claims that the anti-Nazi resistance consisted of only a handful of genuine heroes, while at the opposite end of the political spectrum, the group of pro-German villains was equally small.[21] The overwhelming majority of the Dutch population, instead, presumably lived in the hoary spaces of indifference in between these two extremes. He cites an eyewitness account to highlight the widespread apathy among Dutch onlookers when Jews in The Hague were deported in bright daylight, written by a controversial World War II interlocutor:

> I regularly saw them walking in groups of eight, sometimes in groups of twenty. They wore backpacks and often also carried extra suitcases, always followed by at least two or more police officers. These groups moved through the center of the city. I saw them trudging along in the middle of throngs of women who were shopping and simply continued shopping; they did not even look up. Yes, sometimes a child turned around to observe the strange procession, but the mother would quickly pull her child along. Shopping was more important. It was as if Jews were nothing but air.[22]

Van der Heijden's work has reignited a vibrant—sometimes vitriolic—debate about remembering and rendering account of World War II in the Netherlands during the past decade. He has done so, in part, by criticizing the "*Shoahisering*" (Shoahization) of thinking and writing about World War II, which he blames for perpetuating an ethical discourse concerning human conduct in World War II as too rigidly divided between victims and perpetrators. Indirectly, Van der Heijden echoes the exhortation of the Australian historian Inga Clendinnen, who in her book *Reading the Holocaust* (2002) also urges historians to cast aside their tendency to moralize because "in the face of a catastrophe on this scale so deliberately inflicted, moral judgment is an indulgence we cannot afford."[23] Van der Heijden may adhere to the notion that the historian's most basic task is first to parse, and then to reassemble, the social contexts and political sensibilities of historical actors during World War II in order to try to understand the varieties of wartime exploits of "ordinary people in ordinary situations."[24] He is inexact, however, about how historians can infer the likely intentions behind those actions by relying, for example, on a generic fund of knowledge about the varying human motivations that prevailed during the chaotic times of war. At the same time, his texts are imprecise about the intricate relationship between individual behavior and how it may be extrapolated to the population at large.

In an attempt to construct World War II as a chaotic or even nihilistic historical event, further compromised by his sometimes deceptive deployment of historical evidence, Van der Heijden has tried to convey the Dutch experience during the Nazi occupation as an unprincipled quagmire, divorced from any moral grounding or political convictions in daily life. In his vision, the majority of people merely engaged in self-interested and opportunistic behavior that was sometimes heroic and sometimes blameworthy but always geared toward survival. In his wake, another writer has recently accused members of a particular World War II resistance group in the Rotterdam region of having committed armed criminal acts.[25] It seems as if Van der Heijden tries to reiterate writ large Ian Buruma's incidental but appropriately contextualized comments in *The Wages of Guilt: Memories of War in Germany and Japan* (1994). Buruma has described the Nazi occupation of the Netherlands as "humiliating business," as an era when human weakness was common and heroism was rare. Buruma insists that only "fools" would place themselves in a pantheon of heroes, because most sensible people, instead, tend to understand more easily "the ugly little compromises people make to save their own skin."[26]

In a well-argued and documented response titled "Everyone a Bit of a Victim, Everyone a Bit of a Perpetrator: The Dutch Historikerstreit concerning the Gray War," the Dutch historian Evelien Gans criticized Van der Heijden for trying to equalize and thereby neutralize good and evil conduct during World War II especially with regard to its principal human calamity, the Holocaust. She proceeded to raise the issue of secondary anti-Semitism because of Van der Heijden's charge that some historians indulge in an "unhealthy Holocaust obsession."[27] Gans defines secondary anti-Semitism as a process of transference by blaming the continued presence of Jews in our contemporary world for keeping alive the painful memories of the Shoah—and thereby Germany's singular culpability—rather than allow the mass murder of Jews to pass into oblivion; the unrelenting commemoration of the Shoah nurtures what the German historian Ernst Nolte has described as "Die Vergangenheit die nicht vergehen will" (the past that does not want to go away).[28]

Meanwhile, the "keen relish of Anne Frank's descriptive powers" in her diary—and the museum located in an otherwise unexceptional house on the Prinsengracht in Amsterdam that reverently commemorates her life—functions as an essential element in this transnationally disseminated Manichean imaginary of World War II.[29] In the first decade of the twenty-first century, books continue to appear trying to identify the shadowy person(s) who informed the German authorities about the secret hiding place of the Frank family in central Amsterdam, thereby sending young Anne to her death in Bergen-Belsen.[30] Her short life has been transformed into the embodiment of human innocence and victimhood, even if it sustains a tradition of cultural remembering and history writing that incorporates judgments about heroes and villains. Because the Frank family in their Prinsengracht hideout was supported by a small coterie of Dutch friends who brought them food and daily necessities at considerable personal risk, the idealized memory of Anne Frank continues to reinforce a spurious sense that, with a few exceptions, most members of Dutch society had courageously, even "altruistically," tried to help Jewish fellow citizens during the Nazi occupation.[31] This dubious conviction is further bolstered by the Israeli Yad Vashem Foundation's extraordinarily long list of Dutch men and women (5,108) honored as "The Righteous Among Nations."[32]

However, 75 percent of the Dutch Jewish population was murdered, a death toll that provides a grim comparison, for a variety of complicated reasons, with the 40 percent and 25 percent of Jewish citizens in neighboring Belgium and France who were deported and killed in Nazi extermination camps.[33] Even in Germany, a relatively larger percentage of the Jewish population survived the Nazi era, in part because a considerable proportion of German Jews had fled abroad before the outbreak of the Blitzkrieg in 1940. Until the beginning of the new millennium, Anne

Frank's centrality in Dutch historical memory has perhaps obfuscated some salient facts about popular sensibilities during the Nazi occupation. Approximately two hundred thousand civil servants were required to fill in an ancestry form as early as 1940, without objections from the Dutch government in exile in London. Schoolteachers, police officers, and municipal administrators throughout the country as well as bureaucrats in the central government in The Hague were compelled, in order to guarantee employment, to submit a formal statement about the religious background of parents and grandparents; only several dozen people refused to do so. That the goal of the "declaration of Aryan origins" was to create an inventory of Jewish civil servants was public knowledge during the fall of 1940; nonetheless, the Dutch response was compliance with the Nazi order.[34] To the average Dutch citizen, it was apparently tolerable that, soon thereafter, young Jewish students were separated into haphazardly created schools and then forced to wear yellow stars in public spaces starting in late April 1942.[35] Even when members of the resistance tried to help Jewish families with finding a place to hide, a contentious eyewitness reported in 1944, they sometimes refused to help children whose appearance was too distinctively Jewish, as if they "evaluated people as they might at a cattle market or a slave auction."[36] During the remainder of World War II, a large number of Dutch citizens "ideologically collaborated" with, or "passively acquiesced" to, the Nazi authorities to the extent that approximately 15 percent of the adult population of the Netherlands was charged in 1945 with having betrayed fellow citizens by actively supporting the Nazi occupiers or having voluntarily fought alongside German army troops on the eastern front.[37] Among a total Dutch population of 9 million citizens in 1945, about half a million criminal dossiers were compiled concerning people suspected of alleged war crimes; in October 1945, one hundred thousand Dutch citizens accused of Nazi collaboration were held in jail.[38]

Although it is reasonable to argue that in the contemporary Netherlands a new awareness has emerged that the moral record of the Dutch population during 1940–45 was definitely a mixed one, Anne Frank's iconic place in memories of the Nazi-occupied Netherlands continues to capture the imagination of not only the Dutch public but also international readers of the diary as well as millions of foreign visitors to the Anne Frank house in Amsterdam. While the historiographical debate about the relative merits of a black-and-white versus a shades-of-gray historical narrative of World War II is still unfolding, the memory of Anne Frank provides a site of consensus. In post–World War II culture, the personal has become not only political but also historical: modern selfhood is frequently based on a self-conscious appropriation of the antagonistic human experiences of parents or grandparents during the Nazi era, consisting of either victims and resistance heroes or family members who had belonged to the Dutch National-Socialist Alliance (NSB) or volunteered for the Waffen SS.[39] Anne Frank's memory, instead, constitutes a peaceful "angle of repose" and a reprieve from the overheated discussion in the contemporary Netherlands about the legacies and meanings of World War II.[40]

Her preeminence was again evident in 2007 when the 150-year-old chestnut tree she could see from a window in the secret hiding place in 1943 and 1944, as described in her diary, was seriously damaged by a storm. Despite public pressure to try to preserve the ancient tree, in due course it had to be removed because of safety concerns. Since then, saplings of the giant horse chestnut tree have already been planted elsewhere in Amsterdam and in other cities such as Paris, Madrid, and Montreal. During the planting ceremony in Amsterdam in 2010, city councilor Marijke Vos said, "This tree has a special meaning for Amsterdam but also for people all over the world. It is a symbol of hope and freedom, and with these saplings we can share that hope and freedom with the whole world."[41] Shoots of Anne Frank's chestnut tree will also be planted in places such as Little Rock Central High School in Arkansas, the embattled site of forced desegregation in 1957, and at several Holocaust centers throughout the United States. Not surprisingly, plans are under way to donate a sapling of Anne Frank's tree to Ground Zero in New York City as well.

DIVIDED MEMORIES: SUKARNO AND WORLD WAR II IN DUTCH COLONIAL INDONESIA

In *The Voice of Asia*, the widely read American author James A. Michener recounted a conversation in 1951 with a "crying Dutchman" in Djakarta (Jakarta today), the renamed capital of the independent Indonesian Republic. According to the disgruntled Dutchman, "They [Indonesians] are good-for-nothing stupid people." He allegedly told Michener that "when communism was fashionable, they were communists. When Japanese fascism was popular, that's what they were. Then American dollars bought them to be staunch democrats. Next they'll be devout Muslims killing everyone who isn't. And pretty soon they'll be communist again. A fine thing you damned meddlers have done. You have destroyed Java."⁴² This weepy colonial Dutchman was repeating an intractable historical myth. He was articulating a view shared by many people in the postcolonial Netherlands. Many Dutch citizens continue to bemoan, even today, Washington's presumably misguided and ill-informed foreign policies during the years 1945–49 as being responsible for the premature decolonization of the Dutch East Indies, even though the archival record shows that the Truman administration firmly backed the Dutch government, both politically and financially, until the fall of 1948. This inebriated Dutchman was also voicing a negative opinion about Indonesians that only the most conservative segments of the colonial community had embraced during the prewar years but which had become more prevalent during and after World War II, in part because two of the most prominent anticolonial leaders—Sukarno and Mohammad Hatta—had decided to collaborate with the Japanese invaders, albeit with different degrees of enthusiasm. Only the third member of the leadership of the fragmented nationalist movement, Sutan Sjahrir, withdrew into "internal exile," as the postwar German prime minister Konrad Adenauer called it, by living a secluded life throughout the Japanese "interregnum" in his sister's house in the Bandung region, where he listened to clandestine Allied radio broadcasts.⁴³

In the immediate postwar years, as the standoff between the Indonesian Republic, unilaterally proclaimed on August 17, 1945, and the Dutch government in The Hague degenerated into a bloody colonial war, discussions about the iconic meaning of Sukarno's complicity influenced Dutch East Indies policy and military interventions. His personality also entered the fray of electoral politics in the Netherlands itself. During the 1948 parliamentary elections, for instance, the People's Party for Freedom and Democracy (Volkspartij voor Vrijheid en Democratie, or VVD) featured campaign posters with Sukarno's face, referred to with the title of his academic engineering degree ("ir," short for *ingenieur*) and the slogan "Are you also fed up? Then vote List 6" (*Hebt u er ook genoeg van? Stemt dan Lijst 6*). The VVD was a brand-new center-right party founded in early 1948 on the primacy of individual freedoms and laissez-faire economic principles.⁴⁴ The VVD poster also impressed upon the voters—as a challenge of the social-democratic Labor Party's (Partij van de Arbeid) electoral appeal—that "socialism protects communism in the Indies" (*socialisme beschermt communisme in Indi"*) and that "a new course" (*het roer moet om*) in colonial policy vis-à-vis Sukarno's radical Indonesian Republic was essential.

The elections yielded sufficient parliamentary seats for the fledgling VVD party to enter the next coalition government dominated by representatives of the Labor Party and the Catholic People's Party (Katholieke Volkspartij). The new minister of foreign affairs, in fact, was VVD member Dirk Stikker, immediate past director of Heineken Breweries, who would play a crucial role in the dismantling of the Dutch colonial empire in Southeast Asia by negotiating the sanctions threatened by the United Nations (UN) Security Council—such as the withholding of Marshall Plan aid to the Netherlands government formally designated for the economic recovery of the Dutch East Indies—in the wake of the second "police action" in late December 1948. Although he tried to withstand the pressures imposed on the Netherlands by the UN, the United States, and Australia in particular, Stikker was compelled to help lay the groundwork for the transfer of sovereignty to the Republic of the United States of Indonesia in late December 1949.

Conservative and social-democratic critics alike, whether in the Netherlands or the Indies, invoked as a source of "trauma" the transfer of sovereignty to an Indonesian government led by Sukarno and Hatta as former henchmen of the Japanese—expressed in the slogan "Indië verloren, rampspoed geboren" ("The Indies Torn, Calamity Born" or "The Indies Lost at Disastrous Cost")—even among those who accepted that the end of Western colonial hegemony in Asia was legitimate and inevitable.[45] The otherwise pro-independence Dutch anthropologist J. P. B. de Josselin de Jong, for instance, remarked during the immediate postwar period that Sukarno had been nothing but a vile "Jap collaborator" (*Jappencollaborateur*) who lacked any kind of consistent "ideational motivation" and had wholeheartedly contributed to "reprehensible terror."[46] The subsequent struggle over the end of the Dutch-controlled western half of New Guinea during the late 1950s and early 1960s was again perceived as a rehearsal of the "trauma of decolonization" because it entailed yet another surrender to, and defeat by, the hated figure of Sukarno.

The collective trauma was caused not only by an almost pathological Dutch attachment to its colonial "social engineering" project in the Indonesian archipelago; it was also nurtured by a primal ressentiment of Sukarno as person and leader of the Republik Indonesia.[47] In postwar memories in the Netherlands itself as well as in the Dutch East Indies, the visceral hatred of Sukarno yielded a newly invented notion that Indonesia's anticolonial nationalism constituted, above all, a by-product of the

Japanese occupation. The Japanese were held responsible for single-handedly nourishing the nationalist movement among the educated native elite with Sukarno as primary accessory to, and iconic embodiment of, all the Japanese cruelties and humiliations imposed on hapless European settlers of the archipelago, whether hailing directly from the Netherlands or born into biracial Indies families. Having been an accomplice of the Japanese regime of terror in 1942–45, Sukarno was shunned as a Dutch negotiating partner during the struggle for independence in 1945–49. In the appraisals of Dutch historical memory since World War II and the transfer of sovereignty in 1949, the figure of Sukarno has been reviled over time more often as an "elusive *wayang* character" (*wayang* is the popular Javanese shadow puppet theater) or an unprincipled "sorcerer's apprentice" than he has been described with genuine efforts to understand and explain his pro-independence aspirations.[48] In Indonesia's collective memories, his role as founding father and leader of the Indonesian Republic was denigrated during the Suharto era from 1965 to 1998. Since the fall of the Suharto regime, however, his reputation has been gradually rehabilitated as Indonesia's first president who was also a worthy "heir to world culture," as in the title of a new book focusing on the Sukarno era.[49] Similarly in 2009, a commercial publisher in Jakarta issued an Indonesian translation of a book titled *American Visions of the Netherlands East Indies / Indonesia: US Foreign Policy and Indonesian Nationalism*. On the cover, the picture of Sutan Sjahrir was replaced, without consultation of the authors, with an image of Sukarno with a cameo of George Washington in the background, appearing above the title *Indonesia merdeka karena Amerika?* (Indonesia Independent Because of America?), as if Sukarno should be remembered as the primary founding father of the Indonesian Republic and perhaps also as the politician who had been responsible for mobilizing American support for Indonesia's independence in the post–World War II era.[50]

THE HISTORICAL CONTEXT OF THE ASIA-PACIFIC WAR IN COLONIAL INDONESIA

The Pacific War in Southeast Asia was the beginning of the end of the profitable Dutch imperial management of the Indonesian archipelago, with the islands of Java and Sumatra as its colonial heartland. It also terminated the Netherlands' rightful claim to the status of second-tier player in world affairs—"a mouse that could roar" in the international arena—purely based on its command of a vast and lucrative empire in Southeast Asia.[51] Since 1906, when the first semi-nationalist organization Budi Utomo (Beautiful Endeavor) was established, a fragmented but significant anticolonial movement had burgeoned. For its part, the Dutch colonial regime had kept nationalist sentiments under tight control through a wide range of effective surveillance techniques and preventive incarcerations often justified by arbitrary judicial measures.[52] As recorded in *Lukisan revolusi rakjat Indonesia* (Pictures of the Indonesian People's Revolution), a triumphant verbal and photographic account of the history of Indonesia's liberation from Dutch colonial mastery published by the Indonesian Republic's government printing office in Yogyakarta in December 1949, "A person suspected of being dangerous could be exiled without previous investigation and without awaiting a court sentence."[53] American diplomats stationed in Batavia, Surabaya, and Medan during the 1930s, meanwhile, criticized the Indies government for "summarily banishing," purely as a preemptive measure, any Indonesian Nationalist "without due process of law" even if he or she was not suspected of Communist sympathies.[54]

During the 1930s, however, Japan's territorial expansion became a genuine threat to Dutch colonial society in the Indonesian archipelago. As a consequence, the newly appointed governor general in 1939, as World War II in Europe was unfolding with Germany's invasion of Poland in September, devoted concerted attention to strengthening the colony's inadequate military defenses. Due to the archipelago's possession of rich oil deposits and refineries in Sumatra and Borneo (now called Kalimantan), an eventual Japanese occupation appeared highly likely because the Japanese nation and its war machine were entirely dependent on imported oil. In the United States, a relatively positive image of colonial Indonesia resurfaced during the late 1930s: several laudatory articles appeared in the American press including a lengthy, nicely illustrated article in the *Christian Science Monitor* in 1938, which claimed that "sturdy Hollanders" had exploited their empire with "characteristic moderation ... frankly paternalistic, but wise and just." Military planners in the West had to concede, however, that this dexterously woven "fabric of empire" was "the work of a third-class European power" that maintained only a third-rate army and navy.[55] In 1941, an embargo of American oil exports to Japan was added to an already existing ban on exports of scrap iron and steel, producing a general expectation that a Japanese invasion of the Dutch East Indies was downright unavoidable.[56]

When it finally happened in early 1942, Japan's military juggernaut defeated the Royal Netherlands Indies Army and Navy in a mere two months. According to *Lukisan revolusi rakjat Indonesia*, despite their vow "to die upright rather than to succumb on their knees... the Dutch forces could only resist for seven days while the Dutch–Indies government had already fled earlier in disorder."[57] Once ensconced as rulers of the Dutch East Indies, Japanese authorities quickly seized the instruments of violence and subjugation that were left behind by the Dutch colonial state. As their Dutch forerunners had done, the Japanese also proceeded to draft the well-entrenched network of native notables (*priyayi*) at the regional level into their military administration; many among the *priyayi* proved sufficiently pliable to submit to the new overlords from Japan by simply perpetuating their previous positions in the colonial civil service. The co-optation of *priyayi* regents, law-enforcement officials, and other native retainers in the different administrative districts of Java and elsewhere, in turn, endowed Sukarno's fervent collaboration with a gloss of normalcy. Indigenous leaders employed their personal stature and authority to adapt from "representing the colonial power vis-à-vis the colonized" to a transformed world in which they could begin, indirectly due to Japanese machinations during the Asia-Pacific War, to speak for "their own people vis-à-vis the metropolis."[58]

Since precolonial times, exalted indigenous rulers and chiefs among the numerous "*adat* circles" (ethnically defined groups with shared customs and traditions) populating the Indonesian archipelago had maintained control over their subordinates through a monopoly on violence coupled with "theatrical" displays of power formalized in rituals of command and obeisance.[59] Such ethnically diverse political entities were contest states that, in the face of recurrent intra-local competition and strife over manpower and resources, maintained interior cohesion through threats of physical punishment, whereas the hierarchical practices of the ritualized "theater state" served merely ancillary purposes.[60] In the late nineteenth century, however, the Dutch colonial regime had embarked on a "wave of violence" in order to introduce a modern colonial system of governance, coupled with open-door investments and laissez-faire capitalist production, by gathering and wielding an "unprecedented arsenal of modern tools" of coercion.[61] Around the year 1900, military expeditions took place in the eastern archipelago (Lombok, Bali, Ceram, Flores), in Borneo and Sumatra. Particularly in Aceh in North Sumatra, a protracted colonial war sent at least seventy-five thousand Acehnese warriors and civilians to their deaths and recorded a range of incidents of brutal civilian massacres and summary executions. The twentieth-century colonial state in the Dutch East Indies, in other words, employed technologies of surveillance and intimidation that were imposed, in turn, upon an indigenous world in which revenge, robbery, and fighting were endemic, despite persistent Dutch constructions of colonized subjects in the Javanese heartland and many other areas as peaceful but primitive or as childlike but compliant and thus in need of "uplifting" paternal guidance.[62]

As soon as they had settled in as sovereign rulers of the Indonesian archipelago, Japanese military administrators employed the Dutch East Indies' state apparatus left behind in January 1942, in order to nurture a range of public organizations designed to foster pride among Indonesians in their "nation/race" (*bangsa/kebangsaan*). They made "promises resembling high mountains" to fellow Asians who wished to evict European colonizers. *Lukisan revolusi rakjat Indonesia* commented on the appeal and pledges of the Japanese: "Many Indonesian nationalist leaders were tempted by the propaganda of the Japanese . . . [and] they agreed to cooperate with the Japanese due to their hatred of Dutch colonialism. . . . There were some leaders, however, who were suspicious of Japanese policy that was known to be fascist."[63] The prescient Javanese poet Noto Soeroto, for example, had earlier admonished fellow Indonesians that the "tragedy" of Japan's colonial "rape and pillage" of Korea should serve as a cautionary tale for all Asians yearning for an end to European colonial rule.[64] Nonetheless, Japanese military authorities also provided a multitude of young Indonesians—approximately 2 million men—with basic military training.[65] They instilled in Indonesian youth a "visceral anti-Western bias that bordered on sheer hatred." As an American Office of Strategic Services (OSS) briefing report stated in July 1944, from the very first moment the Japanese took control of the Indonesian archipelago, "the natives" had been inculcated with the conviction that in the brave new world of the Greater East Asia Co-Prosperity Sphere "they are the masters and white people are only dirt."[66] However, Sukarno and Hatta and a few others who were members of an advisory council to the Japanese military occupiers played only a nominal role in policy. The Javanese leaders were granted permission in Java to indulge in mostly perfunctory symbols of national unity—flying the red-and-white Indonesian flag, singing the "Indonesia Raya" national anthem, gathering for carefully monitored political rallies. The new Japanese rulers actually envisioned a future in which Japan and the oil-rich islands of Sumatra and Borneo in particular would constitute an "indivisible unity."[67]

Lukisan revolusi rakjat Indonesia joined other commentators who asserted that, at first, many Indonesians greeted with a mixture of excitement and dread "the militaristic typhoon of a small yellow race" that had descended from the north in early 1942 and quickly brought the ill-equipped Royal Dutch East Indies Army to its knees. Most ordinary Indonesians were astonished by the sight of the Dutch regime crumbling so quickly; as the beleaguered Indonesian Nationalist and Communist Tan Malaka recorded in his diary, Dutch colonial rulers were blown away like "grains of sand on a rock."[68] In a similar vein, a Japanese military officer recalled afterward that toppling the Dutch colonial government required no more than a gentle breeze because the resistance of the Dutch East Indies Army and Navy was as ineffectual as "the war games played by boastful little boys."[69] A few years later Mohammad Rum, a government official of the Indonesian Republic who was incarcerated by Dutch authorities on the island of Bangka after the second military assault on the republic in Yogyakarta in late December 1948, sent an eloquent handwritten letter in English to the Good Offices Committee of the UN charged with mediating the Dutch-Indonesian conflict on behalf of the UN Security Council. He wrote on January 20, 1949, that the Indonesian Republic was not "born as a result of a rebellion against the Dutch." Instead, the most salient historical fact was that the Dutch military establishment had succumbed to the Japanese "without any shadow of a proper attempt to defend the Dutch East Indies." Since the Dutch colonial regime had completely neglected its responsibility to safeguard Indonesians against foreign aggression, the "alleged historic right" of the Netherlands in the Indonesian archipelago lapsed the very moment it failed in 1942 to fulfill its obligations. By surrendering to the Japanese within less than two months, Rum asserted that Dutch rulers had expedited Japan's ability to convert the political and economic tools of colonial mastery into lethal weapons of war and occupation. The independent republic was born only after "Indonesians had paid a very high price in pain and bloodshed, as a great number of her sons fell in their efforts to wrest power from the Japanese."[70] This declaration, however, was an overstatement. Although members of Pembela Tanah Air, or PETA (Defenders of the Country, a Japanese-created army of volunteers), had engaged in daring but small-scale uprisings in Indramaju, Tasikmalaja, and Blitar toward the end of the war, the Japanese maintained firm control even if the suffering of the Indonesian people had reached its "climax" under the Japanese.[71]

Sukarno, for his part, rejoiced in the invasion of the Japanese, who promptly released him from detention in Bengkulu in Sumatra, where he had been held separately from other important Nationalists incarcerated in Boven Digoel, located in a swampy malarial region of western New Guinea. He later remembered that he could all of a sudden envision an independent Indonesia to be achieved alongside Dai Nippon (Greater Japan) because, as he recalled, "for the first time in all my life I saw myself in the mirror of Asia." This statement revealed a new and honest picture of himself.[72] Sukarno argued that the convex mirror of Dutch colonialism had grotesquely magnified the master-servant relationship embedded in Java's "feudal" culture. During the colonial era, a slave mentality (he used *slavengeest* when he wrote in Dutch or *jiwa budak* in Malay, which would become Bahasa Indonesia, the national language of independent Indonesia). This ingrained way of thinking was etched into Indonesians' souls as a counterpoint to Europeans' master mentality (*herengeest* in Dutch, *jiwa ksatriya* in Malay). Dutch colonial culture had forged a complicity with the entrenched patterns of lordship and bondage in Java and elsewhere. This kind of symmetrical conspiracy, he asserted before World War II, had endowed Dutch East Indies society with an aura of coherence. Emboldened by the effortless Japanese defeat of the Dutch army and navy in 1942, he proceeded to call upon his fellow citizens in September 1942 to banish the slave mentality from their hearts and minds; true independence, he implored, could only happen when Indonesians learned to exult in their noble spirit and *jiwa ksatriya*.[73] Sukarno sometimes appealed to the ancient Javanese Jojobojo legend, a story describing yellow monkeys descending from the north to unshackle the island from oppressive white water buffaloes in order to inaugurate a golden age led by a "just prince" (Ratu Adil). In his incendiary rhetoric, when he invoked his own status as Ratu Adil, he was careful not to disparage his Japanese sponsors, who, for their part, had announced via leaflets in early 1942 that they had arrived in Java "to liberate the Indonesian people from enslavement by the Hollanders" and emphasized their own "yellow complexion."[74]

During the following three years, Sukarno indulged his rhetorical skills in "rousing speeches" to mobilize the masses, pursuing two goals simultaneously: "stoking nationalism and stroking the Japanese as the liberators of Asia."[75] He was allowed to establish a semi-military youth organization under his guidance, the Barisan Pelopor (Corps of Pioneers), which reconfirmed his confidence in political centralism and the value of highly personalized structures of authority and deference.[76] He also helped to recruit millions of labor "volunteers"—some estimates suggest 2 million, while others put the number at 4 million or even higher (*sukarela* in Malay, *romusha* in Japanese). They were sent overseas to Japanese-held territories in Southeast Asia such as Burma, where 80 percent died while constructing the Burma-Siam railroad. *Romusha* were also put to work in Java, Sumatra, and New Guinea on infrastructural projects such as railroads and airstrips or in mines, resulting in an alarmingly high death toll as well.[77]

As a result, a Dutch official in Batavia during the fall of 1945 threatened Sukarno with a potential prosecution for war crimes, "for having used fascistic and terrorist methods" against European residents as well as indigenous populations of the archipelago on behalf of his Japanese partners in crime.[78] Sukarno himself would later describe his actions during World War II as shameful: "It was I, Sukarno, who sent [my people] to work. . . . I shipped them to their deaths. . . . And it was I who gave them to the Japanese."[79]

A Dutch-trained Indonesian jurist, Mas Slamet, condemned Sukarno's wartime conduct in no uncertain terms, denouncing Sukarno as a "Japanese mercenary who, through pillage, murder, and kidnapping now tries to consign to oblivion his treachery and immeasurable guilt." As he wrote in an open letter to Queen Wilhelmina on December 28, 1945: "Your people have been liberated from the shouts of 'Heil Hitler' and the stretched arms of deluded Teutonic hordes [*Teutonendom*]. But my people are still suffering from shouts of 'Merdeka' [Independence] and the clenched fists of deluded young men egged on by the ambitions of their imagined leaders who, in reality, are nothing but [Japanese] lackeys in our times of sorrow."[80]

In contrast to Sukarno's unambiguous embrace of the Japanese as long-awaited catalysts of Indonesian independence, Mohammad Hatta's reasons for collaborating with the Japanese occupiers during 1942–45 entailed a range of mixed emotions. He was known as a devout Muslim and bookish personality; critics described him as an "insipid" public speaker and an "ornery" politician.[81] He was a capable economist, however, academically trained in Rotterdam in the Netherlands. He understood that Japan's meager natural resources and its reliance on oil imports from abroad would, in the long run, not be able to withstand America's immense resources, technological sophistication, and productive potential. In Hatta's view, it was likely that Japan's hegemony in Asia would merely be a short-lived "interregnum." Nonetheless, Hatta thought that the Japanese might transform his life-long quest for independence from the realm of dreams into a sphere of realpolitik, enabling Indonesians to create "a state within a state" and bring the goals of an independent new society (*masyarakat baru*) within reach.[82]

Tan Malaka, an equally astute observer of the geopolitical situation during the early 1940s, concurred with Hatta's assessment. He also predicted that America's "staying power" would be far greater than Japan could ever muster. He wrote in his autobiographical diary during the Asia-Pacific War that even though Japanese society had been whipped into a war frenzy, while its soldiers and sailors displayed astonishing "stamina, courage and bravery," Japan would not be able to challenge the United States in "geography, population, finance, production, raw materials, technology and science." He prophesied that Japan's military successes constituted nothing but a "soap bubble" that would undoubtedly burst within a few years. As an Indonesian Nationalist with Trotskyite leanings, he rebuked studious Hatta and flamboyant Sukarno—whom he labeled *banteng besar* (great wild bull)—for aiding the predatory Japanese who "devoured" Indonesia's rice supplies, precious metals, and the bodies of young men and women even faster than the Dutch had done.[83]

POSTWAR MORAL JUDGMENTS ABOUT WORLD WAR II AND SUKARNO'S REPUBLIC

During the German occupation of the Netherlands in 1940–45, illegal newspapers and anti-Nazi political propaganda began to circulate. In the face of a brutal German regime, activists in the Dutch resistance risked life and limb—and the safety of family and friends—by writing, printing, and distributing not only clandestine political pamphlets and insurgent propaganda but also nationalistic poems and songs invoking historically grounded notions of freedom and independence that were presumably typically Dutch.[84] In asserting newly invented forms of national solidarity vis-à-vis the German oppressors, they inspired and legitimized their anti-Nazi activities. At the same time, scores of Dutch resistance fighters could not fathom that Indonesian anticolonial intellectuals might be able to claim nationalist sentiments that were equally legitimate in the wake of more than three hundred years of Dutch colonial subjugation. Dutch "resistance heroes" during World War II, Jeroen Dewulf and Jennifer Foray have recently argued, justified their actions by appealing to lofty democratic ideals in their opposition to Nazi totalitarianism; many among the anti-Nazi writers and activists, however, revealed doubts about granting the same legitimacy to Indonesians' claims in the face of Dutch colonial domination.[85] Equating German oppression with Dutch colonial exploitation in the Indonesian archipelago was a taboo and continues to be viewed, even today, as a problematic assertion or even a "forbidden metaphor."[86]

Already before the outbreak of World War II in Southeast Asia, however, the homology between the emerging Third Reich and Dutch colonial mastery in the Indonesian archipelago had been elaborated when the thoughtful Indonesian Nationalist Sutan Sjahrir wrote in 1936 that "in the Indies, the official idea of a concentration camp has not yet been institutionalized; it thus lags behind Nazi-Germany. But Germany could learn a lot about the creation of such institutions by studying the Dutch practices in Boven Digul."[87] Sjahrir defined the predicament of the colonial relationship as being enacted compulsively by "psychopathic participants: on the one hand, the sadists and megalomaniacs and, on the other hand, the [native] souls that are warped by inferiority complexes."[88] In an oft-repeated observation, he also noted that "the West signifies forceful, dynamic and active life. It is a sort of Faust that I admire, and I am convinced that only by utilization of the dynamism of the West can the East be released from its slavery and subjugation." He underscored the tensions between Occidental notions of "life as a struggle and striving" versus the Oriental embrace of "serenity" and an aversion to change, which he identified as the core of the emerging conflict between West and East.[89]

Sjahrir, along with Hatta and other prominent Nationalists had been incarcerated in the notorious penal colony of Boven Digoel in western New Guinea, where the Indonesian Nationalists considered most dangerous to the Dutch state (*staatsgevaarlijk*) had been placed under lock and key during the 1920s and 1930s. Although the camp allowed for sports, reading, and musical entertainment and where family members could join the prisoners, in this "phantom world" inmates routinely died of malaria or went mad because of the isolation.[90] The prison camp of Boven Digoel was subsequently described in the *New Republic* during the fall of 1945 as "one of the world's most terror-ridden concentration camps in a swampy, malaria-infested jungle."[91] Published after Allied troops had broadcast their horror upon liberating the Nazi death camps in Central Europe during the spring of 1945, this American assessment of Boven Digoel was certainly hyperbolic and tendentious. The article invoked, however, a comparative trope that would become controversial in postwar debates. The editor of the anti-Nazi underground newspaper *Vrij Nederland*, Henk van Randwijk, for example, was at first quite cynical about Sukarno's intentions. In October 1945, he dismissed the proclamation of independence as a "subtle Japanese game" and refused to express support for Sukarno.[92] However, in July 1947 he wrote that "two years after Hitler's defeat, we have not forgotten that armed violence can be used to defend injustice and ungodliness... because I am a Dutchman, I say NO to the brutality we currently perpetrate in Indonesia." With this statement, Van Randwijk implicitly harked back to the famous peroration of Soewardi Soerjaningrat, who in 1913 had rebuked the Dutch colonial regime for the commemorations in the Indies of the Dutch liberation from Napoleon's "foreign domination" in 1813; Soewardi wrote, "If I were a Dutchman, I would not organize an independence celebration in a country where the independence of the people has been stolen."[93] Van Randwijk continued to invoke the "highest standard" of moral integrity he had used during the war to condemn the Nazi regime; in 1947, he applied the same ethical principles to Dutch military actions in Indonesia. Despite his stature as a major anti-Nazi resistance figure, his comparison between the Dutch police action in the Indies in June 1947 and Hitler's Germany prompted a split in *Vrij Nederland*'s editorial board and a reduction in its subscriptions.[94]

During a meeting of the UN Security Council in Paris in late December 1948 in the wake of the Dutch army's second military attack on the Indonesian Republic, an Australian delegate used the same proscribed metaphor: he condemned the Dutch government for committing acts of cruelty in Indonesia that "were worse than what Hitler had done in the Netherlands."[95] And, more recently, when a journalist wrote about Dutch military personnel in postwar Java and Sumatra, stating that "they were not SS officers, no, but because of the things they did, they may be compared [with SS officers]" or that Boven Digoel had been established long before the Nazis founded Buchenwald and Bergen-Belsen, an association of Indies military veterans accused him of libel, after which he was tried in court; his acquittal was later reconfirmed by an appeals court.[96]

CONCLUSION: ICONS OF MEMORY, POSTWAR DILEMMAS, AND "POSTCOLONIAL DEFICITS"

An apparently urgent need to arrive at moral judgments about guilt and victimhood continues to infuse the divided memories of World War II as it unfolded in both the Netherlands and the Dutch East Indies.[97] Different groups of stakeholders in Dutch society derive their contemporary identities from clinging to a particular vision of the past, in general, and of World War II, in particular. After all, historical commemoration in a modern democratic nation—as an element of what is now also called cultural memory—is socially "constructed" and politically "situated," conceptual notions that have long since settled in as platitudes. This recognition implies that any assertion about a society's memorial practices must be parsed, deciphered, and reconnected to the "collected" memories of distinct social communities, which tend to make their own strategic claims.[98] Such intellectual and existential maneuvers, however, are formulated within the constraints of sociopolitical institutions and rhetorical conventions that facilitate certain historical visions while obstructing others. At different moments in time, an informal agreement prevails as to which analogies and metaphors are appropriate and may achieve privileged status versus which figures of speech are forbidden.[99]

Postwar memories of World War II in the European metropole are saturated with abstractions, consisting of dry statistics that confirm civilian and military death tolls, judicial records revealing betrayal and collaboration, or ominous names of places such as Auschwitz, Bergen-Belsen, and Sobibor where murder was carried out on an industrial scale. But the emblematic meaning and emotional resonance of Anne Frank's "child's voice" rose above the din of these abstractions, as if she had ascended from the "the mass grave," holding the memories of millions of anonymous casualties of World War II, by assuming a transcendent identity of flesh and blood.[100] Despite the lingering acrimony in the contemporary Netherlands about historical narratives either colored in nostalgic sepia tints or else in clear black and white, the public commemoration of Anne Frank affords a consensus—an angle of repose—amid the competing claims of stakeholders who defend the superior validity of their own particular "collected" memories.

A different situation obtains with regard to the public remembrance of the Asia-Pacific War in the Dutch East Indies, an "interregnum" that played such a pivotal role in terminating the centuries-long history of Dutch colonial governance of first Java, then Sumatra, and then the entire vast Indies archipelago. The trauma of loss in 1945–49 in which Sukarno featured as a primary agent of doom—and the subsequent degradation of the Netherlands from second-tier standing in world affairs, thanks to the effective management of its Southeast Asian empire, to the status of a small, relatively insignificant European democracy resembling Denmark—took its toll. A post–World War II Dutch demand that Sukarno be removed from any and all political positions in the Indonesian Republic, because of his criminal servitude to Japan's regime of terror, was dismissed as imperious and therefore ignored.[101] Moreover, the continuing confrontations with Sukarno's Indonesian Republic during the 1950s, such as the nationalization of Dutch economic assets in the archipelago and the crisis over Netherlands-controlled western New Guinea, stunned the Dutch nation into an uncomfortable postcolonial silence. In early 1950, the conservative news magazine *Elsevier* had equated Sukarno's manipulation of public opinion in the Indonesian Republic with Hitler's propaganda machine erected by Joseph Goebbels, revealing that Nazi analogies were only forbidden if applied to Dutch citizens and soldiers.[102]

Meanwhile, approximately three hundred thousand Moluccan and mixed-blood Indo-Dutch immigrants arrived during the late 1940s and 1950s; in the Netherlands they constituted the first wave of immigrants who were of a different skin color and clung to different ethnic or religious cultures or eating habits.[103] Poignant reminiscences of the good old days in the tropical gothic of the Indonesian archipelago—ruptured by the humiliating defeat in 1945–49—were intertwined with these intermittent waves of migration. Organizations such as Tong Tong and other interest groups as well as Indo-Dutch writers such as Tjalie Robinson tried to forge an independent, postcolonial sense of community. They wanted to create a coequal space in a Dutch society that throughout the 1960s continued to be fragmented on the basis of clearly delineated Protestant, Catholic, and secular interest groups and sociopolitical organizations referred to as "pillars" (*zuilen*; the process of fragmentation in Dutch civil society was called "pillarization," or *verzuiling*).[104]

The historical imagination of World War II in Southeast Asia is still dominated by memories of Dutch suffering endured during the Japanese occupation. Eventually, this humiliation and pain experienced in the Japanese prisoner of war camps came to be seen as inseparable from

Sukarno's voluntary participation in perpetrating their abject victimization, first under Japanese rule and then afterward also by radical young Indonesians, whom Sukarno and his cronies had whipped into a frenzy during the frightening *bersiap*. As a result, the actual process of decolonization in the East Indies, grounded in anticolonial grievances encouraged by a new worldwide climate of opinion and high hopes invested in newly created international institutions such as the UN, continues to be linked, either directly or indirectly, to Sukarno's role as an unprincipled Japanese puppet who then manipulated the illiterate Indonesian masses for his own demonic purposes in 1945–49.

Even today, a silent presumption still prevails that the Dutch colonial regime until 1942 had protected the simple folks (*kromo, orang kecil*) in the villages and rice fields of hundreds of islands in the Indonesian archipelago from the abuses perpetrated by local potentates and by showing respect for local customs and traditions (*adat*) and pursuing a gradual policy of "uplifting" them to eventual maturity. However, this development process might take as much as another three hundred years, as the penultimate governor general had predicted in 1933.[105] In a contemporary public imagination, Dutch colonial rule is sotto voce also represented, every now and then, as benign and "ethical" due to the rigorous Indological (Orientalist) academic training bestowed upon twentieth-century Dutch civil servants at universities in Leiden and Utrecht. The impressive linguistic skills and knowledge about religion and cultural traditions displayed by most Dutch civil servants presumably surpassed the meager local knowledge at the disposal of British, French, or American colonial administrators in Southeast Asia. Instead, Dutch colonial governance of the Indonesian archipelago is remembered as having "accomplished something great over there," as emblazoned in the title of an extravagant scholarly book that appeared in 1939.

Rather than engage in a genuine postcolonial reckoning with the meaning of Dutch imperialism in Asia, current discussions are too often trapped in questions about the specifics of Dutch political and cultural policy making during the colonial era, military strategy during the independence struggle, or whether the Dutch government in The Hague was engaged in a genuine process of decolonization.[106] Such an obsessive preoccupation with empirical detail, erupting in allegations back and forth between colonial scholars at universities in Leiden and Amsterdam about the existence of a *"doofpot"* (cover-up), may be viewed as an instance of what the feisty essayist Rudy Kousbroek called "the mystical marriage between a typically Dutch formalism and a typically Dutch hypocrisy."[107]

While Anne Frank's iconic positioning in contemporary memory practices is able to function as a site of reconciliation, Sukarno's iconic presence does the opposite: it has contributed to a reluctance to examine the validity of nationalist claims during the first half of the twentieth century as the Indonesian population struggled to free itself from the shrewd economic management of the archipelago's natural resources and labor power for the financial benefit of the mother country—what French visitors during the colonial era called the efficient exploitation of the economic value (*mise en valeur*) of the Netherlands East Indies. Whether explicitly or implicitly, Sukarno is held responsible for mobilizing a revolutionary mass hysteria among fanatic young Indonesians (*pemuda*). Republik Indonesia leaders such as Sukarno, in other words, are sometimes remembered as having undergone an alleged metamorphosis from first being an ungrateful educated native, and then after 1942 a minion of the Japanese, and finally to suddenly thinking he belonged to, quoting a Dutch psychoanalyst in 1949, "a new species of Super Indonesians suffering from a splitting of the super ego, infantile regression and secondary narcissism."[108]

As a result, the lingering ambivalence in Dutch memories about the controversial figure of Sukarno before, during, and after World War II may be viewed as an element in a general "postcolonial deficit" in the Netherlands. Another contributing factor is the obsessive focus of twenty-first-century neoconservative or populist politicians with the nefarious role of Muslim immigrants from Morocco and Turkey in contemporary Dutch society. Obviously, the second- and third-generation descendants of guest workers, brought to the Netherlands beginning in the 1960s, have no personal connection to the history of Dutch colonial mastery in Southeast Asia or in Suriname and the Caribbean. During the past decade, right-wing politicians such as Geert Wilders have deliberately fanned the flames of xenophobia by portraying Moroccan-Dutch and Turkish-Dutch citizens as a threat because they fail to adjust to secular Western values and they constitute a financial drain on the resources of contemporary society at the expense of Dutch-born workers and middle-class citizens.

In the process of designating the "tsunami" of Muslims from the Near East and North Africa as problematic, immigrants from the former Dutch East Indies and Suriname are often reinvented as model immigrants, whose integration in the Netherlands was smooth and efficient due to their linguistic and cultural knowledge.[109] Ironically, their reconstruction as exemplary immigrants in the postwar Netherlands also has the effect of postponing any real discussion about the multiple implications of the Dutch colonial past for the contemporary postcolonial and increasingly multiethnic and multireligious society that now exists in The Netherlands.[110]

1   The phrase "divided memory" was used by Jeffrey Herf in his book *Divided Memory*, which analyzes the differential historical memories of the Holocaust and the "Jewish question" in West and East Germany in the postwar era. The notion of instrumental amnesia concerning a "usable past" is also helpful. See Maier, *The Unmasterable Past*; more recently, see Shevel, "The Politics of Memory in a Divided Society"; also Morina, *Legacies of Stalingrad*.
2   Schulte Nordholt, *Een staat van geweld*, 1–31.
3   As Bijl has recently explored in "Emerging Memory."
4   Kritzman and Nora, eds., *Realms of Memory*. See also Boym, *The Future of Nostalgia*, 49–55.
5   Rigney, "Plenitude, Scarcity, and the Circulation of Cultural Memory," 16.
6   With thanks to Paulus Bijl, whose recent dissertation has effectively elaborated on these issues; see "Emerging Memory."
7   I am indebted to Bijl for this formulation.
8   The term "café au lait" was used by Justuk van Maurik in *Indrukken van een totok*. He also described the Indo-Dutch population as having a "complexion bathed in the color of milk chocolate" (140). All translations from other languages are mine unless otherwise noted.
9   Romein, "Een kinderstem."
10 Boers, "Wees niet bang voor het grijs."
11 As the Dutch sociologist Abram de Swaan proposed in 2010 on the occasion of the fiftieth anniversary of the Anne Frank House in Amsterdam and the inauguration of a new exhibition space.
12 Ribbens, "Anne Frank as Global Comic Book Hero."
13 Boehling, *A Question of Priorities*. See also Friedrich, *Die kalte Amnestie*.
14 Van der Heijden, "Moordenaars onder ons."
15 Gordon, "The Guilty," review of Lipstadt, *The Eichmann Trial*.
16 Quoted in Van der Heijden, "Moordenaars onder ons."
17 Snel, "De grijze massa was goed."
18 Ibid.
19 Köbben, *De tijdgeest en andere ongemakken*, 17–26.
20 Van der Heijden, *Grijs verleden*. See also his recent dissertation at the University of Amsterdam, titled "Dat nooit meer."
21 See Köbben's critique, *De tijdgeest en andere ongemakken*, 17–26.
22 Quoted in Weinreb, *Collaboratie en verzet*, 486–87. In the quotation, Van der Heijden has combined sentence fragments from several paragraphs.
23 Clendinnen, introduction to *Reading the Holocaust*, 5.
24 Van der Heijden, "De oorlog als mensenverhaal." See also Dean, "Against Grandiloquence."
25 For a recent monograph arguing that resistance fighters engaged in criminal activities, see Van Buuren, *De afrekening*.
26 Buruma, *Wages of Guilt*, 6.
27 Van der Heijden, "Het einde van historische correctheid."

28 Quoted in Gans, "De Nederlandse Historikerstreit over de grijze oorlog."
29 Hampl, "The Whole Anne Frank."
30 Müller, *Anne Frank*; Lee, *The Hidden Life of Otto Frank*; Van der Zee, *Vogelvrij: Wie verraadde Anne Frank?*
31 Moore, in *Survivors: Jewish Self-Help and Rescue in Nazi-Occupied Western Europe*, effectively contests the motive of altruism. An earlier indictment was offered by Bovenkerk in Moerings, ed., *Morele kwesties in het strafrecht*.
32 Haan, "Nederland deportatieland?"
33 Ibid.
34 See Verzetsmuseum, "Tweede Wereldoorlog."
35 See Köbben, *De tijdgeest en andere ongemakken*, 17–26.
36 Weinreb, *Het land der blinden*, vol 1. of *Collaboratie en verzet*, 578.
37 Paxton, *Europe in the Twentieth Century*, 464–69.
38 Groen, *Fout en niet goed*; Romijn, *Snel, streng en rechtvaardig*; and Belinfante, *In plaats van bijltjesdag*.
39 Kolthoff, *Veilige afstand*, 88.
40 As in the title of Wallace Stegner's prize-winning historical novel *Angle of Repose*; see also Kees Kolthoff's calm and reasonable analysis of the history of World War II memories in *Veilige afstand*.
41 *Jewish World*, "Anne Frank Tree Saplings."
42 Michener, *The Voice of Asia*, 128–29.
43 "Interregnum" was Mohammad Hatta's phrase. Quoted in Gouda and Brocades Zaalberg, *American Visions*, 114.
44 Van Leeuwen, "De wreker van zijn Indische grootouders."
45 Prins, "In Memoriam Victor Emanuel Korn," 192–202.
46 Jan Petrus, "Benjamin Josselin de Jong, the 'Founding Father' of Structural Anthropology in the Netherlands," quoted in Kuitenbrouwer, *Tussen Oriëntalisme en Wetenschap*, 166.
47 Lijphart, *The Trauma of Decolonization*. The Dutch colonial enterprise as a social engineering project is derived from Van Doorn, *De laatste eeuw van Indi"*.
48 Bank, "Contouren van een ongrijpbare wajang figuur." The three major biographies of Sukarno are Dahm, *Soekarno en de strijd om Indonesië's onafhankelijkheid*; Giebels, *Soekarno*, vol. 1, *Nederlandsch onderdaan*, and vol. 2, *President*; and, in English, Hering, *Soekarno*.
49 Lindsay and Liem, eds., *Heirs to World Culture*.
50 Gouda and Brocades Zaalberg, *Indonesia merdeka karena Amerika?*
51 Quoted in Gouda, *Dutch Culture Overseas*, 23.
52 For a detailed empirical study of the Dutch colonial police, see Bloembergen, *De geschiedenis van de politie in Nederlands-Indi"*. For a more profound analysis of issues of criminality and law enforcement in the culture of the Dutch East Indies before and especially after World War II, see Cribb, *Gangsters and Revolutionaries*.
53 Samsudin in Tjondonegoro, ed., *Lukisan revolusi rakjat Indonesia*, 30.
54 U.S. consular personnel such as Walter Foote, Sidney Browne, Kenneth Patton, and Erle Dickover in reports sent to the U.S. Department of State during the 1930s, cited in Gouda and Brocades Zaalberg, *American Visions*, 89–99.
55 Stoddard, "Spice Islands."
56 For a general discussion of the issue of oil in Japanese war strategies, see Ienaga, *The Pacific War*, 131–32; and Bussemaker, *Paradise in Peril*.
57 Tjondonegoro, *Lukisan revolusi rakjat Indonesia*, 50.

58 Westad, *The Global Cold War*, 82.
59 As in Geertz, *Negara*. The notion of "ethnic circles" is derived from Cornelis van Vollenhoven's arguments concerning *adat* (customs and traditions). See the discussion in Gouda, *Dutch Culture Overseas*, 52–60.
60 Adas, "From Avoidance to Confrontation." See also Schulte Nordholt, *Staat van geweld*, 5.
61 Schulte Nordholt, *Staat van geweld*, 5. See also Schulte Nordholt, *The Spell of Power*.
62 See, among others, Gouda in Damousi and Plotkin, eds., *Transnational Unconscious*. See also Van Till, *Batavia*.
63 Tjondonegoro, *Lukisan revolusi rakjat Indonesia*, 50.
64 Noto Soeroto, "Aziatisch Imperialisme," *Wederopbouw*, 16–17.
65 Tjondonegoro, *Lukisan revolusi rakjat Indonesia*.
66 OSS report, "General Conditions in Java," No. M-212, July 20, 1944, quoted in Gouda and Brocades Zaalberg, *American Visions*, 110.
67 Van den Doel, *Afscheid van Indi"*, 67.
68 Malaka, *From Jail to Jail*, 3:72.
69 Fusayama, *A Japanese Memoir of Sumatra*, 20.
70 Mohammad Rum, "Your Excellencies Members of the United Nations Good Offices Committee and Company," personal letter, January 20, 1949, United Nations Archive Group DAG, Missions and Commissions, subgroup 13, Good Offices Committee (GOC), 1947–49, quoted in Gouda and Brocades Zaalberg, *American Visions*, 124–25.
71 Tjondonegoro, *Lukisan revolusi rakjat Indonesia*, 51.
72 Sukarno quoted in Friend, *Blue-Eyed Enemy*, 82–84.
73 Statement by Sukarno, September 15, 1942, quoted in Friend, *Blue-Eyed Enemy*, 11.
74 Dahm, *Soekarno en de strijd om Indonesië's onafhankelijkheid*, 199–200.
75 Friend, *Indonesian Destinies*, 28.
76 Dahm, *Soekarno en de strijd om Indonesië's onafhankelijkheid*, 268–69.
77 Van den Doel, *Afscheid van Indië*, 68.
78 The Dutch official was Charles O. van der Plas, quoted in Gerbrandy, *De scheuring van het rijk*, 121.
79 Sukarno, *Sukarno: An Autobiography*, 192. See also Frederick in Raben, ed., *Beelden van de Japanse bezetting van Indonesië*, 30.
80 M. Slamet, "Open brief aan Hare Majesteit de Koningin der Nederlanden," December 28, 1945, quoted in Gebrandy, *Scheuring van het rijk*, 272.
81 Opinions reported by Malaka, *From Jail to Jail*; Rose, *Indonesia Free*; and Friend, *Blue-Eyed Enemy*, quoted in Gouda and Brocades Zaalberg, *American Visions*, 114.
82 Rose, *Indonesia Free*, 92, 93, 96; Benda, *The Crescent and the Rising Sun*, 203.
83 Malaka, *From Jail to Jail*, 2:143, 154.
84 Dewulf, "The Many Meanings of Freedom."
85 Dewulf, "Zes kaarsen voor Indi"." See also Foray, *Visions of Empire*.
86 Dommering, "De Nederlandse politieke discussie en de politionele acties in Indonesië," 285.
87 Sjahrir, *Indonesische overpeinzingen*, 85.
88 Sjahrir, *Out of Exile*, 144.
89 This succinct statement is quoted in Gardner, *Shared Hopes, Separate Fears*, 6; Abernethy, *The Dynamics of Global Dominance*, 386; and Westad, *The Global Cold War*, 77.
90 Shiraishi, "The Phantom World of Boven Digul."
91 *New Republic*, October 29, 1945 (unsigned editorial).
92 Van Randwijk, "Tegen het opkomend onweer," quoted in Dewulf, "The Many Meanings of Freedom."

93 Van Oldenburgh, *A Well Respected Man, or Book of Echoes*, 62.
94 Mulder and Koedijk, *H. M. van Randwijk*, 591.
95 Quoted in Gouda, *Dutch Culture Overseas*, 20.
96 Boomsma, *De laatste tyfoon*, 55; interview in *Nieuwsblad van het noorden*, March 6, 1992. See also Meijer, *Oostindisch doof*, 175–84.
97 The term "colonial deficit" is Lizzy van Leeuwen's. See her *Ons Indisch erfgoed*.
98 The term "collected memories" is Christopher Browning's. See his *Collected Memories: Holocaust History and Postwar Testimony*.
99 Gouda, "The Unbearable Lightness of Memory."
100 Buruma, *Wages of Guilt*, 90.
101 Scagliola, *Last van de oorlog*, 25.
102 *Elseviers Weekblad*, January 1950, cited in Meijer, *Den Haag-Jakarta*, 177. Today, the right-wing populist politician Geert Wilders regularly recycles World War II metaphors. He has referred to Islam as fascism and to the Koran as *Mein Kampf*. He has also labeled Osama bin Laden a new Hitler and contemporary notions of Islamist jihad a blitzkrieg. In some of his speeches he has dismissed U.S. president Barack Obama as "the Neville Chamberlain of the 21st century." See Fennema, "Laat de oorlog even rusten."
103 Goss, "From Tong-Tong to Tempo Doeloe."
104 For a poignant description of a response among Indo-Dutch immigrants to their new segregated lives in the Netherlands during the 1950s, see Willems, *Tjalie Robinson*, 309–17.
105 B. C. de Jonge to W. Röell, in Van der Wal, ed., *Herinneringen van Jhr. Mr. B. C. de Jonge met brieven uit zijn nalatenschap*, 423.
106 See, for example, the impressively researched biography of the commander in chief of the Royal Dutch Army during the war of independence, General Simon Spoor, published in May 2011, by Jaap de Moor, *Generaal Spoor*. For an insightful analysis of the historiographical solipsism prevailing among Dutch historians, see Coté, "Strangers in the House."
107 Rudy Kousbroek, interview with Remco Meijer, in Meijer, *Oostindisch doof*, 193. The contentious debate about the existence of a colonial *doofpot* emerged around a book by the University of Amsterdam sociologist Jan Breman, titled *Taming the Coolie Beast*. Breman's book was based on the "Rhemrev report" concerning the dehumanizing conditions imposed on contract laborers on tobacco and rubber plantations on the east coast of Sumatra, a report that was allegedly "lost" in the archives after a Leiden colonial historian had consulted it.
108 P. M. van Wulfften Palthe, *Psychological Aspects of the Indonesian Problem*, quoted in Gouda in Damousi and Plotkin, eds., *Transnational Unconscious*, 90.
109 "Tsunami" is the term used by Wilders, a right-wing politician who is the descendant of an Indo-Dutch family from East Java; hence, his bleached blond hair has been described as an effort to hide his "Indo roots." See Van Leeuwen, "Wreker van zijn Indische grootouders."
110 Van Leeuwen, *Ons Indisch erfgoed*. See also Boehmer and Gouda, in Keown, Murphy, and Proctor, eds., *Comparing Postcolonial Diasporas*.

Chapter 5

France and the Memory of Occupation

JULIAN JACKSON

There are significant differences between the way that the memory of war and occupation has evolved in Northeast Asia and Western Europe. In Europe, beginning in the early 1950s the logic of the Cold War contributed toward Franco-German rapprochement; in Asia, it acted as an obstacle toward reconciliation between China, Japan, and Korea. In Europe, as Auschwitz became, from the 1960s on, the paradigm of absolute evil it became an insuperable impediment to the development of a sustainable narrative of German victimhood despite the short-lived controversy aroused by the *Historikerstreit* (historians' conflict) in the mid-1980s;[1] in Asia, by contrast, there is no similar consensus about the significance of the Nanjing massacre or the Japanese "comfort women," and Japanese war crimes can be counterbalanced by a plausible countervailing narrative of Japanese victimhood in the bombings of Hiroshima and Nagasaki.

Franco-German reconciliation started once it became clear to more farsighted French personalities like Jean Monnet that America would never underwrite France's original aspirations toward the dismemberment of Germany. Making a virtue of necessity, Monnet conceived, and the French premier Robert Schuman fronted, the idea of the European Coal and Steel Community, which was signed in 1951. Reconciliation was not an entirely linear and uncomplicated process: the idea of allowing German rearmament through a kind of European army (the European Defence Community) aroused violent debate in France and was rejected by the French Parliament in 1954. But in retrospect this was only a blip in a longer-term process of reconciliation marked by a number of symbolic events such as the signing of the Treaty of Rome in 1957, the establishment of the Franco-German friendship treaty of 1963, or the meeting of September 1984 when President François Mitterrand of France and Chancellor Helmut Kohl of Germany held hands at the historically charged site of the Battle of Verdun. Indeed, the relationship between successive French presidents and German chancellors—Charles de Gaulle and Konrad Adenauer, Valéry Giscard d'Estaing and Helmut Schmidt, Mitterrand and Kohl, Jacques Chirac and Gerhard Schröder, and even, after a difficult start, Nicolas Sarkozy and Angela Merkel—has been the motor of European unity. What started as what could be called a "thin" reconciliation has gradually become "thicker." For a number of years now, the majority of French and Germans consider each other's country as their closest ally and the one in which they have the most confidence.[2] One remarkable sign of this close relationship is the project, launched in 2003 on the anniversary of the 1963 Franco-German Treaty, to produce a three-volume Franco-German history school textbook, cowritten by French and German historians. Two volumes have so far appeared.[3] If we are to study the memory of the war and occupation in France today, it must be therefore not as a problem in Franco-German relations but as a contemporary problem of French identity.

A CONTEMPORARY OBSESSION

On the day of his investiture as president of the French Republic on May 16, 2007, Nicolas Sarkozy attended a ceremony in the Bois de Boulogne at a monument commemorating the shooting on April 16, 1944, of thirty-four resisters by the Germans. A schoolgirl read out the letter that a seventeen-year-old Communist resister, Guy Môquet, had written to his mother on the eve of his execution along with twenty-six other hostages at Châteaubriant, north of Nantes, on October 21, 1941, as a reprisal for the shooting of the German Feldkommandant of Nantes two days earlier. Afterward, Sarkozy announced that every year on October 21 Môquet's letter should be read out in all French lycées as an example of youthful patriotism, civic virtue, and courage. Some commentators wondered whether Sarkozy, a Gaullist president, had realized, when choosing to celebrate the memory of Môquet, that this young resister had in fact been a Communist; others denounced this annexation of left-wing patriotic memory by a politician of the Right.[4] But many on the left, including the leader of the French

Communists, commended the ceremony.[5] Since Sarkozy was pursuing a policy of *ouverture* to the Left, he probably did know what he was doing in annexing the symbol of Môquet—but there was another purpose to this highly symbolic ceremony. One theme of Sarkozy's rhetoric before his election was that the French should be prouder of their past and abandon their current obsession with "repentance" and apologizing for their history. He had said in Paris during his election campaign on January 14, 2007: "I detest this repentance that wants to prevent us from being proud of being French, which opens the door to a kind of competition between different memories, which pits the French of different origins against each other."[6] He had meant this particularly in relation to the Algerian War and the controversy at the time about whether the French should celebrate the positive aspects of colonization as well as the negative. Sarkozy viewed this as a way of courting the extreme right voters of Jean-Marie Le Pen. But in choosing to inaugurate his presidency with the ceremony around Môquet, Sarkozy was also entering into an implicit dialogue with his predecessor, Jacques Chirac, whose presidency had opened with a no less symbolically charged ceremony—which remains the single moment for which Chirac's presidency is best remembered.

On July 16, 1995, two months after his election, Chirac had attended an anniversary commemoration of the notorious *rafle du Vél d'Hiver* on July 16, 1942, when almost 13,000 Jews (4,051 of them children) had been rounded up in Paris. Chirac's speech was the first time that a French president had acknowledged French responsibility for this terrible crime. He declared that, indeed, the criminal madness of the occupier was supported by the French and their state. This violated, as Chirac explained, France's Enlightenment tradition, its commitment to the rights of man, and its tradition as a country of asylum and welcome. This crime was therefore an irreparable act. This was a theme to which Chirac returned many times. During the trial of the Vichy official Maurice Papon for crimes against humanity in 1998, Chirac inaugurated a memorial to the *"Justes"*—those French who had saved the life of Jews during the occupation—and proclaimed that France had to face its entire history: the good, the bad, and the gray areas. In the last days of his presidency, unveiling a plaque at the Pantheon commemorating 2,727 French *Justes*, he talked of the "sombre shroud of resignation, cowardice and compromise" of the Vichy regime.[7]

That the two most recent French presidents should have opened their periods in office with two such solemn ceremonies relating to the period of the occupation is evidence of the way in which the memory of this period looms large—ever larger one might say—in contemporary French consciousness. The presidency of François Mitterrand, which had begun with a visit to the Pantheon, where he placed a rose on the tomb of the Resistance hero Jean Moulin—a way for Mitterrand of reappropriating the memory of Moulin from Gaullism—had ended with bitter controversies over the revelation of Mitterrand's youthful contacts with the Vichy regime and the fact that until the end of his life he had remained on good terms with the Vichy police chief René Bousquet, one of the masterminds of the very roundup for which Chirac had apologized in 1995.[8] Mitterrand's predecessor, Valéry Giscard d'Estaing, had aroused controversy when he proposed, in a spirit of Franco-German reconciliation, that May 8, the anniversary of the end of the war, should no longer be an annual public holiday. His own predecessor, Georges Pompidou, had got into serious trouble, as we will see below, when it was revealed that he had amnestied the former collaborator Paul Touvier.

Each of these issues had aroused considerable polemic and public discussion, and there are many other signs of the way in which the memory of the occupation continues to haunt the French today. To take a few examples: in November 2010, the French state railway company (SNCF) for the first time—after many efforts and court cases by the children of deportees—expressed publicly its profound "pain and regret" for its role in transporting Jews; one of the most successful films in France in 2010 was a melodramatic blockbuster about the *rafle du Vél d'Hiver*; two current best sellers, which can be found in most train station bookshops, are a pamphlet by the former resister Stéphane Hessel arguing that the values of the Resistance need to be reactivated in contemporary French public life and a violent pamphlet by the novelist Alexandre Jardin denouncing the presumed role played by his grandfather Jean Jardin, the *directeur de cabinet* of Pierre Laval in 1942, in the *rafle du Vél d'Hiver*.[9] Jardin announced in this book, which has itself been denounced by his own family, that he wishes to purge himself of his own DNA.[10]

FRENCH SPECIFICITIES

One could possibly identify four specificities of the French experience that continue to make the memory of the war and occupation so acute and so complicated.

1. The catastrophic defeat of 1940 remains a national trauma. It is true that the defeats of Belgium, Norway, Holland, and so on were no less total and no less dramatic, but the case of France is different because of the country's position as a world power, because of the contrast between the debacle of 1940 and the heroism of 1914–18, because of the completely unexpected nature of the defeat (which surprised the Germans as much as anyone) and because the defeat was accompanied by a complete social and political implosion of which the most striking manifestation was the *Exode*: that extraordinary human tidal wave of millions and millions of civilian refugees who fled the advancing Germans. Their panic about what the Germans would do to them was compounded by a feeling that they had been entirely abandoned by their political leaders. It was on this sense of abandonment and humiliation that the Vichy regime of Philippe Pétain drew much of its initial moral and political legitimacy.[11]

2. Thanks to the political skill and bluff of General de Gaulle, the French found themselves in some sense accepted as one of the victorious powers in 1945: French forces had fought in the final stages of the war both in Italy and in Germany, and they had a zone of occupation in Germany and a permanent seat in the United Nations. How to match up these two completely contrasting facts—the catastrophe of 1940 and the "victory" of 1945? De Gaulle's solution, first outlined in a speech of September 1941, was to propose a reading of the war that inscribed it as part of a thirty-year conflict that had started in 1914 and would end in Berlin in May 1945. So as he had already put it in July 1940, France in 1940 had lost a battle but not the war. This bold claim, however, meshed uneasily with the memory of the debacle of 1940.

3. The French case is further complicated by the particular circumstances of that country's occupation. Unlike Holland and Belgium, France was not directly administered by Germany. About two-thirds of French territory constituted a "free zone" with an independent French government based at Vichy and headed by the venerable hero of the Great War, Marshal Pétain. It is true that over time the autonomy of the Vichy government was whittled away. From 1942 on, the Germans interfered increasingly in policing to combat the development of the Resistance, and they started to impose harsher policies toward the Jews. They also began drafting ever-larger numbers of French workers to work in German factories under the system of compulsory labor service (Service du travail obligatoire, or STO). In November 1942, after the Allies landed in French North Africa, the

Germans also occupied the previously free zone, although Vichy retained theoretical autonomy there. Finally, at the end of 1943, Vichy effectively lost any remaining independence when the Germans forced Pétain to take into his government French pro-Nazi ultra-collaborationists who had previously been based in occupied Paris. Nonetheless, up to the start of 1942, the Vichy government had enjoyed considerable freedom of maneuver.

Thus, France's status in occupied Europe resembled less Holland, Belgium, or Norway—in those countries day-to-day administration was certainly carried out by local civil servants and officials, but they were working under the authority of the occupier—than Denmark, where the Germans allowed an independent government to exist until August 1943. But although the Danish government did collaborate with Germany in many areas, it left Danish political structures largely intact—such that there were even democratic elections in 1943. By contrast, the Vichy government proceeded to carry out a kind of internal conservative counterrevolution (dubbed the "National Revolution") that repudiated many of the values of the previous republican regime: the motto "work, family, fatherland" replaced "liberty, equality, fraternity." Thus, although all countries occupied by Germany have had to confront painful memories relating to the extent that their populations collaborated with the occupiers, in France that memory was even more painful because of the existence of an authoritarian and collaborating regime that was not imposed by the Germans. Furthermore, the head of that regime, Pétain, was hugely popular and became the object of an almost semireligious cult. For these reasons the Vichy period requires the French to confront difficult questions about the nature of their own political culture. It cannot easily be written off as an occupation parenthesis.[12]

4. There are also complex links between the memory of the Algerian War of 1954–62 and that of the occupation. It is extraordinary the degree to which these two complex experiences have become entangled in French national memory. Even during the Algerian conflict itself the resonances and echoes with the occupation were present: some former resisters like Claude Bourdet denounced the French state for torturing Algerians as the Gestapo had tortured the French; others, like the former resister Georges Bidault, claimed that to abandon Algeria was an act of treason equivalent to the acceptance of defeat in 1940. Many young supporters of the Algerian National Liberation Front (FLN) saw themselves as in some sense engaged in the same struggle as the Resistance generation of their parents.

François Maspero, one of the most important and visible supporters of Third World liberation movements, begins his memoirs by invoking the memory of his own father in the Resistance.[13] During the trial of Maurice Papon, present in the minds of his accusers and of the public was the fact that he had also been the prefect of police of Paris in October 1961 when a pro-FLN demonstration was brutally repressed, leading to the deaths of scores of Algerians in the very heart of Paris.[14] If the French state—and a republican state at that—could commit such crimes in Algeria, did that not also invite reflection on other episodes of the French past? The curious avenues into which anticolonialism would later lead are demonstrated in their most exaggerated form by the lawyer Jacques Vergès, who entered public life as the defender of the victims of French colonialism in Algeria and then moved on twenty years later to defending the German Gestapo chief Klaus Barbie on the grounds that, whatever crimes Barbie might have committed, the French needed to carry out their own *auto-critique* before throwing stones at others.[15]

THE GAULLIST NARRATIVE

For all these reasons, the French memory of occupation has generated a massive historical literature—almost a historical subgenre in itself. This started with the now classic work of Henry Rousso in 1987, and the most recent addition is a book by Olivier Wieviorka in 2010.[16] Most of these studies offer a similar broad narrative arguing that after 1945 de Gaulle created a national myth, with three components: (1) apart from a small band of traitors, most of the French people had more or less actively supported the Resistance, and France could therefore be said to have been a nation of resisters; (2) Vichy was a regime both illegal and illegitimate (when asked to declare that the republic was restored in Paris in August 1944, de Gaulle refused on the grounds that the republic had never ceased to exist because Vichy was "nul et non advenu" (null and void); and (3) France had liberated itself.

This version of history was also subscribed to by the Communist Party, which put the emphasis on its own alleged seventy-five thousand "martyrs" and developed after the liberation a veritable cult of its resistance heroes.[17] The Gaullo-Communist celebration of the Resistance received, it is said, a kind of official apotheosis in 1964 when Jean Moulin's remains were moved to the Pantheon by the Gaullist regime in a ceremony presided over by the minister of culture, André Malraux. Then—so the argument continues—at around the end of the 1960s and in the early 1970s, everything changed: the Gaullist myth was shattered, and the pieces could never be put together again. The change in public attitudes was of course linked obliquely to the massive cultural upheaval of 1968. One of the main targets of the protestors of 1968 was the regime of de Gaulle, but they were equally opposed to the Communist Party, which was viewed as sclerotic and conservative. Many on the left had never forgiven the party its lukewarm opposition to the war in Algeria. Given that the Communists and the Gaullists were the two main custodians of the prevailing historical consensus on the occupation, and indeed owed their postwar ascendancy in French politics to their association with the Resistance—the Gaullists as the party of the leader of the Free French movement and the Communists as the party of the seventy-five thousand "martyrs"—it was inevitable that the contestation of their political hegemony in 1968 should also involve a reevaluation of their interpretation of the past. The "generation of '68" was bound to contest the historical myths on which it had been raised.[18]

Two events in the early 1970s are generally seen to symbolize the generational shift in memory. The first was the famous film *The Sorrow and the Pity*, directed by Marcel Ophüls. This artfully constructed documentary showed a vision of occupied France very different from the official Gaullist narrative. If it did not go as far as to portray the French as a society of "collaborators," it showed them to be mostly "attentiste" (wait and see) opportunists, and pointedly it made hardly any reference to de Gaulle. The best evidence of how subversive the film was considered at the time is the fact that, although it was made for French television, the authorities refused to allow it to be broadcast. The head of the French broadcasting organization declared that certain myths had to exit for the sake of domestic political tranquillity. This form of semi-censorship gave Ophüls's film a kind of advance notoriety, which influenced the way it was received and interpreted once it was released in cinemas in 1971. In fact, the message of the film is not as completely debunking—or at least more nuanced—as its reputation suggests, but the sense that something was being hidden obscured some of these subtleties.[19]

The second event was the publication of the French translation of Robert O. Paxton's book *Vichy France* in 1973. For its impact and brilliance, Paxton's work is the single most important book to have been published on twentieth-century French history by any historian. It showed that the

Vichy regime had sought to collaborate with Germany and that the regime had had an internal project for French renewal that was not imposed by the Germans: thus, Vichy was reinserted into a longer narrative of French history. Not all that Paxton said was totally new—although he said it with great force—but the book appeared at a moment when the French public was ready to hear and receive the message it contained. By a curious reciprocal process, Paxton's book gave a kind of academic legitimacy to the very polemical *The Sorrow and the Pity* even if in fact their messages were actually somewhat different, since Paxton, although offering some observations on the minimal role that the French people, in his view, had played in the Resistance, was primarily concerned with the Vichy *regime*.

The way in which the memory of the war suddenly exploded uncontrollably into public debate was demonstrated by the notorious "Touvier affair" when in June 1972 it was revealed that de Gaulle's successor, Pompidou, had secretly pardoned the former French ultra-collaborator Paul Touvier. Although he had been sentenced to death in absentia at the liberation, Touvier had been protected for years by Catholic clergymen motivated by a mixture of charity and right-wing ideology. In fact, the death penalty had lapsed under the statute of limitations in 1967, and Pompidou's pardon affected only some secondary penalties still outstanding. Pompidou had presumed that the measure would pass uncontroversially. Instead, it caused outrage when the news slipped out only a few weeks before Pompidou was due to inaugurate a massive memorial in honor of his predecessor, de Gaulle, at Colombey les deux Eglises. Pompidou was denounced by many former resisters and by many Gaullists of betraying the memory of the Resistance and the legacy of de Gaulle himself. After weeks of polemic, Pompidou tried to defend his decision: "Are we going to keep the wounds of our national discord bleeding eternally? Hasn't the time come to draw a veil over the past, to forget a time when Frenchmen killed one another?"[20] The irony was that that although many Gaullists had themselves been outraged by Pompidou's action, it was in fact very much in the line of de Gaulle's own strategy, which was not to dwell unduly on the memory of Vichy and collaboration. The problem was that this approach became less sustainable at a time when the population was less interested than it once had been in healing the wounds of the past than in picking at them. Pompidou was completely out of phase with the expectations of the population. He further complicated the task by a number of remarks downplaying the glorification of the Resistance and the Free French, which had always been a central part of the Gaullist vision, and compensated in some sense for the position of benign forgetting with which de Gaulle approached Vichy.[21] The Touvier affair rumbled on for another two decades until Touvier ended up in 1994 being the first Frenchman to be found guilty by the courts of crimes against humanity.[22]

THE MYTH OF THE GAULLIST MYTH

It is possible, however, to question whether the so-called Gaullist myth of the Resistance was ever as dominant as is often alleged—except possibly in the very immediate postliberation period and possibly in the period when de Gaulle returned to power in 1958.

1. In the first place, when in 1945–46 rules and protocols were established to determine who had the right to call themselves former resisters—an issue with, of course, material consequences as well as symbolic ones—the definitions adopted were in fact comparatively restrictive and centered around very much a military and activist conception of resistance, which did not include the more informal kinds of civil and supporting roles that individuals might have played—but also therefore implicitly contradicted the idea of an entire nation in resistance.[23]

2. The real experience of the French population has been a highly fragmented one—in this respect quite different from the Great War. One illustration of this is the trial that took place in 1953 in Bordeaux of the perpetrators of the terrible massacre carried out by elements of the Waffen SS at the village of Oradour sur Glane, near Limoges, in June 1944. It turned out that a few of the defendants were actually from Alsace and had been enrolled forcibly into the SS: they felt themselves to be also victims of the war. The trial pitted two French regional memories against each other: when the Alsatians were quickly amnestied after the trial there was outrage in the Limoges area.[24] The fragmentation of French experience during the war was embodied in the postwar period by the proliferation of associations representing different sectors of the population. These associations existed both to defend the material interests of their members—access to pensions and compensation for sufferings endured—and, no less importantly, to claim their place in the collective national memory. These associations included of course former resisters but also former prisoners of war (of which there had been 1.6 million during the occupation), former deportees/internees in concentration camps, and former labor deportees

(i.e., those who had been conscripted to go and work in German factories from 1943 on under the STO scheme). Statutes defining the status of each of these categories were laboriously elaborated starting in the late 1940s. Among "deportees/internees" a distinction was made between "resistance deportees"—those who had been arrested because of their active participation in the Resistance—and others who had been arrested for other reasons and were designated "political deportees." The latter were considered to be victims who deserved recognition and compensation, but in the hierarchy of recognition they came below the resistance deportees, who were heroes as well as victims. The category of "political deportee" did not, however, distinguish between all the different categories of deportees and thus offered no distinctive status to those approximately two thousand Jews who had survived the concentration camps and were assimilated absurdly into the overall category of "political" deportees. Since in this period a specifically Jewish memory of the occupation had not yet found much public voice, this assimilation did not at the time give rise to any debate, unlike some of the other categorizations that were being established.[25]

The most contested and painful debate concerned those who had been conscripted to work in Germany. In 1945, they had organized themselves into the National Federation of Labor Deportees (FNDT), with a membership of about half a million. But in May 1951, when their status and rights were legally codified, they were allowed to describe themselves not as deportees but as "requis" (requisitioned), that is, "people constrained to work in enemy territory." This ranking was a retrospective demotion since during the occupation BBC and Resistance propaganda had described them as "deportees." Now they were downgraded to the bottom of the hierarchy of recognition—below the resisters, of course, but also below the deportees, whose suffering was judged to have been greater than theirs. The FNDT continued until 1974 to try to hold on to its name, but this position was contested in the courts by representatives of the associations of deportees. Their objection was upheld by the courts in 1979, and the FNDT had to change its name to the National Federation of Victims and Survivors of the Nazis' Forced Labor Camps.[26]

Overall, then, even during the apogee of the so-called Gaullist myth, the figure of the victim was as central in French consciousness as the hero, the deportee as much as the resister, perhaps even more so. In April 1954, Parliament unanimously voted to create a Journée nationale de déportation (National Day of Deportation)—and this commemoration has taken place every year since then on the last Sunday of April—but it is interesting that there was no (and still is no) similar day to commemorate the memory of the Resistance.

3. This relative marginalization of the Resistance perhaps reflects the very complex relationship that had always existed between the resisters and the population as a whole. In some sense the Resistance had always been the bad conscience of the French, and the resisters themselves had always had an ambivalent view of the population as a whole. From the beginning, the resisters had enjoyed a sense of themselves as in some way representing, and speaking for, the mass of the population—they were the *true* French— but also as a tiny and heroic elite who despised the passivity of the population as a whole. Resisters were thus torn between their contempt for the French and their ambition of winning them over. This position was compounded after the war by a prevailing sense among former resisters that their aspirations for the renewal of French society had been betrayed.

The marginality of the Resistance is nicely symbolized by the geographical situation of two important monuments that were set up in Paris to commemorate different aspects of the occupation. The first is the Mémorial de Mont Valérien set up at the Fort of Mont Valérien, west of Paris, where about one thousand resisters had been shot during the war. In November 1946, the bodies of fifteen resisters and Free French fighters were buried there, and it became an annual site of commemoration for the Gaullists during the Fourth Republic. De Gaulle, after his return to power, ordered a proper memorial to be built on the site, and it was inaugurated in 1960: the crypt containing the fifteen bodies was surmounted by a huge Cross of Lorraine. The second monument is the Mémorial de la déportation, which was set up at the initiative of a number of associations of deportees and was inaugurated in 1962. It is situated at the tip of the Île de la Cité in the very heart of Paris, unlike the monument of Mémorial of Mont Valérien, which is on the outskirts of the city.

1968 AND THE MEMORY OF THE OCCUPATION

So if the broad narrative established by Rousso and others would seem to be correct, it does need to be nuanced. The same is also true of the impact of 1968 and the *The Sorrow and the Pity*. The film is often seen as showing how the upheaval of 1968 was translated into the politics of memory of the war. It is indeed true that the film's makers did position themselves explicitly as contesting the heroic Gaullist narrative. But ironically, although the film presented a ferociously negative vision of Vichy—for example, challenging the claims that Vichy had done anything to save Jews—it did, despite now being interpreted as a "left-wing" critique of Gaullism, perhaps unwittingly chime in with the apologias of former right-wing defenders of Vichy by presenting a vision of the French population as *attentiste* and pro-Pétainist. At the same time, it is not quite true to say that the 1968 generation was set on challenging the conventional image of the heroism of the Resistance. Its relationship to that period was more complicated. One of the most famous slogans of 1968—which in fact had already been used in the Algerian War—was "CRS [French riot police] = SS." At the Avignon Theater Festival in September 1968, radical protestors used rhetoric drawing on the occupation to make parallels with their critique of contemporary politics. One of their posters showed geese being fed "Kultur," as if the Gaullists in 1968 were no better than the Germans in the 1940s. But the radicals of 1968 were concerned less with attacking the myth of the Resistance than with reappropriating it for themselves and taking inspiration from it. In 1970, the Maoists of the Gauche prolétarienne founded a direct-action group dubbed the New Popular Resistance (NRP). Their song was a new hymn of partisans, and in 1971 they went to the memorial of Mont Valérien to lay a wreath—even if the exact meaning of this gesture was ambiguous: were they reclaiming the Resistance from de Gaulle's successors, or were they in fact reclaiming de Gaulle posthumously from his successors?[27] It is certainly ironic that those who had so violently contested de Gaulle in 1968 should three years later make a kind of pilgrimage to a site of memory so associated with him. In this complex relationship to the Resistance and even the Gaullist past may lie one of the reasons why the French extreme Left stepped back in the early 1970s from terrorist temptation, unlike the cases of Italy (the Red Brigades) or Germany (the Red Army Faction, or RAF).[28] Their German and Italian equivalents were driven by a similar desire to bring their parents' generation to account, but in neither country was there a usable countervailing national memory. One could not imagine German radicals deploying, say, the memory of Claus von Stauffenberg (a conservative aristocratic officer who had tried to assassinate Adolf Hitler in the summer of 1944 to save Germany from total defeat) as a rallying point or a source of inspiration.

One of the extraordinary features of the evolution of the German extreme Left is the way in which their obsession with the Nazi past led them in some cases to a marginalization of the Holocaust and indeed to a new form of anti-Semitism through their identification with the Palestinians and rejection of Zionism as a new form of fascism.[29] This did not occur in France, and the killing at the Munich Olympics in 1972 of eleven Jewish hostages by Palestinian commandos was an important moment in the evolution of the French extreme Left away from a flirtation with revolutionary violence. It is interesting how many French militants of 1968 were the children of Jews who had suffered or died under occupation—and the Munich massacre was a catalyst for a sharper awareness of their Jewish identity.[30]

FRENCH JEWISH MEMORY

The transnational emergence of a specific Jewish identity around the Holocaust is a story that has been told many times, starting with the immediate postwar period when Primo Levi's memoir of his time in Auschwitz hardly found any readers up to the contemporary sense of the Holocaust—or Shoah—as the central event of the Second World War. As for the specific case of France, it is not quite true that the issue of the persecution of the Jews was entirely ignored at the liberation or that there was no attempt by the French Jewish community to keep alive the memory. One can mention in this regard the setting up of the Tomb of the Unknown Jewish Martyr (Tombeau du martyr juif inconnu) inaugurated in the Marais district of Paris in October 1956 at the initiative of Isaac Schneersohn, who in 1943 had conceived the idea of establishing a clandestine organization to collect and preserve documentation relating to the fate of the Jews in the war. This organization subsequently became the Centre de documentation juive contemporaine (CDJC). But although its publications were important, their impact was limited, and so Schneersohn proposed creating something that would be noticed outside the world of scholarship. This was the purpose of the Tombeau du martyr juif inconnu, whose first stone was laid in 1953, and it is indeed the first monument of its kind in the world to commemorate what has come to be known as the Shoah.[31]

The ceremony inaugurating the monument of course highlighted the responsibility of Germany in the fate of the Jews of France. And, as we have seen, the Jewish deportees continued to be assimilated into the general category of "political deportees": at this time the central symbol of deportation was Buchenwald, not Auschwitz, and the monument to Auschwitz inaugurated at Père Lachaise cemetery in 1946 did not specifically mention the Jews at all. When Alain Resnais directed his important 1955 film on the concentration camps, *Night and Fog*, the deportation of the Jews—as opposed to resisters—was barely mentioned at all.[32] This would simply not have been possible twenty years later, and the film that perfectly illustrates the sensibility of the 1980s is Claude Lanzmann's *Shoah*.

Of course, in the first years of its existence, even Israel avoided constructing its identity and its legitimacy on Jewish suffering in the Holocaust: the new state wanted heroes not victims. It was only beginning in the 1970s that the issue of the Holocaust came to loom more and more centrally in the memorial politics both of Israel and of the West. Among the events that contributed to this change in perception in France were the Adolf Eichmann trial in 1961 (which for the first time gave a public and international voice to the survivors); the Six-Day War; the controversy surrounding de Gaulle's declaration about the Jews as a "dominating" people, made during that 1967 conflict; and, finally, a notorious interview in 1978 with Louis Darquier de Pellepoix, Vichy's former commissioner for Jewish affairs, who from his exile in Spain told journalists that only fleas were gassed at Auschwitz.[33]

The specificity of the French case in this emergence of Jewish memory was the increasing focus on the role of the Vichy state in the Holocaust— and particularly the participation of the French police in the arrests that took place in Paris on July 16, 1942. A perception developed that the French perpetrators of these crimes had not been properly tried at the liberation. It is striking that at the liberation Xavier Vallat, who had been Vichy's commissioner of Jewish affairs until April 1942, had proudly claimed in his defense that he could not be accused of collaboration since his anti-Semitism long predated the occupation. This claim was true, but this defense also made strategic sense in 1944 when people were looking to prosecute collaborators, not anti-Semites. It would have seemed very odd in 1994 when the public and the country were looking for French anti-Semites, not French collaborators. So when Maurice Papon was put on trial in 1998, his defense was exactly the opposite: that he did what he did because he had had no choice. Papon had only been a junior official of the Vichy regime during the occupation, and if he found himself on trial, it was because the more senior figures were dead. He was there as a kind of proxy for Vichy. The problem with the trial, however, was that his case, quite apart from his junior status, was not simple. Although he was a servant of the Vichy regime, some resisters testified that he had secretly helped them. In theory, this had no bearing on the crimes of which he was accused, but it did muddy the waters: it pitted Resistance memory against Jewish memory.[34]

In 1993, it was officially decided that July 16 should become a national day of mourning to remember the Jews who had died in France. But this was no longer enough for some, and there were demands that Mitterrand should also formally admit the responsibility of France in the Holocaust. This admission Mitterrand refused to make on the grounds that the Vichy state was not "'France"—and in this he was being faithful to the Gaullist interpretation that Vichy was a German parenthesis in France's history. Paradoxically, it was a Gaullist president who two years later took the decision, as we have already seen, to accept formal responsibility for the role of the "French people and the French state" in the Holocaust. One problem with this decision, as noted by the historian Henry Rousso, was that, however barbaric the events of 1942, the logic that underpinned them was primarily one of collaboration—an awful bargain by Vichy to keep control of its police—rather than the logic of Vichy anti-Semitism (even if Vichy's own anti-Jewish attitudes made this bargain easier for the regime to accept).[35] But centering attention on the French participation in the roundups deflects attention both from Vichy's own traditions of anti-Semitism and from collaboration. Chirac's speech certainly was extraordinarily important because in effect—and this was recognized by some historic Gaullists who were far from happy—it undermined the entire Gaullist reading of France's history.

FRENCH NATIONAL IDENTITY AND THE OCCUPATION

This part of the Gaullist narrative—that Vichy was not "France"—seems now to have been definitely buried. But it is not clear what exactly has replaced it. The stakes of this debate are of course about much more than what the French did or did not do in the occupation. They are at the heart of questions of national self-identity in France today. One remembers Ernest Renan's famous 1882 comment in his lecture "What Is a Nation?" that "forgetting, even historical error, are a necessary factor in the creation of a nation, and thus the progress of historical studies are often a danger for nationhood."[36] One effect of the concentration on Vichy has been in the same spirit to destroy the intelligibility of the national past. Pierre Nora, in the summing-up essay to his massive series *Lieux de mémoire*, asks why what had been in some sense designed as an alternative to commemorative history had ended up being incorporated into the very official history it had sought to demystify. One of his answers was that the French were living the end of a national myth that had linked the future to the past. How do the French live in a post-Gaullist present? He concluded that few eras had experienced so much doubt about the coherence and continuity of the national past. He was not discussing only or even mainly the memory of Vichy, but that was certainly part of the story.[37]

In 1993, a sociologist, Paul Yonnet, published a strange book in which he lamented the way that French national identity was under threat from multicultural antiracism, which was undermining national identity by celebrating cultural and ethnic diversity. He partly blamed post-1968 historians for subverting existing accounts of the French national story about its past through their concentration on Vichy's anti-Semitism, which he considered to be an excessive focus on that particular aspect of what had happened.[38] These were not the writings of some marginal crank, since the book was published by Gallimard and seriously discussed in the columns of the respected review *Le Débat* of which Nora was in fact the editor. The debate goes on without coming to any resolution. Finding the appropriate tone, and the appropriate balances between history and myth, denigration and celebration, is very difficult—not least because of the very complex and uneasy relationship that the French have to the Resistance and its memory.

This takes us back to where we opened: Sarkozy's attempt to overcome the culture of repentance with one of restoring pride in the French past. He has done this partly by linking himself to the memory of the Resistance by annual pilgrimages to the plateau of Glières, where a famous Resistance uprising had been crushed by the Germans in March 1944, by his visit to Normandy beaches in 2008, and, of course, by his celebration of Guy Môquet as a symbol of resistance to Hitlerian barbarism.[39] But what kind of resistance hero was Môquet in reality? His father, Prosper, was a prominent French Communist activist who had been arrested by the French government in October 1939 because, at that time, owing to the Nazi-Soviet nonaggression pact, the Communist Party was considered to be a defeatist organization: the leader of the party, Maurice Thorez, had indeed deserted from the army on October 4 and made his way to Moscow. After the defeat of France, Prosper's son Guy had been arrested for distributing Communist propaganda at the train station, Gare de l'Est in Paris. He was found guilty and interned at the camp of Choiseul, near Nantes. But at the time of his arrest, the official line of the Communist Party was still that the war was an imperialist conflict, and this position did not change until the Nazi attack on the Soviet Union in June 1941. The tracts and poster that Môquet was arrested for distributing and posting were not in any sense a call to resistance or indeed even anti-German, and it was simply Môquet's misfortune already to be in prison when the Germans selected hostages for execution once the Communists had launched their attacks against German soldiers. After the war these details were obscured by a Communist Party that needed to reinvent its very sinuous policy in the period between 1939 and 1941—and turning Môquet into a martyr of resistance was symbolically important because it implicitly ratified the party's line that in reality it had been in the Resistance from the beginning.[40] Of course, there is every reason to believe that Môquet, had he managed to escape from prison, would have joined the Communist Resistance, but for Sarkozy to select him as a symbol of his strategy for the French to overcome their culture of repentance is an object lesson in the perils of mobilizing history to serve the ends of contemporary politics.

1. Maier, *The Unmasterable Past*.
2. Rosoux, *Les usages de la mémoire dans les relations internationales*.
3. François, "Le manuel franco-allemand d'histoire," 73–86.
4. Joffrin, "Oui il faut lire la lettre de Guy Môquet"; Azéma, "Guy Môquet, Sarkozy et le roman national," 6–11.
5. Sarkozy's revival of the memory of Môquet gave rise to a number of books of which the most forensic is Berlière and Liaigre, *L'affaire Guy Môquet*. Others were more pious: Streiff, *Guy Môquet: Chateaubriant, le 22 octobre 1941*; Bosson, *Guy Môquet: J'aurais voulu vivre*; Etiévent, *Guy Môquet: J'aurais voulu vivre*; Nils, *Guy Môquet mon amour de jeuenesse*; and Rayski, *Le cadavre était trop grand*.
6. *L'Humanité*, "Tel quel: Sarkozy 'Je deteste la repentance.'" See also *Discours 2007*, available through the Université Aix-Marseille (formerly the Université de Provence). This online site lists public talks by prominent French politicians running for president in 2006–7 and contains many of Sarkozy's similar speeches given in different places (see bibliography, under Université Aix-Marseille).
7. Jackson in Oulmont, ed., *Les 18 juin*, 226.
8. Péan, *Une jeunesse française*.
9. On the film, *La rafle*, which opened in March 2010, see Jackson, "*La Rafle*"; and also Hessel, *Indignez-vous!*
10. Jardin, *Des gens très bien*.
11. Diamond, *Fleeing Hitler*.
12. For a comparative study of the memory of occupation, see Lagrou, *Mémoires patriotiques et Occupation nazie*.
13. Maspero, *Les Abeilles et la guêpe*.
14. Golsan, "Memory's *bombe à retardement*."

15 For the contortions of Vergès, see Vergès and Bloch, *La face cachée du procès Barbie*.
16 Rousso, *The Vichy Syndrome*; Wieviorka, *La mémoire désunie*. Other books published in between include Namer, *Batailles pour la mémoire*, and Barcellini and Wieviorka, *Passant souviens-toi!* On the memory of the Resistance, see Douzou, *La résistance française*. On the political uses of the past, see Andrieu, Lavabre, and Tartakovsky, *Politiques du passé*.
17 On the memory wars between the Communists and Gaullists, see Nora in Nora, ed., *Les lieux de mémoire*, vol. 2.
18 Vigna, "Le crible de la mémoire."
19 Rousso, *The Vichy Syndrome*, 114–29. For a recent attack on the *The Sorrow and the Pity*, see Laborie, *Le chagrin et le venin*.
20 Quoted in Rousso, *The Vichy Syndrome*, 123.
21 Ibid., 129–41.
22 Golsan, ed., *Memory, the Holocaust and French Justice*.
23 Wieviorka, "Les avatars du statut de résistant."
24 Farmer, *Martyred Village*.
25 Wieviorka, *La mémoire désunie*, 79–92. On prisoners of war and the STO, see Cochet, *Les exclus de la victoire*; and Lewin, *Le retour des prisonniers de guerre français*. There are several essays on the role played by the various associations in Wahl, ed., *Mémoire de la seconde guerre mondiale*.
26 Wieviorka, *La mémoire désunie*, 90–92.
27 Le Dantec, *Les dangers du soleil*.
28 Sommier, *La violence politique et son deuil*.
29 Kundnani, *Utopia or Auschwitz?*
30 For one May 1968 protester's reaction to the Munich massacre, see Geismar, *Mon mai 1968*.
31 Wieviorka, *Déportation et génocide*.
32 Lindeperg, *Nuit et Brouillard*.
33 Rousso, *The Vichy Syndrome*, 148–63; Wieviorka in Becker and Wieviorka, eds., *Les Juifs de France*. See also Fania Oz-Salzberger's chapter in this book.
34 On the Papon trial, see Golsan, ed., *The Papon Affair*; and Wood, *Vectors of Memory*, 113–42.
35 Rousso, *Vichy: Un passé*, 64.
36 Renan, *Qu'est-ce qu'une nation?*, 7–8.
37 Nora, *Les lieux de mémoire*.
38 Yonnet, *Voyage au centre du malaise français*.
39 Berlière and Liaigre, *L'affaire Guy Môquet*, 11; Raymond, "Recycling the Resistance Myth."
40 Berlière and Liaigre, *L'affaire Guy Môquet*, 85–123.

PART III

PATHS TO RECONCILIATION

Chapter 6

Historical Reconciliation in Northeast Asia

Past Efforts, Future Steps, and the U.S. Role

GI-WOOK SHIN

As with many other cases around the world, regional reconciliation in Northeast Asia first occurred between governments in the postwar era. Japan established diplomatic relations with countries it had once invaded or colonized: with the Republic of China in 1952, with the Republic of Korea (ROK) in 1965, and with the People's Republic of China (PRC) in 1972. The ROK normalized relations with former enemies, the PRC and Russia, in the early 1990s.

Yet historical reconciliation in Northeast Asia has been "thin," as these nations have failed to come to terms with their intertwined pasts. Disputes over war responsibilities, territories, and Japan's colonial rule continue to shape regional relations in Northeast Asia. Anti-Japanese sentiments remain salient in China and Korea, even among the younger generation with no direct experience of colonialism or war. The Japanese suffer from "apology fatigue," questioning why they must continue to repent for events that took place six or seven decades ago. From Japanese atrocities in China to the American decision to drop atomic bombs on Japan, no nation is immune from the charge that it has formed a less than complete view of the past. And all nations, sharing a reluctance to fully confront the complexity of that past, tend to blame others.

To be sure, there is widespread recognition of the need for reconciliation and the final resolution of historical injustices. In fact, many Asians have sought to achieve that goal through various means—apology politics, litigation, joint history writing, and regional exchanges. Yet wounds from past wrongs—committed in times of colonialism and war—are not fully healed and have become highly contentious diplomatic issues.

Northeast Asian nations need to promote "thick" reconciliation to foster a shared vision for the region that transcends victimhood and exclusive notions of national history. In doing so, it is crucial to understand the complex layers of Northeast Asian history and reconciliation. While Japan is often contrasted with Germany—it is blamed for its failure to come to terms with its past wrongdoings and urged to follow the steps that Germany has taken—it would be misleading to mechanically compare Northeast Asia to Western Europe in their respective ways of dealing with the past as both regions have distinctive histories, experiences, and memories. Instead, we must continue to search for a Northeast Asian method of reconciliation, while learning from European experiences. The United States should also be a key variable in this model since it has played an instrumental role in shaping postwar regional order in Northeast Asia, including the history question.

PAST EFFORTS AT RECONCILIATION

While European nations grappled with the history question as an international relations issue from the earliest days of the postwar period, such was not the case in Northeast Asia. The "history problem" between Japan and its Asian neighbors began only in the 1980s, triggered by the so-called textbook controversy of 1982. Up to that point, textbooks were mostly a domestic issue within Japan. Yet, with the emergence of civil society in Japan's neighboring countries in the 1980s, issues of historical injustice were no longer monopolized or controlled by governments. Civil society and transnational nongovernmental organization (NGO) groups became increasingly involved in issues of historical injustice and reconciliation. Growing global attention to national identity, human rights, and historical injustice has also contributed to the recognition of the "history problem" in Northeast Asia.

Those changes in domestic and international environments brought the history question to the forefront of Northeast Asian relations, prompting the nations to search for means of reconciliation. As Yoichi Funabashi notes, however, there is no uniform or universal formula for reconciliation; it is a multifaceted process requiring varied inputs and action at many levels.[1] As such, it is worthwhile to review each of the modes of reconciliation — apology politics, litigation, common historiography, and regional activism/

TABLE 6.1 List of Official Apologies Made by a Japanese Head of State or Government

Year	Speaker	Addressed to	Context	Key terms
1984	Emperor Hirohito	Korea	Korean president Chun Doo-Hwan's visit	"regrettable" "unfortunate past"
1989	Prime Minister Takeshita Noboru	Korea	Speech to the National Diet of Japan	"deep regret and sorrow"
1990	Emperor Akihito	Korea	Korean president Roh Tae Woo's visit	"feel the deepest remorse"
	Prime Minister Toshiki Kaifu			"we are sorry"
1992	Prime Minister Kiichi Miyazawa	Comfort women	Press conference	"apologize from the bottom of my heart and feel remorse"
		Korea	Miyazawa's visit to Seoul, on the "comfort women" issue	"heartfelt remorse and apology," "truly sorry"
	Emperor Akihito	China	Visit to China, vocally expressed, on the suffering inflicted on the Chinese by the Japanese	"remorse"
1994	Prime Minister Tomiichi Murayama	Neighboring Asian nations	Statement on the "Peace, Friendship, and Exchange Initiative"	"profound and sincere remorse and apologies"
	Emperor Akihito	Korea	Korean president Kim Young Sam's visit	"deep regret"
1995	Prime Minister Tomiichi Murayama	All Asian nations	Fifty-year anniversary of the end of World War II	"deep remorse and heartfelt apology," "profound apology"
1996	Prime Minister Ryutaro Hashimoto	Korea	Hashimoto's visit to Jeju Island	"deep remorse and heartfelt apology"
1997	Prime Minister Ryutaro Hashimoto	China and other Asian nations	Summit: "Seeking a New Foreign Policy toward China"	"deep remorse and heartfelt apology"
		China	Hashimoto's visit to China	"deep remorse and heartfelt apology"

TABLE 6.1 *(Continued)*

1998	Emperor Akihito	Korea	Korean president Kim Dae Jung's visit	"deep sorrow," "heartfelt apology"
	Prime Minister Keizo Obuchi	Korea	Japan-ROK joint declaration	"deep remorse and heartfelt apology"
		China	Signing of a joint declaration officially recognizing Japan's responsibility for past atrocities	"keenly conscious of the responsibility," "deep remorse"
2001	Prime Minister Junichiro Koizumi	Korea	Koizumi's visit to Seoul	"remorse and apology"
			Letter addressed to former "comfort women"	"sincere apologies and remorse"
2002	Prime Minister Junichiro Koizumi	North Korea	Japan–Democratic People's Republic of Korea Pyongyang declaration	"deep remorse and heartfelt apology"
2003	Prime Minister Junichiro Koizumi	All Asian nations	The fifty-eighth memorial ceremony for the war dead	"profound remorse"
2005	Prime Minister Junichiro Koizumi	Nations involved in World War II	The Asian-African Summit	"deep remorse and heartfelt apology"
		Victims of Japanese aggression	Sixty-year anniversary of the end of World War II	"deep remorse and heartfelt apology," "feelings of mourning"
2010	Prime Minister Naoto Kan	Korea	One hundred–year anniversary of the annexation in 1910	"deep regret," "feelings of deep remorse and heartfelt apology"

Note: For apologies directed at countries including China, see Rose, *Sino-Japanese Relations*, 101-2.

exchanges—to assess their achievements and shortcomings before exploring the next steps.

Apology

Apology diplomacy has been a major tactic in the reconciliation process. As table 6.1 shows, since 1984 there have been eleven apologies directly made by Japanese heads of state or the Japanese government—four from emperors and seven from prime ministers—to the people of Korea, including North Korea. Japan has also made direct apologies to China several times during this period in an effort to ease past diplomatic tensions. Notably, there exists a clear pattern in the terms used in Japan's apologies. Until the early 1990s, the key terms had been "regret" and "remorse," which did not necessarily signify an apology on Japan's part. The word "apology" first appeared in 1992, when then prime minister Kiichi Miyazawa, during his meeting with ROK president Roh Tae Woo, stated, "I, as prime minister, would like to once again express heartfelt remorse and offer an apology to the people of your nation." In retrospect, the mid-nineties—centered as they were on Prime Minister Tomiichi Murayama's leadership—were a high point in apology diplomacy between Japan and Korea.[2]

Yet despite Japan's repeated use of the term "apology" from that point on, its neighbors have continued to view the Japanese with skepticism. From their perspective, as Caroline Rose points out, Japan's various efforts to "apologize" for wartime atrocities have not been backed up by actions to "reinforce the apologies"; instead, they are often coupled with ambiguous wording and counterproductive statements and behavior on the part of the government.[3] For instance, by repeatedly using the ambiguous phrase "deepest remorse" (*tsusetsu na hansei*), which is perceived by Japan experts in Korea as a phrase more widely used when someone passes away rather than when one acknowledges one's wrongdoings and apologizes, Japan cannot avoid the criticism by the recipients of such an "apology"—South Korea and China—that it lacks sincerity. As Chinese president Jiang Zemin said during his 1998 visit to Japan, "No matter how beautifully the words are written, if they are not put into effect then they mean nothing."[4] In fact, throughout the 1990s, Japanese political elites showed ambivalence between formal apology and frequent statements that glorified their colonial rule.[5] Furthermore, the renascent Japanese Right mounted vocal attacks on officials and officially inspired apologies, directing their fire in particular at Murayama's

TABLE 6.2 Examples of Japanese Officials' Statements Denying Wartime Responsibility

Year	Person	Excerpt from quotation
1980–1989	Masayuki Fujio, education minister (1986, 1988)	Suggested that the Rape of Nanking wasn't a big deal: "It is not murder under international law to kill in war.... The conflict in China started accidentally.... Japan fought to protect itself at a time when the white race had turned Asia into a colony."
	Okuno Seisuke, director of the General National Land Agency (1988)	"It was the Caucasian race that colonized Asia.... If anybody was the aggressor, it was the Caucasians. It is nonsense to call Japan the aggressor or militaristic."
1990–1995	Shintaro Ishihara, Japanese writer and politician (1990)	"People say that the Japanese made a holocaust there [in Nanking], but it is a lie."
	Hashimoto Ryutaro, Liberal Democratic Party (LDP) president (1993)	"Whatever better options may in hindsight appear to have existed--I cannot bring myself to dismiss curtly as a war of aggression."
	Michio Watanabe, foreign minister	"Japan's annexation of Korea in 1910 had been done amicably, with Korean consent."
1996–2000	Shigeto Nagano, justice minister (1997)	"The so-called Rape of Nanjing and related atrocities supposedly committed by the Japanese military are fabrications."
	Nobukatsu Fujioka, professor of education, Tokyo University (1997)	"The Americans brainwashed the postwar Japanese into believing they had committed terrible war crimes."
	Seiroku Kajiyama, chief cabinet secretary (1997)	"Foreign 'comfort women' conscripted for Japanese army brothels were prostitutes."
2001–2010	Toru Toida, governing party lawmaker (2007)	"We are absolutely positive that there was no massacre in Nanjing."
	Shinzo Abe, prime minister (2007)	"There is no evidence to prove there was coercion, nothing to support it." (Referring to the "comfort women" accusation.)
	Toshio Tamogami, former chief of staff, Japan Air Self-Defense Force (2008)	"It is often those who never directly saw the Japanese military who are spreading rumors about the army's acts of brutality.... It is certainly a false accusation to say that our country was an aggressor nation."

TABLE 6.2 *(Continued)*

2011–present	Yoshihiko Noda, former prime minister (2012)	"The matter [compensation for the comfort women] is closed." South Korean criticism that Japan's previous offerings were insufficient "hurt the feelings of conscientious Japanese, and it is a pity."
		"There are no records confirming that women were taken away by force and there are no accounts [by former Japanese soldiers], but the Kono statement came out based on the accounts of comfort women."*
	Jin Matsubara, chairman of the National Public Safety Commission (2012)	"I think Cabinet members must discuss revising the Kono statement, since no direct evidence has been found proving that comfort women were taken away by force by the military."
	Shinzo Abe, prime minister (2012)	"If the LDP returned to power, it would be necessary to review the Kono Statement."

SOURCES: See Cropsey, "On the Pearl Harbor Anniversary." For a list of several compiled quotations from Japanese officials, see "Japanese War Crimes: Introduction," http://www.users.bigpond.com/battleforaustralia/WarCrimeIntro.html. Specifically looking at LDP president Hashimoto Ryutaro, see *LDP Monthly*, October 1993, as quoted in Wakamiya, *The Postwar Conservative View of Asia*, 21. For Seisuke's comments, see *Asahi Shimbun*, April 26, 1988: 2, as quoted in Lind, *Sorry States*, 49.

The Kono Statement of 1993 was an apology to comfort women issued by then chief cabinet secretary Yohei Kono on August 4, 1993.

efforts to express the kind of apology that would satisfy Asian sentiment. Instead of acknowledging culpability in colonial/imperial aggression, some senior Japanese officials blatantly defended Japan's position so as to evade responsibility for wartime misdeeds. As one official states: "It is nonsense to call Japan the aggressor or militaristic. . . . I still think it is wrong to define [The Greater East Asia War] as a war of aggression. . . . The objective of the war itself was a justifiable one, which was permissible in principle in those days. . . . I think the Rape of Nanking is a fabrication."[6] Another is quoted as justifying Japan's role in annexing Korea in terms of "Asian liberation" from voracious Western powers (see table 6.2).

Japanese former prime minister Junichiro Koizumi's ostentatious visits to the Yasukuni Shrine in his official capacity provided another revealing illustration of the confusing message conveyed to Asian neighbors. As one Chinese intellectual noted, "When he [Koizumi] was here, he said—and I remember this clearly—'I express profound regret/apology for the suffering caused by the Japanese invasion of China,' . . . but after he got home, he continued visiting the Yasukuni Shrine."[7] Similarly, the outpouring of Japanese books, films, and magazines raising doubts about the Nanjing massacre, along with Prime Minister Shinzo Abe's recent attempt to revisit the Kono Statement, leads many Asian neighbors to question the sincerity of the Japanese apology.[8] Not surprisingly, according to 2005 surveys of South Koreans and Chinese, "Japan's apology" was still considered to be "the most important element to solve the disputes over history between the two countries" (42.6 percent for Koreans and 48.2 percent for Chinese).[9] A more recent public opinion survey by *Seoul Shinmun*, conducted on December 21-23, 2012, also shows that 94 percent of Koreans do not think that Japan reflects on its past aggression.[10] Such critical attitudes by Koreans and Chinese toward Japan's apology, in turn, have led to a negative response in Japan, even to the extent of "apology fatigue," according to the conservative Japanese press *Sankei Shimbun*. The *Seoul Shinmun* survey shows that 63 percent of Japanese find the ROK's demand for apology incomprehensible, implying a widening gap between the perception of the people of the two countries. Criticism from Koreans and Chinese has also provoked reactions from nationalistic Japanese. For instance, in December 1996, the Society for Creating New Textbooks (Atarashii Kyokasho Tsukurukai), a symbol of rightist neo-nationalism in Japan in the mid-1990s, was organized in reaction to this general trend toward repentance and reconciliation.[11]

In the end, the Japanese failed to recognize past wrongs and move forward. People in Korea and China have slowly but gradually realized that the formal ritual of apology is but one element in the complexities of the politics of remembrance. It is questionable that apology diplomacy has much utility left as a means of furthering historical reconciliation. Politics surrounding state-issued apologies have largely negated the putative intent of apologizing and, if anything, have set Japan back in terms of actually reconciling with its East Asian neighbors. Overall, the political value associated with an apology for historical issues in Japan has superseded substance and frustrated victim consciousness. As an East Asian "apology failure" (apologizing for the past as a means of capitalizing on this for the future)—not its failure to apologize—this has the general effect of only perpetuating "a disastrous policy failure."[12] Decades of this kind of apology failure have created a deadlock in the East Asian reconciliation process that cannot be broken until one state is able to pinpoint and address its own "identity mythmaking" and redirect the process altogether to benefit rather than belittle wartime victims.

Litigation

Compensation for the victims of Japanese aggression has been another contentious issue between Japan and its neighbors. Most Koreans and Chinese believe that Japan has yet to compensate victims, while Japan has objected to such compensation on legalistic grounds. In seeking a settlement between the victims and those responsible for crimes against them, litigation has been adopted as a major tactic in redressing historical injustice. Unlike in the West, however, its efficacy has proven to be very limited. Almost all lawsuits that Asian victims filed in Japanese courts were either thrown out or left unresolved, though courts have recognized the fact of victims' suffering. Victims who filed cases in American courts fared no better. Generally speaking, the fate of Japanese war crime victims seeking redress is one of "betrayal punctuated by glimmers of hope."[13]

Beginning in late 1991, forty women, represented by an NGO called the Association of Pacific War Victims and Bereaved Families, filed the first suit against the Japanese government addressing systematized sex slavery during the war. The following year another group of former sex slaves (this time primarily Korean women) filed suit in the Yamaguchi District Court in Fukuoka, demanding an official apology from the government along with $2.3 million in reparations. In April 1993, another group, consisting largely of Filipinas, asked the Tokyo District Court for 20 million yen per plaintiff. After years of litigious battling, the Tokyo District Court rejected the demands made by both the NGO-represented group and the Filipina group. As discussed below, Article 14 of the 1951 San Francisco Treaty of Peace was cited as the primary legal ground. Surprisingly, in 1998 the Fukuoka District Court ruled in favor of the Korean group, citing United Nations legal terminology concerning slavery. The court concluded that the Japanese government had violated basic human rights by "forcing them into sexual slavery" and found the government in violation of statutory and constitutional law.[14]

However, in 2001 the Hiroshima High Court overturned the Fukuoka decision, turning to the articles of reparations in the postwar treaties with the United States and holding that the government was not legally required to apologize or compensate. The court ruling was based on the following premise:

(a) ... International criminal law may not be applied retroactively; (b) the comfort station system did not involve the crime of slavery, and even if it did, the prohibition of slavery was not a customary norm of international law at the time; (c) rape was not prohibited during wartime by either the Hague Convention or by customary norms of international law; and (d) as Korea was an internationally recognized annexed part of Japan's empire during World War II and thus not considered an adversary, the laws of war are inapplicable to Korean nationals.[15]

While the task of gaining legal accountability for these war victims has wholly failed to result in official reparations, thousands of people have been mobilized and suits continue to be filed. Additionally, some who failed in Japan have taken their plight to the United States in hopes of finding a more sympathetic legal ear.

The legal basis by which foreigners may file outside claims in American courts is the two-century-old Alien Tort Claims Act (ATCA) of 1789. This statute provides a means for noncitizens to seek recourse in the United States for violations of standing international law and has been the legal hook utilized in recent decades by a variety of non-American plaintiffs. Since comfort women had anticipated little if any chance of success in Japanese courts, they saw ATCA as a window of opportunity. In 2000, fifteen former comfort women filed a class action suit in the District of Columbia Court. The plaintiffs of *Hwang Geum Joo, et al. v. Japan* hoped to circumvent previous rejections by Japanese courts by arguing that the Japanese military had engaged in a commercial activity through the setting up of a network of "comfort" stations and collecting money for their services.[16] As a response to these claims of "systematized sex," however, the Japanese government filed a counter-motion to dismiss. When the case was heard by the Supreme Court, Associate Justice Ruth Bader Ginsburg reaffirmed the district court's judgment in 2005, finding that the Japanese government did indeed enjoy sovereign immunity from such claims as set forth at the San Francisco Peace Conference and that the legal interpretation of peace treaties must remain at a "government-to-government level."[17]

Korean forced laborers' unsuccessful litigation struggle using the

Hayden Bill of California State between 1999 and 2004 further proved the limits of the litigation tactic. Introduced in the California State Legislature by longtime civil rights activist turned politician Tom Hayden, the Hayden Bill provided what was initially seen as a means of circumventing "an international legal deadlock" resulting from the American and Japanese governments' official positions regarding war reparations and the specific terms of the postwar settlements. In the years leading up to the Hayden Bill, petitions to both governments had been consistently rejected by citing the previous state-to-state normalization treaties.[18] However, the legislation eliminated—at the level of state law—the statute of limitations and redefined "war crimes victims" to include those affected by allies of Nazi Germany. This resulted in a number of California-filed suits against the Japanese government by forced laborers, American prisoners of war, and comfort women. While this legislation initially encouraged and mobilized victims groups to file their claims in California courts, it ultimately failed to secure a new forum for compensation as the Supreme Court did not recognize the individuals' claims.

To further complicate the matters, in May 2012, the South Korean Supreme Court ruled in favor of eleven South Koreans who demanded Japanese firms pay them for forced labor during Japan's colonial rule of Korea, marking the first legal victory of South Korean forced laborers. The Court repealed lower court decisions that ruled against South Koreans seeking unpaid wages and financial redress from Mitsubishi Heavy Industries Ltd. and Nippon Steel Corporation for forced labor from 1941 to 1945, paving the way for South Korean forced laborers to seek compensation for their work nearly seven decades after Korea gained independence from Japan.[19] Japan's response still remains to be seen, but the two involved companies have not yet taken any measures to comply with the ruling.

Shared History

Collaborative history writing has been another approach to achieving historical reconciliation. The frequent clashes over history textbooks in Northeast Asia, in 1982, 2002, 2005, and 2011, for example, demonstrate that history is not simply about the past but also about the present and future. One approach to solving this problem has been to form both official and unofficial committees to produce jointly written history.

The first official attempt to deal jointly with history textbooks was undertaken in October 2001 by Japan and South Korea. Prime Minister Koizumi and President Kim Dae Jung officially agreed to establish the Japan-ROK Joint History Research Committee as a gesture of commitment to a state-sponsored effort toward placing a reconciled view of the past in a new regional history framework. The committee, while not entirely a failure, has yet to attain the success that was envisioned at its commencement. Even though it adopted the United Nations Educational, Scientific, and Cultural Organization (UNESCO) model of writing a "parallel history," when it finished the first phase in May 2005, both sides failed to come to a consensus on what exactly should be incorporated into the textbooks. Apparently, there was significant disagreement over how to interpret Japan's colonial rule, including the question of Japan's role (or lack thereof) in Korea's modernization.[20]

Following Koizumi's controversial visits to the Yasukuni shrine, the work of the joint committee was put on hold until October 2006 when then prime minister Abe and President Roh Moo Hyun agreed to relaunch efforts. The committee met on April 27, 2007, in Seoul, reaching an agreement to form a new subgroup—in addition to the three existing groups studying ancient, medieval and contemporary history—to study history textbooks. The idea reportedly was to try to narrow differences between the textbooks of the two nations. The Japan-ROK Joint History Research Committee released another report in 2010, but once again the two sides failed to reach a consensus view on Japan's 1910–45 colonial rule of the Korean Peninsula, most notably on its recruitment of Korean laborers and comfort women, as well as the drafting of Koreans into the Japanese military.[21]

Japan and China launched a similar effort as part of the thaw in relations that followed the leadership transition in Japan from Koizumi to Abe. During Abe's October 2006 visit to Beijing, the two countries announced an agreement to form the China-Japan Joint History Research Committee to put the history issue in the hands of historians rather than politicians. Modeled after the Japan-ROK format, the China-Japan committee of twenty leading historians from both countries aimed to write parallel histories utilizing the UNESCO model. Led by Bu Ping, Chinese director of the Institute of Modern History at the Chinese Academy of Social Sciences, and Shin'ichi Kitaoka, a Japanese professor at Tokyo University, both sides agreed to conduct a joint study and produce an account of two thousand years of Sino-Japanese interaction by 2008. This would be in time to mark the thirtieth anniversary of the signing of the Japan-China Peace and Friendship Treaty.

From the first meeting convened on December 26, 2006, in Beijing, however, it became clear that their goals were nothing short of daunting. Not surprisingly, the Japanese wanted to focus on the postwar era, while the Chinese were more interested in taking their own inventory of the colonial and wartime periods.[22] Members agreed that each side would separately write its own version of bilateral history texts ("parallel history") and exchange written comments on controversial issues. They agreed on a list of major historical events to be discussed, including the Nanjing massacre and Japan's "Twenty-One Demands" on China.[23] The final report was completed and made public in January 2010, with one and half years delay, only to show that the two sides could not resolve differences on controversial modern events including the 1937 Nanjing massacre.[24]

Such official efforts make for a complex, long-term process, and it is too early for any sort of final judgment of their efficacy. While this approach of writing a shared history is fraught with difficulties and has yet to come close to achieving reconciliation, it has offered many important lessons for those nations involved. By and large, it seems almost impossible to arrive at a common rendition of historical events, particularly regarding the most controversial aspects of history. Writing a shared regional history might be feasible intellectually, but not politically. In Northeast Asia, the government still has considerable influence in textbook making, and with such heavy state involvement, the resulting history textbooks can easily turn into issues of diplomacy and international relations. It is no coincidence that textbooks have become a nexus for significant international tension in the region, especially between Japan and China and between Japan and the two Koreas.

Regional Exchanges and Activism

Finally, there have been increased intersocietal exchanges as part of efforts to redress historical injustice. The official opening of a cultural exchange between Korea and Japan in 1998, their cohosting of the 2002 World Cup Games, and the pop-culture industry boom between them, which even resulted in the coining of the term "Hallyu" (or "Korean wave"), have all helped to ease deep-seated antagonism, mistrust, and fear. Many young Japanese are aware of the recent Korean cultural blossoming in TV drama and filmmaking, and the Japanese media are increasingly buying these Korean cultural products. High school history teachers and students of both countries are holding joint summer camps every year to learn more about Japanese and Korean history. More and more Koreans study in China and Japan, while China has been attracting an increasing number of Japanese and Korean tourists. Such multilevel cultural interactions across borders will be useful resources in achieving the ultimate grace of forgiveness, liberation from the old victim/aggressor identity, and the development of a new regional identity based on a vision of peaceful coexistence—but this, of course, will be a gradual process.

In addition, a growing number of scholars and civic activist groups, especially in Japan and South Korea, have worked together in history writing, including data and testimony collection, documentary filmmaking, and public history propaganda work. Besides official efforts to compile joint history books, for instance, scholars of Northeast Asia have worked together toward a mutual understanding of regional history. The first such effort was the Japan–South Korea Joint Study Group on History Textbooks, which was organized in the late 1980s, long before the official efforts. In early 2005, scholars, teachers, and activists from China, Japan, and South Korea published the first-ever East Asian common history guidebook, *A History That Opens to the Future: The Contemporary and Modern History of Three East Asian Countries* (in Japanese: *Mirai o hiraku rekishi*; in Korean: *Miraerŭl yŏnŭn yŏksa*).[25] It is hoped that such publication of jointly written history will help achieve one of the most challenging, long-term goals of regional reconciliation: the teaching of a reconciled past to the young people of Japan, Korea, and China.

Bilateral, state-oriented approaches to the history issue have now expanded to multifaceted, transnational activism in which the government, civil society, academia, and the media have all become involved. Several Asian NGOs have collaborated to address the issue of comfort women by jointly sponsoring events such as the International Women's Tribunal of December 2000. This was preceded by the groundbreaking creation of the Asian Women's Fund—the first time Japan sought to confront its past through a public-private collaboration.[26] A sort of ripple effect took place as civil society in both Korea and Japan enlisted several NGOs to the cause of confronting the two states' divided conceptions of their shared history. In November 2004, a group of Korean and Japanese scholars formed the Hanil Yondae 21 (Korea-Japan Solidarity 21) with a clear aim to promote deep introspection and build regional solidarity between the two nations for future generations. Research centers in Korea, Japan, and China often hold joint workshops and conferences in addressing historical and territorial issues. All these efforts reflect the hopes of a growing civil society that East Asia can confront its future as a regional collaborative entity, rather than as a region wracked by division and conflicting interpretations of history.

JAPAN VERSUS GERMANY

Before discussing further steps toward historical reconciliation, it is worth comparing Western Europe with Northeast Asia, especially with a view to the frequently asked question of why Japan failed to emulate Germany in dealing with its past wrongdoings. Many have compared Japan unfavorably to Germany in this respect and have maintained that East Asia is lagging far behind in achieving a substantive reconciliation with the victims of its unfortunate past. One explanation for this difference is that central governments in East Asia wield greater influence in shaping discourse on history issues and hinder civil society's ability to address these issues.[27] Although some NGOs have been engaged in redressing historical injustices, in comparison to Europe civil society has been weak (Japan), almost nonexistent (Communist China), or not much interested in historical issues (Korea). There exists no major transnational organization or culture that might play a central role in achieving historical reconciliation.[28] Besides, while Germany had to address the history issue in order to be part of a new Europe, Japan saw no such need. The United States did not press Japan to reconcile with its neighbors either—as it had Germany, in the years following 1945. Instead, as Japan's importance as a bulwark against Communism in the region increased with the intensification of the Cold War, the United States sought to put aside issues of historical responsibility, as seen in the case of Japan-ROK normalization of 1965. In fact, Washington supported the purging of leftist, pro-Communist officials, even though it was the political Left that had opposed Japanese imperialism and "was more likely to favor justice and remembrance."[29]

Japan was unquestionably a major aggressor in the region and must acknowledge unequivocally its responsibility. Still, it is worth considering Japanese psychology in dealing with historical injustices, as there exists a strong sense of victimhood among Japanese. Nazi war crimes were well documented and could not be denied, such that the German right-wingers lacked the political ammunition to engage in any kind of denial politics. On the other hand, there have been controversies over the extent and responsibility of Japanese war crimes, and victim consciousness has led to the rise of rightist nationalism in Japan. The most significant lesson of the apology tactic was that it revealed a weakness in the Japanese political elites' commitment to the cause that may have reflected their own victim identity. Besides the well-known atomic bombings of Hiroshima and Nagasaki that killed approximately 140,000 and 70,000 civilians, respectively, the United States killed far more civilians through the massive firebombing of Japanese cities. For instance, the firebombing of Tokyo alone on March 9 and 10, 1945, led to the death of about 100,000 people and the destruction of one million homes.[30] Even at the time, the targeting of entire cities for destruction with conventional weapons (known as "area" or "carpet" bombing) was controversial, and Japan to this day remains the only country hit by nuclear weapons.[31]

Although these bombings may have been necessary to defeat the Japanese military while minimizing American (and Japanese) casualties, there existed dissenting views of the American actions. Justice Radhabinod Pal of India argued during the Tokyo trial that "in the war in Asia the only act comparable to Nazi atrocities was perpetrated by the leaders of the United States."[32] Nevertheless, no discussion of American bombing on civilians was ever allowed at the Tokyo Tribunal, and the question of wartime responsibility has been put on the back burner throughout the postwar period for the sake of strengthening the Japanese-U.S. alliance.[33] In fact, to this day, other than a 1995 visit by Ambassador Walter Mondale to Tokyo's March 10 "Peace Day" (a memorial for those killed and injured in the fire bombings), a visit by Nancy Pelosi, Speaker of the House of Representatives, to the Hiroshima Atomic Bomb Memorial in 2008, and the recent visit by Ambassador John Roos to the Hiroshima Peace Memorial Park in August 2010, the United States has made only limited acknowledgment of human sufferings.[34]

Japanese victim identity is well reflected in the media and school textbooks as well as in well-known museum displays. Justice Pal's dissenting view, which was dismissed at the time of the tribunal, has been given attention in Japanese history textbooks.[35] This idea of American guilt and Japanese victimhood is a prevalent theme in the Yushukan Annex Museum inscriptions at the Yasukuni Shrine. Prepared in the early 2000s, the displays make no reference to invasion, aggression, massacres, or atrocities committed by Japanese troops. Instead, they blame American president Franklin D. Roosevelt for provoking war with Japan. As Jeff Kingston points out, "Japanese suffering is the only suffering on display."[36] While less explicit than the Yasukuni Museum language, even historical museums addressing the atomic bomb present a view that questions America's justification for the bombs and leaves open the question of general responsibility for the war. The Hiroshima Peace Memorial Museum, for instance, asserts that "the atomic bomb had cost 2 billion dollars and mobilized, at its peak, over 120,000 people. Linking this weapon to the end of the war would help justify that expenditure. In addition to the desire to force Japan's surrender, these considerations led the United States to proceed with the atomic bombings." This general accusation is backed by depictions of American behavior immediately following the bomb and characterizations of perceived American insensitivity to the resulting damage. At one point, the exhibits devote several captions to the suggestion that the horrific casualties had inspired an American reaction more attuned to scientific research than medical and humanitarian aid.

With this frame, often employed by progressive media elements, the Japanese highlight the suffering of their own citizens during the Asia-Pacific War, while ignoring Asian victims of Japanese aggressions. In addition, they have employed a "displacement" frame, claiming that other Western nations were committing equally terrible—or worse—violations of human rights in their respective colonies. This discourse, often favored by Japanese conservatives, downplays the severity of Japan's war crimes.

In addition to the Japanese sense of suffering, postwar geopolitics had a profound impact on the ways in which Northeast Asia and Western Europe dealt with the historical injustices of the prewar period. American leaders of the Allied forces in Japan believed that keeping the emperor as a social institution, but deprived of political power, would facilitate the occupation and reconstruction of postwar Japan. Unlike in Europe, where key Axis leaders of the war and the Holocaust were punished for their atrocities and crimes, the opportunity to address the personal and institutional role of the emperor in Japanese historical injustices was clearly lost. However, as historian Herbert P. Bix acutely notes, "As long as Hirohito remained on the throne, unaccountable to anyone for his official actions, most Japanese had little reason to question their support of him or feel responsibility for the war, let alone look beyond the narrow boundaries of victim-consciousness."[37] In fact, the Japanese elite attempted to "protect the throne, its occupant, and their own rule" by linking Hirohito to "the idea of peace," and the campaign to promote the myth that the emperor was innocent or a victim of the militarists only strengthened Japanese victim consciousness and impeded the search for historical truth.[38] As Jennifer Lind asserts, "Psychological warfare officials and Occupation authorities alike crafted a mythology of Japanese victimhood in which the public had been duped by a militarist clique into launching an ill-fated war." This "military clique thesis," according to Lind, pardoned the Japanese of guilt and helped to foster an already ubiquitous "sense of self-pity."[39]

The failure to confront and address war responsibility then "provided fertile soil for the growth of a postwar neonationalism" in Japan.[40] An exemplary case in point is an award-winning essay by the then chief of staff of the Japanese Air Self-Defense Force, General Toshio Tamogami, in the fall of 2008. In what the *Economist* labeled a "barely warm hash of thrice-cooked revisionism," Tamogami claims that the war was Japan's attempt to defend its legally held territories of China and Korea against Communist conspirators, Pearl Harbor was nothing but an American trap, and Japanese colonial rule was a benevolent undertaking viewed with gratitude by its East Asian neighbors.[41] Any accusation of wartime atrocity is nothing more than a misconceived "rumor," and Japan must fight to "reclaim its glorious history... for a country that denies its own history is destined to fall." Tamogami has advocated a rather extremist view, but his accusatory essay strongly suggests that unless the United States addresses its own history issue with Japan, this kind of rightist view will continue to find ground in Japan.

Another product out of geopolitical considerations is the San Francisco Peace Treaty of 1951. It was an agreement between the Allied powers and Japan that formally ended the war, settling Japan's obligations to pay reparations for its wartime acts. However, Asian nations that were the primary victims of Japanese aggressions were not included in the formal process of settling Japan's responsibilities: Neither the ROK nor the PRC was invited to the San Francisco Peace Conference, and neither was party to the 1951 treaty. By then, the PRC had become an enemy of the United States, and Korea was weak, divided, and in the midst of a war. The Republic of China (Taiwan) signed a separate peace treaty with Japan in 1952.

Nevertheless, the 1951 treaty became a major basis for later court rulings on wartime atrocities and crimes. For instance, in April 2007, Japan's

Supreme Court foreclosed all pending and future lawsuits arising from actions taken by Japan in the course of colonialism and war. The court cited as its main ground the relevant provisions of the San Francisco Treaty, especially Article 14, which states that "except as otherwise provided in the present Treaty, the Allied Powers waive all reparations claims of the Allied Powers, other claims of the Allied Powers and their nationals arising out of any actions taken by Japan and its nationals in the course of the prosecution of the war, and claims of the Allied Powers for direct military costs of occupation." The article gave no separate mention of Japan's reparations for its Asian victims, and the article has been interpreted as waiving those victims' rights to claims altogether. Article 14 has been cited in American cases as well.

In addition, deficiencies of the San Francisco Treaty disallowed a resolution to the current territorial disputes in Northeast Asia. For instance, early drafts of the treaty specified that Dokdo/Takeshima (referred to as "Liancourt Rocks" by the American government) was initially Korean territory, but later changed to Japanese territory in 1949, and in the end omitted any reference to the area. Similarly, the Soviet Union was initially specified as the recipient of the Kurile Islands, but this was deleted in the final stage of treaty drafting as well. The lack of specification was neither a coincidence nor an error. Instead, as Kimie Hara points out, "Various issues were deliberately left unresolved due to the regional Cold War."[42] The United States commanded responsibility for designating sovereignty over the islands but sidestepped this.[43] As Hara explains further: "Earlier drafts were consistent with the 'punitive peace' plan and the Yalta spirit of inter-Allied cooperation. However, with the emergence of the Cold War, the peace treaty changed from punitive to generous as United States' strategic thinking focused on securing Japan within the Western bloc and assuring a long-term US military presence in Japan, particularly in Okinawa."[44]

There was an opportunity to remedy the deficiencies of the San Francisco Treaty when Japan and South Korea normalized relations, but the issues were once again put aside. In 1965, under heavy pressure from a United States anxious to solidify its Cold War security alliance system and bolster the South Korean economy, the ROK agreed to normalize relations with Japan despite intense domestic protests. In exchange, South Korea received substantial Japanese economic assistance, but Japan refused to term this assistance "reparations." Issues such as disputed territories and Japan's colonial rule were again swept under the rug. Unlike in Western Europe, where the United States established a multilateral security arrangement (i.e., NATO) and pushed for Franco-German reconciliation, in Northeast Asia the United States established a bilateral "hub and spoke" alliance system with Japan and the ROK and did not press for a fundamental historical reconciliation between the two allies of the United States. As a result, "normalization" occurred at the governmental level but without addressing popular demands for the redress of historical injustices. As one former U.S. senior diplomat notes, "For American policy makers, strategic considerations have consistently trumped issues of equity in historic disputes involving Japan since World War II."[45]

NEXT STEPS: CAN THE UNITED STATES PLAY A ROLE?

As shown above, many efforts toward historical reconciliation in Northeast Asia—from apology to litigation to joint history writing—have seemed promising, but none has succeeded. Even when the governments of Japan, China, and South Korea have tried to move away from being held hostage to history, public perceptions have not always followed or supported the political lead. Not only in democratic societies like Japan and South Korea but even in China, political leaders must accommodate popular perceptions and demands in their policy making. As scholars and experts have noted, reconciliation is a long-term, multifaceted process, involving various groups and actors. Above all, it requires patience, especially in Northeast Asia, where efforts toward historical reconciliation did not begin until the 1980s. We can and should learn from other successful experiences of reconciliation, such as the European one (see Fania Oz-Salzberger's chapter in this volume). Ultimately, though, we must develop a model or strategy that acknowledges more recent historical experiences and the complex politics of contemporary Northeast Asia. In this context, it is worth considering whether or not the United States can play a constructive role in breaking the current stalemate and in facilitating a renewed effort toward historical reconciliation in the region.[46]

There has been some debate in American academic and policy-making circles about the role that the United States might play in helping resolve historical disputes and achieve reconciliation in Northeast Asia. A predominant view has been that this is primarily a matter for Asians and better left to historians. By taking a specific position, many fear that the United States could be pulled into the Sino-Japanese rivalry or be forced to take sides between its key allies in the region, Japan and South Korea.[47] In this vein, the American State Department has consistently taken a position that the San Francisco Treaty protected Japan from demands for compensation from victim nations.

Yet despite its proclaimed neutrality, the record shows that the American government has not always acted so. When former forced laborers filed claims against Japan, for instance, it took a position very different from the one it had taken in the German case. Instead, the government pressed hard to force the reluctant German government and German corporations to admit their role and responsibility, offer a public apology to the victims, and provide compensation. Toward the Japanese government, however, the American position was precisely the opposite, protecting it against claims at every step, even prior to the San Francisco Treaty.

The contrary view contends that the United States can hardly afford to stand outside these disputes, particularly as it was a key player in their formation. Referring to the recent dispute over the naming of Dokdo/Takeshima, Alexis Dudden aptly points out that it has "brought us back to 1952, when America's occupation of Japan ended, and the United States determined who owned what in East Asia and the Pacific."[48] Gil Rozman argues that American efforts in the region need to be directed more toward narrowing the historical divide in East Asia, while acting as the impetus for increased mutual understanding. The United States should exercise proactive leadership, contending that "benign neglect of Japanese nationalism threatens to unravel the spirit of reconciliation in East Asia."[49]

Contrary to the policy stance adopted by the executive branch, the United States House of Representatives took up Asian history issues more proactively by introducing bills on Japan's responsibility regarding wartime comfort women. For instance, the House in 2007 passed a resolution (H. Res. 121) criticizing the Japanese handling of the comfort women issue. Introduced by Representative Mike Honda, a Japanese American legislator, the resolution called on the Japanese government to "formally acknowledge, apologize, and accept historical responsibility in a clear and unequivocal manner for its Imperial Armed Forces' coercion of young women into sexual slavery, known to the world as 'comfort women,' during its colonial and wartime occupation of Asia and the Pacific Islands from the 1930s through the duration of World War II." The resolution urged that Japan "should educate current and future generations about this horrible crime while following the recommendation of the international community with respect to the 'comfort women.'"⁵⁰

As many have noted, any reexamination of the United States' "national myth" with respect to wartime atrocities is most likely to provoke controversy and spirited rebuttals within the United States. Understandably, there are objections to any efforts that could open this Pandora's box, as it could become easily and overly politicized. Still, Washington must not overlook the issues at hand and should reconsider its "hands-off" posture and take a more proactive role. The United States not only has a responsibility for helping resolve the disputes but also has a clear interest in ensuring that the peace and prosperity of a region so vital to its future is not undermined by controversies rooted in the past. In other words, resolving the history issue is not simply a matter of helping Asians achieve overdue reconciliation; it is important, if not imperative, for the United States' alliance relations and strategic equities in the region as well. As the recent dispute between South Korea and Japan over Dokdo/Takeshima illustrates, the history question can easily spill over into the American policy arena.

How, then, can the United States become involved in facilitating historical reconciliation in the region? Some experts advocate an active American intervention in Asian history issues by pressing Japan to confront its past. For instance, G. John Ikenberry argues that Japan's history problem is an American problem and therefore "Washington should encourage Japan to pursue [a] German path, tying 'normalization' to redoubled commitments to regional security cooperation."[51] It is a noble aim but not an effective strategy. It would not be convincing in the eyes of the Japanese who have their own victim consciousness vis-à-vis the United States, desiring first "true closure."[52] In addition, many in the region, especially in Korea, want the Americans to take a clear position on contested historical and territorial issues. However, that does not appear to be a sensible approach either, since the Americans would be forced to take sides between two vital allies.

Instead, I would argue for a *self-critical, self-reflective approach*. That is, the United States needs, first and foremost, to acknowledge any responsibility that it has in handling or mishandling of history issues. For instance, it can express regret for having paid scant attention to Asian issues during the Tokyo Tribunal and put geopolitics over regional reconciliation throughout the Cold War period. Unlike the Nuremberg court, the Tokyo trial was not sufficiently represented by judges from those nations that suffered the most from Japanese aggression: only three of the eleven judges at the trial represented Asian countries, and there was no representative from Korea. The American-led tribunal failed to appreciate the massive suffering of Chinese and Koreans at the hands of Japanese invaders and colonizers and the need to dry up the deep well of anger left behind. The proceedings paid only cursory attention to Japanese aggression against Asians, such as Japan's invasion of Manchuria in 1931, the Nanjing massacre, the use of forced Korean labor in Japanese mines and factories, "and the 'comfort women'" coerced by the Japanese military.[53] Instead, the tribunal focused on the Japanese actions that had most directly affected the Western allies—the surprise attack on Pearl Harbor and the mistreatment of Allied prisoners of war. Moreover, the United States provided immunity to those Japanese who tested biological weapons on live prisoners of war and civilians, in exchange for information obtained from the experiments.[54] These flaws and specific omissions "discredited the evidence of war crimes that the trials did uncover, tainted the concept of postwar justice, and restored the legitimacy of the very leaders the trials had sought to impugn."[55] Looking back, the American approach made sense from a geopolitical perspective, but not in terms of historical reconciliation.

The United States could go further by recognizing the sufferings of Japanese victims of the atomic bombing, with an official presidential visit to the site of the nuclear attacks. In fact, it appears that in 2005 the government considered just such a proposal, having President George W. Bush stop in Hiroshima before or after the Asia-Pacific Economic Cooperation (APEC) meetings held in November 2005 in South Korea. However, Japan's relations with China and South Korea were chilly due to then prime minister Koizumi's repeated visits to the Yasukuni Shrine, and so the United States reportedly forwent the Hiroshima visit to avoid any misunderstanding that it had sided with Japan.[56] The American government contemplated a similar plan in 1995, the fiftieth anniversary of the end of the war, but President Bill Clinton canceled his participation in the APEC meetings due to a crisis over the passage of the nation's budget. He did visit Japan the following year but did not travel to Hiroshima.[57]

Recently, the call for the president to visit Hiroshima or Nagasaki has gained new momentum, given President Barack Obama's 2009 Prague speech advocating a nuclear-free world. The visit fits nicely with Obama's vision for a nuclear-free world; his official visit to Hiroshima or Nagasaki could be seen as an important step toward demonstrating his leadership in implementing a new nuclear-free policy. Such an action by the president would also enhance America's international image as champion of human rights and peace, one that has been tainted in recent years with a resulting sharp rise in anti-American sentiment in many parts of the world. It could certainly aid in removing the "historical thorn" that exists between the United States and Japan.

To be sure, an Obama visit must be carried out with great caution and care. It should be an occasion to acknowledge human sufferings in the larger context of Obama's vision for creating a nuclear-free world. If a Hiroshima visit were to be construed as an official apology, it would draw strong resistance from the conservatives in the United States and be counterproductive in achieving reconciliation.[58] It should be made very clear from the outset that his visit is not meant to vindicate Japan's victim identity or support rightist views that hold the Americans as responsible for wartime atrocities. Otherwise, it could have the unintended consequence of strengthening the historical amnesia that overlooks Japan's own responsibility for wartime atrocities toward its Asian neighbors.

Thus an Obama visit should be aimed at activating a larger process of historical reconciliation that includes Northeast Asian nations as well as the United States. However, if an Obama visit were taken only to reaffirm the alliance with Japan, it would create grave and widespread concerns, particularly among Chinese and Koreans, that the Americans prioritize Japan among its East Asian relationships. It was for this reason, as noted above, that the possible Bush visit to Hiroshima in 2005 did not take place. As Fumio Matsuo suggests, in order for such a visit by the American president to be successful, it should be followed by similar actions on the part of the Japanese toward its Asian neighbors. For instance, the Japanese prime minister could undertake a similar visit to Nanjing to pay tribute to the victims of the 1937 massacre. Only when an American president's visit occurs in the larger regional context can the United States avoid alienating China and South Korea and play a constructive role in facilitating historical reconciliation in Northeast Asia.

Finally, the United States can aid in efforts to reinterpret Article 14 of the San Francisco Peace Treaty so as to allow victims to file claims against the Japanese government and Japanese corporations, as was done with Germany. Generally, cases brought by individual victims of Japanese war crimes in American courts have been dismissed on the ground that they would have uncertain but predictably negative consequences for healthy bilateral and economic relations. Robert Bork, former solicitor general and defeated nominee for the Supreme Court, asserts that individual tort cases filed against governments will have a "certain potential to interfere with United States foreign policy."[59] However, the general American aversion to consideration of such cases begs the question of the difference between the Japanese and the German cases with regard to the American role in reparation and reconciliation. The Americans played a facilitating role in the negotiations between Nazi slave-labor victims and the German government and German companies that led to the creation of the German Slave Labor Foundation.[60] In contrast, the American government filed a statement of interest in the cases of litigation against the Japanese government and Japanese companies favoring the Japanese government.[61] In other words, the United States took a largely *political* approach toward the German case, encouraging both parties in the litigation to make settlements, whereas it took a strictly *legalistic* approach toward the Japanese case by denying the rights for individual claims with reference to the San Francisco Treaty.[62]

As John W. Dower, the author of the Pulitzer Prize–winning 2000 study *Embracing Defeat* asserts: "We wanted Japan on our side because China was now seen as an enemy. And this meant not burdening Japan with reparations (any more than necessary), not burdening Japan with future claims. That's the treaty of 1951. . . . And it also meant the Americans set about whitewashing and sanitizing Japan's war responsibility and war crimes."[63] In this context, one can legitimately question the validity of the strictly legalistic interpretation of the treaty born out of political considerations. In recent years, there has been a call for a new interpretation of international law, challenging the traditional state-centric view that individuals lack any independent standing and only states possess rights. Although this new approach still faces a great deal of difficulty, it could open up new possibilities, and the United States could seriously consider a possible reinterpretation of the 1951 treaty. Such proactive actions, it is hoped, would encourage the Japanese to explore with greater sincerity and depth their own record of the past and overcome their sense of victimization. This could instigate a new process of reconciliation in the region — one that is badly needed.

CONCLUDING REMARKS

It is a critical time for a new Northeast Asia. Increased regional interaction in recent years has not diminished the importance of the past. On the contrary, the past has become even more contentious as nations vie for regional leadership. In fact, as Daniel Sneider points out, the emergence of history textbooks as a diplomatic issue in the early 1980s was a response to Japan's bid for regional leadership, propelled by its economic success.[64] The multiple layers of disputes among Northeast Asian nations over history and territorial issues in the region should give rise to concern among American policy makers. Now, as China emerges as an economic power and competitor with Japan for leadership in an integrated Northeast Asia, interpretation of the past seems even more critical than ever.

In searching for a model of reconciliation, we must understand the complex layers of Northeast Asian history. It is misleading to mechanically compare, as many casual observers do, the ways that Northeast Asia and Western Europe have dealt with World War II. It cannot and should not be expected that Northeast Asia will simply repeat or emulate Western Europe. The regions have distinctive histories, experiences, and memories and perhaps even different cultural modes of reconciliation. Accordingly, we must search for a Northeast Asian method or strategy, while using the European experiences only as a reference. This will require a certain level of patience with the rather slow progress made so far; as the next chapter in this volume shows, even in Europe it took a long time to achieve significant progress, and efforts in Northeast Asia are relatively recent. Reconciliation is inherently a complex, long-term process involving multiple actors, including the state, civil society, and international organizations. In this context, the United States can be a useful and facilitating player, but for this it has to examine its own history in the Pacific more carefully.

> I am grateful to Hilary Izatt and Joyce Lee for research assistance and to Don Keyser, David Straub, Jonathan Greenburg, and Fumio Matsuo for their insightful comments.

1. Funabashi, ed., *Reconciliation in the Asia-Pacific*.
2. Murayama created the unofficial Asian Women's Fund to compensate comfort women, showing his administration's commitment to the cause (although the Korean government ultimately rejected the effort). In June 1996, every one of the seven new middle-school history textbooks selected by the Education Ministry included a one-line description of the comfort women issue. It was a significant gesture of repentance by the Japanese political leadership to resolve the comfort women controversy.
3. Rose, *Sino-Japanese Relations*, 102.
4. *Asahi Shimbun*, "Mirai o hiraku nitchū kankei ni (Opening up a Future for Sino-Japanese Relations)," November 24, 1998, 5, as quoted in Rose, *Sino-Japanese Relations*, 108.
5. For more on Japanese conservatives' view of Asia, see Wakamiya, *Sengo hoshu no Ajia kan*.
6. *Mainichi Shimbun*, May 5, 1995, as quoted in Wakamiya, *The Postwar Conservative View of Asia*, 11–13.

7   Interview with Li Zongyuan on April 22, 2010.
8   For instance, see Higashinakano, *Top-Secret Chinese Nationalist Documents Reveal the Truth about the Nanking Incident*. According to Higashinakano, "An examination of those documents reveals that the provenance of accusations that Japan perpetrated a massacre in Nanking is wartime propaganda initiated by the Nationalist intelligence organization. They also expose European and American Nationalist agents who were intimately involved in the concoction of 'Nanking Massacre' propaganda."
9   *Dong-A Ilbo*, "Opinion Poll on Chinese and South Korean Attitudes toward Japan and Other Nations."
10 Ahn, "Ninety-Four Percent of Koreans."
11 See *Han'guk Ilbo*, October 16, 2001.
12 Dudden, *Troubled Apologies*, 33.
13 Lee, "In Search of Redress for Historical Injustice," 144.
14 United Nations Commission on Human Rights: *Update to the Final Report on Contemporary Forms of Slavery; Systematic Rape, Sexual Slavery and Slavery-Like Practices during Armed Conflict: Report of the Special Rapporteur, Gay J. McDougall*, U.S. ESCOR, 52nd Sess., Prov. Agenda Item 6, UN DOC E/CN.4/Sub2/2000/21 (2001), as quoted in Vanderweert, "Seeking Justice for 'Comfort' Women," 161.
15 Vanderweert, "Seeking Justice for 'Comfort' Women," 160–64.
16 Memorandum of Points and Authorities in Support of Plaintiffs' Motion for Declaratory Judgment That Japan Cannot Claim Sovereign Immunity in Defense of Claims of Systematic Sexual Slavery during World War II in *Hwang Geum Joo, et al. v. Japan*, no. 00-CV-2288, renumbered 00-CV2233 (D.D.C. motion filed March 5, 2001), as cited in Vanderweert, "Seeking Justice for 'Comfort' Women," 176.
17 United States District Court for the District of Columbia, Civil Action 00–02233 (HHK), *Hwang Geum Joo, et al. v. Japan*, Henry H. Kennedy Jr., United States District Judge, Memorandum: October 4, 2001, 23.
18 Yoneyama, "Traveling Memories, Contagious Justice," 62–64.
19 *Chosun Ilbo*, "Supreme Court Rules Japanese Firms Must Pay for Forced Labor."
20 International Crisis Group, *North East Asia's Undercurrents of Conflict*, 13.
21 *Japan Times*, "Japan, S. Korea Researchers at Odds."
22 In his opening speech, Bu Ping proclaimed: "In Japan, speeches and activities not admitting the responsibility for the war of aggression and denying the historical facts of the war have existed until now. Those irresponsible words and actions going against the common interests of the two countries have constantly hurt the public sentiment of a war victim nation." See the morning edition of *Mainichi Shimbun*, December 27, 2006; and Dickie and Pilling, "Sino-Japanese Historians Battle to Find Consensus."
23 See *Japan Times*, March 21, 2007; and *Xinhua*, March 21, 2007. The "Twenty-One Demands" refers to a set of demands that were issued by the Japanese Empire to the nominal government of China on January 18, 1915, and included the confirmation of Japan's acquisitions in Shandong Province; the formal recognition of Japan's spheres of influence in Manchuria, in Inner Mongolia, and over various railways, mines, metallurgical complexes, and so forth; and the barring of China from conceding any additional coastal or island territories to any foreign power other than Japan. The Demands resulted in two treaties between China and Japan, agreed upon on May 25, 1915.
24 *People's Daily*, "China-Japan Scholars' Report Completed"; *Agence France-Presse*, "New Study."
25 Even in this book, complete agreement was not possible to achieve. According to a key participant in the project, all three nations are producing slightly different version of the com-

mon history book. For instance, when referring to "comfort women," the Korean version uses "sex slaves," while the Japanese one uses "ianfu" (Japanese for "comfort women").

26. See Horvat in Shin, Park, and Yang, eds., *Rethinking Historical Injustice and Reconciliation*, 222.
27. Ibid.
28. For instance, Christian groups, imagery, and language played an important role in the Franco-German reconciliation, and even the concept of reconciliation has Christian overtones (i.e., forgiveness). It is difficult to envision an entirely analogous movement toward international reconciliation in Northeast Asia, which does not have the same degree of presence of transnational Christian groups. See Cole's introduction in Cole, ed., *Teaching the Violent Past*.
29. Lind, *Sorry States*, 32.
30. *Wikipedia*, "Bombing of Tokyo."
31. Selden, "Japanese and American War Atrocities."
32. Dower, *Embracing Defeat*, 473–74.
33. President Ronald Reagan signed the Civil Liberties Act of 1988, which offered apologies and reparations to survivors among the 110,000 Japanese and Japanese Americans who had been interned by the U.S. government in the years 1942–45. In this case, however, as Mark Selden notes, "the victims' descendants are American citizens and apologies proved to be good politics for the incumbent." Selden, "Japanese and American War Atrocities," 14.
34. While Mondale did not speak at the event in Tokyo, he told reporters following the visit that he "wanted to come ... to say how sorry we are for how people had to suffer and the destruction here." Mondale quoted in Herman, "Burning Memories," 40. Additionally, Pelosi's visit was significant in that she was the highest ranking U.S. official to visit any Japanese site memorializing victims while still in office. Former president Jimmy Carter visited the Hiroshima Memorial several years earlier but not in an official capacity. See *BBC News*, "Pelosi Visits Hiroshima Memorial."
35. See Ishi, Itoo, and Kasahara, "Tokyo War Crimes Tribunal," in the popular *Yamakawa Japanese History B* textbook.
36. Kingston, "Nanjing's Massacre Memorial."
37. Bix, "War Responsibility and Historical Memory," 17.
38. Ibid., 12.
39. Lind, *Sorry States*, 30–32.
40. Dower, *Embracing Defeat*, 444.
41. *Economist*, "The Ghost of Wartimes Past."
42. Hara, "Cold War Frontiers in the Asia-Pacific."
43. Dudden, "Dangerous Islands," 2.
44. Hara, "Cold War Frontiers in the Asia-Pacific." See also Hara's book, *Cold War Frontiers in the Asia-Pacific*.
45. Straub in Hasegawa and Togo, eds., *East Asia's Haunted Present*, 215.
46. For a more detailed discussion of the U.S. role in Northeast Asian historical reconciliation, see Shin, "Historical Disputes and Reconciliation."
47. See Straub in Hasegawa and Togo, eds., *East Asia's Haunted Present*.
48. Dudden, "Dangerous Islands," 2–3.
49. Rozman, "Japan and Korea," 26.
50. H.R. 121, 110th Cong. (2007).
51. Ikenberry, "Japan's History Problem." See also Shin, "Beyond Apology, Moral Clarity."
52. Matsuo, "Tokyo Needs Its Dresden Moment."

53 In Dower's view, the Tokyo trials focused on "crimes against peace" but ignored "crimes against humanity," including "murder, extermination, enslavement, deportation, and other inhumane acts committed before or during the war, or persecutions on political or racial grounds in execution of or in connection with any crime within the jurisdiction of the Tribunal, whether or not in violation of the domestic law of the country where perpetrated." Many war crimes against Asians such as forced labor, "comfort women," and mass killings of civilians belong to the second category. See Dower, *Embracing Defeat*, 473–74, 456.

54 A former judge at the Tokyo trial, B. V. A. Röling, recalled in 1983: "The prestige of the trial has also been severely damaged by the revelation of the existence in Manchuria of a Japanese laboratory for research into bacteriological weapons. These weapons were tested on prisoners of war and cost thousands of lives. This incident would have provided a case, rare at the Tokyo trial, of centrally organized war criminality. But everything connected with it was kept from the tribunal. The American military authorities wanted to avail themselves of the results of these experiments, criminally obtained by Japan, and at the same time to prevent them from falling into the hands of the Soviet Union. The judges in Tokyo remained ignorant. The Japanese involved in these crimes were promised immunity from prosecution in exchange for divulging the information obtained from the experiments." See Röling's introduction in Hosoya et al., eds., *The Tokyo War Crimes Trial*, 18.

55 Lind, *Sorry States*, 30–31.

56 Takino, "Visit to Hiroshima by President Bush Considered."

57 Straub in Hasegawa and Togo, eds., *East Asia's Haunted Present*, 215. As Takino of the *Mainichi* reports, "The plan did not materialize because a schoolgirl in Okinawa was raped by three U.S. marines in September that year."

58 See Kozak, "LeMay and the Tragedy of War."

59 Bork quoted in Vanderweert, "Seeking Justice for 'Comfort' Women," 181.

60 There was no specific legal reference to reparations from Germany, unlike with Japan, through the San Francisco Treaty.

61 See Tokudome, "POW Forced Labor Lawsuits."

62 One reason for the contrasting response by the U.S. government action may have to do with the difference in political mobilization of the respective ethnic communities. The Jewish American community has been better organized and continuously pressured the U.S. government to be proactive in dealing with this history issue. See Bazyler, *Holocaust Justice*; Sanua, *Let Us Prove Strong*; Shafir, *Ambiguous Relations*; and Shain, "Ethnic Diasporas and U.S. Foreign Policy." By contrast, the Asian American community is newer to the country and has been far behind in addressing the history issue in its members' home countries, though they were quite successful in redressing the wartime internment of Japanese Americans. However, recently they have been more active as illustrated by the case of House Resolution 121 on the comfort women. Mike Honda, a Japanese American legislator, introduced the resolution, and the Chinese and Korean American communities were mobilized in support. It is likely that Asian Americans will become more active on the history issue in the coming years and that, as American citizens, they can press the U.S. government to be more forthcoming. Activism among Asian Americans is an area that merits more careful attention as far as the U.S. role in dealing with the history question in Northeast Asia is concerned.

63 Dower quoted in Tokudome, "POW Forced Labor Lawsuits," 11.

64 Sneider, "The War over Words."

Chapter 7

Israelis and Germany after the Second World War

Is Reconciliation Possible?
Can Universal Lessons Be Drawn?

FANIA OZ-SALZBERGER

Israeli-Jewish readers are often surprised when they come across references to the Holocaust in East Asian literature. Such references are quite rare, but they are not expected to be otherwise. While Western, more specifically European, and in particular German remembrance of the genocide of the Jews by Nazi Germany is deemed historically necessary and morally essential, East Asia is not part of this set of expectations. Both geographic and cultural differentials keep spheres of remembrance apart, and while World War II is a common, indeed global, sphere of memory, its genocidal aspects are more circumscribed. Some scholars have at times *compared* the Jewish calamity to atrocities that took place in China or in Cambodia, but East Asian scholars and artists do not often ponder the Holocaust per se.[1] Haruki Murakami's short but poignant mention of the Adolf Eichmann trial in his novel *Kafka on the Shore* is, from an Israeli-Jewish perspective, a refreshing exception to the rule.[2]

Let us consider a stronger formulation of this absence of expectation: East Asia is deemed exempt from understanding the horror of the Holocaust, because the German atrocity toward Jews is seen by many descendants of both victims and perpetrators as historically unique and culturally singular. According to this approach, neither Japanese war atrocities in occupied lands nor Pol Pot's massacre of many of his own people can compare to the premeditated, systematic, highly technologized, and ideologically nurtured German bid to annihilate the Jewish nation en bloc.[3] Nor can the Holocaust be measured against Joseph Stalin's systematic massacre of Russian "antirevolutionary" dissidents, intellectuals, and even whole economic classes.[4]

This claim for the uniqueness of the Jewish genocide conducted by Nazi Germany has grown stronger in the past three decades, as scholars and intellectuals—Jewish and gentile—have argued against moves to "relativize" the Nazi atrocity by placing it on the same level as Stalinist extermination policies or other totalitarian horrors. In Germany, the ensuing debate became known during the 1980s as the *Historikerstreit*—the historians' conflict.[5] In subsequent years, numerous historians have published research and historiographical analyses offering evidence and theoretical considerations supporting the singularity of the mass murder of Jews under Nazism.[6] But as the term *Holocaust* has become commonplace for the genocide of the Jews, it has also been borrowed for numerous other crimes, including mass killings perpetuated in East Asia.[7] Many authors have voiced their aversion to this universalization of the terminology of the Holocaust, while others have opted for the more specific term *Shoah*, a Hebrew word taken from the Bible and deployed specifically, first in Israel and later elsewhere, to denote the German crime against the Jews. The word *Shoah* has become more commonplace for denoting the Holocaust in the wake of Claude Lanzmann's monumental 1985 documentary of the same name.[8] At present, many research centers, periodicals, conferences, and books aiming at comparative analyses opt for the combination "Holocaust and Genocide," which allows universalizing comparisons alongside an ongoing emphasis on the specificity of the German-Jewish case.

This uniqueness accrues not only to the sheer extent of the massacre but also to the aim to wipe a whole nation from the face of the earth: not just some of its members, or the residents of a geographic zone, or a particular social class. The singularity of the Holocaust stems from Germany's standing as a "nation of culture," steeped in European history and manners, and accommodating numerous Jewish people, Jewish texts and ideas, even Jewish names and words, deep within its cultural legacy.[9] Consider the Hebrew Bible, essential to Christianity in general and to Lutheran Protestantism in particular; consider the impact of Jewish thinkers such as Baruch Spinoza and Moses Mendelssohn on the German Enlightenment and indeed the gradual entry of German Jews into academic and scientific life in Germany following the Enlightenment and the nineteenth-century liberalization and emancipation. By the time Adolf Hitler came to power in 1933, a flourishing German culture—epitomized and peaking in the Weimar Republic—incorporated German-Jewish thinkers and scientists, writers and artists, lawyers and teachers at an ever-growing pace. Thus, anti-Semites were obliged to make a vast effort, both pseudoscientific (race theories mobilized to prove the inhumanity of the so-called Jewish race, economic theories purporting to prove their "parasitical" nature) and ideological (Hitler's *Mein Kampf* [1925] and its numerous offshoots), to position the Jews as the uttermost enemies of the German nation. The bureaucratic and logistical organization of the Final Solution was spearheaded from Berlin under the command of Eichmann, in full cooperation with the regime's senior leadership, and spread throughout Nazi-occupied and Nazi-sympathizing lands in a highly efficient network of evacuation, transportation, ghettoization, imprisonment in labor camps, and collective annihilation in death camps. The technology of multiple murders reached its evil nadir in the infamous gas chambers, where a specially adjusted chemical formula, Zyklon B, accomplished the fastest mass killing of the largest numbers of human beings in history. Perhaps the most poignant reminder of the total "otherness" came from the Holocaust survivor Yehiel Dinur, who wrote his novels under the pseudonym *Kazetnik 135633* (derived from the German acronym KZ for "concentration camp," along with his prisoner's serial number tattooed on his arm). In his testimony on the witness stand of the Eichmann trial, Dinur was asked by Attorney General Gideon Hausner about his unusual pseudonym. The trial protocol is as follows:

Q. What was the reason that you hid your identity behind the pseudonym "K. Zetnik," Mr. Dinur?

A. It was not a pen name. I do not regard myself as a writer and a composer of literary material. This is a chronicle of the planet of Auschwitz. I was there for about two years. Time there was not like it is here on earth. Every fraction of a minute there passed on a different scale of time. And the inhabitants of this planet had no names, they had no parents, nor did they have children. There they did not dress in the way we dress here; they were not born there and they did not give birth; they breathed according to different laws of nature; they did not live—nor did they die—according to the laws of this world. Their name was the number "Kazetnik."[10]

Shortly after making this statement, Dinur collapsed on the witness stand. His testimony became a traumatic collective memory among Israelis, and the term he coined in his testimony and in his novels for the Auschwitz concentration camp, the "other planet," became a pivotal part of Israeli Holocaust discourse. Auschwitz was not the only extermination camp, and not the only place where Zyklon B gas chambers were deployed, but it was the largest death complex. In Israel and beyond it has sunk into collective memory as the ultimate abode and symbol of evil.

Thus, apart from the vast dimensions and total annihilation policy of Nazi Germany's extermination of the Jews, the Holocaust is singled out by the devious sophistication of its intellectual sources and mass murder mechanisms: never has such an elaborate and "modern" ideology been executed in such a well-administered and technologically advanced manner.[11]

Another aspect of its uniqueness, which is highly relevant to the current context, is the deep affinity—especially in spheres of "high culture" such as scholarship, science, and the arts—and the intimate social proximity of the perpetrator and victim cultures. There were 505,000 Jews in Germany when the Nazi party ascended to power, and 80 percent of them held German citizenship. The majority of them, like hundreds of thousands of Jews in other Western and Central European countries, were thoroughly immersed in the national culture and shared in almost every aspect of its economic and social life. Numerous Jewish men had fought in the German army during the First World War, some of them lost life or limb, and many of them won medals of distinction. Most German Jews considered themselves proud Germans, and their collective legacy was German as well as Jewish, with both aspects often overlapping. No wonder that Nazi policies were primarily aimed at disassociating "Jewish" elements from the deepest bowels of German history and culture: burning Heinrich Heine's books, alongside many others, and purging numerous professors and scientists from the universities are just two examples of the significant effort to empty German culture of its great Jewish building blocks.[12] By the same token, a deep sense of belonging to the German nation and culture, like the First World War medals proudly toted by Jewish-German veterans, did not save any German Jew from Nazi persecution.

To this day, Israel's polity and culture are marked by the German legacy of some of its founders and builders. Israel's first university, the Hebrew University of Jerusalem, was established in 1925 largely by scholars educated in German universities of the Second Empire and the Weimar Republic eras. Main branches of learning, on both university and school levels, were directly influenced by German (including German-Jewish) scholarly traditions: philosophy; law; literature; ancient, medieval and modern history; biblical criticism; Jewish history; music; and art, to name but a few. Among the governmental branches of the young state of Israel, the Ministry of Justice and the Supreme Court were most deeply influenced by German legacies of jurisprudence, brought and developed by the German-born and German-educated founders of the top echelons of the Israeli judiciary. In the parliamentary sphere, several important parties, among them the Liberal Party and the Orthodox Agudat Yisrael, hailed from a German-Jewish ideological ancestry. Other aspects of the Israeli public sphere, including the extra-parliamentary movements for Jewish-Arab reconciliations beginning with Brit Shalom in the 1930s, the Israeli Civil Rights Association, and other rights-orientated nongovernmental organizations, were founded and led by German-born and German-educated activists. Modernizing approaches in Israel's Orthodox Jewish communities, too, were often based on the intellectual fruit of earlier generations of German-Jewish reformers.[13]

The cultural affinity is of particular interest in the present context because it pertains not only to the Holocaust itself but also to the post-Holocaust dialogues between Germans and Jews, and especially between Germans and Israeli Jews. As we shall see, that long-gone cultural intimacy, overshadowed by its horrific aftermath, remained a constant factor in Israeli engagement with the German past and in present-day relations. Germans, too, are deeply aware of the lost German-Jewish fabric of social and intellectual cohabitation.

The history of Israeli relations with postwar Germany and with its dark past covers four main periods, divided by watershed events; although complex processes such as those discussed here do not transform overnight, these events both symbolized and perpetuated subtle shifts in the ways that Israelis have thought and acted on matters pertaining to Germany and to the Holocaust. Certain elements in the history of German-Jewish-Israeli engagements with the Holocaust legacy might compare, correspond, or offer more universal lessons to other post-conflict societies dealing with their own memories of conflict and atrocity.

Alive are the *Nibelungen*.
Fire. Darkness. And *Judenrein*.
In the battlefields fall *die Jungen*

Und ruhig fliesst der Rhein.[14]
[...]
East, east, the battalions are riding!
But they know that the day is near,
Other rivers will flow pure and tidy.
But the Rhein will stay red. Never clear.

Thus wrote Nathan Alterman, perhaps the greatest of modern Hebrew poets, in Tel Aviv in 1942.[15] The poem was titled "The Liberation of Lorelei." It evoked the medieval German poem *Nibelungenlied* as well as Heinrich Heine's famous *Lorelei*: the nymph Lorelei combs her hair atop the eponymous rock above the river Rhine. The Nazis were steeped in this sort of Germanic lore, and while dispensing with Heine himself—he was a Jew by birth, his conversion to Christianity counted for nothing in the Nazi racist worldview—the legendary Germanic contents, which Heine made famous (despite his hidden and modern irony), were very much alive again in Hitler's Germany.

Alterman's poem, which like many other of his political essays in verse first appeared as a newspaper column, was engraved in the collective consciousness of the Israeli nation-in-making. Most memorable was the bottom line: Germany's rivers, like Germany's hands, can never again be cleansed of innocent blood.

How is Alterman's legacy faring in present-day Israel? In 1999, about 150,000 Israelis traveled to Germany for purposes of tourism, business, and study. Over the past decade that number has steadily grown to over 350,000 every year. Even in 2009, when global economic depression negatively affected the influx of tourists into almost all countries, the number of Israelis arriving in Germany grew by 8 percent compared to the previous year. Thousands of Israelis permanently reside in Berlin. German visitors, products, and cultural artifacts are welcome and commonplace in Israel.[16] Is there anything left of Alterman's bloody Rhine or of Kazetnik's "other planet"—namely, of the Israeli-Jewish commitment never to forget or forgive the Holocaust?

My answer to these questions, in a preliminary nutshell, is that a great deal has changed, and much has persisted. Israelis have not "normalized" their relation to Germany, but we may be witnessing a new type of anomaly.

In order to track and explicate the long process of Israeli postwar attitudes toward Germany, I would like to propose four major historical stages.

The first stage begins in the 1940s and ends with the Eichmann trial of 1961. This was a stage of absorption in two senses of the term: the arrival and reception of Holocaust survivors from Europe to Israel and a slow, halting process of collective awareness among Israeli Jews of the enormity and horror of the Holocaust. The year 1961 marked a colossal watershed, when the trial of Eichmann, a senior Nazi war criminal kidnapped in Argentina and brought to justice in Jerusalem, profoundly altered the collective remembrance of the Holocaust in Israel and elsewhere. The second stage, that of heightened awareness, shock, and reworking of memory, encompasses the trial and its immediate aftermath. But the same era paved, somewhat paradoxically, the road to diplomatic normalization of the relations between Israel and the "other Germany." In 1965, the Federal Republic of Germany and the state of Israel established full diplomatic relations, and shortly afterward the retired federal chancellor Konrad Adenauer visited Israel. These events—colossal, controversial, and consciousness heightening—open a third stage, in which Israeli discourses of Holocaust remembrance matured in several different channels: governmental, educational, literary, and artistic. While public engagement with the Shoah was increasingly ritualized, embedded in museums, school curricula, annual ceremonies, and official speeches, "private" discourses of Holocaust remembrance grew and flourished. Thus, the 1970s and the 1980s were an era of ritualization of memory but also of individual engagement with the past. Writers, filmmakers, and artists of the younger generation began reworking Holocaust memory in their individual ways. This process, at first slow and scattered, became highly significant in the 1990s and especially in the 2000s. The fourth stage in my proposed timeline begins in 1989, when the fall of the Berlin Wall and the ensuing unification of Germany a year later opened new floodgates, both geographic and psychological. The past two decades have witnessed an unprecedented rise in the number of Israelis visiting Germany, studying German, and taking an interest in numerous aspects of German politics, economics, society, and culture. The current stage is characterized by broad human encounters and intensification of relations, but also a new surge of remembrance and reworking of past legacies.

1945/48/49–1961: ABSORPTION

Our periodization begins with a triple entry—there were three "year zeros" in the history of German-Israeli relations. The Third Reich collapsed in

May 1945, the state of Israel was established in May 1948, and the Federal Republic of Germany came into being in May 1949. (Its eastern counterpart, the German Democratic Republic, established in October 1949, never had an official relationship with Israel.)

The establishment of Israel followed a vote of approval at the United Nations (UN) General Assembly in November 1947. This was the apex of six decades of efforts by the Zionist movement to create, develop, and legitimize a modern Jewish polity in the ancestral Land of Israel. While our present context does not enable us to dwell on the highly complex history of Zionism and the Jewish-Arab conflict over the Ottoman- and British-occupied region known as Palestine ("Land of Israel" for the Jews), the basic point is that the UN resolution granting sovereign statehood to both Jews and Palestinian Arabs crumbled soon after its issue. A bloody war of independence (from the Jewish standpoint) and *Nakba* ("calamity," from the Palestinian standpoint) were initiated in November 1947 by the Palestinian leadership's wholesale rejection of the UN partition plan. The war was internationalized in May 1948, immediately following Israel's Declaration of Independence, by several neighboring Arab nations that sent their regular armies to invade the new Jewish state. This conflict was a messy end to almost thirty years of British mandate in Palestine, a former region of the Ottoman Empire that had never been sovereign in modern times.[17]

In the immediate aftermath of the Holocaust, the horror and enormity of Nazi Germany's crimes against the Jews were reported by occupying forces, including Jewish fighting and rescue personnel, units recruited by the British army in Mandatory Palestine, and Jewish death camp survivors and refugees, many of whom strove to reach safety in the Jewish homeland. But the three years between the fall of the Third Reich and the establishment of Israel were marred by escalating Arab-Jewish conflict under the increasingly ineffective British mandate rule, and the flux of Holocaust survivors met with a resolute British refusal to grant entry to the thousands of refugees. The Jewish community in Mandatory Palestine, known as the Yishuv, was busy developing a political as well as a military infrastructure. Among the Yishuv's civil and paramilitary acts of anti-British defiance, a sustained effort was made to ship thousands of Jewish refugees from Europe, smuggle them onto the shores, and accommodate them in Jewish communities. Some of the attempts succeeded, and others failed, most famously in the case of the ship *Exodus* in 1947. Historical accounts of the role of Holocaust refugees in the politics and culture of pre-state Israel and early Israel have varied considerably: some scholars have argued that the Jewish leadership of the Yishuv exploited the plight of Europe's Jews to buttress the case for Israeli independence, making political, at times cynical, use of human tragedy for political ends.[18] Others have shown that the Zionist ideal of creating a Jewish homeland in Israel was powerfully shared by many of the Holocaust survivors and also by numerous European Jews among the 6 million who did not survive. A clear majority of over a quarter of a million Holocaust survivors who gathered in temporary postwar refuges in Europe were self-motivated to reach the Land of Israel and join in the building of a Jewish homeland.[19]

The main point in the present context is that the postwar Yishuv and the young state of Israel were not intensely preoccupied with the events of the Holocaust or with dealing directly with the defeated Germans. Instead, the main thrust of Israeli Jewish energy and awareness was aimed at achieving a Jewish nation-state, ousting the British mandate government (which was adamantly blamed and opposed for ignoring the plight of Jewish Holocaust refugees trying to migrate to their ancestral homeland), and pursuing the ascending paramilitary and military conflict with the Palestinians and their supporters in neighboring Arab countries.

During the 1950s, in the aftermath of 1948, the young state of Israel was concerned with building a political and economic infrastructure, absorbing a million Jewish immigrants (including both Holocaust survivors and refugees from Arab and other Islamic countries). It was an era of future-orientation and optimism, offering a healing experience of sorts for many survivors who were physically and psychologically strong enough to take part in the national project and mood. Here was a factor distinguishing Holocaust survivors in Israel from their counterparts in other countries, including the United States: they were able to experience and participate in a phase of nation building, shelving or postponing their dealings with their personal traumas and sharing a collective sense of meaning and mission.

On the other hand, many survivors were unable to make the requisite mental and cultural transition into the Israeli society-in-the-making, struggled with horrific private memories, and met with all too little sympathy and support in a society too busy with its own narrative of war and independence to heed the sad memories of Europe's annihilated Jewry. An extreme version of this collective repression of memory was the sense that European Jews were somehow partially responsible for their plight because they had allowed themselves to be passively victimized rather than join the Zionist movement and migrate to the Land of Israel ahead of the calamity. In this vein, early Israeli commemorations of the Shoah were particularly attuned to acts of active heroism and paramilitary opposition to the Nazis, favoring the narratives of the Warsaw Ghetto Uprising (1943) and the Jewish partisans.

In general, the memory of the Holocaust during this period was characterized by an "official" approach, created and disseminated by government institutions in charge of education and public rituals.[20] It is important to note that individual Holocaust narratives were not wholly absent—Israeli poets, in particular, began to represent the Holocaust in their work, some survivors started to tell their stories in public, and some private commemoration initiatives had begun—but such narratives were not yet central to pubic-sphere awareness. In retrospect, individuals as well as the Israeli collective related to the Holocaust in a way not dissimilar to what scientists later described in terms of post-traumatic repression. It took many years for Israelis, as well as Germans, to undo the silence and rework and articulate their experiences, or their parents' experiences, of the Nazi-perpetrated mega-trauma.

The two postwar German states were not in any way partners in remembrance: the German Democratic Republic, part of the Soviet bloc, was alienated from the Jewish state because the USSR had cut its ties with Israel when the latter opted for a Western orientation. The Federal Republic of Germany offered financial and technological aid to Israel in 1951, under the unfortunate title of "reparations." Israel's dire economic need brought David Ben-Gurion's government to accept the offer. A fierce debate ensued in the Israeli public arena, peaking in a violent demonstration near the Knesset (Israeli Parliament) on January 7, 1952. The reparations agreement, officially named the Luxembourg Agreement, was signed by German chancellor Konrad Adenauer and Israeli foreign minister Moshe Sharet on September 10, 1952.[21] But there was no talk of diplomatic rapprochement, moral closure, or human reconciliation. The vast majority of Israelis, throughout the 1950s and in many cases also during the following two decades, were averse to any contact with persons or things German: brand names, merchandise, and the German language itself were practically (though not legally) banned from public view. Nathan Alterman, in another famous political poem, insisted that "reparations" be replaced by "return of looted property": indeed, Israelis could not see the German payments made to Jews in the 1950s and thereafter as any manner of compensation; rather, it was seen as a disproportionately small part of the stolen property and the destroyed lives of 6 million Jewish victims. Nor did Israelis, or Germans, or indeed the international community, cast doubt on Israel's entitlement to receive part of the returned loot. Israel was generally conceived as direct heir to the dead Jews of Europe (though victims and their descendants who relocated to other parts of the world were not deprived of their individual entitlements). As we have seen, this collective entitlement, albeit questioned in recent years by Israeli scholars and anti-Israeli polemicists, is nevertheless deeply rooted in the sense of yearning and belonging to Israel expressed by numerous victims and survivors.[22]

Paradoxically, Israeli Jews were at this stage far more "European" in their collective orientation than the ensuing generations; in 1960, after the mass immigration of Jews from Muslim countries, over 50 percent of Israel's Jewish population was still European-born.[23] For many of them, German legacies continued to figure prominently in their literary, musical, and intellectual preferences. Thousands of German-born Israelis spoke and read, in the privacy of their homes, a language whose very sound was considered an abomination in the public sphere. Significantly, German books—especially but not exclusively by anti-Nazi prewar authors and by the new postwar generation of West German authors—were translated into Hebrew and avidly read and discussed during the early postwar decades when all other importations from Germany were frowned upon.[24] The postwar Israeli reception of German books proved more tolerant than parallel attitudes in other cultural fields: while the nineteenth-century German composer Richard Wagner, beloved by the Nazis, was (and to a large extent still is) collectively shunned by Israeli audiences, children's books from Germany (especially by Erich Kästner and Karl May) were translated into Hebrew as early as the 1950s.[25] The writings of philosopher Friedrich Nietzsche, another Nazi favorite, were taught at the Hebrew University in Jerusalem and serially translated into Hebrew beginning in the mid-1960s. Thus, the main cultural legacy of the early phase, still powerfully prevalent in Israel today, is a deep cultural ambivalence about Germany—and, by extension, Europe as a whole.[26]

Thus, the prewar phase of Jewish-Israeli attitudes toward Germany's Nazi past was marked by collective and individual ambivalence, typifying a very gradual process of "absorption": an influx of survivor-refugees were invited to join the fresh and energetic Israeli narrative rather than relate their own stories. Governmental acceptance of payments from the Federal Republic of Germany alongside a partial "official remembrance" overshadowed individual narratives of memory. While some historians have fiercely criticized this collective, nation-centered attitude to the Holocaust, others (including myself) see this process in terms of an understandable delay, collective as well as individual, to come to grips with the enormity of the German genocide of the Jews. It took almost two decades after the end of the World War II for Israeli Jews—along with other Jews, many Germans, and the global community—to begin to delineate and grasp the vast dimensions of Nazi atrocities. The Eichmann trial, discussed below, was to become a major estuary for the release of memory and engagement.

1961–1970S: HEIGHTENED AWARENESS, DIPLOMATIC RAPPROCHEMENT

The trial of a senior Nazi perpetrator of the Holocaust, Eichmann, in Jerusalem in 1961 was a watershed moment in the history of Holocaust remembrance in Israel and one of the most important chapters in global recollection and understanding of the genocide of the Jews.

Eichmann (1906–1962) was a senior SS officer, ranked Oberstürmbannführer, who was appointed by the SS commander General Reinhard Heydrich and by the senior civil authorities of the Nazi regime to organize and coordinate the various phases of the Final Solution, the systematic annihilation of European (and subsequently world) Jewry as resolved at the Wannsee Conference in 1942. A dedicated Nazi ideologue and highly capable bureaucrat, Eichmann masterminded the deportation of Jews to ghettos, concentration camps, and death camps throughout the German-occupied territories of Europe. After fleeing to Argentina following the collapse of the Third Reich, he was traced and abducted by the Israeli security service known as Mossad, indicted and tried by the Jerusalem District Court, sentenced to death, and hanged in May 1962.[27] The impact of the Eichmann trial for Israeli collective memory was from the very beginning, and has remained, nothing less than momentous.

For the world, the trial's most famous outcome was Hannah Arendt's book *Eichmann in Jerusalem*, first published in 1963. But the Israeli interpretations of the trial were, on the whole, radically different from Arendt's understanding of Eichmann's stature as an ordinary "small man" in the clutch of historical events, exemplifying what she called the "banality of evil."[28] The witnesses at the trial, Jewish victims conveying firsthand testimonials, and the numerous courtroom viewers and hundreds of thousands of radio listeners encountered a different Eichmann, ideologically prepared and consciously active on behalf of an exceptionally evil political strategy of mass murder.

The testimonies aired in the trial came to constitute the first corpus of eyewitness accounts ever to reach the Israeli public. The materials filtered into classroom syllabi and rituals of remembrance. An important shift gradually took place in the public image of the survivors: no longer passive victims and "sheep to the slaughter" but individual heroes of epic dimensions. Sensitivity to private narratives and to human differences grew in time. A new generation of writers and artists growing up in the 1950s and 1960s recalled the Eichmann trial as a major childhood event. Sons and daughters of survivors began listening more closely to their parents' stories, or—very often—questioning their parents' silence and encouraging them to articulate their memories for the benefit of posterity.

Heightened awareness of the Holocaust was also fed by a growing sense of existential anxiety among Israelis. By the mid-1960s, it became clear that the Armistice Agreement of 1949 between Israel and its hostile Arab neighbors was not maturing into peace but rather deteriorating into impending war. The years prior to the 1967 Six-Day War were characterized by attempts of Palestinians in exile to return to their old homes either by individual attempts at penetrating the border or, increasingly, through political and paramilitary organization. The larger Arab states bordering Israel—Egypt, Syria, and Jordan—armed themselves in preparation for open warfare, diplomatically and sometimes militarily supported by the rest of the Arab world. Many Israelis, including numerous survivors of the Holocaust and of earlier anti-Semitic pogroms, were thrown back to darker times. A new understanding of and sympathy for the constantly threatened Diaspora Jewish life began replacing the old Israel-born haughtiness toward Diaspora victimhood.

At the same time—and of great relevance to the present context—a new awareness of postwar Germany was emerging. Israelis began to turn their gaze, and heighten their curiosity, about present-day Germans. It was too early a time for person-to-person dialogue, but the governments of Israel and the Federal Republic were deep in discussion over the establishment of diplomatic ties. Israel's pre-1967 sense of international isolation and strategic weakness was a weighty factor in the willingness of Israel's leaders to reach for the friendly hand of the German Federal Republic. The two countries established full diplomatic relations in 1965, in an agreement signed by Prime Minister Levi Eshkol and Chancellor Ludwig Erhard. But when they exchanged ambassadors, the absence of "normality" was reflected even in the two envoys' biographies: the German ambassador to Jerusalem, Rolf Pauls, was a former Wehrmacht soldier, and the Israeli ambassador in Bonn, Asher Ben-Natan, was a Vienna-born Jew whose mother tongue was German. Immediately after the official ceremony in Bonn, Ben-Natan drove to Cologne to attend a memorial ceremony for the murdered Jews. Meanwhile, in Jerusalem, as Pauls handed his credentials to President Zalman Shazar, a large group of demonstrators stood outside the residence, crying, "Six million times no!"[29]

Former prime minister Ben-Gurion and former chancellor Adenauer, both retired by 1965, were the true architects of Israeli-German rapprochement. As founding fathers of their young countries, and drawing on their enormous prestige in their respective nations, neither was particularly reliant on public opinion. Both leaders were awake to the profound historical and moral dimension of their step, and both were also attuned to politically pragmatic considerations. Israel needed strong international allies and suppliers of civil and military commodities, while Adenauer's coalition was tottering. In the broader context of the Cold War, Israel's Arab enemies were sponsored by the Soviets, and Egypt had become closely linked with the German Democratic Republic. West Germany was urged to take sides. Moral and utilitarian considerations, government interests, and public opinion were uniquely entangled in the German-Israeli rapprochement.[30]

Within Israel the onus was, of course, on Ben-Gurion, who faced intense and emotional opposition to reconciliation with Germany. Still, Israeli public opinion and (more poignantly) Israeli society in general proved mature enough to offer polite hospitality to the aging Adenauer, who visited Ben-Gurion in his home in the Negev desert in 1966. Increasingly, Israelis were becoming aware of a new generation of Germans. They encountered the "other Germany," an expression made popular by Ben Gurion himself. Young Germans began arriving in Israel in the mid-1960s, volunteering to work in kibbutzim and health and community institutions. Those young people, representing a process of remembrance and repentance taking place in West Germany, were made welcome, although not all kibbutzim and institutions were willing to accept German volunteers. Those first encounters between Germans and Jewish Israelis were the humble beginning of a people-to-people interaction that has increasingly characterized, and nowadays overwhelmingly defines, German-Israeli relations.[31]

However, a great many Israelis neither applauded nor trusted the "other Germany." Testimonials of the Eichmann trial were too fresh and too painful to ignore. German products, especially those with brand names pointing to companies with a Nazi past, such as Siemens and Volkswagen, were unpopular with consumers.[32] But present-day Germany was not merely "guilty by association." As a small number of Israelis began visiting West Germany, in some cases also the East, and committing their impressions to print, it transpired that German institutions still employed former Nazis and that the legal system had allowed many murderers to walk away unpunished (or, in some prominent cases, under-punished). From Bonn, the Israeli journalist Amos Elon sent stories to his newspaper, *Haaretz*, describing the numerous Nazi fingerprints, the ex-Nazis still present in the German juridical system, and the painfully light sentences given, in those days, to former SS and Gestapo members by the federal courts.[33] For many Israelis, the "other Germany" remained far from "other."

THE 1980S: INDIVIDUAL ENGAGEMENT

The best way to chart the subtle change that took place during the 1980s, mainly among the younger generation of Israelis, is to consider one book, one film, and one musical album. There were other effective books, films, and works of music and art relevant to our story, but the three singled out here lead and reflect a new stage in Israeli dealings with Germany and its Nazi past.

David Grossman's second novel, and his first international best seller, appeared in 1986. *See Under: Love* presented an unusual engagement with the Holocaust and the destroyed Jewish European past, authored by a thirty-two-year-old former radio broadcaster.[34] In a highly original way, the book juxtaposed an Israeli child growing up in the sad and unspeaking home of Holocaust survivors with two Jewish-Polish writers and Holocaust victims, one historical (the author Bruno Schulz) and the other fictitious. The novel's final part, an encyclopedia-like account of a Jewish baby's short life, completes the novel's unusual journey into pain, memory, and fragile rationality. *See Under: Love* is considered by many Israeli readers to be one of the masterpieces of modern Hebrew literature. In a sense, it reinvented

Holocaust fiction, helping to bring marginalized earlier authors (including fine novelists such as Aharon Appelfeld) to center stage and paving a road for a generation of younger writers to wrestle, in disparate ways, with the Holocaust and its aftermath. Increasingly, they also wrestle with present-day Germany and Germans; Grossman himself was historically more circumscribed, but his effective articulation of both horrors and remembrance opened a veritable floodgate.[35]

Two years later, in 1988, filmmaker Orna Ben Dor-Niv created her documentary film *Because of That War*, focusing on the album *Ashes and Dust* produced in the same year by singer-songwriter Yehuda Poliker and his partner, lyricist Ya'akov Gilad. Both filmmaker and musicians were born to Holocaust survivors, and the songs in the album tackle the stories of the musicians' families and their own feelings as members of the "second generation." A blend of rock, pop, and Greek folk music, it was the first Israeli album to tackle the Holocaust directly and persistently. Ben Dor-Niv interviewed the musicians and their parents and showed one of the sons traveling to Auschwitz and one of the mothers narrating her horrendous experiences to an audience of young schoolchildren. The novelty in Ben Dor-Niv's film was its wholly personal vista. It was neither "educational" nor "ideological" and made no references to Zionism; Israel is present in the Gilad-Poliker songs only by delicate insinuation: a small room overlooking the Mediterranean, a private safe haven for tormented refugees rather than a national homeland for a persecuted people. The personal angle of *Ashes and Dust*, gently highlighted in *Because of That War*, corresponded to the unique individual voice of Grossman. To be sure, *See Under: Love* employs broader lenses, addressing Jewish identity, the Hebrew language, and European literature in its complex plot. But Grossman's work, like that of Poliker, Gilad, and Ben Dor-Niv, enabled a generation of young artists and audiences to come to grips with the German-Jewish past through individual, informal, and nonideological prisms.

After the fall of the Berlin Wall in the autumn of 1989, followed by Germany's unification, this newly personalized sphere of Israeli encounters with the Nazi past took a significant new turn. An era of individual travel and personal encounters began in the 1990s and gained social and cultural momentum in the 2000s. It brought Israelis and Germans, especially the younger ones, children and grandchildren of persecutors and victims, into a proximity, even familiarity, that had not existed between Jews and Germans since the collapse of the Weimar Republic.

1989–PRESENT: HUMAN ENCOUNTERS AND INTENSIFICATION

The fall of the Berlin Wall was not the sole reason for the new influx of Israeli visitors into Central and Eastern Europe, particularly into Poland and Germany. Other contributing factors include the significant improvement in the Israeli economy and its rising quality of life and the shift toward independent travel abroad in all age groups. In particular, younger Israelis have been traveling the world, often as backpackers to East Asia and South America but also as students, artists, and cultural tourists. In the 2000s, this generation discovered Germany, especially Berlin.[36]

In earlier decades, very few Israelis went to Germany. The vast majority of Holocaust survivors never even revisited their countries of origin, let alone the land of the erstwhile perpetrators. Israelis were not avid travelers during the 1960s and early 1970s, for economic as well as cultural reasons. Their engagement with the genocide of European Jewry and the loss of a millennium of European-Jewish life took place at home, in Israel. It was conceived through books, stamped into rituals, informed by an ever-weakening flow of personal memories of immigrants and survivors. For those born in Israel, Europe was a dim, shady, verbal, bookish memory: part dream, part nightmare.[37]

This is no longer the case. Europe today, specifically Germany, is host to many thousands of Israeli tourists, businesspeople, artists, students, and even schoolchildren. Many of those are part-time or full-time "history tourists," travelers of memory. To be sure, most Israelis would not imagine Europe as their home. It is, rather, a new journey into the past. This symbolic revisitation of Europe, and in particular of Germany, has nurtured recent literature, cinema, political debate, and conceptions of identity.

Israeli-German encounters among young people as well as academics, intellectuals, and artists have been greatly facilitated by several philanthropic foundations, mostly German or German-Israeli ones, that initiate and sponsor numerous educational projects, scholarships, conferences, and dialogue groups in both countries. Interestingly, the individual itineraries and the philanthropically funded encounters often overlap. The German effort to conserve memory and encourage dialogue seems to correspond to a real fascination with Jews, and the same is true of Israeli interest in Germany and the Germans. A geographic dimension has been added to the historical one: previous generations of Israelis merely read; today's

Israelis visit the sites, rediscovering the lost landscape of their ancestors.

Israeli literature has never before been so preoccupied with Germany. In recent years, not only young writers but also several major Israeli authors have dedicated novels and essays to Germany and Berlin. The list includes novelists A. B. Yehoshua, Amos Oz, Yoram Kaniuk, and Chaim Be'er. All these authors have published fiction or nonfiction describing visits to Germany and close encounters with Germans in recent years. The books display various attitudes toward Germans today, but they all share a sense of place, especially of Berlin, that has been absent from Israeli literature for many years.[38]

The plot of the successful Israeli film *Walk on Water* (2004) culminates in Berlin. Director Eytan Fox and writer Gal Uchovsky endow present-day Berlin with a strong sense of place, because for them and for their generation of young, cosmopolitan Israelis, Berlin is indeed *the* place where things are happening, where lives are transformed. *Walk on Water*, like its literary counterparts, does not evade or dwarf the Nazi past; it conjoins the past and the present, including the deep fascination and attraction mutually felt by young Israelis and Germans, into a story of generations, dark secrets, and humanity.

Films, novels, travelogues, media reports, websites, and blogs all seem to tell many variations of one story: Berlin is becoming, for Israelis today, the greatest portal into Europe, the European past, and particularly the Jewish European past. It is, to be sure, a past-haunted portal, but it is also future oriented. Berlin is a globalopolis in which Israelis and Germans will be talking and writing, shooting films, and observing one another, perhaps for generations to come. To a certain extent, Tel Aviv is Berlin's natural counterpart in this quest: an increasing number of Germans have recently been traveling to Tel Aviv or settled there, although it does not match the number of Israelis drawn to Berlin. This phenomenon teaches an important lesson about the particular role of cities, rather than countries, to post-conflictual human encounters and interactions. Large and cosmopolitan cities are more open and future oriented, less xenophobic and nationalistic, than other parts of their respective countries.

To some degree, this human interaction has been marred in recent years by a problematic political climate for Israel. Israel's governments in the 2000s came under severe criticism from many European, including German, observers of the Middle Eastern situation. The unresolved Jewish-Arab and Israeli-Palestinian issues have made attitudes toward Israel increasingly polemical. Legitimate criticism is sometimes tainted by anti-Israeli sentiments that border on anti-Semitism, and at times downright anti-Semitism is at play. Unfortunately, critique of government policies on the Palestinian issue—a critique often shared and openly voiced by moderate Israelis too—becomes a wholesale denunciation of all Israelis, even a denial of Israel's right to exist.[39] At its most extreme, it links Israel's controversial policies with statements about the general features of the Jews. In some quarters in Germany, Nazi statements are sounded once again. While this climate of opinion is not directly related to our topic, it does affect day-to-day encounters between Germans and Israelis. While some Israelis naturally join in some criticisms of their own government, others fear that a deep, unchanged anti-Semitism is affecting political discourse and casting a shadow over the German ambition to overcome the sinister past.[40]

But the current phase of Israeli-German encounters, especially in Berlin, can have surprising effects on the Arab-Jewish conflict. In particular, Arab citizens of Israel (who amount to 20 percent of Israel's population) who arrive in Berlin as part of the recent wave of tourists and temporary residents discover their Israeli identity afresh. I interviewed several Arab Israelis in Berlin who spoke of a new sense of understanding of the historical plight of the Jews. In Berlin, they reconsidered the Israeli part of their identity, became closer to their Jewish countrymen, and shared with them a sense of historical displacement and remembrance.[41]

The present phase in Israeli-German relations is about re-familiarization rather than reconciliation, forgiveness, or "normalization." More Israelis and Germans meet and talk than ever before, and past as well as present relations are evoked in scholarship, literature, and art. The German word *Normalisierung*, used in some quarters to express the wish of the present generation to leave the dark aspects of German-Jewish history behind, is not part of the Israelis' lexicon. Rather than normalization, one might talk of a new level of anomaly. Civil societies, rather than governments, are conversing directly and intensely. Whatever political issues are raised or will be raised in this ongoing conversation, it has already achieved a great deal by inspiring creativity and allowing numerous individuals a closer look into the lives and minds of their interlocutors, the descendants of their grandparents' worst enemies.

What, if anything at all, can an East Asian observer derive from the unique story of the Jewish-Israeli-German encounter? This chapter has placed great emphasis on the singularity of this case. Does this mean that no lessons can be drawn for other post-conflictual cultures exploring routes of reconciliation and re-familiarization?

I do not think so. The German-Israeli relationship may indeed have untranslatable aspects, but it also has a great deal to suggest to other sites of historical-cultural rapprochement. In each of the stages of the evolving relationship, some elements are universal, or at least potentially applicable to other societies.

The first stage, the earliest phase of Jewish-Israeli engagement with the Nazi past, should offer the simple lesson that calamities are slow to sink in. Prior to reconciliation, the affected societies must come to grips with their immediate past, either as victims or as perpetrators. They also need to sort out the inner divisions within them—for example, between survivors and others in the victim nation or, on the side of former perpetrators, between culprits, innocents, and the numerous "bystanders" who were aware of atrocities but did nothing to stop them. In short, post-conflictual societies must conduct inner dialogues before (or at least during) any attempt at dialogue with former enemies, persecutors, or victims.

The second stage in the Israeli-German case is difficult to convey to other parts of the world, because the Eichmann trial was an unusually poignant turning point in collective consciousness. Perhaps the nations of former Yugoslavia, or some African nations, in the wake of juridical processes of war criminals may experience some of the intense disclosure felt by Israelis (and to some extent by Germans) during and after the Eichmann trial. In other societies, similar effects might come from other kinds of testimonials—memoirs, biographies, and fiction—that address the human need both to tell of past events and to learn about them.

Another important lesson has to do with the differing pace of governments and civil societies in their parallel paths for rapprochement. Diplomatic reconciliation might be easier to accomplish than societal reconciliation, as the Israeli case suggests. But, conversely, there may be cases in which post-conflictual societies were mutually more forgiving than their respective governments. My main point here is that "official" and "unofficial" processes of reconciliation are seldom synchronized. Historically, governments have often led the way and set agendas of both war and peace, but in recent years, in cyberspace and in real space, individuals and social groups are capable of affecting collective agendas.

The third stage is, in my mind, both crucial and universal. It pertains to the removal of "post-conflict management" from governmental monopoly to a spectrum of individuals, perhaps heralded by writers and artists, and followed by numerous private persons. Both memory and the prospects of reconciliation (or re-familiarization) are individuated and made personal. Public rituals of remembrance may continue and even expand, but they too can be fed by artistic and personal expressions of memory and future hope.

Finally, the fourth and current stage of interaction between Israelis and Germans covers new ground, again universally applicable, of travel and encounter at close quarters. Cities and their social and cultural venues become the best arenas for interaction. Books, music, and the visual arts can flourish in a globalized urban climate, which still retains distinct national and individual narratives. This stage not only enhances interpersonal encounters but also promotes cultural energy and creativity. The past is neither forgotten nor forgiven, and there is no "normalization." Instead, a young generation with a stronger hold on global networking and cross-border interaction can find new ways of exploring, expressing, and challenging the past. And, for the first time, their immediate audience can comprise the "others," members of the previously hated opponent, grandchildren of their grandparents' worst enemies.

The German-Jewish-Israeli case is indeed unique, both in the monstrosity of the crimes committed by Germans against Jews and in the past cultural intimacy of the lost German-Jewish existence. While the former singularity cannot and should not be pushed into comparative debates, the latter is relevant to many other parts of the world. Cultural familiarity is a hideous basis for genocide, but it can also make re-familiarization a great journey of discovery. This, I hope, is a lesson capable of crossing continents and oceans.

1   Ma, "Contrasting Two Survival Literatures"; Simon, *Laws of Genocide*.
2   Murakami, *Kafka on the Shore*, 131–32.
3   Simon, *Laws of Genocide*, 103–12.
4   Kershaw and Lewin, eds., *Stalinism and Nazism*, 1–25.
5   Augstein, *Historikerstreit*; Evans, *The New Nationalism and the Old History*; Baldwin, ed., *Reworking the Past*.
6   See especially Broszat and Friedlander in Baldwin, ed., *Reworking the Past*; and Bauer, *Rethinking the Holocaust*.
7   For recent examples, see Chang, *The Rape of Nanking*; and Morelli, *Trauma and Healing*.
8   Felman in Hartman, ed., *Holocaust Remembrance*.
9   Elon, *The Pity of It All*.
10 The Nizkor Project, "The Trial of Adolf Eichmann: Session 68," pt. 1.

11 Friedlander, *The Years of Extermination*; Bauer, *Rethinking the Holocaust*.
12 Elon, *The Pity of It All*; Grunfeld, *Prophets without Honor*.
13 Gelber, "A New Homeland"; Oz-Salzberger and Salzberger, "The Secret German Sources of the Israeli Supreme Court."
14 *Nibelungen*—a legendary royal dynasty celebrated in a medieval German epic, *Nibelungenlied*. *Judenrein*—Jew-free, official Nazi title for the annihilation of Jewish populations. *Jungen*—youngsters. *Und ruhig fliesst der Rhein*—and calmly flows the Rhine (quoted from Heinrich Heine's poem, *Lorelei*).
15 Alterman, *The Seventh Column*, 2:226–27 (translation is mine).
16 *Israel Central Bureau of Statistics Report*, 2010; Oz-Salzberger, *Israelis in Berlin*; Bartos, "Israeli-German Relations."
17 For general histories of Mandatory Palestine and Israeli independence, see Gilbert, *Exile and Return*; Sachar, *History of Israel*; and Segev, *One Palestine, Complete*. For accounts of the 1948 war exemplifying the ongoing historical debate and "clash of narratives," compare Gelber, *Palestine 1948*, with Pappé, *The Making of the Arab-Israeli Conflict*.
18 Zertal, *From Catastrophe to Power*; Zertal, *Israel's Holocaust*.
19 Bauer, *Rethinking the Holocaust*, 242–60.
20 Don-Yehiya, "Memory and Political Culture"; Shapira, "The Holocaust."
21 Sagi, *German Reparations*.
22 On Israeli scholars' questioning of collective entitlement, see Zertal, *Israel's Holocaust*. On victims and survivors and collective entitlement, see Bauer, *Rethinking the Holocaust*, 242–60.
23 Oz-Salzberger in Persson and Sträth, eds., *Reflections on Europe*.
24 Sheffi, *Vom Deutschen ins Hebräisch*; Oz-Salzberger in Ollov, ed., *The Legacy of the German-Jewish Religious and Cultural Heritage*.
25 On Israelis and Wagner, see Sheffi, *The Ring of Myths*.
26 Reinharz and Shavit, *Glorious, Accursed Europe*; Oz-Salzberger, *Israelis in Berlin*.
27 Yablonka, *The State of Israel vs. Adolf Eichmann*.
28 Arendt, *Eichmann in Jerusalem*.
29 Oz-Salzberger in Feinberg, ed., *Rück-Blick auf Deutschland*.
30 Deutschkron, *Israel und die Deutschen*; Ben-Natan and Hansen, eds., *Israel und Deutschland*.
31 Oz-Salzberger, *Israelis in Berlin*; Bartos, "Israeli-German Relations."
32 My personal experience may be of relevance here: our family never buys Siemens products. My mother-in-law and her sister were teenage slave workers at a Siemens plant in the Ravensbrück concentration camp.
33 Elon, *Journey through a Haunted Land*.
34 Grossman, *See Under: Love*.
35 Morahg, "Israel's New Literature of the Holocaust."
36 Oz-Salzberger, *Israelis in Berlin*; Oz-Salzberger in Feinberg, ed., *Rück-Blick auf Deutschland*.
37 Reinharz and Shavit, *Glorious, Accursed Europe*; Oz-Salzberger in Persson and Sträth, eds., *Reflections on Europe*.
38 Oz-Salzberger in Feinberg, ed., *Rück-Blick auf Deutschland*.
39 Gerstenfeld, "Anti-Israelism and Anti-Semitism."
40 Joffe in Gerstenfeld, ed., *European-Israeli Relations*; Bartos, "Israeli-German Relations," 73–91.
41 Oz-Salzberger, *Israelis in Berlin*.

PART IV

THE PAST AS PRESENT AND THE PSYCHOLOGICAL RESPONSE TO DIFFERENT KINDS OF MEMORY

Chapter 8

Historical Memories and International Relations in Northeast Asia

GILBERT ROZMAN

As Daniel Sneider argues in this volume, when debates on the past resumed after the Cold War, instead of contributing to reconciliation, they exacerbated distrust through distortions aimed at rallying domestic support behind a narrowly contentious cause. Igor Torbakov, in a later chapter, explains for Eastern Europe how politicizing history serves the construction of a national identity that maximizes public support for the powers that be. He describes recent nationalization of history at the expense of the histories of other nations, which is also the pattern in Northeast Asia, where, just as the economic basis for regionalism is strengthening, the necessary shared memories are being jeopardized by the search for national pride pitting one state against another. In comparison to the tensions over historical narratives in Europe, those in Northeast Asia pose a more serious threat to peace, as seen especially in the linkage drawn in China to a territorial dispute with Japan.

Europeans look back to a closely shared history and civilization as well as postwar alliance cooperation to achieve shared goals. When the subject of historical memory arises, there is broad consensus limiting it to a single period and one chief transgressor, Nazi Germany. Postwar Germany clearly differentiates itself from the crimes attributed to Adolf Hitler and those who rallied behind him, but important too is the fact that today no state sees an advantage in international relations in dredging up the history of Nazi aggression, let alone in dwelling on transgressors further back in history, or in demonizing the United States for its conduct during the Cold War. In the case of Northeast Asia, historical memories are much more complex, while the significance of historical comparisons for current international relations and perceived regime legitimacy is much greater. For China, it continues to grow.

One historical memory has overshadowed all others in its impact on bilateral relations in Northeast Asia for the past two-thirds of a century. It is, of course, the recollection of Japan's colonialism and imperialist aggression prior to 1945, exacerbated by anger over revisionist episodes of rationalizing its conduct and denying both the full measure of suffering of its victims and the importance of avoiding additional offense. In turn, the Japanese became obsessed with the way China and South Korea played the "history card" without due recognition of Japan's transformation in the postwar era and its legitimate right to defense, confusing reasonable realism with offensive revisionism.[1] Yet two other historical memories are gaining ground with potential to overtake the fixation regarding Japan's past. One is the narrative of the United States as an imperialist state with racist attitudes, which imposed its culture as well as its view of critical historical events on skeptical Asian audiences. To some extent, Japan and South Korea are influenced by this theme, and China is making it a cornerstone of a more assertive national identity. The other narrative drawing close scrutiny is that of China as a Sinocentric and Communist state that arrogantly claims the right to reconstruct a hierarchical order and discipline states critical of its values and behavior.[2] This view is spreading in South Korea and Japan, and elsewhere too.

To assess how the third of these historical memories is influencing current international relations in the region, selected writings from China, from 2010 and 2011 are used. The absence of Chinese refutations on the historical themes covered makes it clear that these sources convey an approved worldview, which can be appreciated by avoiding narrow coverage of one period. History informs the broader concept of national identity with consideration of retrospective views of three eras: (1) the premodern era, to the extent that it is deemed responsible for the second era; (2) the modern era leading up to the latter half of the 1940s; and (3) the Cold War era, to the degree that it is considered an extension of the second era. The second period has, of course, proven the most provocative: Japan's militarism, China's Communist revolution, and American imperialism and wartime conduct in 1945. Yet the earliest era matters too as the time of China's tributary system and, in many Chinese accounts, the incubation period of Japanese militarism, South Korean impudence, and American imperialism/hegemony. Further, the Cold War era consists of more than two decades of virulent U.S.-Soviet and Sino-U.S. enmity, since Chinese depict it anew as the time of the Korean War and engrained rivalry rooted in the second era with lasting consequences in the post–Cold War, which, despite a prevailing positive image of relations in this region apart from North Korea, sparks unexpected controversy. If one era were treated in isolation, we would miss the way the three periods together shape thinking about the past, notably at times of a spike in national identity, as in the late 1980s in Japan, the early 2000s in South Korea, and, most relevant today, 2009 through 2012 in China.[3] Chinese views fixed in memories centered on East Asia are stressed here rather than the obvious U.S.-Soviet competition.

Serious professional historians and international relations experts in China, as in Japan and South Korea, are reluctant to parrot revisionist historical claims, at least in the extreme manner they are now presented. China's leadership is still in a position to sever some of the assumed linkages, for instance by positively evaluating new developments in Sino-U.S. relations and downplaying the idea that the United States' policy is to contain China. In that case, experts would be freer to present differing arguments, and at the grassroots level historical memories that may not have taken firm root could lose some of their tenacity. Academic exchanges and joint projects may still give foreigners some opportunity to counter extreme viewpoints. Yet hopes for challenging the emergent national identity narrative with decidedly one-sided historical memories are faint, given recent trends and the nature of China's politics.

The political elites of Northeast Asia are concerned with regime legitimacy. Japan's elite, primarily in the Liberal Democratic Party (LDP) but not limited to that party, decided that only through historical vindication, however interpreted, could Japan become a "normal state." Although maintaining U.S. alliance relations and "reentering Asia" matter too as the international mechanisms for Japan to shed the stigma of a "defeated power," they do not substitute for new historical judgments as the breakthrough objective. When in December 2012 the LDP won a landslide victory and Shinzo Abe returned as prime minister, ardent revisionists were heartened that their champion would realize the long-sought historical "normalcy." South Korea's elite, predominantly in conservative parties, have contended with the rival claims of the North Korean regime to be the legitimate heir to the Korean state. If South Korea enjoys an advantage in international recognition and various symbols of a successful state, those do not obviate the drive to transform the narrative of the past in order to strengthen the South's legitimacy, leading toward reunification. While Park Geun-hye in December 2012 defeated the progressive candidate, reducing the role of national identity in dealing with North Korea and Japan, she had to be sensitive to criticism of her father, Park Chung Hee, being too soft on Japan. The Chinese Communist Party has the most problems with regime legitimacy, in light of the record of the Mao era and the absence of democratic elections. Much more than the other two East Asian states, it is obsessed with constructing a historical narrative in support of the regime's continued rule. Its recent, far-ranging reconstruction of the history of East Asia, the United States, and Western roles in the region merits close attention.

Brief mention should be made of the joint history project between China and Japan that took place between 2006 and 2010. As seen in a delay in the joint commission's work and, later, a lack of results, the postwar era proved most controversial, ostensibly due to Japanese insistence on discussing the 1989 Tiananmen massacre of Chinese democracy demonstrators by China's government. Later, it was Japan that took the lead in lifting sanctions on China. Whereas for other periods there was agreement to publish papers with differing interpretations, China refused to allow any coverage of the sensitive history of the People's Republic of China (PRC). While the Chinese assessment emphasized a divide on the Japanese side as rightists insisted on covering up Japan's aggression or opted for neutral language on the character of the war, it also disagreed with references to the accidental and intermittent nature of Japan's foreign policy from the Meiji era, insisting instead on continuity in militarism and expansionism. Arguing that Japan's scholars could not see the forest for the trees, the Chinese side proceeded from a coordinated, holistic approach.[4] This is indicative of how Japan's wartime history has been put in a broad context of national identity. Japanese commentary on the divergent results of the joint research commission also draws attention to China's overall framework: treating premodern Japan as a vassal state, refusing to accept the Ryukyu Islands (Okinawa) as Japanese in the Meiji era (1868-1912), rejecting evidence that moves such as the Mukden invasion were not planned in Tokyo as part of an effort to fit the causes of the Sino-Japanese War into a desired narrative, and putting the history of the PRC off-limits.[5] Whereas Japan's maneuvering to limit acknowledgment of bad intentions and atrocities fits a predictable pattern, China's approach to historical memory is less understood, going well beyond exposing the Japanese cover-ups.

THE PREMODERN ERA

In the heady days of optimism about reconciliation, the Confucian tradition appeared to be a unifying force in East Asia.[6] During the 1980s, there was much talk of "Confucian capitalism," unleashed by Japan, then the "four little tigers," and last by China.[7] South Koreans, in the euphoria of normalization with China and Japan in the expectation that it could become the bridge between China and the West, viewed China as a historical partner with shared traditions more than as a Communist state that had tried to eliminate its Confucian legacy and supported North Korea. As plans emerged for establishing an East Asian community of these three states and the member states of the Association of Southeast Asia Nations (ASEAN), there was further interest in looking to the past for shared values.[8] Yet China had different ideas about the utility of Confucianism. Instead of focusing on how it could draw the region together, China glorified it as well as China's own record at the center of East Asia, entitling China to define Eastern civilization.[9] Combining into one ideological amalgam socialism, Confucianism, and anti-imperialism, China was indifferent to how this use of the past alienated countries fearful of Sinocentrism.[10] By 2010, China was trumpeting its superior history as a model for the future, Japan was recalling China's premodern arrogance and the need to break free, and South Korea was stressing two millennia of strife associated with Chinese invasions and *sadae* (the concept of a weaker state obliged to serve the greatness of a stronger one) dependency.

Despite the lingering popularity of Confucian themes among Japanese and South Koreans seeking to rediscover their roots, premodern history is now one of the most divisive sources of national identity gaps in East Asia. Prime Minister Fukuda Yasuo and President Hu Jintao had spoken in trips to the other's civilizational crucible—Qufu and Nara—of shared cultural memories, but the values gap did not narrow.[11] Instead, China disregarded the advice in its "new thinking" publications of 2003 on how to win Japan's trust, while presenting such a one-sided recounting of its own history that Japanese, South Koreans, and others are unable to find common ground.[12] As for the initial historical divide with South Korea, China seemed in 2004 to step back from aggressively propounding its claim to the ancient Korean Kingdom of Koguryo, but a few years later it was assertively pressing this outlook in ways that were reinforced by deepening distrust in South Korea.[13] While China has long been critical of Japan's premodern history as a factor contributing to its militarism, and has lately intensified criticism of Western, including U.S., history as a factor leading to imperialism, the image of Sinocentrism is now the foremost barrier to mutual respect over premodern ties.

Chinese sources today idolize the order led by imperial China, known as the tributary system. They see it as a "harmonious world" based on mutual trust rather than coercion. Instead of aiming for messianic leadership or resorting to cultural and then all-out imperialism, China was content to lead by example and to export its culture only through emulation in accord with its benevolent self-image. Eschewing wars of conquest, China demonstrated no interest in gaining an economic advantage through foreign relations. Given these "memories," China finds useful precedents for the future of international relations and especially for regionalism, which is poised to draw on the same geographical propinquity and cultural roots.[14] With legitimacy sought as the successor to the harmonious Confucian order, China has turned Maoist history on its head while stirring doubts about joining the "East Asian community." Maoism vilified Confucianism and strove for revolution in striking contrast to these recent views.

Among other states, Korea appears as the principal beneficiary of China's beneficence, spared being conquered or having to prepare for costly military self-defense. Japan also benefited, successfully borrowing from a more advanced culture without suffering from military, economic, or cultural expansionism. If this self-contained international system fell short in opening boundaries to the outside and adjusting to conditions of the modern era, Chinese advocates do not question its success or the lost opportunity to endure and evolve into a new regional order. After all, they argue that a geographic and cultural foundation existed for regionalism even if military and economic circumstances remained unfavorable for a period.[15]

Of late, Chinese writings on South Korea have charged that it is failing to present an objective view of its history prior to the Japanese annexation. This is not limited to the controversy over Koguryo, which over the past decade has become a staple of criticism against South Korea. Rather, the charges have broadened to complaints over haughtiness to the point that South Koreans are alleged to view their own culture, language, and history as indicators of the most superior civilization.[16] Charging that this leads to a mixture of myths and facts, the critics see a direct challenge not only to China's civilization and its positive influence but also to mutual understanding at a time when South Koreans are proceeding to erase traces of its legacy, especially by removing the name Han (which suggests it was a Chinese name) from the city of Seoul and rewriting the character for Han in order to lessen the association with China.[17] While Chinese are pressing for the rise of Eastern civilization to assert itself at last after a long period of Western dominance, the fact that South Koreans, the nation most shaped by Chinese civilization, are distancing themselves should pose a troubling challenge.

Recent Chinese sources apply a civilizational test to Japan, arguing that it is conveniently forgetting two thousand years of history when Japan often was unfriendly to China and had expansionist ambitions, as it alternated cooperation with conflict. Even now as it superficially is friendly to China, it reverts to its customary mode in allying with the United States for unfriendly purposes. In this vein, Chinese sources since the mid-1980s have railed against unwarranted Japanese aspirations to become a great power politically and even militarily.[18] Such arrogance is traced to the Sui dynasty (581-618), when a Japanese emissary sought equal treatment; the Ming-era (1368-1644) disparagement of Chinese customs by Japan; Toyotomi Hideyoshi's interest in conquering China in the 1590s; and the continuous ambition from 1868 to 1945 to use force to expand in Asia. By recognizing a common culture with China (rather than the West) and embracing an East Asian community (led by China), Japan at last can put these ambitions (and containment) behind it, argue Chinese commentators.[19]

Japanese sources are ambivalent in assessing this Chinese-led premodern order with the important caveat that they view it in increasingly negative terms in the later premodern centuries. While recognizing value in Japanese borrowing from China, they find that correctives were necessary in order to reassert the priority of the preceding Japanese culture. Invasion attempts by the Yuan dynasty (1271-1368, the period of Mongol rule of China) are depicted as Chinese aggression, not just as atypical actions prompted by Mongol power holders. The tribute system imposed by China on its neighbors with it obligatory kowtowing and deference appears in a mostly negative light, justifying Tokugawa Japan's refusal to participate. The Tokugawa ruled Japan from 1600 to 1868. Praise is reserved for the Tokugawa success in carving out Japan's own mini-tributary system, while championing nativist cultural claims and looking with disdain on the Manchu or Qing dynasty's (1644-1911) claims to be continuing China's political and cultural hegemony in East Asia.[20] Advocates of *Nihonjinron* (the theory of Japaneseness, which gained a broad following in the 1980s and endures) find purity in the Tokugawa-led domestic order in combination with a reassertion of imperial rule in a more centralized polity capable of extending Japan's cultural influence elsewhere. Intrusions from other states are viewed ambivalently, opening new possibilities but also soiling society's purity. If China's Communist leadership in a 180-degree turnabout following the Mao era has found a model in the Confucian past for an ideological rebirth, Japan's revisionist politicians and writers, with frequent support from the LDP leadership and doubtful relevance for international relations, have indulged mostly in divisive nostalgia. Yet Abe's platform in 2012 threatened provocative moves offensive to South Koreans as well as to Chinese.

While *Nihonjinron* is narcissistic without demonizing other nations, as is the South Korean *minjok* (this term for "the nation" became associated with an obsession with exclusivity supposedly dating from Tangun, the legendary founder of Korea in the third millennium B.C.E.), Sinocentrism has been riddled as of late with demonization of the West, especially the United States. Whether comparisons are drawn between warmongering, imperialist Western states and the harmony-seeking premodern China or the rising, imperialist United States of the nineteenth century and China's current peaceful rise, the conclusions are similar. U.S. isolationism was no more than a response to weakness; the "open door" policy was really U.S. expansionism disguised as an "isolationist" state rejecting imperialism by the other powers; America is driven by a messianic mission to save the world and spread its civilization, which again is manifest after the Cold War after the restraining force of the Soviet Union was lost.[21] This contrasts with China's long-term support for an autonomous, peaceful foreign policy without any aspirations for hegemony or expansion. If South Koreans are ungrateful to China's record of benevolence and Japanese worse in taking pride in early signs of militarism that contributed to a feeling of superiority toward China, the main premodern problem lies in Western civilization, epitomized by the United States.[22] In today's Chinese national identity narrative, problems of the twentieth century are rooted in premodern civilizational defects elsewhere, unlike China's praised history.

THE MODERN ERA TO THE SECOND HALF OF THE 1940S

Sino-Japanese differences in interpreting the war period of the 1930s through 1940s and the preceding decades have been well documented for a quarter of a century. The onus has been on Japan, the aggressor, to acknowledge forthrightly its past conduct without hiding under the excuse that it has already apologized and China just keeps playing the "history card" for nationalist reasons and diplomatic one-upmanship. Japanese charges against China's manipulation of historical memories ring hollow; yet in 2010, as China's self-confidence rose, the full range of Chinese revisionist thinking came to the surface. There are commonalities between the thinking of the two sides, as well as big differences.

Chinese and Japanese revisionists both criticize Western imperialists for endangering their country, including threats to colonize them that were forestalled only with difficulty. Just as both sides are prone to idolize their premodern era, they are in basic agreement in rejecting the humiliating treatment by the West beginning in the mid-nineteenth century. For Chinese, this rejection is more far-reaching, grouping Japan with the Western powers. They allow no ambiguity about their country as a victim, never guilty of imperialism. The fact that the postwar period after 1945 is now treated as a time of continuity with the past, leaving unresolved the legacy of imperialism adds poignancy to their arguments. Since the "century of humiliation" lives on, Chinese raise the profile of the pre-PRC era not only for Japan but also for the United States, which is deemed responsible for Taiwan's status. In some ways, this era has yet to conclude, not only for Japan, which has not faced up to its crimes, but also for the United States, whose hegemony and heavy Asian presence is a holdover too of the age of imperialism.[23]

Japanese revisionists also put the pre-1945 period at the top of their history agenda. They insist that Japan's conduct must be reinterpreted in a more positive light. While they accept some criticism, they make at least three qualifying claims: (1) in the age of imperialism Japan behaved normally, including in its competition with the United States as an imperial power; (2) Japan's excesses in Asia are exaggerated for current nationalist purposes without acknowledgment of positive contributions to economic development; and (3) Japan was motivated by the admirable objective of liberating Asia from Western, racist imperialists. With this reasoning, revisionists refuse to draw a line between positive postwar Japan and negative imperialist, wartime Japan (using the vague label "prewar" for the years prior to 1945 serves this aim) or to make a sharp distinction between the world before 1945 and the postwar era.[24]

Revisionists in Japan disagree with the verdicts reached on this period by insisting that their country has been done an injustice. In contrast, revisionists in China perceive the international system and its civilizational foundation as deeply flawed, agreeing with the Japanese that Asia was victimized while going further in a full-fledged rejection of the political and cultural tenets that drove Western states.

Obviously, China and Japan have been unable to bridge their differences in looking back at their intertwining histories from the 1890s to 1940s. The Chinese Communist Party has a big stake in demonizing Japan totally, while also putting the behavior of the West in as negative light as possible. In this respect, revisionists in Japan can find some accord. The more negatively they depict Western imperialism—even when it was on the wane, led by the United States—the more easily they can excuse their country's conduct and reinforce claims to idealistic motives in Asia. In this way, Japan's interest in this period is largely limited to salvaging national pride, while China's interest is driven by today's obsessive policy objectives, transforming the regional order and the international system. Many of Japan's revisionists focus on reinterpreting the attack on Pearl Harbor and the causes of the war with Western countries as well as the Tokyo Tribunal and the enduring judgments about the conduct of the war, including the American use of two atomic bombs against Japan. They seek justice in history for national identity, but China's leaders now construct an assertive national identity, drawing on this era to gain legitimacy for the Communist Party and achieve a fundamental transformation of international relations.

On the surface, the gap between China and Japan concerning this period is over how far-reaching the criticism of Japan's conduct should be. Yet the Chinese aim seems to be to demonize Japanese civilization and Japan's entire history and, by extension, to condemn the international system as a whole. After Japan's leaders appeared to take historical memory off the table with Prime Minister Abe's visit to China in the fall of 2006, and China's leaders reciprocated with an upbeat appraisal of relations to the spring of 2008, China decided to renew criticisms, even ignoring the arrival of a new Democratic Party of Japan (DPJ) government inclined to keep revisionists out. No longer was the Yasukuni Shrine a focus (on this issue, see Daniel Sneider's chapter in this volume). Instead, it was in this situation that China's leaders broadened the narrative in order to demonize Japanese history and civilization, reject Korean history and civilization, support North Korea no matter how provocative its conduct, and also demonize the United States and Western civilization. It is unlikely, given this far-reaching shift, which I have discussed in two chapters of my recent book, that Japan's conduct was a driving force.[25]

Japanese aggravatingly are mostly apathetic to their country's ruinous action. South Koreans are so convinced of Japan's negative legacy in the early twentieth century that they largely ignore anything positive. Yet despite being justly aroused by Japan's rightist provocations, China has pushed its interpretation of the modern era toward a much broader revisionist agenda. It is keen on linking Japan to the other imperialist powers, condemning the war years of the 1930s and 1940s along with all of modern history in Japan and the West, and insisting that the war ended without resolving the problems of colonial imperialism. With this increasingly adamant perspective, Chinese authorities are not inclined to historical reconciliation. Confident of China's superior economic position, despite the need for reform, the Chinese mainstream appears to have shrugged off warnings by some experts in 2011 that keeping a low profile was needed for the immediate future until China's economy and international status have grown stronger.[26]

THE COLD WAR ERA

Japan stopped being prominently disparaged after Chinese Communists took power in 1949, allied with the Soviet Union against the United States, and entered the Korean War on the side of the aggressor, North Korea in 1950. Then it was America that was the enemy, but beginning in 1972 China's perspective was to downplay the gap that had existed between China and the United States and Japan since the 1950s, while concentrating blame on Soviet "revisionists." Once Chinese leader Deng Xiaoping had put his country on course to join the world economy after 1977, there was little need to rehash the Mao-era narrative toward prior enemies, which had become essential partners. A residue of criticism of American imperialism and Japanese militarism lingered in the background without being taken very seriously. Yet in the 1990s this residue turned into a wellspring, and in 2010 it was a torrent. Nationalism replaced abandoned Marxism as the source of Communist Party legitimacy. The Cold War in Asia was again an important national identity theme for China, including the Korean War, with relevance for the ongoing crisis over North Korea's nuclear weapons program and the U.S. alliances with Japan and South Korea having an impact on Chinese aspirations for regionalism based on Sinocentrism.

In a Chinese about-face, the Cold War reemerged as a significant factor in the competition with the United States. During the 1970s, the Chinese obsession with Soviet revisionism and the fragility of normalizing relations seemed to suspend serious examination of the earlier period of antagonism and the 1950–53 war against the United States. In the 1990s, China's patriotic education movement identified 1940s Japan as the main transgressor. Yet after 2000, as a sharper line was drawn against the United States and the pointed criticisms of Mao Tse-tung in 1978–81 receded from memory, the Chinese took a broader approach to resuscitating socialism as a form of national pride in China. This meant stressing the period of 1949–71, especially with respect to foreign policy, and rekindling charges against the United States in this period. (The United States was accused of an ideological Cold War mentality driven by anti-Communism, which has persisted across periods.)

An obsession in Chinese coverage of the Cold War is the notion that the United States' plots to undermine the resolve of Communist supporters were a determining force, as they could be in our era without extraordinary vigilance and discipline. This theme is evident in the coverage of the late 1950s and early 1960s when Nikita Khrushchev ruled the Soviet Union, reigniting Maoist accusations that the Soviet Union went on the wrong track ideologically when it dropped its guard against the West. America's "peaceful evolution" had no chance during Joseph Stalin's lifetime, we are told. He was successful in strengthening the state, building a strong economy, and blocking the pernicious effects of U.S. ideology, even if his cult of personality and dogmatism left problems that a successor would need to resolve. By completely repudiating Stalin, who died in 1953, Khrushchev (and later Mikhail Gorbachev in the 1980s) committed the gravest of errors, among which was destroying the reliability of Communism and opening the door to American machinations. One error was to propose that the aim of Communism is the withering away of the state. Another was to support all-around cooperation with the United States. Above all, Khrushchev undermined belief in Communism among the Soviet people and created an environment that nurtured Gorbachev and others who worshiped the American capitalist system and democratic socialism.[27]

Writings on the Korean War ignore the North's invasion of the South, only indicating that a civil war had begun and the United States intervened, invading Korea as an imperialist state. The United States then proceeded to extend its imperialism by intervening in China's civil war through protection of Taiwan. These events in 1950 are seen as the key moment in all post–World War II East Asian international relations. China's involvement at the request of North Korea after warning the United States not to approach the Yalu River is fully justified as an anti-imperialist move, according to writings marking the sixtieth anniversary of China's entry into the war.[28] Indeed, the crux of these reassessments of the Korean War is threefold: (1) China's humiliation beginning in the nineteenth century persists, and the war was one important step in its shift from weak victimization to proudly fighting back; (2) 1945 is not a true watershed because Japan's defeat and the rollback of its conquests and Western imperialism was incomplete, as were the results of the Korean War; and (3) the Cold War U.S.-Soviet rivalry in Asia is secondary to the struggle against the unjust regional order, which endured after the end of the Cold War and is largely due to the United States and its alliances, especially with Japan and South Korea. The glorious nature of the Korean War may have drawn scant mainstream attention in the 1990s when some tried to expose the fact that North Korea attacked South Korea with approval from Stalin and Mao, contrary to long-standing claims, but in 2010 it was an essential narrative.[29]

Recollections and analysis on the sixtieth anniversary of the war served the purpose of glorifying the military and its current priorities and refocusing on the memory of American imperialism at a time of intensified warnings about U.S. plans to contain China. If North Korea had been occupied (the outcome of defeat, rather than unification through South Korea), the United States would have turned its evil plotting for invasions toward China, one source explains.[30] In this reasoning, the U.S. alliance with South Korea continues to be a negative element, along with intentions to achieve "regime change" in North Korea and apply pressure limiting China's rise.

Today in Chinese eyes, the Cold War appears much less as two hegemonic powers striving for an advantage than as the United States, driven by anti-Communism, opposing China. The Soviet Union is credited in the Korean War with countering American airpower to the extent that China was reassured to enter the war and then benefited by learning how to defend itself. Recollections of this war serve to paint the Soviet Union in a more positive light and make a critical linkage in demonizing the United States.[31] The fact that South Koreans now perceive China through the lens of the Sino–North Korean alliance and as "red" shows the importance of a divide in historical consciousness, which is blamed on the South without recognition that China is the one reviving it.[32]

Discrediting postwar South Korean history, Chinese sources blame the United States military and South Korean president Syngman Rhee (1948-60) for relying on the *shinilpa* (the pro-Japan faction during Japan's colonial rule), which had gained from collaboration and ideological support for Japan's annexation of Korea, as the new pro-U.S. faction and the backbone of anti-Communism. Controlling both the economic and cultural levers of society, the descendants of the pro-Japan faction made anti-Communism the essence of nationalism.[33] Rather than true nationalism, this construct, which Chinese sources fail to see as a response to any action of North Korea or China, is associated with dependence on the United States and weakness toward Japan. It suggests continuity between pre-1945 (when Korea was a Japanese colony) and post-1949 South Korea, which is reinforced by a distorted view of history and leads to disrespect of China.

Chinese criticism of South Korea after 1987 makes democracy seem like a problem amid the legacy of the previous period. Given Korean victimization by Japan from 1905 to 1945, sympathy is the main attitude toward the pre-1945 era. But for the post–Cold War era, South Korea is faulted for a large gap between aspirations to be a great power and the absence of material prerequisites. This is attributed to factors such as confusion over national identity introduced by the mixture of a rapid decline in Confucianism and Buddhism and expansion of Christianity as well as a U.S.-style free, democratic culture. Indeed, the spread of democracy in a society troubled by sharp inequalities is treated as an impetus to political pandering to elicit mass support. Along with a spiritual vacuum has come pride in the "Korea fever," which has come with the popularity of South Korean dramas, leading to what the Chinese call a superiority complex. While the Chinese may acknowledge the impact of this complex on attitudes toward Japan over history and a territorial dispute over some islands between Japan and South Korea, they express a great sense of betrayal at what is seen as accelerating South Korean determination to rid their culture and historical memory of Chinese cultural elements.[34] Disconnecting the past of the two countries is treated as an unforgiveable crime now that China glorifies its civilization as the real glue in the region's history, which can serve as a model for the rise of a shared culture. Abnormal South Korean development since 1945, they claim, interferes with building an East Asian community.

There are two striking omissions from the writings on South Korean cultural ingratitude. If the impact of North Korea does get mentioned in passing and a divided nation's thirst for unification are presumed to have an impact, there is no effort to analyze how changing attitudes toward North Korea or its approach to the South matter. Likewise, there is complete silence about the effect of China's behavior and cultural narrative on perceptions of the Sino-Korean cultural gap. While the South is subject to intense criticism, China is not in the least criticized, nor are there any hints about how it might develop a more effective strategy for addressing this hiatus.

The Chinese critique of Japan has long traced deeply embedded nationalist failings, much more serious than those now identified in South Korea, far back in history.[35] In the 1980s, when learning from Japan was in vogue, this was somewhat downplayed, and in the brief 2003 appeals for "new thinking" toward Japan, critics of this approach aired their concerns.[36] In 2007, Hu Jintao spoke positively during his visit to Japan of its ancient culture, pointing to commonalities with China. Yet most Chinese publications kept castigating Japan's premodern past, and this grew more pronounced in the 2010 downturn in relations after a Chinese boat rammed a Japanese cutter and China applied maximum pressure to free the captain. What was clearer in 2010 was that Japan's views on the Yasukuni Shrine and its wartime atrocities were, after the understanding reached in 2006, no longer the primary focus.[37] Instead, Japan's guilt centered on its continuing role in aiding the U.S. military in separating Taiwan from the PRC, its preference for the U.S. alliance over the East Asian community, and its resistance to China's revisionist thinking on international relations in Asia. Given such charges, there was no Chinese inclination to praise postwar Japan as peace loving or post-1972 Japan as supportive of China's rise. Instead, a negative image of Japan in the Cold War serves the argument that the results in 1945 were incomplete.

Recent reviews of Sino-Japanese relations up to 1972 prioritize the Taiwan issue. While Hatoyama Ichiro and Ikeda Hayato are seen as exceptions for their interest in forging better relations, Yoshida Shigeru, Kishi Nobusuke, and Sato Eisaku are deemed antagonistic to China. Under U.S. pressure they accepted subordination in a Cold War anti-Communist strategy. Setting aside resentment of the United States, they cynically sought benefits from sticking close to Japan's ally. Even in the 1960s, they failed to seize the opportunity of the Sino-Soviet split. Their aim was to ride the U.S. coattails to gain leadership in Asia, as well as to prevent Taiwan from joining the PRC through a U.S.-Japanese-Taiwanese triangle. This was, allegedly, dependent on the persistence of pre-1945 popular thinking, which had been shaped by imperialism, as well as on rightists with an agenda including China, historical consciousness, territory, and Taiwan.[38] After Sino-Japanese normalization, thinking about Taiwan did not significantly change. In this sense, 1945 was not a sharp dividing line, nor was 1972. The legacy of Japanese extremism survives today, nurtured in the Cold War era, according to Chinese views.

In 2010, Chinese writers took a firmer line against the notion that the history issue was resolved. Even more important than continuing the tradition of friendly exchanges, one author explained, is the need to draw lessons from Japan's wars of aggression. This call to intensify the struggle over history came amid accusations that Japan was hardening its position toward China, joining in Barack Obama's decision to contain China's rise in the guise of "returning to Asia."[39] In turn, Japanese welcome more American involvement in the territorial disputes over the East China Sea, in the manner of its historical alignment with other powers in pursuit of expansionism. Connecting the history matter to current issues in international relations stokes the emotions of Chinese readers and serves a wide-ranging national identity narrative. Abe's return as prime minister might have given Chinese reason to pause at the start of 2013 to await his policy choices, but his positions on strengthening the alliance and Japan's military compounded warnings against his extremist view of history.

Of course, the Soviet Union figures prominently in Chinese coverage of the Cold War, as a problem and as a source of cautionary tales for China in its defense of socialism. One point in Chinese criticisms of Soviet leadership in the 1950s through 1980s is a lack of geopolitical prioritizing with awareness that a vast country was very exposed and needed to avoid conflicts on all sides. By antagonizing China, spending heavily to fortify its eastern border, and entering a war in Afghanistan that alienated countries in all directions, the Soviet Union ignored the priority of facing the challenge of the United States and the West. Gorbachev compounded the problem by retreating in an unprincipled manner in foreign policy and relaxing control over Eastern Europe too quickly.[40] The implication of this analysis marking twenty years since the Soviet collapse is that China has learned the lessons of failure in defending the socialist cause. It has a longer-term perspective and will not abandon North Korea or lose focus on the need to weaken the United States in order to regain Taiwan and revive its authority in Asia.

SINO-JAPANESE COMPARISONS AND
INTERNATIONAL RELATIONS

Historical memory has a lengthy pedigree in East Asia as a mechanism in the service of regime legitimacy and bilateral relations. During the 1980s, Japanese were turning again to history in pursuit of the elusive goal of a "normal Japan" and with an eye to gaining equality with the United States and "reentering Asia" as its leader. Despite a growing sense that these goals were beyond reach, revisionists continued over the next two decades to rewrite history while reconstructing the national identity. Some prime ministers offered their support, while others, whether sympathetic or not, did not see the project as being in the interest of Asian regionalism or the U.S. alliance. Japan's record of historical revisionism is filled with stops and starts and discontinuities. It infuriates Chinese and South Koreans without any end in sight, but it need not be a barrier to improved relations, as Japan finds a way to keep its offenses under control such as in 2006–8 as Chinese ties thawed and 2010 as South Korean ties improved. Yet in 2013 the danger of a downward spiral due to Japan's moves was greater than previously.

The joint history project with China reached too far not only because Japan's academic contingent proceeded with extreme caution in light of national sentiment, but also due to China's hardened position on a wide range of historical memory. Nevertheless, one Chinese assessment of this joint research project found constructive results despite academic divisions and political barriers. Citing Japanese newspapers following the project's launch in late 2006, the assessment found a strong interest in narrowing differences, apart from the right-wing *Sankei Shimbun*. Pointing to the final results, it also noted some success in Japanese recognition of a war of aggression rather than liberation and of Nanjing as a massacre. After years of Japanese calls for ending "apology diplomacy" and boosting nationalist pride by avoiding textbook references to atrocities and colonialism, these acknowledgments were welcomed. In turn, the article claimed that Chinese histories had in recent years shifted from a focus on revolution to one on civilizations and their interactions, adding that China needs to do a better job of covering post-1945 Japan and its peaceful development path. Yet the source lacked any candor about the nature of China's history coverage and how it was evolving in 2009 and 2010, while only stressing the history-consciousness deficit and the victimization consciousness in Japan.[41]

However justified the criticisms of Japan, the failure of the joint history project was due in large part to the rigidity of China's views and the nature of the new civilizational approach as it grew increasingly extreme by 2010.

The mainstream Sinocentric worldview visible during the spike of national identity inside China around 2010 contrasts sharply with the revisionist historical outlook that accompanied the spike in Japan's national identity around 1990 and, in some respects, kept gaining traction under LDP rule over the following two decades. Comparisons of reasoning about the above three eras reveal similarities—veneration of the premodern era, distortion of the modern era to claim victimization far beyond what is accurate, and a sense of abnormality about the Cold War era tied to unmet aspirations for regional leadership. But more emphasis should be placed on fundamental differences. If Japanese are seeking redemption with only modest interest in challenging the foundations of the international system, Chinese are now obsessed with radically reinterpreting the way the history of the world is presented and forging a different system of international relations, while vilifying Western civilization with stress on the lingering presence of imperialism. Those preoccupied with history in Japan seek vindication, while their counterparts in China are intent on radical transformation of historical studies and the overall international system.

The history issues central to Japanese and South Korean concerns need not be preoccupations in a rapidly changing regional environment. While many focus on Dokdo/Takeshima, it remains securely under Korean control, with Japan's challenge likely to stay pro forma in nature, serving a national identity debate. It is a diversion to dwell on this matter. In keeping alive ambitions to accuse the United States with regard to World War II—Pearl Harbor, the Tokyo Tribunal, the two atomic bombs, and the partition of Korea—some in the region are also distracted from what really counts. There is no benefit from raising these sensitive issues, which Americans will fail to appreciate, except to salvage some hopes for national identity. Damaging trust in vital alliances is unwise in the current atmosphere of China's drive for hegemony.

The Senkaku/Diaoyu issue, the assessment of premodern Sinocentrism, and various historical issues linked to the legitimacy of the Chinese Communist Party are of much greater significance in the struggle over Asian reorganization. China treats these as actionable, serving to justify policy choices with far-reaching consequences. In 2012, the Chinese position grew more assertive, backed by military challenges to Japan's positions, using the pretext of Japan's nationalization of the territory in response to a right-wing attempt to purchase it and provoke China. Japanese as well as South Koreans and Americans must pay close attention to how revisionist historical memory is being employed on behalf of an aggressive stance toward returning China to its past glory and relegating its neighbors to a lower status.

CONCLUSION

The Chinese Communist Party has bided its time on some matters, but its objectives are consistent, and the recent burst of historical revisionism is in line with a trend that can be traced back to debates of the 1980s. Thus, in 1989 demonization of the United States intensified; in the mid-1990s, accusations against Japan became more vitriolic; and from the mid-2000s on, South Korea was targeted more directly. At first the charges narrowly centered on specific historical issues—American anti-Communism, Japanese historiography of the war, and South Korean claims to Koguryo. By 2010, the full scope of China's revisionism of the histories of the United States, Japan, and South Korea became clear. It serves three broad objectives: legitimation of the rule of the Chinese Communist Party, Sinocentric reorganization of Asia, and reinterpretation of both world history and the international system in opposition to the long-accepted status quo.

Although Chinese claims to have been victorious against Japan understate the role of the United States in forcing that country's surrender and the role of the anti-Communist Chinese nationalist regime in leading China's resistance, they require rewriting the history of relations with not only pre-1945 Japan but also post-1945 Japan. While North Korea launched the attack against South Korea that caused the Korean War and did so only after both the Soviet Union and China had given their consent, glorification of this war remains important for legitimacy, contributing to supporting North Korea today and identifying South Korea in negative ways. Insistence on American anti-Communism and containment intentions toward China requires hostility toward the United States too, even if American leadership is striving to narrow this. China's historical memories serve to obscure many blank spots in historical coverage of the party's horrendous human rights record, while making it difficult to find common ground with other states.

The Sino-Soviet dispute started with the difference in 1956 over how to evaluate Stalin's rule. In the 1980s, China was caught in a struggle of its own over how, in a period of reform, to reevaluate the key turning points in the history of Soviet as well as Chinese socialism before it became alarmed that Gorbachev's reforms in the 1980s opened the Pandora's box of revelations about what really had transpired in collectivization, purges, and abuse of absolute power.[42] First allowing some criticisms of the Cultural Revolution (1966-76) and then shutting the door on them, China's leadership revealed its hypersensitivity to history. Drawing lessons from the collapse of the Soviet Union, it has gone further in reconstructing the past to serve didactically the reinforcement of party rule through information control.

At the core of Japanese revisionism is the notion that Japan's motives in the pre-1945 search for Asianism were pure. Chinese reasoning about regionalism goes further by regarding it as the natural revival of traditional relations in Asia, which were marked by harmony and interrupted only by imperialism. In 2010, prior calls for Sino-Japanese cooperation and even ASEAN leadership in forging a community were overshadowed by warnings that the U.S. "return to Asia" backed by Japan was a threat to economic and cultural integration. This historically based argument sees U.S. hegemony as the heir to nineteenth-century Western imperialism followed by Japan's imperialism. In 1945, the war ended without restoring the rightful order; so only now, with China's rise, can history resume its natural course. There is no "end of history," since the Chinese reject universal values in favor of a "return of history."

Civilizational analysis pits China at the head of Eastern civilization, battling against the United States and its partners in support of Western civilization. Japan and South Korea have become too enamored of the West to embrace their destiny within an integrated East Asia. Beginning with the U.S. occupation of both states in 1945, they fell under an alien orbit. Only by loosening and, ideally, rejecting alliance ties with the United States and joining China through ASEAN +3, or the China-Japan–South Korea Free Trade Agreement, leading to a community, will the historical hiatus in civilizational development be ended, as economic integration proceeds.

As a nation proud of its democracy, Japan's grievances are limited to being treated fairly regarding an age when imperialism was acceptable. Seeking regional leadership after the Cold War, Japan sought recognition of its status and culture, but it had little idea about how its vague support for "Asian values" would translate into a regional framework distinct from the international system. After all, in the 1980s it still regarded itself as part of the West. In contrast, China's ideological amalgam of socialism, Confucianism, and anti-imperialism coalesces around a rejection of the past two hundred years of global integration apart from economic cooperation. In the 1980s, China was again hostile to the notion of "humanism" after castigating the Soviet leaders in the 1950s for accepting this theme from the European Enlightenment. Rediscovering "harmony" from China's cultural tradition, Chinese offered it as a contrast to the principles of Western civilization. Moreover, by linking hegemony to imperialism, they denied the positive nature of American leadership in the Cold War and post–Cold War eras, seeing the end of World War II as well as the end of the Cold War more as continuities than as turning points. Given this approach to national identity, China has no interest in striving for a shared historical outlook. A wide identity gap serves its ambitions.

In the 1980s, when Japan was at its peak in relative power, it was well positioned to lead in historical reconciliation with a reforming China and a democratizing South Korea. Overconfidently assuming that these states were dependent on Japan and that it was free to pursue its historical revisionism, Japan missed the opportunity to lower the impact of historical memories. In the 2010s, China's relative power has reached a peak, and it too is prioritizing revisionism over reconciliation despite improvements in Japan's posture from Abe to Hatoyama and more intense wooing by George W. Bush after 2006 and Obama beginning in 2009. Some observers see growing insecurity in this shift toward demonization of other states or direct civilizational rivalry. Others perceive overconfidence as China's economy rose amid a global financial crisis and its military made unexpectedly rapid breakthroughs. Whatever the combination of alarm over domestic imbalances and deepening problems and arrogance over the failures of the American and Japanese economies, China's rejection of building a regional community consistent with the international community has deep historical roots.

In Germany, France, and other European states, the Nazi regime is an isolated exception to a proudly shared history. In Japan, South Korea, and especially China, the war era from the 1930s to the Korean War is a brief part of a contested history with no end in sight. Unless the gap over other periods is bridged appreciably, the divide over the war era is unlikely to be narrowed. While for a time it appeared that Japanese provocative language was the main factor in keeping the gap wide, China is now at the forefront of the issue. Unless Chinese leaders make an abrupt change of direction in the way they conceive of national identity, there is no prospect for other nations to have a significant impact in addressing the historical gap. Idealism will do no good in the face of determined opposition by the most critical actor, which is bereft of it.

Prospects for reconciliation of historical memories rest less on historians than on politicians who prioritize diplomatic objectives and, at times, reconsider national identity priorities in consideration of domestic politics. While attempts to convince others of the empirical evidence in support of one's arguments cannot be relaxed in academic circles, scholars are unlikely to convince those intent on utilizing historical memories to arouse the public. When Japanese politicians were guilty of distortions offensive to many, reconciliation seemed to depend on supporting the substantial community in Japan active in resisting them. The situation in China is more difficult due to authoritarianism, censorship, and the absence of a civil society. Along with efforts in support of serious academics, a different strategy is necessary to expose not only the distortions but the increasingly divisive agenda behind them.

1   Hasegawa and Togo, eds., *East Asia's Haunted Present*.
2   Rozman, ed., *U.S. Leadership, History, and Bilateral Relations*.
3   Rozman, ed., *East Asian National Identities*.
4   Tao, "Haiyuan lishi, zhaoyue lishi."
5   On the actual complicated history of who was or was not a Chinese vassal state, earlier disputes about the Ryukyu Islands, and past diplomatic relations in the region, see Toby, *State and Diplomacy in Early Modern Japan*, particularly chap. 3. On the very recent revival of the historical controversy over who owns Okinawa (the main island), see Nagamoto, "Who 'Owns' Okinawa?"
6   Hahm, "How the East Was Won."
7   Rozman in Borthwick, ed., *Pacific Century*.
8   Rozman, "Cultural Prerequisites of East Asian Regionalism."
9   Zhao, "Hexie linian yu Zhongguo heping jueqi."
10 Rozman, "Chinese National Identity."
11 Rozman in Gong and Teo, eds., *Reconceptualising the Divide*.
12 Cohen, *Retracing the Triangle*.
13 Chung, "China's 'Soft' Clash with South Korea."
14 Rozman, "Chinese Strategic Thinking."
15 Han, "Zhongguo jueqi yu Dongbeiya de anquan zhanlue xuanze."
16 Rozman, "History as an Arena of Sino-Korean Conflict."
17 Wang, "Shixi dangdai Hanguo minzuzhuyi."
18 Rozman, "China's Changing Images of Japan."

19 Hou, "Guanyu Zhongri guanxi de shikong weidu tantao."
20 Jun, *Chugokuka suru Nihon (bunmei no shototsu) issennenshi.*
21 Wang, "Meiguo jueqi jinchengzhong de waijiao zhengce xuanze jidui Zhongguo heping fazhan de qishi."
22 Rozman, ed., *National Identities and Bilateral Relations.*
23 Rozman, "Invocations of Chinese Traditions."
24 Kawai, *Kyokasho kara kieta Nihonshi.*
25 Rozman, "Chinese National Identity and East Asian National Identity Gaps"; and Rozman, "Chinese National Identity and the Sino-U.S. Civilizational Gap."
26 Wang, "China's Search for a Grand Strategy."
27 Zhang, "Meiguo shi ruhe cong yishixingtai yingxiang Heluxiaofu de?"
28 Song and Luo, "Lun kangmei yuanchao zhanzheng zhengyixing."
29 Xia and Qi, "Chaoxian zhanzheng yu Dongbeiya geju."
30 Wang and Tang, "Kangmei yuanchao zhanzhengzhong dang de lingdao jiti zhanju kongzhi sixiang yanxi."
31 Zheng and Peng, "Kangmei yuanchao zhanzhengzhong Zhongsu kongjun hezuo shimuo."
32 Dong, Wang, and Li, "Hanguo gongzhong dui Zhongguo jueqi de renzhi yu taidu fenxi."
33 Wang and Wang, "Lun Meijunzheng yu Hanguo chinripai dezhuanxing."
34 Guo and Ling, "Minzuzhuyi yu Hanguo waijiao zhengce."
35 Yang, Liu, and Gao, *Riben baike cidian.*
36 See the journal *Shijie Jingji yu Zhengzhi*, no. 9 (2003).
37 Ba, "Cong wenhua shijiao touxi Riben waijiao zhengce de zhanlue xuanze."
38 Wang, "Luelun fujiaoqian daozhi Zhongri guanxi didui taishi de yinsu."
39 Feng, "Zhongri liangguo lishi wenti de zhengjie."
40 Li, "Yao jinji Sulian diyuan waijiao de jiaoxun."
41 Gao, "Lishi jiaokeshu wenti."
42 Rozman, *The Chinese Debate about Soviet Socialism*; Rozman, in Bernstein and Li, eds., *China Learns from the Soviet Union.*

Chapter 9

Divisive Historical Memories

Russia and Eastern Europe

IGOR TORBAKOV

There appears to be a consensus among professional historians and political analysts that over the past several decades, the "politics of history" has become a significant aspect of domestic politics and international relations, both within Europe and in the world at large.[1] This trend toward politicizing and instrumentalizing of history might take on various shapes and forms in different countries, but there are basically two main objectives that are usually pursued. The first is the construction of a maximally cohesive national identity and the rallying of the society around the powers that be. The second is eschewing the problem of guilt.[2] The two are clearly interlinked: having liberated oneself of the sense of historical, political, or moral responsibility, it is arguably much easier to take pride in one's newly minted "unblemished" identity based on the celebratory interpretation of one's country's "glorious past," which is habitually regarded as "more a source of comfort than a source of truth."[3] It is therefore extremely important to investigate the vital links between history, memory, and national identity.

The main objective of this chapter, then, is to explore how the memories of some momentous developments in the tumultuous twentieth century (above all, the experience of totalitarian dictatorships, World War II, the "division" and "reunification" of Europe, and the collapse of the Soviet Union) and their historical interpretations relate to concepts of national identity in Eastern Europe and Russia. Identities are understood here not as something immutable; by contrast, I proceed from the premise that identities are constantly being constructed and reconstructed in the course of historical process. "As communities and individuals interpret and reinterpret their [historical] experiences . . . they create their own constantly shifting national identities in the process."⁴ But national "remembering" is a tricky and controversial business. As the late Tony Judt argued, "Memory is inherently contentious and partisan: one man's acknowledgement is another's omission."⁵ Any interpretation of the past based on national "remembering" would inevitably involve not only the self-image of a given nation but the latter's relations with the other nations as well. A clash between national memories is thus prone to lead to the growth of tensions between states. This explains, the Estonian analyst Maria Mälksoo points out, why any "national memory" has a "foreign policy dimension and context to it."⁶

> As states seek to strengthen not only their physical security but also their self-perception and self-image in international relations, while they desire to have their stories reinforced by significant others, it is under the umbrella of memory politics that identity policies and security policies meet. If identity is a security issue, it is often the case that memory also becomes a security issue—or is securitised. In addition to classic security dilemmas, new ontological security dilemmas emerge: the certainty of "our" story undermines the ontological uncertainty of "them"; they consider our interpretation of history to be hostile to theirs, which is why they launch memory political counterattacks against us.⁷

WHY ESCALATION?

All is *not* quiet on the Eastern (European) front. The past two decades following the collapse of the Soviet Union have witnessed an escalation of *memory wars* in which Russia has largely found itself on the defensive, its official historical narrative being vigorously assaulted by a number of the newly independent ex-Soviet states. Suffice it to recall just the most important episodes of this monumental "battle over history." Following the Soviet collapse, Museums of Occupation were set up in Latvia and Estonia; one of the museums' main objectives is to highlight the political symmetry between the two totalitarian regimes that occupied the Baltics in the twentieth century—German national-socialism and Soviet Communism.⁸ In May 2006, a Museum of Soviet Occupation opened in Tbilisi, Georgia, following the Baltic states' example. The same month, the Institute of National Memory was established in Ukraine, inspired by the Polish model.⁹ In November 2006, the Ukrainian Parliament passed a law recognizing the Holodomor (the disastrous famine of 1932–33) as genocide of the Ukrainian people perpetrated by the Soviet Communist regime.[10] In May 2009 a landmark academic and political event took place in Vilnius—over eighty representatives of European cultural journals convened in the Lithuanian capital to discuss the topic of "European histories." The event's participants agreed that a comprehensive twentieth-century European history has yet to be crafted, and that the first step toward this goal should be the integration of Eastern Europe's tragic totalitarian experience into the overall European narrative.[11]

There appear to be two sets of reasons behind the increasingly acrimonious disputes over history in which Russia is pitted against the former imperial borderlands. The first is what might be called the "classical" politics of identity following the collapse of a multinational empire. Second, there is a specific geopolitical conjuncture primarily connected with the expansion of the European Union (EU) and the growing rivalry between the EU and Russia over their overlapping neighborhoods. An important subplot linked with both the Soviet Union's unraveling and the EU's eastward thrust is the struggle over the contested issue of Russia's own shifting identity.

Students of anthropology, political science, and postcolonialism have long explored history writing (and mythmaking) as part of an overarching problem of nationalism, national identity, and nation building. Their key premise has been that (re)writing history and (re)making myths is what nation-states generally do, history being a principal tool to construct national identity.[12] It has also been argued (particularly forcefully within the field of postcolonial studies) that any regime change inevitably entails a confrontation with the past: "A new future requires a new past."[13] In cases when regime change, state creation, and nation building coincide, the confrontation with the past becomes particularly acute. This is precisely the situation in which the countries that emerged from under the rubble of the Soviet Union found themselves.[14]

The key problem here is this: new states have emerged from the debris of the Soviet Union, but in many cases they exist without clear-cut identities or links to logically conceived "nations." Yet identity is decisively a question of empowerment. So what were, realistically, the available strategies that the newly independent ex-Soviet countries could resort to?

Under Communism, studies of nationalism or national identities were not a terribly popular topic. "National question" in the Soviet Union was routinely explored as an aspect of class paradigm. As it has famously been postulated, liquidation of class distinctions (creation of classless society) would automatically lead toward the solution of national problem—through the creation of the "new historical entity" (the "Soviet people") in which national/ethnic differences would be preserved in their harmless (i.e., nonpolitical) ethnographic form. National histories of the Soviet Union's multifarious peoples were secondary (and highly controlled) narratives—the component parts of the Soviet grand narrative.

Following the demise of Communism and the Soviet Union's unraveling, the incipient nation-states either returned to national historiographic tradition (where it existed) or hastily set about creating one. One common feature has been the "nationalization of history" whereby the history of a newly born post-Soviet state is conceptualized as the history of a titular nation, the latter being associated with the titular ethic group.[15]

Yet this strategy of nationalizing history inevitably leads to strains—both internally and externally. Thus, "nationalization" of history centered on titular nation cannot help but produce what can be called "mutually exclusive" histories, whereby national minorities are excluded and/or designated as *Others*. In the situation when all post-Soviet states are multiethnic and multicultural, the exclusivist narrative is counterproductive at best and outright dangerous at worst.

In fact, as many students of nationalism have pointed out, the construction or reconstruction of identity is indeed a violent and dangerous process for all those involved—both *within* the newly emerged state and *without*. The making of one nation entails the unmaking of another: for example, the rise of particularist identities in the ex-Soviet republics leads to the demise of the overarching Soviet identity; nation building in Ukraine compels the remaking of the Russian nation.

A recent Russian study based on the examination of nearly two hundred school history textbooks and teacher guides from Russia's twelve post-Soviet neighbors demonstrated that the trends toward nationalizing history and "othering" are gaining momentum in most new independent states. The report, released in Moscow in the end of 2009 and titled "The Treatment of the Common History of Russia and the Peoples of the Post-Soviet Countries in the History Textbooks of the New Independent States," argues that Russia's neighbors are now using textbooks that present Russia in all its historical incarnations as the enemy of the peoples of these countries. The study's authors note "with regret" that "except for Belarus and (to a lesser degree) Armenia, all the remaining countries have moved to present the rising generation with a nationalistic view of history, based on myths about the antiquity of one's own people, about the high cultural mission of its ancestors and about 'the cursed enemy'": the Russians. "If these tendencies continue," the report concludes, "then after 15 to 20 years, the events of the 20th century will be completely forgotten by the population. In the consciousness of the peoples of the former USSR will be formed an image of Russia as an evil empire which for centuries destroyed, oppressed and exploited them."[16] Remarkably, several surveys of history textbooks from the ex-Soviet republics conducted by local scholars (e.g., the analyses carried out in Ukraine by Viktoria Sereda and Natalya Yakovenko, respectively) revealed the same prevalent trend—namely, the active use and abuse of the negative images of the Other.[17]

Some Russian historians appear to have been unpleasantly surprised, even hurt, by what they called the blatantly nationalistic and viciously anti-Russian interpretations of Russian imperial and Soviet history by non-Russian scholars from neighboring states. "It is a revisiting, at a new level, of the theory of 'absolute evil' which used to be popular during the early Soviet period," contends Moscow University professor Aleksandr Vdovin. "Back then, this nefarious role in Soviet historiography was played by the [Russian] Tsarism that 'oppressed the peoples of the empire.' Now it is Russia that is painted as the 'absolute evil.'"[18] But more perceptive Russian and international commentators seem to agree that a certain degree of anti-Russian bias in the new independent countries' historiographies was all but inevitable. It should not be treated as an "unexpected phenomenon," argues one Russian analyst; rather, it should be understood as a "norm."[19] In their efforts to assert their still shaky and fragile national identities and root them in the (re)invented national traditions, the new countries were bound to "push against" Russia's official historical narrative. "The shaping of an image of the ethnic or cultural Other has become an inalienable part of the cultural and political mobilization as well as of the politics of memory pursued by the newly independent states," writes the prominent Ukrainian historian Georgiy Kasyanov.[20] It should come as no surprise, adds Kasyanov, that in the post-Soviet space it was "Russia and the Russians" who ended up being the "absolute champions" as far as the forming of negative ethnic stereotypes and "othering" are concerned. Thus the ground for "history wars" was in fact inherent in the postimperial situation. These conflicts could have been somewhat attenuated had Russia—a former imperial overlord—had at least a modest success in what Germans call *Vergangenheitsbewältigung*, or "coming to terms with the past."[21] But it hadn't.

EUROPE'S SHIFTING MEMORY LANDSCAPE: FOREIGN POLICY IMPLICATIONS

There is also an important geopolitical angle to this already tangled story. The tectonic shifts in European geopolitics caused by Communism's collapse and the Soviet breakup—above all, the EU's eastward expansion and the accompanying change in Russia's position in Europe—inevitably led to the shifts in European memory landscape. The unraveling of the Eastern bloc, the unification of Germany, and the subsequent EU enlargement have undermined a historical consensus that used to exist—throughout the entire period of the Cold War-era "stability"—within Europe (including Soviet Russia) with regard to World War II and postwar experiences.[22] As history is written by the victors, two principal historical narratives for decades dominated the scene—one advanced by the Western Allies, the other by the Soviets. These narratives had quite a lot in common—both highlighted the glorious victory over Nazi Germany, successful postwar reconstruction and the long period of postwar peace and economic development. Other (potentially dissenting) European voices were hushed up and basically inaudible. But the crumbling of the Cold War order revealed the plurality of Europe's "mnemonic communities." Some scholars refer now to the three main narratives, adding an East European story to the previously dominating two.[23] Others suggest that there are actually four stories as they single out the unique German experience within the Western European group.[24] Still others, arguing that East-Central Europe seen as a single entity is a "fiction," distinguish within this broad region at least four areas. The latter are defined according to their memorial modes—largely based on the regional countries' attitudes toward their Communist past.[25] Finally, there are commentators who contend that in Europe there are as many memories of World War II and postwar experiences as there are nations.[26] In the words of Claus Leggewie, "If Europe has—or is developing—a collective memory, it is just as diverse as its nations and cultures."[27]

For our purposes, what is particularly important is that some of the new EU entrants' attempts to correct the "European mnemonic map" are perceived in Moscow as putting Russia's self-understanding, prestige, and international status into jeopardy. Arguing that "Eastern European memories of World War II are still *les lieux d'oubli* [sites of forgetting] rather than parts of *les lieux de mémoire* [sites of memory] of the officially endorsed collective European remembrance of the war," some Eastern Europeans—particularly the Balts and the Poles—assert that in today's EU "the integration of historical perceptions and interpretations is still out of sync with institutional integration."[28] But make no mistake—this is not a mere historiographical issue. The champions of the new European historical consensus are fully cognizant of the fact that historical narratives and collective memories are also "a source of power" and thus aspects of power relations. "This is why the memory war over the meaning of Communist heritage simultaneously represents a fight for symbolic power and for the right to define the frontiers of the joint memory community in Europe."[29] Most East European nations now view the wartime and postwar period as a "useable past"—crucial for strengthening separate identity, giving a boost to populist nationalism, externalizing the Communist past, and casting their particular nation as a hapless victim of two bloodthirsty totalitarian dictatorships. As East Europeans are pushing for the reintegration of their disastrous war and postwar experiences into a (pan-)European narrative, two main pillars of the erstwhile historical consensus—the ones particularly cherished by Russia, namely, the notions of the antifascist good's triumph over the Nazi evil and of the Red Army's liberation of Eastern Europe—have come under severe attack. By contrast, the new interpretation advances the notion of the Nazi-Soviet equivalence and rejects the Soviet/Russian claim to the mantle of "Europe's liberator" by branding the Soviet postwar policies in Eastern Europe as an act of occupation. Again, this is not just an academic controversy. In a number of East European countries, the new historical narratives are used to justify certain political moves in what can be called a perfect example of history politics. As Mälksoo notes,

> East European MEPs [members of the European Parliament] have made it their political mission to devise a framework for the treatment of Communist crimes similar to that of Nazi crimes. This has led to the adoption of relevant resolutions by the European Parliament and political declarations by the Parliamentary Assembly of the Council of Europe and the OSCE [Organization for Security and Co-operation in Europe]. The

European Commission has organised hearings on "Crimes committed by totalitarian regimes." These hearings are hoped to develop into a concrete institutional instrument in the longer perspective.³⁰

Moreover, as if to additionally underscore the *political* dimension of the ongoing memory wars, East Europeans assert that "these debates are conducted, and lances are broken, *in the name of Europe*—and, of course, *for Europe*—to make one's historical narrative 'more European.' This also serves to highlight one's Europeanness to the detriment of the opposing party's Europeanness."[31]

This is exactly how the matter is perceived by Russia's ruling elites. As Moscow sees it, what is at stake in the acrimonious debates over historical narratives with the former Eastern bloc satellites and ex-Soviet republics is no less than Russia's status as a "European nation" and great (European) power. When a number of Western and Eastern European historians and policy makers set forth a thesis about the "Soviet occupation" and then pile on top of it another thesis about the "Adolf Hitler–Joseph Stalin equivalence," this is viewed by Moscow as something very much akin to adding insult to injury. It's not difficult to understand the reason for Russia's nervous reaction to the new historical narratives of the origins of World War II and the interaction between Europe's two totalitarian regimes as well as to the reinterpretations of the relationship between the totalitarian states and the "free world." The traditional overall representation of World War II based on the erstwhile historical consensus has been that this was a global confrontation between good and evil—with Nazi Germany being habitually associated with absolute evil. "Thirty years ago there seemed to be no doubt" as to what the Second World War was about, notes the Russian historian Yaroslav Shimov. "The Russians, the Americans and the majority of the Europeans perceived World War II as a colossal tragic epic—the history of the joint struggle against global evil and of the victory over this evil that was won due to the enormous sacrifices in blood and treasure."³²

In the new narrative, though, the picture gets somewhat more nuanced and the new accents appear: World War II has come to be interpreted not only as the struggle between good and evil but also as the struggle between freedom and tyranny, democracy and totalitarianism—with the notions of democracy, freedom, and liberalism being unambiguously equaled with the notion of good. Seen through this (updated) conceptual optics, the following storyline is emerging. Two equally vicious totalitarian empires secretly divided up their respective spheres of influence in Eastern Europe and, having jointly attacked Poland, triggered the pan-European conflict that subsequently became global. Following Nazi Germany's invasion of the Soviet Union, the liberal West pragmatically allied itself with one totalitarian predator against the other. The victory over Nazism was attained thanks to the massive Soviet war effort in the European theater, which in turn led to Stalin's occupation of half of Europe, with the enfeebled West (particularly the war-ravaged Western European nations) being unable to adequately respond to what was the brazen act of Soviets building their "outer empire" against the will of the "captive nations" in Europe's East. However, the confrontation between good and evil continued in the postwar period, having taken on the form of the Cold War waged for several decades between the democratic Western nations, on the one hand, and the Communist USSR ("the evil empire") and its satellites, on the other. The "liberation of Eastern Europe" and the Soviet breakup appear to symbolize the ultimate triumph of good (i.e., freedom and democracy) over evil (i.e., tyranny and totalitarianism). The bottom line seems to be this: the West has made an enormous contribution to the liberation of humankind from the "curse of the twentieth century"—totalitarianism in its dual form of Nazism and Stalinism. For its part, post-Soviet Russia, not unlike the (vanquished) postwar Germany, has yet to go through the painful process of repentance, atonement for the committed crimes, and thorough de-Stalinization.

It's difficult not to see how these historiographical debates over the "correct" interpretation of past events are effectively the struggle over power. The thing is that so long as the old historical consensus remained intact, Russia's victory over Nazism legitimized its great power status in Europe and its sphere of influence in the eastern part of the continent. The new historical controversies over the nature of Soviet "liberation" of Eastern Europe and over Stalin's purported equivalence with Hitler effectively undermine Russia's status as the "liberator of Europe" and erode whatever symbolic capital it might claim to prop up its "Europeanness." What we are witnessing is basically a "clash" of two very different notions of "liberation." In today's Europe (and, for that matter, the United States), the liberation of Europe in World War II is inseparably welded with the idea of democracy—the restoration of democratic order in that part of Europe which was cleansed by Western Allies of the "brown plague." Such interpretation presupposes that whatever the Soviet Union did in the eastern half of Europe that fell under Stalin's control could be called anything but "liberation."

What had actually happened "on the ground" was, of course, much less neat than the descriptions offered by the traditional "totalitarian" model or than a stark dichotomy of the "Western liberation" and the "Soviet suppression" that is currently being advanced by many Western policy makers and ideologues. The Hitler–Stalin comparison has kept analysts busy ever since the 1930s. However, the totalitarian model, as its contemporary critics rightly note, mainly "focused on similarities rather than differences [between the two dictatorships] and . . . contained far more description than explanation."[33] As the recent historical research has demonstrated, "While the two regimes often rested on similar power structures and methods of control, nevertheless they were the product of entirely different social forces, ideas and aspirations."[34] Moreover, some scholars argue that the thesis of the Nazi-Soviet equivalence and of a "double genocide"—which, for instance, figures quite prominently in Timothy Snyder's acclaimed recent study *Bloodlands*[35]—blurs the undeniable fact that ultimately it was Nazi Germany and not the Soviet Union which was responsible for the outbreak of World War II and the ensuing carnage. The critics also assert that Snyder and other like-minded scholars unwittingly help the Far Right politicians in the Baltic region (and in some other "new accession" states in the eastern half of the EU) to pursue their "politics of history" fueled by anti-Russianism and the desire to exculpate the region's Nazi collaborators and participants in the Holocaust.[36] Notably, the leading Stanford historian Norman Naimark—who, in his latest book, seeks to forcefully make a point that Stalin was a mass murderer and an exceedingly brutal dictator of the worst kind—appears to concede that the Stalin-Hitler equivalence thesis is flawed. Although Naimark concludes that "the points of comparison between Stalin and Hitler, Nazism and Stalinism, are too many to ignore," he also admits that there are key differences and that the Holocaust was, on many counts, "worse."[37]

Nor is the issue of the "Soviet occupation of Eastern Europe" that straightforward. Stalin *is* the main culprit, for sure. But the Western powers are not unblemished either. In Eastern Europe, for more than half a century, "Yalta" has become a grim symbol of betrayal, with Western Allies being perceived as accomplices in Stalin's expansion and, in Milan Kundera's words, the ensuing "tragedy of Central Europe."

The criticism of the Allies' compliance with the demands of the Stalinist Soviet Union at Yalta and the consequent Western moral responsibility for the closing off of Eastern Europe behind the Iron Curtain during the Cold War thus runs as a red thread through the mnemopolitical discourse of Poland and the Baltic states.[38]

Eastern Europeans have a point. After all, John Kenneth Galbraith, then a top official in the U.S. Office of Price Administration, who appeared to consider the Soviet Union a compelling social experiment, suggested that "Russia should be permitted to absorb Poland, the Balkans, and the whole of Eastern Europe in order to spread the benefits of Communism." For his part, George Kennan, at the time a counselor of the American embassy in Moscow, privately advised Charles Bohlen, Franklin D. Roosevelt's interpreter and adviser on Soviet affairs in Yalta, to "divide Europe frankly into spheres of influence—keep ourselves out of the Russian sphere and the Russians out of ours." Ultimately, it was realpolitik and not the lofty ideals of freedom that defined the contours of postwar Europe.[39]

Notably, some East European pundits readily admit that their countries heavily exploited Western Europe's feeling of guilt and the sense of owing a debt to Eastern Europeans in their nations' quest to join the Euro-Atlantic institutions. As a result, they assert, all counterarguments notwithstanding, the dual North Atlantic Treaty Organization (NATO) and EU enlargement "was framed *entirely* as the undoing of historic injustice towards Eastern European states."[40]

Having thus received some satisfaction from the erstwhile Western supporters of the despised "Yalta order," the "political historical" activists in ex-Communist countries have set their sights on the East. At a minimum, their objective appears to be as follows—to force post-Soviet Russia, too, to face up to its "dark past" and to apologize for the crimes of Soviet totalitarianism. To this end, East European lawmakers had pushed hard for the adoption, in 2009, of two international documents that couldn't fail to rile official Moscow—a resolution of the European Parliament titled "On European Conscience and Totalitarianism" and a resolution passed by the Parliamentary Assembly of the OSCE titled "Divided Europe Reunited: Promoting Human Rights and Civil Liberties in the OSCE Region in the Twenty-First Century."[41] Both resolutions branded Nazism and Stalinism as similar totalitarian regimes, bearing equal responsibility for the outbreak of World War II and the crimes against humanity during that period. The resolutions strongly called for the unconditional international condemnation of European totalitarianism. Moscow's reaction to all of this was unambiguously negative. In particular, Russian lawmakers, incensed at Stalinism and Nazism being lumped together, called the OSCE resolution an "offensive anti-Russian provocation" and "violence over history."[42] It is also no mere coincidence that in May 2009 Russia's president, Dmitry Medvedev, announced the formation of a new presidential commission dedicated to "analyzing and suppressing all attempts to falsify history to the detriment of Russia's interests."[43]

RUSSIA'S AMBIGUOUS SYMBOLIC POLITICS

Russia's irascible response is instructive in that it accurately reflects the Russian elites' utter discomfort at being pressured as well as their appreciation of the sensitive history-foreign policy nexus. The country's governing elites appear to perceive memory and history as an important ideological and political battleground: Russia's detractors—both foreign and domestic—allegedly seek to spread interpretations of past events that are detrimental to Russia's interests, and there is an urgent need to resolutely counter these unfriendly moves. Several elements of such politics of history have already been introduced in Russia: a set of officially sponsored and centrally approved textbooks with the highly pronounced statist interpretation of twentieth-century Russian history, the attempts to establish the "regime of truth" using legislative means, and the creation of a bureaucratic institution to fight the "falsification of history."[44]

The Kremlin's official position was well epitomized in Vladimir Putin's remarks at the June 21, 2007, meeting with the participants of the all-Russian history teachers' conference. Putin's main message was twofold: "Past events should be portrayed in a way that fuels national pride" and "We cannot allow anyone to impose a sense of guilt on us."[45] In general, the transcript of the meeting makes a fascinating read in that it gives an intriguing picture of the attempts to forge a broad consensus within Russia's ruling and intellectual elites—the picture in which the emotional, the historical, and the political are closely intertwined. The academics who took part in the gathering at Putin's countryside retreat expressed their firm conviction in the *political* significance of the past. The latter, as one pundit put it, is not some curiosa assembled in an antiquarian's store but rather a vital "mechanism, functioning within the structure of the present." After all, the argument goes, all taken decisions are nothing but a projection of a worldview that is formed within the consciousness of those who take decisions. For its part, an individual's worldview is shaped, to a significant degree, by history—the dominant master narratives about the past. Thus, history might well be understood as the past politics, and politics—as the present history. No wonder, then, that Putin's guests found themselves in a unanimous agreement with the famous Orwellian maxim: He who controls the past also controls the present and the future.[46]

Likewise, the meeting's participants agreed that particular interpretations of the past can be (and often are) the effective instruments of power politics and levers deployed to influence the other nations' position. At one point, a scholar bemoaned Russia's "humiliating" treatment by the West, which allegedly sees it as an eternal apprentice. "How long will we continue putting up with being treated as pupils? We are a country, a gigantic country that can take pride in its extraordinary achievements, but we are still perceived as pupils," the political science professor Leonid Polyakov complained. Responding to his remark, Putin was quick to note that it's truly intolerable when "someone takes on the role of a teacher and starts lecturing us." But, he pointedly added, besides being an irritant, "this is undoubtedly an instrument to influence our country's conduct."[47]

Putin's concluding remarks at the gathering with historians are noteworthy for both their defiance and his attempt to normalize and relativize Russian history—in particular the Soviet period. "As far as the problematic pages of our history are concerned, they were a reality," Putin said. "But they were a reality in the life of any state! And in fact we had less of them than some others, and they were not as horrible as those inscribed in the history of some other countries . . . other countries had even more horrible things." In a word, this was Putin's advice to Russia's detractors to leave it alone and mind their own business. "Let them think about themselves," he blurted.[48]

Against this backdrop, it would seem that historical interpretations began to be increasingly viewed in Moscow as the means that various international actors use to assail Russia's international standing, seeking to undermine its symbolic power—possibly with the view of extracting concessions. A number of leading Russian historians have argued that following the geopolitical shifts of the late 1980s and early 1990s, Russia became the chief object of Western pressure as the leading Western nations and their new East European allies seek to cast Russia as the ultimate loser in the Cold War and a country that could now be presented with all sorts of claims. "The most vicious attacks are directed at the [Russian-supported] interpretations of World War II and at the Yalta-Potsdam system," write Aleksandr and Yelena Senyavsky in the journal published by the prestigious Moscow State Institute of International Relations (MGIMO). The reason for this, they explain, lies in the fact that this system had confirmed the results of the war, making the Soviet Union the dominant power in Europe. Moreover, having recognized the immense Soviet war losses and the USSR's decisive role in defeating Nazi Germany, its Western wartime allies had also recognized its significant role in the construction of the postwar "modern Europe." Following the Soviet breakup, Russia has found itself in a much less favorable geopolitical situation, the authors concede, but, they contend, "the new Russia's principal interest is in the maximally possible preservation and perpetuation of those aspects of the system of international relations" that had emerged in the wake of World War II.[49]

Indeed, to get a better sense of why Moscow is so uneasy about the attempts to "reinterpret World War II results" one has only to recall three things: the persistence of Russia's self-image as a great power, its constant concern about falling behind relative to its main (Western) competitors, and the simple fact that 1945 represented the absolute pinnacle of Russia's geopolitical might. Some scholars have long argued that following its defeat in the Crimean War in 1856 and until the Soviet victory in World War II, Russian power has been in a relative decline.[50] The USSR's triumph over Nazi Germany—associated with Stalin's policies—reversed this trend and restored Soviet Russia to an enviable position of a country "without whose permission not a single gun in Europe could fire a shot," as Prince Aleksandr Bezborodko, Russia's eighteenth-century top diplomat, had once colorfully put it. We appear to be dealing here with a remarkable case of geopolitical continuity. "Don't forget," Judt reminded us,

> that as seen from a historian's perspective, a historian of contemporary Europe, Stalin was in many ways the natural successor to Catherine the Great, and the tsars of the 19th century, expanding into the Russian near west, and to the Russian southwest in particular—territories that Catherine began her expansion into, which have always been regarded as crucial by Russian strategists, both because of access to resources, access to warm water ports, and because it gives Russia a role in Europe, as well as in Asia.[51]

Just consider two plain historical facts: Russia was among the biggest losers in World War I and saw its statehood crumbling and the borderlands seceding, while World War II results confirmed at Yalta and Potsdam turned Russia (in the form of the Soviet Union) into the world's second superpower—a status that included Moscow's immense geopolitical clout in Europe. Remarkably, a history textbook that was unveiled at the 2007 historians' conference opens with the telling phrase: "Moscow, between 1945 and 1991, was the capital not only of a country but of an entire world system."[52] However, Russia's four-decade-long dominance over Eastern Europe was brought down in a series of "velvet revolutions" in 1989. As one pithy comment put it, "Russia was the main victor in World War II and the main loser in 1989."[53]

That is the crux of the matter: Russian elites felt tremendously aggrieved by the loss of international influence following the collapse of the Soviet Union. But now, twenty years on, "Russia is back"—having lived through the decade of "national humiliation" (1990s), it has rebounded and experienced a significant revival in the 2000s. The Russian leadership's "historical political" moves are meant to complement the country's increasingly assertive foreign policy—in particular, to reclaim the lost historical moral high ground. Yet Russia's international identity remains—possibly intentionally—highly ambivalent. On the one hand, it claims legitimacy in Europe as a post-Soviet *European* state; on the other, it presents itself as the direct successor to the Soviet Union—a stance that entails two important implications: Russia's claim to a status of great power with a sphere of "privileged interests" and its reluctance to fully recognize Soviet/Stalinist crimes. However, nothing undermines trust and sours the relations between Russia and its neighbors more than the reluctance of Russian policy elite to fully come to terms with the Soviet past, recognize the crimes of the Stalinist regime, and acknowledge all the wrongs it did both to the Russian people and the other peoples of the former USSR and Eastern Europe. Some Russian commentators and politicians argue that the Kremlin leadership has already condemned Stalinism and, besides, Russia is one of its many victims. Indeed, certain liberal-minded segments of Russia's political leadership who are interested in the strengthening of their country's ties with the West seem to have embarked on their own, as yet rather feeble, de-Stalinization campaign.[54] In an apparent attempt to politically mend fences with Poland, the Russian Duma officially recognized that the

Katyn crime—the execution in 1940 of about twenty-two thousand Poles by the Soviet security police—was committed on direct order by Stalin and other Soviet leaders. Prior to this unprecedented statement, the Polish film *Katyn* was shown on Russian television, and President Medvedev, on his visit to Warsaw in September 2010, awarded the Order of Friendship to Andrzej Wajda, the film's celebrated director.[55]

But these declarations are definitely not enough. Russian human rights activists have long asserted that in Russia, the memory of Stalinism is invariably a memory of *victims* but not of the committed *crime*. Twenty years after the end of Communist rule, there isn't even one legislative act in which the state terror would be unequivocally characterized as crime.[56] Nowhere is it stated that the extrajudicial bodies created during the Soviet period were a bad thing: since they were formed on the orders of the supreme organs of the Soviet power, they are deemed to be perfectly legal. As a result, Russia finds itself in a vicious circle. Without the legal assessment of the crimes committed by the Soviet regime, it is impossible to advance public education based on the liberal values, but the present-day Russian authorities are reluctant to pass a legal judgment on the Stalinist misdeeds.[57]

Some more enlightened members of the Russian elite, however, appear to clearly see where the problem lies. It is rooted, the former chairman of Russia's influential Council on Foreign and Defense Policy, Sergei Karaganov, states bluntly, in "the legacy of Soviet socialism"—that is, "Stalinism" and its consequences. In his recent essay published in the government newspaper under the telltale title "A Russian Katyn," Karaganov argues that, so far, Russians "have not found in themselves the strength to recognize that *all Russia is one large Katyn*" filled with "the nameless graves of millions of victims of the regime" that ruled over the Soviet Union for most of the previous century.[58] "Over the past year," Karaganov noted,

> Both the president and prime minister have condemned Stalinism. And all the same, we have not dared to fully reject its inheritance, to repent for the outrages committed by us and our ancestors over ourselves and our own people.... Without bowing before the victims of Stalinism and without recognizing the guilt of their own country before them, we will remain inheritors only of another part of our people—their executioners, guards, and snitches, of those who voluntarily de-kulakized [the country] and destroyed the churches.[59]

Remarkably, Karaganov has made a direct link between Russia's inability to face up to its "dark past" and the country's international image: "The anti-Russian sentiment is strong also because we ourselves are unable to part with the worst in our history." This is what Russia's liberal scholars and rights activists have been arguing for years. But such a statement, coming from a person of Karaganov's stature and appearing in a government daily, becomes significant.[60] It appears to indicate that, although in today's Russia there is no open and nationwide discussion of the country's unpalatable past comparable to the famous *Historikerstreit* (historians' conflict) in Germany in the 1980s, the acute struggle over the interpretation of history does take place even within the establishment.[61] This largely internal struggle accounts for the seemingly contradictory moves that the Russian authorities are making. Notably, President Medvedev who signed the infamous decree on the creation of the "commission against falsifications of history," appointed in October 2010 Mikhail Fedotov, previously head of Russia's liberal-leaning Union of Journalists, the Kremlin's top human rights advisor. Upon his appointment, Fedotov wasted no time to declare his sweeping de-Stalinization agenda. Russia has no future, he argued, unless it can overcome its totalitarian mind-set and understand the full scale of Stalin's repressions. He further contended that Russia's Soviet legacy was inextricably linked with its main problems such as corruption and lack of press freedom. He also announced that he would soon present Medvedev with a package of proposals to eradicate "totalitarian thinking."[62] This was apparently done at the meeting of the Council on Civil Society and Human Rights in Yekaterinburg on February 1, 2011, which was attended by President Medvedev. There a group of liberal intellectuals headed by Karaganov and Arseny Roginsky, head of *Memorial*, announced the launch of an ambitious project titled "On the Perpetuation of the Memory of the Victims of the Totalitarian Regime and on National Reconciliation." This project, which should become a "mass movement for restoring historical memory and justice," is aimed at no less than the radical transformation of the consciousness of both Russian society and the Russian elite. Remarkably, what is at stake, according to the project's leaders, is the (re)creation of a *new Russian identity*, without which, they contend, "progress will be impossible."[63]

The direct link that is made between de-Stalinization and the forging of Russia's new post-Soviet identity is instructive. Drawing on the German postwar lessons, liberal-minded Russian intellectuals and political thinkers argue that, like the denazification and the campaign of the collective guilt in Germany following the Nazi era, the ideology and politics of de-Stalinization should become an instrument of the thorough reforming of Russia's political and social system. For Russia, this de-Stalinization agenda is both urgent and strategic as it should constitute, according to one comment, an important aspect of the country's "new identity, new 'national idea,' if you wish."[64] Ultimately, a new social norm should take root that would reject excessive violence and the primacy of the state interests over those of the individual and instead uphold the principles of tolerance, compromise, and societal dialogue. As a result, Russia's entire political culture will have been transformed. It would appear, though, that Russia is in for a long haul. The country's elites seem to be divided over the kind of identity they wish for Russia: either that of a *derzhava* (great power) that bosses around in its geopolitical backyard or that of a law-governed European state at peace with its neighbors. Thus Russia's contradictory "politics of history" is likely to continue. If anything, Medvedev, judging by his remarks at the Yekaterinburg meeting of the Human Rights Council, was not terribly impressed by the proposals advanced by a group of Russian liberal thinkers. He reiterated that both he as president and the Russian Parliament have already made political statements with regard to the Stalinist period and its crimes, while it is up to the courts to pass any legal ruling in these matters. So it's unclear, he argued, what else could be done here.[65] On the other hand, Russian public attitudes also indicate that there is an uphill struggle ahead. According to the 2009 survey of the Levada Center, Russia's well-respected independent pollster, around 49 percent of Russians believe that Stalin played a largely positive role in the country's history, while only 33 percent hold that he was a negative historical figure.[66] In a sense, suggests the liberal political analyst Kirill Rogov, Russia "finds itself in a situation similar to the one that West Germany experienced in the beginning of the 1950s, when seven years after the destruction of Hitler's Third Reich and the actual completion of the denazification campaign it turned out that Nazism had remained part of the national political consciousness, and one-third of Germans were ready to justify it one way or the other."[67]

CONCLUSION

Is it realistic to believe that ex-Communist Eastern European states will ever do without politics of history and that the memory wars between them will eventually end? While national images of the past will never fully coincide, it appears feasible to reach some reconciliation between them and thus avoid creating negative identities. Such reconciliation can be achieved in the course of a broad and mutually respectful dialogue between national memories and historical narratives. All the participants of this dialogue would agree that while national memories are not congruent and historical narratives might diverge, one's image of the past could only be enriched through the knowledge of alternative interpretations.

Such dialogue, however, will only be possible if three formidable obstacles are overcome. The most important obstacle is authoritarian political culture. As Karl Schlögel argues, "Authoritarian conditions are hostile to memory. A mature historical culture and a civil culture belong together."[68] Indeed, scholars have noted the close correlation between regime type and the degree of a regime's reliance on historical myths.[69] True, all regimes resort to and rely on mythmaking. But in liberal democracies, political legitimacy is much less dependent on the unifying historical narrative that would foster compliance with government policies than it is in authoritarian regimes. Genuine democracies are thus much more tolerant of dissent, controversy, and competing ideas and can afford the luxury of treating history that challenges habitual assumptions with relative equanimity. This trait, in the words of the eminent British historian Michael Howard, is a mark of maturity. By contrast, authoritarian leaders prefer to feed their subjects with what Howard calls "nursery history." In his view, "[A] good definition of the difference between a Western liberal society and a totalitarian one—whether it is Communist, fascist, or Catholic authoritarian—is that in the former the government treats its citizens as responsible adults and in the latter it cannot."[70]

The second problem is the widespread perceptions that mass publics hold about what history actually is. Sociological surveys demonstrate that in most post-Soviet states, people are largely unaware of one fundamental thing—that studying history is a complex and continuous process in the course of which what used to be perceived as "historical truth" can (and should) be refuted as new evidence emerges or new interpretations are advanced. According to the recent data provided by the All-Russian Center for the Study of Public Opinion, or VTsIOM, a Russian pollster,

60 percent of the respondents hold that history should not be revised, that past events should be studied in such a way that would exclude "repeat research" leading to new approaches and interpretations. Only 31 percent of those polled believe that the study of history is a continuous and open-ended process. Furthermore, 79 percent spoke in favor of using one single textbook when teaching history course in schools—lest the young minds get confused by alternative interpretations. Symptomatically, 78 percent supported the creation of the presidential commission charged with fighting "falsification of history," and 60 percent said the passing of a "memory law" criminalizing the "revision of WWII results" would be a good thing. Ironically, when 61 percent of Russians say that "national interpretations" of the past are inadmissible, they appear to be oblivious of the fact that their own interpretation is no less "national."[71]

This picture of public attitudes should correct an oversimplified perception of symbolic politics in the post-Soviet lands as basically a one-way street whereby the discourse that serves the interests of ruling elites is being imposed upon society. In more ways than one, the prevalent attitudes toward history and memory demonstrate the meeting of the minds between the rulers and the ruled in Eurasia.

It would appear that these attitudes can be changed only slowly through the changes in the way national histories are written in Russia and other ex-Soviet republics. And this is the third big problem that needs to be tackled. It would be naive to believe that national governments (or die-hard nationalists, for that matter) will one day stop regarding (and exploiting) historical narrative as a useful means of nationalist mobilization. After all, common history is what holds the imagined community together. So an ethnic-centric, "nationalized" history is likely to persist. But what is needed, assert some leading historians, is to supplement a traditional national narrative by a *multiethnic* or, better still, *transnational* approach. "Transnational" or "transcultural" history, argues Andreas Kappeler, would be based on "multiperspectivity and comparison" and would "investigate interactions, communications, and overlapping phenomena and entanglements between states, nations, societies, economies, regions, and cultures."[72]

These new approaches would probably still not help overcome the divide between memories in the post-Soviet world. But there is no need to try bridging the gap between national memories. This goal is unattainable. The objective to be pursued is much more modest: to promote understanding of other perspectives and interpretations.

1. Carnegie Moscow Center and the Shigabuddin Mardzhani Institute, "The Politics of History and Its Variations in Post-socialist Countries," seminar; Greene, ed., *Engaging History*.
2. Rachinsky, "Istoriia kak pole boya," 47.
3. Snyder, introduction, *East European Politics and Societies*, 4.
4. Purcell, "War, Memory, and National Identity," 188–89. For a detailed discussion of the interrelation between history and identity, see MacMillan, *Dangerous Games*, particularly chap. 4.
5. Judt, "From the House of the Dead."
6. Mälksoo, "The Memory Political Horizons."
7. Ibid.
8. See, e.g., Michel and Nollendorfs in Ruge, ed., *Der Kommunismus im Museum*; and Nollendorfs, *Museum of the Occupation of Latvia*.
9. See Kabachiy, "Ukradennaya pamyat."
10. Maksymiuk, "Ukraine: Parliament Recognizes Soviet-Era Famine as Genocide"; Kasyanov, "Golodomor i stroitel'stvo natsii." For a more detailed treatment of the politics of history in Ukraine, see Marples, *Heroes and Villains*; Olszanski, "Yushchenko's Historical Policy"; and Rodgers, "Compliance or Contradiction?"
11. *Eurozine*, "Eurozine Conference Held in Vilnius."
12. See MacMillan, *Dangerous Games*; Friedman, "The Past in the Future."
13. Foner, *Who Owns History?*, 77.
14. See Abdelal, "Memories of Nations and States"; Kuzio, "History, Memory, and Nation Building"; Kuzio, "Nation Building, History Writing"; and Wolczuk, "History, Europe, and the 'National Idea.'"
15. Bordiugov and Bukharayev, *Vcherashnee zavtra*.
16. For their part, authors of Russian history textbooks often seek to depict Russia as a homogeneous civilization, which leads to the biased representation of certain non-Russian ethnic communities. See Shnirelman, "Stigmatized by History or by Historians?"; and Shnirelman, "Rossiiskaya shkola i natsional'naya ideya." Unless otherwise noted, the translations in this chapter are mine.
17. See Shnirelman, *Shkil'na istoriya ochyma istorykiv-naukovtsiv*; and Yakovenko, "Kontseptsiya novogo uchebnika ukrainskoi istorii." To get a sense of how heated the public debate over the concept of school history textbooks in Ukraine is, see the polemic between Yakovenko and Professor Yuri Mytsyk: Mytsyk, "Novoe ili podzabytoe staroe"; and Yakovenko, "Likbez dlya professor."
18. Vdovin quoted in Samarina, "Istoriya umolchaniya."
19. Karavayev, "'Novy istoricheskii mif' i konflikty interpretatsii."
20. Kasyanov, "Natsionalizatsiya istorii ta obraz inshoho."
21. The vigor of the German debate on the country's terrible past is as yet unimaginable in today's Russia. The latest example of the frank process of national self-scrutiny in Germany is the exhibition *Hitler and the Germans: Nation and Crime* that opened in the German Historical Museum in October 2010. The show, the first to focus on Hitler since 1945, explores the sensitive issue of how German society nurtured and empowered the Nazi dictator. See Slackman, "Hitler Exhibit Explores a Wider Circle of Guilt"; and Paver, "Exhibiting the National Socialist Past." One should not forget, though, that it took the Germans at least twenty years to start debating the Nazi past in earnest. See, e.g., Mommsen, "Changing Historical Perspectives of the Nazi Dictatorship"; Kansteiner in Lebow, Kansteiner, and Fogu, eds., *The Politics of Memory in Postwar Europe*; and Frei, "Preodolennoe proshloe?"
22. Lebow, Kansteiner, and Fogu, eds., *The Politics of Memory in Postwar Europe*; Gledhill,

"Integrating the Past"; Kattago, "Agreeing to Disagree"; Esbenshade, "Remembering to Forget"; Judt, "The Past Is Another Country."
23 Snyder, "The Historical Reality of Eastern Europe"; Davies, *No Simple Victory*.
24 Zehfuss, *Wounds of Memory*.
25 Schmale in Faraldo, Gulinska-Jurgiel, and Domnitz, eds., *Europa im Ostblok*; Troebst, "Jalta versus Stalingrad, Gulag versus Holocaust"; Troebst, "Kakoi takoi kover?"
26 Krzeminski, "As Many Wars as Nations." The Polish original is in *Polityka*, March 23, 2005.
27 Leggewie, "Seven Circles of European Memory."
28 Mälksoo, "The Memory Politics of Becoming European," 654; Mälksoo, "The Memory Political Horizons."
29 Mälksoo, "The Memory Political Horizons."
30 Ibid.
31 Ibid. (emphasis in original).
32 Shimov, "Vtoraia mirovaia: Konets eposa."
33 Benn, "On Comparing Nazism and Stalinism," 189. See also Geyer and Fitzpatrick, eds., *Beyond Totalitarianism*; Overy, *The Dictators*; and Bullock, *Hitler and Stalin*.
34 Bullock, *Hitler and Stalin*, 191.
35 Snyder, *Bloodlands*.
36 See Zuroff, "A Dangerous Nazi-Soviet Equivalence"; and Katz, "Why Red Is Not Brown in the Baltics." The German historian Wilfried Jilge specifically points to the tendency of East European intellectuals to construct what he terms the "national Holocausts" and thus confer on their nations a status of victim—and the perceived moral high ground that goes along with it. "From this position of moral superiority, the crimes of one's own nation are justified as defensive actions," writes Jilge in an article tellingly titled "The Competition of Victims"—the phrase he borrowed from the former Polish foreign minister Władysław Bartoszewski. "In this context," Jilge goes on, "national stereotypes serve to distance 'one's own' national history from 'false' Soviet history and thus to 'cleanse' 'one's own' nation of everything that is Soviet." Jilge, "Zmahannya zhertv."
37 Naimark, *Stalin's Genocides*. See also the review of Naimark's book by Hockenos, "The Fine Line of Blood."
38 Mälksoo, "The Memory Politics of Becoming European," 662.
39 Hamby, "Endgame." See also Harbutt, *Yalta 1945*; Plokhy, *Yalta: The Price of Peace*.
40 Mälksoo, "The Memory Politics of Becoming European," 662 (emphasis added).
41 For the texts of resolutions, see European Parliament, "Resolution on European Conscience and Totalitarianism"; and OSCE Parliamentary Assembly, "Vilnius Declaration."
42 Taratuta and Vodo, "Rossiya popala v plokhuyu istoriyu."
43 See the text of the Russian President's Decree no. 549, "O Komissii po fal'sifikatsii istorii."
44 For a detailed analysis of the narratives contained in the Russian history textbooks, see Benn, "The Teaching of History in Present-Day Russia"; Benn, "The Teaching of History in Putin's Russia"; Kaplan, "The Vicissitudes of Socialism in Russian History Textbooks"; Sherlock in Cole, ed., *Teaching the Violent Past*; Ferretti, "Obretennaya identichnost"; and Berelovich, "Sovremennye rossiiskie uchebniki istorii." For a comprehensive discussion of the attempts to pass a "memory law" in Russia, see Koposov, *Pamiat' strogogo rezhima*. For a discussion of history politics in Russia and in some of the ex-Communist states, see Miller, "Istoriya imperii i politika pamyati"; Miller, "'Istoricheskaya politika' v Vostochnoi Evrope"; Miller, "Istoricheskaya politika: Update"; Logvinov, "Istoricheskaya politika na postsovetskom prostranstve"; and the *Russian Analytical Digest* special issue "History Writing and National Myth-Making in Russia." Also see Kasyanov, "Golodomor i stroitel'stvo natsii";

Rachinsky, "Istoriia kak pole boya"; the *Evropa: Zhurnal Pol'skogo Instituta Mezhdunarodnykh Del* special issue "Trudnoe nasledie proshlogo: Rossiia v poiskakh istoricheskoi pravdy"; and Reisner et al., "Writing National Histories." Finally, see also Astrov, "Estonia: Political Struggle for a Place in History."

45 "Stenograficheskii otchet o vstreche s delegatami Vserossiiskoi konferentsii prepodavatelei gumanitarnykh i obshchestvennykh nauk," Novo-Ogarevo. On Putin's personal sense of history, see Hill and Gaddy, "Putin and the Uses of History."

46 "Stenograficheskii otchet." Symptomatically, this appears to be a point of contact of sorts between some Baltic pundits and their Russian ideological opponents. "Let us give another high five to Orwell—who controls the past, controls the future!," notes Mälksoo in her analysis of East European memory wars. Mälksoo, "The Memory Political Horizons."

47 "Stenograficheskii otchet."

48 Ibid.

49 Senyavsky and Senyavskaya, "Vtoraia mirovaia voina i istoricheskaia pamiat," 300.

50 See Baumgart, *Der Friede von Paris*. This thesis is also discussed in Luks, "Predchuvstvie zakata Evropy i strakh pered Rossiei."

51 "Interview with Historian Tony Judt," Radio Free Europe / Radio Liberty.

52 Filippov, *Noveishaia istoriia Rossii*, 6. Notably, Aleksandr Filippov, the principal author of this history manual, is deputy head of the National Laboratory of Foreign Policy, a research institute affiliated with the Kremlin. For an English language review of the book, see Benn, "The Teaching of History in Putin's Russia."

53 *Eurozine*, "European Histories: Toward a Grand Narrative."

54 Lipman, "The Third Wave of Russian De-Stalinization."

55 Dempsey, "Old Foes See Reasons to Get Along"; Trenin, "Rossiya i Pol'sha."

56 See Roginsky, "Pamyat' o stalinizme."

57 Khazanov and Payne, "How to Deal with the Past?"

58 Karaganov, "Russkaya Katyn" (emphasis added in my translation).

59 Ibid. (emphasis added).

60 Remarkably, the 2010 session of the Valdai Discussion Club—a forum cofounded in 2004 by RIA Novosti and Russia's Council on Foreign and Defense Policy, which brings together Russian and foreign scholars, journalists, and public intellectuals—was devoted to discussing the topic of "Russia's history and future development." Some Russian participants have forcefully argued that "without a full realization of Russia's horrific past, without both figuratively and physically burying Lenin, Russia cannot move forward." Zolotov, "The Storm of History"; Lieven, "Reexamining Russian History."

61 Unlike in Germany, the community of professional historians in Russia has not yet evolved into a genuine "expert corporation" that enjoys the trust of Russian society. As some commentators note—to my mind, correctly—in today's Russia, the institutional conditions for the independent scholarly expertise and analysis are still lacking. Indeed, basically, institutions are norms and rules; the latter, however, cannot be abided by in the absence of trust. In a polity where people question (and for good reasons at that) the trustworthiness of the courts, the existence of independent scholarly expertise, the ability of the professional community to pass an unbiased judgment, the possibility of holding an unrestrained discussion in the mainstream mass media, and the very search for truth appear to be problematic. Yet in lieu of the full-blooded *Historikerstreit*, over the past decade Russia did see three big debates on history textbooks: the "Dolutsky affair," the "Filippov affair," and the "Vdovin-Barsenkov affair." On the Filippov affair, see the following articles in *Kritika: Explorations in Russian and Eurasian History*: Brandenberger, "A New Short Course?"; Mironov, "The

Fruits of a Bourgeois Education"; Solonari, "Normalizing Russia, Legitimizing Putin"; and Zubkova, "The Filippov Syndrome." Also of interest are Sokolov, "Vek surka"; and Babich, "Stalin's Methods Revived."
62 Grove, "Russia Must Exorcise Stalin's Legacy."
63 See the speeches by Karaganov and Roginsky at the February 1, 2011, Yekaterinburg meeting of the Council on Civil Society and Human Rights.
64 Rogov, "Destalinizatsiya."
65 "Stenograficheskii otchet."
66 Rogov, "Destalinizatsiya."
67 Ibid. There is, however, a remarkable sign of more salubrious winds blowing in Russian historiography—a recent publication of the two-volume textbook of Russian modern history, *Istoriya Rossii: XX vek*, edited by Andrei Zubov. Three features distinguish this landmark study: it rejects the traditional statist approach by putting the individual at the center of the narrative and by striving to present the history of society rather than the history of the state; it rejects the traditional stance of "wounded nationalism" that used to invariably portray Russia as a victim of foreign aggression; and it rejects the traditional aversion to using foreign accounts. Significantly, it also offers a very untraditional interpretation of World War II: eschewing the use of the symbolically laden term "the Great Patriotic War," the authors suggest a more neutral one—"the Soviet-Nazi war," arguing that the conflict, which started as the war between the two regimes, then evolved into the war between the two peoples. *Istoriya Rossii* has been received with glowing reviews in the West (see, e.g., Pipes, "A New Russian History That's Sensational for the Right Reasons"). Far more important, though, is that the book was supported by some more liberal members of the Russian elite. See Karaganov, "Drugaya nasha istoriya."
68 Schlögel, "Places and Strata of Memory."
69 See Sherlock, *Historical Narratives*, 1–27.
70 Howard quoted in MacMillan, *Dangerous Games*, 39.
71 See *Vedomosti*, "Boyazn' proshlogo." In all fairness, such attitudes are by no means limited to Russia and the post-Soviet lands. History wars in the United States and in a number of other Western countries, notes the American historian Eric Foner, "did underscore the basic differences between historians' understanding of their task and what much of the broader public thinks the writing of history entails. Historians view the constant search for new perspectives as the lifeblood of historical understanding. Outside the academy, however, the act of reinterpretation is often viewed with suspicion, and 'revisionist' is invoked as a term of abuse." Foner, *Who Owns History?*, xvi.
72 Kappeler in Kasianov and Ther, eds., *A Laboratory of Transnational History*, 63–64.

Chapter 10

Guilt, Shame, Balts, Jews

ROGER PETERSEN

Few events have ever brought back the memory of World War II as powerfully as the collapse of Communism and the resurrection of independent Baltic states. Modern Lithuania, Latvia, and Estonia were born from the rubble of World War I and struggled and thrived for about twenty years before being occupied and incorporated by the Soviets and Germans. Lithuania, the focus of this study, was absorbed by the Soviet Union in June 1940, invaded by the Germans in June 1941, and reoccupied by the Soviets in the summer of 1944. During the course of the 1940s, hundreds of thousands of residents of Lithuania were killed and deported by the Soviet and Nazi regimes. As the Soviet grip loosened during Mikhail Gorbachev's glasnost and perestroika reforms, in March 1990 Lithuania became the first of the fifteen Soviet republics to declare independence; it soon gained international recognition after the failed August 1991 coup.

As the newly independent state emerged, the Lithuanian government acted to undo the persecution of the Soviet period by issuing certificates of rehabilitation to individuals convicted by Soviet courts of war-related crimes.[1] Jewish organizations vehemently protested this move. Depending on the estimate, roughly 200,000 of Lithuania's 240,000 Jews perished during the Holocaust. More than almost any other ethnic group in Eastern Europe, Lithuanians are portrayed as willing collaborators in those killings. Rabbi Marvin Hier, dean of the Simon Wiesenthal Center, proclaimed, "What they are doing is an insult to history and a very extreme miscarriage of justice." The Wiesenthal Center portrayed many of those being rehabilitated as including "some of Hitler's worst collaborators."[2] In response, Lithuanians often responded with counturcharges that Jews collaborated with the 1940–41 Stalinist regime that preceded the German invasion.³

The case of interaction between Lithuanians and Jews in the early 1990s is relevant to a more general question: What happens when members of one group ask members of another to admit complicity of their nation in crimes that happened decades earlier? Sometimes the request results in acts of confession, even atonement. Other times such requests are met with a vitriolic backlash. What accounts for this variation? In order to answer this question, we need to understand the emotions that underlie the private discourse that accompanies the public debate during this interaction.

To begin it is useful to use both Aristotle and modern social psychology. Then, two newspaper editorials written in 1990 and 1991 by Jewish authors, both addressing Lithuanian violence against Jews during the Second World War, will illustrate the points about the specific emotions of guilt, anger, and shame. In Aristotle's *Rhetoric*, especially Book 2, he sought to show how and why some speakers succeed in influencing their audience.⁴ He held that in order to persuade one must be able to reason logically, to understand human character, and to understand the emotions. Much of *Rhetoric* is devoted to systematically categorizing the emotions and how they are excited in the course of persuasion. In the opening paragraphs, Aristotle states the potential influence of emotion when he writes, "The arousing of prejudice, pity, anger, and similar emotions has nothing to do with the essential facts, but is merely a personal appeal to the man who is judging the case."⁵ In the historical interpretation of various nations' collaboration with the Nazi German regime, there are indeed essential facts, but also unavoidable arousals of emotion, and an appeal to an audience.

Building on these definitions, we can discuss guilt, shaming, norms against shaming, and a phenomenon I term "backdoor shaming." Guilt attaches to specific actions, while shame is connected to overall character. "Shaming" involves demeaning overall character. Shaming a people is very close to stereotyping and is unacceptable given current norms. But asking for an admission of guilt, that is, an admission of the blameworthy nature of specific actions rather than admission of defective character, has at least a chance to result in productive dialogue. However, the presence of certain rhetorical devices, whether intended or not, may be perceived as a covert attempt to move the discourse from guilt to shame. The presence of these backdoor-shaming devices produces the impression that historical victims are seeking revenge. Rather than productive dialogue, backlash becomes the likely result.

These ideas can be illustrated by an examination of Jewish-Lithuanian discourse that occurred in 1990–91. This case is appropriate for several reasons. First, there is a bloody history; the vast majority of Lithuania's Jews perished in the Holocaust. Second, unlike Swiss confiscation of Jewish assets or protection of the sizable Jewish minority in Hungary, tangible issues of money or safety did not play a prominent role in Baltic-Jewish interactions; rather, as should become clear, the stakes must be primarily seen from the standpoint of emotions. Third, the existence and simmering nature of the private discourse at that time seems indisputable. In one of the op-ed pieces analyzed below, A. M. Rosenthal characterizes the private Jewish discourse when he mentions the personal letters he received from fellow Jews after he wrote articles favoring independence for Lithuania. He writes: "All through the years I was speaking out or writing out for Lithuanian independence, three decades now, I received letters from around the world warning me that I was terribly, unforgivably wrong. . . . The letters predicted that under independence open anti-Semitism would rise again in Lithuania, murderers would become heroes and Fascists move into office—I would see."[6] On the Lithuanian side, private passions ran high as well.[7]

EMOTIONS

The psychologist Nico Frijda treats emotions as changes in "action readiness" to satisfy "concerns."[8] Frijda differentiates between "surface concerns" that are connected with the values of a particular human environment and the concerns hardwired in the species' constitution, although to a great extent the former must derive from the latter.[9] To meet these concerns, the individual possesses a repertoire of activation and deactivation mechanisms that change action readiness. These mechanisms are the emotions. They change readiness physically and cognitively; they alert the individual to modify relationships in the environment. In this view, the defining feature of emotion is the associated "action tendency."[10] Frijda provides examples of alertness, anger, and craving:

> There is a discrepancy or mismatch that initiates the program; decrease in this discrepancy guides and terminates the behavior. . . .

... If, for instance, the situation is seen as an unfamiliar one, action tendency is generated for actions removing that unfamiliarity: alertness, scanning the environment. If the situation is seen as one that blocks freedom of action, action tendency emerges that aims toward removing that obstruction: anger. If mismatch consists of something desirable not possessed, action tendency is toward possession: craving or desire.[11]

In social situations, the concerns and generated action tendencies are usually complex. Here, we are concerned with the emotions relevant to interaction between A and B when A has suffered historically at the hands of B. In effect, these past actions have created concerns for A and imbalances in the relationship between A and B. In this case, at least two equilibrium-restoring emotions work to trigger responses to these problems. First, there is the concern to alleviate one's own sense of loss. The emotion of *grief* addresses this concern by generating an action tendency to seek proper remembrance of the loss as compensation. Aristotle points out the re-equilibrating effects of mourning: "There is an element of pleasure even in mourning and lamentation. There is grief, indeed, at his loss, but pleasure in remembering him."[12]

Second, there is the concern to confront one's negative relationship with the victimizer. The emotion of *reproach*, defined as the disapproval of another's blameworthy action, generates several action tendencies. One such tendency is to request confession, that is, an admission that the acts committed against A were morally wrong. When reproach is combined with *anger* the resulting action tendency is to seek punishment or revenge in some form.[13] For Aristotle, anger was partly defined by the impulse to revenge and could not be separated from it—"No one grows angry with a person on whom there is no prospect of taking vengeance."[14] In some situations, anger is a mixture of pain and pleasure, the pain of being insulted combined with the pleasure of revenge, or at least imagining revenge. In this case, A wishes that B suffer as a result of his or her blameworthy action. The question becomes how B should suffer. As the question of physical or monetary suffering is not of much relevance to the battles of historical interpretation, the worst suffering that can be inflicted in the case at hand is emotional in nature, and the most painful emotion that can be created by historical reevaluation is *shame*.

Shame "involves taking a single unworthy action or characteristic to be the whole of a person's identity."[15] In other words, A wishes that B think of him- or herself as a bad person due to the act committed against A. Shaming involves the pleasure of revenge. The deliberate induction of shame ("shaming") involves an emotion, in which disapproval is "mingled with the pleasure of making you aware of it."[16]

THE INTERPLAY OF EMOTIONS

Unanticipated events, such as the rebirth of Lithuania and its policies of rehabilitation, insert the Second World War into present-day politics. The victim group (A) becomes compelled to address the policies of the perpetrator group (B). The emotions of A—grief and reproach, and possibly anger—drive A to initiate a request for confession from B. How will B respond to that initiative?

B's response to A's initiatives can take at least four forms (remorse, atonement, contrition, and backlash) each of which can again be discussed in terms of emotion and action tendency.[17] In two forms, A's request activates, or possibly produces, *guilt* emotion in B. When this emotion is accompanied by distress toward the committed action, and a strong wish that the deed had never been done, B's response is *remorse*.[18] The related action tendency is toward confession, an act that may help relieve the burden of guilt. Under certain circumstances, in addition to confession, the guilt emotion may also produce an action tendency to compensate the victim, a response of *atonement*.[19]

In two other forms, B's response does not involve the emotion of guilt. In the form of *contrition*, as I define it here, B responds with confession, but it is an emotionless confession. B may confess for purely nonemotional instrumental reasons, for instance, to improve world image to help smooth entry into economic and political organizations. Still, with contrition B does admit that the morally bad acts committed against A indeed happened and are a part of B's history.

The fourth response is emotionally driven, but the emotion is not guilt but *anger*, and the action tendency is toward *backlash*, not confession. Even if B may be willing to admit to certain historical crimes, this willingness is likely to evaporate if B perceives that A is not simply asking for admission of responsibility but engaged in an effort to gain revenge through shaming B. Clearly, no group or individual wishes to be shamed. In very few cases do individuals believe that their group should have to endure the sting of shame or that the collar of shame is justified. If B perceives being shamed, angry historical countercharges may be aimed at A in response.

The distinction between guilt and shame is crucial to the present argument and requires elaboration. First, to repeat, guilt only attaches to the action, not to the general character of the perpetrators.[20] Second, and nearly as important, guilt need not involve an audience, but shame relies on the emotions of observers. In a trivial example, an individual can feel guilty about not being able to carry out a diet. This failure and the emotion it generates may be an entirely private matter. Shame, on the other hand, attaches to one's character as a whole and is social. The grossly obese person is often ashamed because he or she is seen as a fundamentally flawed character not only in his or her own eyes but in the eyes of others and by commonly held social standards.

For the purposes here, shame can be seen as a *social* emotion involving three actors—the victim A, the perpetrator B, and observers C. When A shames B, A wants observer C to also feel that B is intrinsically bad as proven by B's action against A. A desires that C feel *contempt* for B. Furthermore, and this is when the power of shame becomes most intense, A desires that B is aware of C's contempt. Shame, for Aristotle, only exists when our worth is devalued by those whose admiration is prized. It is possible that A may try to shame B even in the absence of observers. However, the strongest act of shaming, and the one most likely to produce backlash, occurs when observers are drawn into the interaction. Related, given the likelihood of backlash by B, shaming strategies aim not so much to directly create the emotion of shame in B, a very difficult task when the tools are historical, but more to damage B through lowering the worth of B in the eyes of C. The case below will closely follow the contours of these abstract points.

The emotions involved in historical reevaluation of B's victimization of A can then follow the paths illustrated in figure 10.1 below. I am leaving out any discussion of the action tendencies of C's emotions. The complexity involved in such a pursuit would go beyond the scope of this chapter, although in the case of contrition the actions of C, or the anticipated actions of C, might be the motivation for B's confession. With contrition, B may confess to blunt any negative emotional reaction of C that is resulting or might result from A's initiative. C's negative reactions could come from a host of emotion/action tendency dynamics. The relevant factor for B, however, is not the specific nature of this interplay but B's estimation of *any* possible negative cost from C that would be higher than the cost

FIGURE 10.1 The sequence of emotions and action tendencies among victims, perpetrators, and observers.

A's initiative		B's response		C's reaction
Emotion	Action tendency	Emotion	Action tendency	Emotion
Grief and reproach	Seek confession	Guilt	Confession + wish that event never occurred (remorse)	Not relevant
		Guilt	Confession + desire to compensate victim (atonement)	Not relevant
		None	Confession, but not due to emotions (contrition)	Various
Grief and reproach + anger	Seek revenge through shaming	Anger	No confession, countercharges (backlash)	Contempt

of confession. Alternatively, with contrition B may confess simply to blunt costs resulting from A's actions without regard to C. In this case, the emotions/action tendencies of C are irrelevant or redundant. In its essence, contrition, as developed here, is basically a cost-benefit function with the costs remaining unspecified. In any event, the most interesting and important interactions are those that center on guilt and shame rather than contrition.

No doubt, A would prefer atonement or remorse over contrition. In many cases, though, A will not be able to distinguish among them. A may be able to gauge the sincerity of B's confession by whether members of B exhibit physical manifestations of the guilt emotion or by B's longer-term actions. In the immediate aftermath of A's initiative, however, the assessment must remain probabilistic.

The murkiness of this politics of emotion extends toward the perceptions of B as well. When the issue is involvement in mass murder, it is reasonable for members of B to assume that some members of A may be driven by anger and the tendency toward revenge. Furthermore, when the issue is involvement in mass murder, some members of B will assume that members of A intend to seek revenge through shaming even when the stated intentions of A are only to seek confession. Again, the assessment is probabilistic.

Here we arrive at the essence of the Baltic-Jewish problem: the anger and countercharges of Balts may arise from their perception that while some Jews and other Westerners explicitly ask for an admission of guilt concerning the role of some citizens, the underlying agenda is actually shaming. Rather than seek atonement or remorse, Balts perceive that the actual goal is revenge gained through developing contempt for them in the eyes of observers.

If B misperceives the intentions of A, the outcome is tragic, one in which misperception of motivation leads to backlash and the breakdown of dialogue.[21] Why might such misperception occur? Why does it seem so common? Before these questions can be answered, the "clouding" effects of what is the "norm against shaming" must be addressed.

THE NORM AGAINST SHAMING

Given the powerfully distressing nature of shame, it is not surprising that norms against shaming an entire people exist. First, strategically searching out shameful acts is often seen as a shameful act in itself. This sense that it is shameful to shame is found across a host of cultures. For example, Robert I. Levy writes of Tahitians: "Although gossip is an important part of 'shame control,' the words designating gossip have a pejorative tone, and gossiping is said to be a bad thing to do. Ideally, the behavior which would produce shame on becoming visible has to spontaneously force its way into visibility; people are not supposed to search out shameful acts."[22]

Second, shaming a collective group such as a race or nation is very close to an act of stereotyping or prejudice and thus particularly inappropriate, at least by current Western standards.[23] Some actions certainly need to be condemned, as do some individuals who commit them, but societies and nations do not deserve blanket condemnation.

The norm against shaming can be seen in the reactions to Daniel Goldhagen's 1996 book *Hitler's Willing Executioners: Ordinary Germans and the Holocaust*.[24] This work helped shape the contours of the widest public discourse on guilt, shame, and the Holocaust. The fact that the book's historical generalizations flirted with breaking the norm against shaming at least partly fueled the enormous controversy over the work. The premise of the book was that the German culture was thoroughly permeated with "eliminationist anti-Semitism," the idea that Jews must disappear from German society. Reacting to early criticism, Goldhagen made extensive efforts after the book's publication to state that the German people are not bad, but rather their pre-1945 culture was bad. For many reviewers of the work, however, Goldhagen's separation of attacking a culture of a people rather than a people was disingenuous. Despite Goldhagen's efforts to restrict his interpretation to a certain time period, they believed his attack on a collective came too close to violating the norm. Typical was the review by Kristen R. Monroe in the *American Political Science Review* in which she concluded her review by stating: "Sadly, ironically, by condemning the German people en masse, Goldhagen comes perilously close to the same kind of cultural and ethnic stereotyping that still leads to anti-Semitism, and which Goldhagen so passionately and rightly deplores."[25] The more popular press produced similar criticisms. In *Foreign Affairs*, Fritz Stern described the parts of Goldhagen's work as "joined by a single intent: the indictment of a people."[26] In the *New Yorker*, Clive James described Goldhagen's desire to "blame the whole population" as having a "retributive impetus that carries him far beyond his proper objective."[27] In important ways, these responses to Goldhagen's historical generalizations about Germans resemble the reactions of some Balts to some Jewish historical initiatives about the Baltic role in the Holocaust. The source of both reactions can be found in beliefs about backdoor shaming.

THE CRUX OF THE PROBLEM:
THE PERCEPTION OF BACKDOOR SHAMING

Due to this powerful norm against shaming, those who actually seek revenge cannot openly shame their target of revenge. Both A and B have a sense of this prohibition. However, there are several techniques that can indirectly accomplish shaming. Here is why misperception becomes so common: both those who seek revenge and those who only seek confession will use a similar form in their public discourse, a form that openly concentrates on blameworthy actions. Yet those who seek revenge can employ several devices within this discourse to move the focus from the specific acts to the general character of the nation whose members committed the acts. In other words, A can attempt to move the underlying emotional content of the historical interpretation from the question of guilt to that of shame. I term the devices that implicitly move the discourse from guilt to shame "backdoor shaming."

The problem of misperception of motive arises when backdoor-shaming devices creep into the public discourse of A even when A's purpose is not to shame. It follows that misperception can be avoided if these devices are identified and conscientiously avoided. The purpose of the following section is to illustrate several of these devices within the text of one short editorial as well as to demonstrate their absence in another similar piece.

IDENTIFYING THE DEVICES OF BACKDOOR SHAMING

Several backdoor-shaming devices are present in an editorial by Benjamin Frankel and Brian D. Kux that was published in the *Los Angeles Times* on April 29, 1990. Frankel, the teaching assistant for a class I took at the University of Chicago in the 1980s, told me shortly after the article was written that it was intended in part to simply prod Lithuanians to admit that the events mentioned were part of their history. I have no reason to doubt his stated intention. However, the article was angrily received by the Lithuanian community (with whom I was conducting field interviews at the time of the article). Frankel was surprised at the intensity of the negative response.[28]

The following passages involve evaluation of the Lithuanian actions against Jews in June 1941.

> It is easy to understand why Lithuania's quest for independence has engendered support in the United States. The spectacle of a small country defying the mighty Soviet empire in the name of self-determination is endearing. But there are three reasons why the United States should pause before embracing Lithuanian nationalism.

Frankel and Kux then state that the United States should not disrupt the peaceful transition occurring in the Soviet Union (reason one) and that the United States should not open a Pandora's box of border disputes (reason two). I have numbered the passages for reference.]

> 1. The third reason to pause before embracing the Lithuanian cause is infrequently discussed, though it is on many people's minds. Lithuanian nationalism has not been particularly enlightened or benign. In fact, it has been manifestly ugly.
> 2. Consider the Lithuanian record during World War II. No other people collaborated with the Nazis more enthusiastically than the Lithuanians and Ukrainians.
> 3. When Soviet troops left Kaunas, the former Lithuanian capital, on June 23, 1941, Lithuanian partisans, led by the national hero [Algirdas] Klimaitis,

began systematically killing Jews. Jewish homes and synagogues were set on fire.

4. Between June 25-29, Lithuanian nationalists murdered 5,000 Jews (3,800 in Kaunas, 1,200 in other towns). The killing method was as primitive as it was effective: hundreds of Jewish men, women, and children were hunted down and clubbed to death in the streets and public squares of Kaunas in full view of a supportive population.

5. On June 28, Lithuanian police, impatient with the slow pace of the killing, released convicts, gave them iron bars and sent them through the cities to kill Jews. Those not beaten publicly or tortured to death were taken by partisans to killing sites outside the city and shot.

6. Some Lithuanian policemen thought the shooting of young children to be too much trouble. So they tossed them alive into the pits, next to their dead parents' bodies.

7. Those Lithuanians who were repulsed by their countrymen's barbarity were discouraged by the Lithuanian religious leader, Bishop Brizgys. He set an example for the entire population by forbidding the clergy "to aid or intercede for the Jews in any way," as the Nazis reported with satisfaction.

8. The thoroughness and zeal of the Lithuanians in rounding up the Jews and handing them over to the Germans was gratefully acknowledged by SS officers. One of the group commanders, Karl Jaeger, reported to SS headquarters in Berlin that the Lithuanian help made killing the Jews "like shooting at a parade." This experienced SS murderer reported that the existence of the partisans made the Lithuanian capital "comparatively speaking, a shooting paradise." Internal SS memos marveled at what they called the Lithuanian "self-cleaning action."

9. Should Lithuania's embrace of the Nazis, and their eager collaboration in killing Jews, be reasons for denying them independence? No. But the ugly character in Lithuanian nationalism should not be overlooked, either. It is absurd for Lithuanians to lecture us on the meaning of morality and betrayal.

10. We should also take the concerns of the Russian and Polish minorities in Lithuania quite seriously. Lithuania's past treatment of minorities is hardly reassuring.

11. The major objective of U.S. foreign policy in the near future is to facilitate a peaceful transformation of the Soviet Union to ensure that the accompanying political changes in Europe will not plunge the continent into a period of nationalistic and ethnic tensions. The unilateral and precipitous steps taken by the Lithuanian leadership undermine this goal.

12. We should support the principle of self-determination. But we should oppose the arrogant, selfish, and irresponsible exercise of that principle. [End of article]

What are the rhetorical elements that move the focus from judgment of the act to judgment of the people and create the perception of shaming? What are the devices that implicitly create the impression that a people is inherently bad?

The most common device, perhaps, is *decontextualization*. There is extensive theoretical and empirical material on attribution, a closely related concept. When a horrific act is described with no context, the audience will likely attribute the cause of the act to the character of the perpetrator rather than to the circumstances or the nature of the situation. In effect, one is left to conclude that only a bad people could produce such bad actions. In this way, the focus easily moves from guilt to shame.

In the article above, Frankel and Kux provide no context for the events of June 25–29, 1941. For these events, context can be provided at three levels. The immediate events of the month of June can provide a first frame. On June 14–21, the Soviets, who had occupied the country for a year, brutally deported about thirty thousand residents, 1 percent of the entire population. Sometimes whole families were forced into the cattle cars, other times family members became separated. In order to avoid shipment to Siberia, thousands of Lithuanians fled their homes and went into hiding in the woods or moved from house to house. When the German invasion was announced on June 21, thousands of underground armed Lithuanians went into action to clear out the Soviets. They were joined by tens of thousands of totally unorganized citizens who wanted to join in the routing of the hated Soviets. Estimates usually place the number of organized rebels at thirty thousand and unorganized joiners at about seventy thousand or more. During the anti-Soviet actions largely taking place in the days immediately before the anti-Jewish violence, over four thousand Lithuanians were killed and eight thousand wounded.[29] To give a comparative perspective, only two thousand Lithuanians were killed in the entire war of independence in 1918–20. In short, this was a highly brutalized and damaged society. Tens of thousands of individuals had just lost family members through deportation and fighting. Thousands had just come out of hiding. The days before the events depicted by Frankel and Kux can only be characterized as incredibly violent and chaotic.

A second possible frame is composed of the wider events of the first Soviet occupation and the entire German occupation, the years 1940–44. Clearly, Lithuanians and Jews perceived different primary enemies. For the Lithuanians, the Soviets, having already occupied the country and eliminated Lithuanian sovereignty, were considered the greatest threat. Lithuanian society was founded on three pillars: the nation, the Catholic Church, and the family farmstead. On each score, ethnic Lithuanians would prefer the Germans to the Soviets. The Soviets had already eliminated Lithuanian national sovereignty; Lithuanians might be able to bargain it back with the Germans. The Soviets held an officially atheist doctrine and had persecuted the Church in the 1940–41 period; the Germans were not expected to follow that agenda. The Soviets' agricultural policy was collectivization; the Germans were less likely to destroy family farming. The Lithuanians were caught between Joseph Stalin and Adolf Hitler and were forced to play a strategic game. While no one wishes to state it openly, for ethnic Lithuanians the Germans were clearly the more promising choice. Even with the Germans, Lithuanians often played a strategic game. At the tail end of the German occupation, Lithuanians clearly resisted opportunities for unconditional collaboration with the Nazis. When the Germans tried to raise a Waffen SS legion in March 1943, only 177 of 3,230 candidates complied with required registration. At the end of the war, many Lithuanians were willing to serve in German-created units, but only under the command of Lithuanian officers and in anticipation of being able to fight, in a replay of the events from the First World War, for Lithuanian independence. The Germans had to abandon their plans for an SS legion and declared that the Lithuanians were "unworthy of wearing the SS uniform."[30]

For Jews, obviously, the Soviets offered a better (although still bad) choice. Within this strategic context, Lithuanians clearly perceived that Jews sided with the Soviets during the 1940–41 occupation and willingly and enthusiastically collaborated with them. I will skip over this critical and controversial issue here.[31] The question here is about inclusion of context. When a victim group asks a perpetrator group for confession of crimes, should there be any mention of the strategic context within which those crimes occurred? In Frankel and Kux's treatment, Lithuanians were enthusiastic collaborators and obsessed with killing Jews; there is no need to provide a "strategic context" that may only serve to make inexcusable excuses for these crimes. Most Lithuanian accounts I have heard stress the strategic context: Lithuanians and Jews had different primary enemies; it's unfortunate that Jews were mass-murdered, but Lithuanians had to take care of their own problems; furthermore, Jews were asking for it because of their collaboration with the Soviets during this strategic game. For Americans, imbued with the centrality of the Holocaust in the events of Eastern Europe during World War II, it may be difficult to understand that for many Eastern Europeans, the Holocaust was more of a sideshow than a main event. However, for nations like the Lithuanians, who would at the end of the war again fall under Soviet domination for the next forty-five years, that is often the case.

Discussing "strategic context" is a particularly thorny issue. The point here is that if victim group A requests that perpetrator group B confess and atone, group B is much more likely to respond positively if some mention of context, which runs against group-based shaming, is included in the appeal. Group A would need to consider the appropriateness and cost of inclusion of "strategic context." This issue played out in the "historians' conflict" in Germany (in effect, a situation in which perpetrator group B considers the appropriateness and cost of inclusion of "strategic context" within its own circles). In that case, the "winning" side argued that stressing strategic context was inappropriate. But Germany created the Nazis, invaded its neighbors, initiated war, and orchestrated the Holocaust. The states between Stalin and Hitler may be another matter.[32]

The interwar period can provide a third, and yet wider, frame. While interwar Lithuanian-Jewish relations were undoubtedly rough in many ways, in comparative context they were relatively healthy for the region. Many historians who specialize in East European and Baltic history do not see Lithuanians and Balts in general as profoundly anti-Semitic in the era before the war. Ezra Mendelsohn, the author of a major comparative study on Central European Jewry, sums up the situation in the following words: "But the 'Jewish question' in Lithuania never was the subject of obsessive attention, as it was in Poland, Romania, and Hungary, and no Lithuanian government attempted to revoke Jewish emancipation. Moreover, Lithuania suffered little of the anti-Semitic violence endemic to Poland."[33] In his authoritative study of the region, Joseph Rothschild states that Jews "were relatively the best-treated of the country's [Lithuania's] interwar minorities."[34] In a recent account, Timothy Snyder specifically discusses the events of 1941 in this larger context (as well as the shorter-term strategic context) and summarizes:

The mass murder of the Jews of Vilnius could not have taken place without the assistance of Lithuanians: the Germans did not have enough men for the job. That said, it is important to remember that the double occupation of Lithuania, by the Soviets and then by the Germans, was an exceedingly violent break with the previous history of Vilnius and Lithuania. Though the Germans had no trouble finding Lithuanians willing to kill Jews, what happened in 1941 had no precedent in prewar Lithuanian policy or in the history of Lithuanian-Jewish relations.[35]

To summarize, providing context prevents shaming in two ways. First, the focus moves away from general categorizations to discussion of specific acts and events. For instance, the third frame casts doubt on the power of long-term cultural/character factors in explaining the specific acts of anti-Jewish violence of June 25–29. The second frame also casts doubt on the unconditional and "enthusiastic" nature of Lithuanian collaboration. Although Frankel and Kux ask us to consider "the Lithuanian war record" during World War II (passage 2), the article actually addresses only the events during the first few days of occupation. In reality, the relationship between Germans and Lithuanians, as indicated by their boycott of the SS legion, was fairly complex and changed over time.[36]

Second, providing context provides the reader with motivations that are closely tied to the blameworthy actions themselves rather than to issues of general character. These motivations are rooted in the circumstances of the first Soviet occupation or, yet more specifically, in the circumstances of June 1941. Of course, each of these motivations may exist alongside a general violent, ignorant, anti-Semitic (and shameful) general character. The situation and its specific circumstances might be seen only as the "trigger," the "match," that set off the violent event. Alternatively, the nature of the immediate situation might be seen as the primary cause. One thing is for certain, without any context at all the reader has no ability to judge the relative weights of circumstances of the act versus general character.

Consider two specific actions within the section from Frankel and Kux's article—the release of prisoners (passage 5) and the statement of the bishop (passage 7). Without context, the article seems to imply that the only reason for these actions was to kill Jews, apparently for reasons of anti-Semitism. When the context is considered, however, other possible motivations become obvious. Given the massive number of deportations and imprisonments occurring in mid-June, the release of convicts was probably aimed more at freeing political prisoners in general than instrumentally and specifically employing convicts to go and specifically beat Jews. When seen in context, the motivation of the statement by Bishop Brizgys also appears more complex than implied by the article. During the first Soviet occupation, the Catholic Church suffered severe persecution. The Germans, who had occupied the country during World War I, were certainly friendlier to Catholicism than the Soviets were in 1940–41. The Church clearly did not wish to antagonize the incoming and extremely powerful German regime, as to do so would not help restore the institutional health and strength of the Church. As presented without context, the Frankel and Kux article implies that the motivation of the Church was to facilitate killing Jews. The more logical conclusion was that the Church was concerned above all with rebuilding its strength and preventing further persecution. Helping Jews, and thus antagonizing the Germans, would have been counterproductive to this fundamental goal. While distancing themselves from the plight of the Jews may have been cowardly or self-centered, motivation toward self-preservation and/or institutional power is far different from the one suggested in the account above.

Without context, Frankel and Kux portray a deeply sick people, ill with rabid anti-Semitism and prone to violence, motivated in most actions by an obsession to kill Jews. The problem seems to be a bad people, worthy of shame. Seen within context, the events are part of a very violent and rapid series of shocks—occupations, deportations, persecutions, and invasion. Within context, Lithuanians may be motivated by cultural and historical anti-Semitism, but they are also powerfully motivated by desires for vengeance against the brutal Soviet regime, for restoration of sovereignty, for reestablishment of basic Lithuanian institutions—motivations created by the situation of 1940–41.

Frankel and Kux may have aimed for confession, an admission that these acts are blameworthy and deserving of guilt, but without the slightest reference to the context of these events they have created the impression that the perpetrators of these acts are blameworthy and defective as a people and deserving of shame. Perhaps the act of participating in brutalization or serving as a cog in a machine of mass murder can have no legitimate reason and should never "be put in context." Perhaps any explanation or detailing of mitigating circumstances for such acts can become a justification for the acts, and some acts should simply not be justified. Still, one must consider the effects and costs of not providing context.[37]

In addition to decontextualization, the attribution of blame is affected by the *choice of specific words and terminology*. Some words implicitly link the blameworthy actions of individuals to the larger collective unit and thus move the focus from the individual action to the character of the group. Consider passage 3 above. By calling Klimaitis a "national hero" Frankel and Kux imply that the actions of this individual are linked to the nation and are admired by the nation. From what little is known about Klimaitis, the designation does not seem justified. By employing the adjective "systematically" and the term "partisans" in the same passage, the implication is that an organized group rationally carried out a plan to beat and kill Jews. As suggested in the discussion of the context above, these days were marked by disorder, if not chaos, as seventy thousand previously unorganized men joined in the rout of the Soviets. While not explicitly discussing the character of Lithuanians, these terms link actions and individuals to the group in the manner of backdoor shaming.

Clearly, the *timing* of a request for confession, as well as the *audience* toward which the request is directed, affects whether a perception of backdoor shaming is likely to occur. Shame is the opposite of the emotion of *pridefulness*. Both are social emotions, the former leading one to sense the negative evaluation of respected peers (*contempt*), the latter reflecting a positive evaluation by respected peers (*liking*).[38] If A wishes to seek revenge on B by creating contempt in C, the ideal *timing* of a release of B's negative history will be when B is most likely to receive a positive evaluation from C. Not only may the negative history create shame in B, but it may prevent B's pridefulness, the negation of shame, by blocking the conferral of positive status from C. If the primary goal in the shaming of B is creation of contempt for B in the eyes of C, then the likely *audience* of the request for confession will be C. If the primary goal is simply confession and guilt-related contrition, atonement, or remorse, the interaction need only involve A and B—no real effort at involving C as an audience need be made.

Frankel and Kux's article seems to shame on both of these scores. Review the beginning and ending passages as a set (the preface paragraph and passage 12): "The spectacle of a small country defying the mighty Soviet empire in the name of self-determination is endearing. . . . But we should oppose the arrogant, selfish, and irresponsible exercise of that principle." In effect, the citizens of the United States (C) are told not to confer positive status on Lithuanians (B), as they are inclined, but rather to see this people as "arrogant, selfish, and irresponsible." The timing of the article was at the height of a revival of pride in the Lithuanian American community; the image of David versus the Soviet Goliath, so dear to Lithuanian self-perception, was coming to life.

Finally, backdoor shaming can result from *linking events across disparate time periods*. If B commits similar acts at different times and under different circumstances, then it must be the nature of B's character, rather than the circumstances of the specific actions, that are at work. Above, Frankel and Kux link the anti-Jewish violence of June 1941 to possible future violence against Russian and Polish minorities (passage 10). The implication seems to be that this was a defective people fifty years ago and character does not change; thus, this is still a defective people capable of violence and hatred even under highly changed circumstances.[39]

In short, Frankel and Kux's op-ed piece includes many devices that tend to indirectly shame an entire people.[40] The response to their piece, in my understanding and interactions with the Lithuanian community, was entirely negative. It did not create enhanced dialogue, but rather acted as an embittering brake on dialogue.

A COUNTEREXAMPLE

This result, however, has not obtained in every Jewish-initiated request for confession. Below, an editorial by A. M. Rosenthal, "Absolution for Killers," published in the *New York Times* on September 10, 1991 is offered as a counterexample. At the time of Rosenthal's article, Lithuania had just gained independence. Rosenthal is directly addressing the issue of blanket rehabilitation.[41]

> 1. All through the years I was speaking out or writing out for Lithuanian independence, three decades now, I received letters from around the world warning me that I was terribly, unforgivably wrong.
> 2. They were letters of indelible pain. They came from Jews in America, Europe and Israel who had been brutalized by Lithuanian Nazis before and during the German occupation of 1941–1944 or whose families had been wiped out.
> 3. The letters told the retching truth about these Lithuanian Fascists. Serving in special terror battalions with the German Army, they murdered scores of thousands of Jews in Lithuania. And as the Germans moved these

death squads about Eastern Europe and the Soviet Union they slaughtered Poles, Russians, Ukrainians, Gypsies—and more Jews.

4. The letters predicted that under independence open anti-Semitism would rise again in Lithuania, murderers would become heroes and Fascists move into office—I would see.

5. I replied that if the world could stomach recognizing Germany and the Soviet empire it could acknowledge the independent existence of three small nations that had suffered under both. I still believe that.

6. I also said that perhaps time, the suffering under Fascism and Communism and the new generation of Lithuanians involved in a freedom movement would prevent the return or exoneration of local Fascists.

7. Now, in the first days of independence, it has become the obligation of the Lithuanian Government to show whether that hope was realistic or delusional. The answer will be heard not only in the West but everywhere in the Baltics, Eastern Europe or the former Soviet Union where Fascists may try to rewrite history so they can crawl back to power.

[Rosenthal then provides some details of the exoneration process and reviews the original news story of Stephen Kinzer, then proceeds.[42]]

8. The Lithuanian Information Center in Washington tried quickly to comply with my specific requests for more information. But responsibility on "rehabilitation" is divided among three Lithuanian departments and Vilnius seems to be reacting defensively instead of in full candor.

9. It is not yet possible to find out how many cases of Lithuanian Nazis are involved and whether the exonerations came from error or a campaign to rewrite history under the pretext of rehabilitating real victims of Nazi and Soviet courts.

10. President Vytautas Landsbergis has issued tart denials of large-scale exonerations. But he says it is possible that "among the individuals repressed by the Soviets were also Holocaust criminals."

11. But the man he is asking to investigate is Artusas Paulauskas, the prosecutor who issued the exonerations in the first place. Neither the U.S. State Department nor the Department of Justice are at all satisfied with the replies from Vilnius.

12. Friends of Lithuanian freedom in Lithuania and abroad can help again now by urging President Landsbergis to do two things: Give full access to witnesses and documents to the Office of Special Investigation of

the Department of Justice, which has deep experience in hunting war and Holocaust criminals. Simultaneously, convene a special board of inquiry, including foreigners, to investigate the charges and the whole exoneration process.

13. Taken quickly, those two steps would be the best independence gifts Mr. Landsbergis could give to his own nation and a world that watches in both hope and pain. [End of article]

In essential ways, the Rosenthal article is similar to the piece by Frankel and Kux. Both list horrific acts committed by Lithuanians (passages 2–3 in Rosenthal); both ask for the recognition of certain historical issues (Rosenthal explicitly mentions the "rewriting of history" in passages 7 and 9); both try to involve a Western audience. Despite these similarities, the results of the articles seem vastly different. Rosenthal's article was not met with the same intensity of Lithuanian anger. Furthermore, it seems that Rosenthal's effort may have led to increased dialogue between Lithuanians and other groups.[43] Although impossible to prove, a strong argument can be made that these differences in reception and creation of dialogue relate to the absence of backdoor shaming devices in the Rosenthal piece.

First, the Rosenthal article does provide some *context*. The author recognizes that Lithuanians have been victims as well as perpetrators (passage 5). He also recognizes the specific bureaucratic context of "rehabilitation" (passage 8). Second, Rosenthal avoids the *terminology* that implicitly links individuals and individual actions to national character. He mentions the key players in the controversy by name and position, President Landsbergis and prosecutor Paulauskas, and does not describe them as representations of the general character of the Lithuanian people. In fact, in passage 12, Rosenthal clearly separates individual leaders from the general population by appealing to that population to pressure their leader. Third, Rosenthal is quite explicit in *not linking past events to present or future ones*. Passage 6 clearly recognizes that intervening events and present circumstances may override any continuing negative cultural traits. Fourth, in regard to *audience*, Rosenthal directs his comments not only to a Western audience but to Lithuanians as well. Importantly, he mentions the basic Lithuanian view of the events (passage 10). By focusing on both the target (B), as well as the audience (C), the author reduces the chance that the article will be seen primarily as an effort to create contempt for the target in the eyes of the audience.

Rosenthal keeps the focus throughout on specific acts. He specifies the problem, specifies the most relevant individuals, and specifies a set of actions that will correct the problem. By doing so, Rosenthal includes context, avoids problematic terminology, evades the equation of actions across historical time periods, and provides respect to the target while still generating pressure from the audience.

CONCLUSION

As their states were being reborn, Balts were asked to come to terms with events from the Second World War. They sometimes perceived that while some Jews and Westerners explicitly asked for an admission of guilt, the underlying agenda was shaming. Rather than seek contrition or remorse, Balts sometimes perceived that requests for confession were really acts of revenge that tried to develop contempt for Balts in the eyes of observers. While this problem probably underlies many situations, it was especially acute for the Baltic states as Communism collapsed. Jewish initiatives were seen as attacks at the very moment when Baltic pride and self-assertion was rapidly rising. Moreover, existing general Western views of the Baltic states exacerbated the problem. As Anatol Lieven has summarized:

> For a hundred years and more, Western journalists had swung between two contradictory stereotypes of Eastern European nations, and would surely do so in their [Baltic] case. The first stereotype is of gallant little freedom-loving peoples, fighting against wicked empires for the sake of independence and liberal democracy. The second is horrid little anti-semitic peasants, trying to involve us in their vicious tribal squabbles.... Where they have criticized the Balts (especially over anti-semitism), the criticisms have been so extreme, biased, and badly supported that they have merely infuriated even reasonable Balts, and discredited Western advice in general.[44]

We can again come back to Aristotle, who in observing the conditions that create shame, wrote: "And men feel shame when they have acts or exploits to their credit on which they are bringing dishonour, whether these are their own, or those of their ancestors, or those of other persons with whom they have some close connexion [sic]."[45] With the rebirth of Baltic independence, Balts were reconstructing their identities. Naturally, on the Balts' side the process concentrated on "acts and exploits to their credit," especially the struggle, both of present citizens and their ancestors, to gain and regain sovereignty in the face of Soviet/Russian might. For Jews, the rebirth of Baltic independence dredged up painful imagery and history, and they felt, and feel, a duty to their ancestors, and survivors, to ask for confession of acts that have the potential to bring dishonor to Baltic history. The current reinterpretation of Baltic history must be a delicate balancing act that allows for Baltic pride with recognition of sensitive historical events. This balancing act will not succeed if shame, contempt, and anger dominate the underlying emotions of the discourse. It will not succeed if a Baltic perception of backdoor shaming exists or if Jews and Westerners remain ignorant of the natural tendency of backdoor shaming to enter into the discourse. If former wounds and antagonisms are to heal, if productive discourse and positive interactions are to obtain, we must work to clearly understand the complex emotions that our rhetoric produces. Although Aristotle understood this point clearly, it seems to often be forgotten in our present age.

1   As early as 1989, Lithuania had passed a law aimed at undoing Soviet convictions in the immediate postwar years. By October 1991, thirty-five thousand individuals had been rehabilitated. See Kamm, "Lithuania Halts the Reversal of War-Crimes Convictions."
2   Both quoted passages in this paragraph are from Kinzer, "Lithuania Starts to Wipe out Convictions for War Crimes."
3   Tomas Venclova's "Jews and Lithuanians," a widely read Lithuanian view from the time, was published in *Cross Currents* and discussed this interchange; in the same issue, also see Zuvintas, "An Open Letter to Tomas Venclova."
4   I am relying on the translation of W. Rhys Roberts from the Oxford edition.
5   Aristotle, *Rhetoric*, Book 2, 95.
6   Rosenthal, "Absolution for Killers." The authors of the other article employed below, Benjamin Frankel and Brian D. Kux, describe the history of this period as "infrequently discussed, though it is on many people's minds." Frankel and Kux, "Recalling the Dark Past of Lithuanian Nationalism."
7   I make this statement largely based from experiences doing extensive fieldwork with the Lithuanian diaspora in 1989-92.
8   Frijda, *The Emotions*. Other generally agreed upon characteristics of emotions less relevant to this study are physiological arousal and expression, valence, nature of intentional object, and cognitive antecedents. I define and address emotion in several of my own works, most recently in *Western Intervention in the Balkans*.
9   Frijda, *The Emotions*, 466.
10 There is a long history of viewing emotion in terms of action tendency orienting individual action to meet concerns. In the sixteenth century, Juan Luis Vives saw emotion as a faculty that helped individuals to seek good and avoid evil. Thomas Hobbes wrote of appetites and aversions in much the same vein. In the twentieth century, Frijda's *The Emotions* is preceded

by Magda B. Arnold's *Emotion and Personality* and followed by Andrew Ortony, Gerald Clore, and Allan Collins's *The Cognitive Structure of Emotions*. In the last work, the authors state their differences with Frijda on the issue of treating emotion as action tendency on page 11. Still, the similarities in usage outweigh the differences.

11 Frijda, *The Emotions*, 76–77.
12 Aristotle quoted in Elster, *Alchemies of the Mind*, 83.
13 On anger, see Petersen and Zukerman in Potegal, Stemmler, and Spielberger, eds., *A Handbook of Anger*.
14 From the translation used in Elster's *Alchemies of the Mind*, 58.
15 Lindsay-Hartz, de Rivera, and Mascolo in Tangney and Fischer, eds., *Self-Conscious Emotions*, 297.
16 Elster, *Alchemies of the Mind*, 207.
17 There is another reaction that I will not discuss, and that is the guilt-driven action tendency to make oneself suffer for the acts that one has committed. On this action tendency, see Elster, *Alchemies of the Mind*, 213. As Jon Elster notes, this reaction plays a large role in psychoanalytic theory.
18 Frijda, *The Emotions*, 201. Relating to the present context, a passage in Kurt Vonnegut's novel *Bluebeard* captures the victim's desire that others feel remorse for genocidal actions, rather than the victim's desire for revenge. At one point the protagonist is asked whether his father, an Armenian survivor of Turkish massacre, desired punishment of the Turks: "She asked me just now . . . if my father wanted to see the Turks punished for what they had done to the Armenians. 'I asked him the same thing when I was about eight years old, I guess, and thinking maybe life would be spicier if we wanted revenge of some kind,' I said. . . . 'Father finally answered the question this way: "All I want from the Turks is an admission that their country is an uglier and even more joyless place, now that *we* are gone"'" (*Bluebeard*, 40).
19 Given the scope of the action, the death of roughly 200,000 of 240,000 Lithuanian Jews for instance, the undoing of the act is impossible, and any act of atonement is more symbolic than corrective. Given these historical realities, confession, either from contrition or remorse, rather than compensation stemming from atonement, is the larger issue at hand in assessing past Jewish-Baltic relations.
20 Elster, in *Alchemies of the Mind* (206–16), devotes a short section on the relationship and differences between guilt and shame, which provides many relevant sources. Among these distinctions is the attachment of guilt to specific actions and shame to one's character as a whole.
21 If B correctly perceives that A is engaged in an effort to shame and responds with backlash, the outcome is certainly a negative one but is not tragic in the sense that it might have been relatively easily avoided.
22 Levy, *Tahitians: Mind and Experience*, 340.
23 This norm may be very widespread both geographically and temporally, although in Western society I believe the qualifier "currently" is appropriate and necessary.
24 Goldhagen, *Hitler's Willing Executioners*.
25 Monroe, review of *Hitler's Willing Executioners*, 212–13.
26 Stern, "The Goldhagen Controversy," 128.
27 James, "Blaming the Germans," 44.
28 Frankel and Kux, "Recalling the Dark Past of Lithuanian Nationalism." All the following passages are from this article.
29 For a discussion of the overall context of the June 1941 events and a detailed history of the Lithuanian uprising, see Budreckis, *The Lithuanian National Revolt of 1941*.

30 See Misiunas and Taagepera, *The Baltic States*, 56.
31 I address this perception and its role in the events of 1941 in depth in *Understanding Ethnic Violence*.
32 These states, and their unfortunate geographic location, are a major focus of Snyder, *Bloodlands*.
33 Mendelsohn, *The Jews of East Central Europe*, 236.
34 Rothschild, *East Central Europe*, 378.
35 Snyder, "Neglecting the Lithuanian Holocaust."
36 German plans and internal political maneuvering over Baltic policy, as well as Baltic reaction to these policies, are described in the following sources: Dallin, "Ostland and the Baltic States"; Reitlinger, *The House Built on Sand*, especially chap. 4. The strategic logic of German policy is discussed in Alexiev, *Soviet Nationalities in German Wartime Strategy*. For a summary of documents, see Mulligan, "The OSS and the Nazi Occupation." Alexander Dallin, in his definitive treatment of German policy in the East, writes, "The internal development of the Baltic States under the Germans is a subject so vast and so distinct from the fate of the 'old Soviet' areas that only the most cursory attention can be paid to it here." Dallin, *German Rule in Russia*, 182.
37 In a point too broad to follow up on here, the failure to provide context might be seen as an abdication from social science, an enterprise centered on identifying causes (circumstances) and effects.
38 I am borrowing Elster's terminology from *Alchemies of the Mind. Guilt*, its opposite *pride*, and its reflection in the eyes of an observer, *admiration*, all relate to an *action* of B. *Shame*, its opposite *pridefulness*, and its reflection in the eyes of C, *liking*, all relate to the *character* of B.
39 As a point of fact, the Freedom House reports on "nations in transit" have long listed Lithuania as free in all respects, and it is now considered to be a "consolidated democracy" along with the other Baltic nations. No other former Soviet Republics score nearly as well. Freedom House, *Nations in Transit 2013*.
40 A few comments about the nature of the reports of SS commanders, Frankel and Kux's basic source, should be made before going on to the second article. I am familiar with the reports of SS commander Franz Stahlecker, who led Einsatzgruppe A, and those of Karl Jaeger, chief of Einsatzkommando 3. The problem with these reports is twofold. First, they are contradictory; second, they may have been written with certain political motivations in mind. For instance, as Frankel and Kux state, "Internal SS memos marveled at what they called the Lithuanian 'self-cleaning action.'" Yet, at another point, Stahlecker writes, "It was astonishingly difficult at first to set into motion an extensive pogrom against the Jews." Arno J. Mayer, in *Why Did the Heavens Not Darken?*, also recognizes that Stahlecker and Jaeger may have had motivations to "spin" their accounts of the June 1941 events in a certain way. Mayer, recognizing the fact that Stahlecker and Jaeger claimed a great deal of credit for the Lithuanian actions (contrary to Lithuanian "self-cleansing") but not believing them, speculates on reasons they had for inaccurate reporting: "Since by the time they drafted their reports the brutalization of war, including the mass killings of Jews, was official policy, probably both Stahlecker and Jaeger claimed excessive credit for what the Lithuanians were inclined and able to do on their own, especially as there was neither army nor police to restrain them." Mayer, *Why Did the Heavens Not Darken?*, 259. Given the ambiguity of these documents, in my own work I use the memoirs of Jewish survivors, which are quite consistent, to determine the basic nature of the June 1941 events.
41 Rosenthal, "Absolution for Killers." The passages cited all come from this article.
42 Kinzer, "Lithuania Starts to Wipe out Convictions."

43 See the related stories in the *New York Times* on September 11, 14; October 17, 20; and November 17, 1991. The *Times* editorial board concluded that "Lithuania now shows a sensitive will to do justice to both the innocent and the guilty (September 14). On November 17, the *Times* reported that thirty-five thousand certificates of rehabilitation had been issued, while five hundred had been denied for war crimes. Alan Dershowitz also weighed in on the issue in his *Contrary to Popular Opinion*, 338–40.
44 Lieven, *The Baltic Revolution*, 381.
45 Aristotle, *Rhetoric*, Book 2, 95 (Roberts translation).

Bibliography

Abdelal, Rawi. "Memories of Nations and States: Institutional History and National Identity in Post-Soviet Eurasia." *Nationalities Papers* 30, no. 3 (2002): 459–84.

Abernethy, David B. *The Dynamics of Global Dominance: European Overseas Empires, 1415–1980*. New Haven, Conn.: Yale University Press, 2000.

Adas, Michael. "From Avoidance to Confrontation: Peasant Protest in Pre-colonial and Colonial Southeast Asia." *Comparative Studies in Society and History* 23, no. 2 (1981): 217–47.

Agence France-Presse. "New Study Fails to Bridge Japan, China History Divide." January 31, 2010.

Ahn Donghwan. "Ninety-Four Percent of Koreans Say Japan Does Not Regret Its Past Wrongdoings." *Seoul Shinmun*, January 4, 2013. http://www.seoul.co.kr/news/newsView.php?id=20130104001010.

Akçam, Taner. *A Shameful Act: The Armenian Genocide and the Question of Turkish Responsibility*. New York: Metropolitan Books, 2006.

Alexiev, Alex. *Soviet Nationalities in German Wartime Strategy, 1941–1945*. Santa Monica, Calif.: Rand Corporation, 1982.

Alterman, Nathan. *The Seventh Column*. [In Hebrew.] Vol. 2. Tel Aviv: Davar, 1954.

Andrieu, Claire, Marie-Claire Lavabre, and Danielle Tartakovsky. *Politiques du passé: Usages politiques du passé dans la France contemporaine*. Aix-en-Provence: Publications de l'Université de Provence, 2006.

Arendt, Hannah. *Eichmann in Jerusalem: A Report on the Banality of Evil*. New York: Penguin Books, 1994.

Aristotle. *Rhetoric*. Translated by W. Rhys Roberts. New York: Modern Library, 1954.

Arning, Matthias. *Späte Abrechnung: Über Zwangsarbeiter, Schlussstriche und Berliner Verständigungen*. Frankfurt am Main: Fischer, 2001.

Arnold, Magda B. *Emotion and Personality*. New York: Columbia University Press, 1960.

Art, David. *The Politics of the Nazi Past in Germany and Austria*. Cambridge: Cambridge University Press, 2006.

Asahi. "Kankoku daitoryo: 'Nihon, shinryaku o seitōka' Takeshima kyokashohihan no danwa." Satellite edition, March 24, 2005.

Astrov, Alexander. "Estonia: Political Struggle for a Place in History." [In Russian.] In "Politics of History." Special issue, *Pro et Contra* 13, nos. 3–4 (2009): 109–24.

Augstein, Rudolf. *Historikerstreit*. Munich: Piper Verlag, 1987.
Azéma, Jean-Pierre. "Guy Môquet, Sarkozy et le roman national." *L'Histoire*, no. 323 (September 2007): 6–11.
Ba Dianjun. "Cong wenhua shijiao touxi Riben waijiao zhengce de zhanlue xuanze." *Riben Xuekan*, no. 4 (2010): 93–106.
Babich, Dmitry. "Stalin's Methods Revived." *Russia Profile*, September 22, 2010.
Baldwin, Peter. *Reworking the Past: Hitler, the Holocaust, and the Historians' Debate*. Boston: Beacon, 1990.
Bank, Jan. "Contouren van een ongrijpbare wajang-figuur: Het turbulente leven van Soekarno." *NRC Handelsblad*, September 17, 1999.
Barcellini, Serge, and Annette Wieviorka. *Passant, souviens-toi! Les lieux du souvenir de la Seconde Guerre mondiale en France*. Paris: Plon, 1995.
Barkan, Elazar. *The Guilt of Nations: Restitution and Negotiating Historical Injustices*. Baltimore: Johns Hopkins University Press, 2001.
Bartos, Helen. "Israeli-German Relations in the Years 2000–2006: A Special Relationship Revisited." Master's thesis, St. Anthony's College, 2007. http://users.ox.ac.uk/~metheses/Bartos%20thesis.pdf.
Bass, Gary. *Stay the Hand of Vengeance: The Politics of War Crimes Tribunals*. Princeton, N.J.: Princeton University Press, 2000.
Bauer, Yehuda. *Rethinking the Holocaust*. New Haven, Conn.: Yale University Press, 2001.
Baumgart, Winfried. *Der Friede von Paris 1856: Studien zum Verhältnis von Kriegsführung, Politik und Friedensbewahrung*. Munich: Oldenbourg, 1972.
Bazyler, Michael. *Holocaust Justice: The Battle for Restitution in America's Courts*. New York: New York University Press, 2003.
BBC News. "Pelosi Visits Hiroshima Memorial." September 2, 2008. http://news.bbc.co.uk/2/hi/asia-pacific/7593298.stm.
BBC News Asia. "Japan and China Trade Barbs over Islands at UN." September 28, 2012. http://www.bbc.co.uk/news/world-asia-19754353.
Belinfante, A. D. *In plaats van bijltjesdag: De geschiedenis van de bijzondere rechtspleging na de Tweede Wereldoorlog*. Assen: Van Gorcum, 1978.
Beller, Steven. *A Concise History of Austria*. Cambridge: Cambridge University Press, 2006.
Benda, Harry J. *The Crescent and the Rising Sun: Indonesian Islam under the Japanese Occupation, 1942–1945*. The Hague/Bandung: W. Van Hoeve, 1958.
Benedict, Ruth. *The Chrysanthemum and the Sword: Patterns of Japanese Culture*. Boston: Houghton Mifflin, 1946.
Benn, David Wedgwood. "On Comparing Nazism and Stalinism." *International Affairs* 82, no. 1 (2006): 189–94.
———. "The Teaching of History in Present-Day Russia." *Europe-Asia Studies* 62, no. 1 (2010): 173–77.
———. "The Teaching of History in Putin's Russia." *International Affairs* 84, no. 2 (2008): 365–70.

Ben-Nathan, Asher, and Niels Hansen, eds. *Israel und Deutschland: Dorniger Weg zur Partnerschaft*. Cologne: Bohlau, 2005.

Berelovich, Vladimir. "Sovremennye rossiiskie uchebniki istorii: Mnogolikaya istina ili ocherednaya natsional'naya ideya?" *Neprikosnovenny Zapas*, no. 4 (2002).

Berger, Thomas. *War, Guilt, and World Politics after World War II*. Cambridge: Cambridge University Press, 2012.

Berlière, Jean-Marc, and Frank Liaigre. *L'affaire Guy Môquet: Enquête sur une mystification officielle*. Paris: Larousse, 2009.

Bijl, Paulus. "Emerging Memory: Photographs of Colonial Atrocity in Dutch Cultural Remembrance." Ph.D. diss. Utrecht University, 2011.

Bischof, Günter. "Victims? Perpetrators? 'Punching Bags' of European Historical Memory? The Austrians and Their World War II Legacies." *German Studies Review* 27, no. 1 (February 2004): 17–32.

Bix, Herbert P. "War Responsibility and Historical Memory: Hirohito's Apparition." *Asia-Pacific Journal: Japan Focus*, May 20, 2008. http://japanfocus.org/-herbert_p_-bix/2741.

Bloembergen, Marieke. *De geschiedenis van de politie in Nederlands-Indïe": Uit zorg en angst*. Amsterdam: Boom, 2009.

Boehling, Rebecca. *A Question of Priorities: Democratic Reform and Economic Recovery in Postwar Germany*. Oxford, U.K.: Berghahn Books, 1996.

Boehmer, Elleke, and Frances Gouda. "Postcolonial Studies in the Context of the 'Diasporic' Netherlands." In *Comparing Postcolonial Diasporas*, edited by Michelle Keown, David Murphy, and James Procter, 37–55. New York: Palgrave Macmillan, 2009.

Boers, Merel. "Wees niet bang voor het grijs." *NRC Handelsblad*, April 30, 2010.

Boomsma, Graa. *De laatste tyfoon*. Amsterdam: Prometheus, 1992.

Bordiugov, Gennadii A., and Vladimir M. Bukharayev. *Vcherashnee zavtra: Kak "natsional'nye istorii" pisalis' v SSSR i kak pishutsia teper'*. Moscow: AIRO-XXI, 2011.

Bosson, Nancy. *Guy Môquet: "J'aurais voulu vivre."* Le Mans: Libra Diffusion, 2007.

Bovenkerk, Frank. "Het Nederlandse aandeel in de jodenvervolging als criminologisch probleem." In *Morele kwesties in het strafrecht*, edited by Martin Moerings, 11–31. Gouda, Netherlands: Quint, 1999.

Boym, Svetlana. *The Future of Nostalgia*. New York: Basic Books, 2001.

Brailey, Nigel. *Thailand and the Fall of Singapore: A Frustrated Asian Revolution*. Boulder, Colo.: Westview Press, 1986.

Brandenberger, David. "A New Short Course? A. V. Filippov and the Russian State's Search for a 'Usable Past.'" *Kritika: Explorations in Russian and Eurasian History* 10, no. 4 (2009): 825–33.

Breen, John, ed. *Yasukuni, the War Dead, and the Struggle for Japan's Past*. New York: Columbia University Press, 2008.

———. "Yasukuni and the Loss of Historical Memory." In *Yasukuni, the War Dead, and the Struggle for Japan's Past*, edited by John Breen, 143–62. New York: Columbia University Press, 2008.

Breman, Jan. *Taming the Coolie Beast: Plantation Society and the Colonial Order in Southeast Asia*. New York: Oxford University Press, 1989.

Broszat, Martin, and Saul Friedlander. "A Controversy about the Historicization of National Socialism." In *Reworking the Past: Hitler, the Holocaust, and the Historians' Debate*, edited by Peter Baldwin. Boston: Beacon, 1990.

Browning, Christopher. *Collected Memories: Holocaust History and Postwar Testimony*. Madison: University of Wisconsin Press, 2003.

Buchholz, Petra. "Tales of War: Autobiographies and Private Memories in Japan and Germany." In *Memories of War: The Second World War and Japanese Historical Memory in Comparative Perspective*, edited by Takashi Inoguchi and Lyn Jackson. Tokyo: United Nations University, 1998. http://unu.edu/unupress/m-war.html#tales.

Buckley, Chris. "China Accuses Japan of Escalating Tensions over Disputed Islands." *New York Times* (Hong Kong), February 28, 2013.

———. "China Leader Affirms Policy on Islands." *New York Times*, January 29, 2013.

Budreckis, Algirdas Martin. *The Lithuanian National Revolt of 1941*. Boston: Lithuanian Encyclopedia Press, 1968.

Bukh, Alexander. "Japan's History Textbook Debate: National Identity in Narratives of Victimhood and Victimization." *Asian Survey* 47, no. 5 (September/October 2007): 683–704.

Bullock, Alan. *Hitler and Stalin: Parallel Lives*. London: Fontana, 1993.

Buruma, Ian. "From Tenderness to Savagery in Seconds." *New York Review of Books* 58, no. 15 (October 13, 2011): 27–28.

———. *The Wages of Guilt: Memories of War in Germany and Japan*. London: Jonathan Cape, 1994.

Bussemaker, Herman. "Paradise in Peril: Colonial Power and Japanese Expansion in South-East Asia, 1901–1941." Ph.D. diss., University of Amsterdam, 2001.

Carnegie Moscow Center and the Shigabuddin Mardzhani Institute of the Tatarstan Academy of Sciences. "The Politics of History and Its Variations in Post-socialist Countries." Seminar, Kazan, March 5–6, 2010.

Chang, Iris. *The Rape of Nanking: The Forgotten Holocaust of World War II*. New York: Basic Books, 1997.

Chang, Jui-te. "The Politics of Commemoration: A Comparative Analysis of the Fiftieth-Anniversary Commemoration in Mainland China and Taiwan of the Victory in the Anti-Japanese War." In *Scars of War: The Impact of Warfare on Modern China*, edited by Diana Lary and Stephen MacKinnon, 136–60. Vancouver: University of British Columbia Press, 2001.

Chirot, Daniel. "Europe's Troubled World War II Memories: Are They That Different?" In *History Textbooks and the Wars in Asia: Divided Memories*, edited by Gi-Wook Shin and Daniel Sneider, 269–85. New York: Routledge, 2011.

Chirot, Daniel, and Clark McCauley. *Why Not Kill Them All? The Logic and Prevention of Mass Political Murder*. 2nd ed. Princeton, N.J.: Princeton University Press, 2010.

Chosun Ilbo. "Supreme Court Rules Japanese Firms Must Pay for Forced Labor." May 25, 2012.

Christensen, Thomas. "China, the U.S.-Japan Alliance, and the Security Dilemma in East Asia." *International Security* 23, no. 4 (Spring 1999): 49–80.

Chung, Jae Ho. "China's 'Soft' Clash with South Korea: The History War and Beyond." *Asian Survey* 49, no. 3 (2009): 468–83.

Ciucă, Marcel-Dumitru, ed. *Procesul Mareşalului Antonescu: Documente*. With a foreword by Iosif Constantin Drăgan. 2 vols. Bucharest: Saeculum I. O. and Europa Nova, 1996.

Clendinnen, Inga. Introduction to *Reading the Holocaust*. Cambridge: Cambridge University Press, 2002.

Cochet, François. *Les exclus de la victoire: Histoire des prisonniers de guerre déportés et STO (1945–1985)*. Paris: Kronos, 1992.

Cohen, Danielle F. S. *Retracing the Triangle: China's Strategic Perceptions of Japan in the Post–Cold War Era*. Maryland Series in Contemporary Asian Studies, no. 2. Baltimore: University of Maryland, School of Law, 2005.

Cole, Elizabeth A. "Introduction: Reconciliation and History Education." In *Teaching the Violent Past: History Education and Reconciliation*, edited by Elizabeth A. Cole, 1–28. Lanham, Md.: Rowman and Littlefield, 2007.

Coté, Joost. "Strangers in the House: Dutch Historiography and Anglophone Trespassers." *Review of Indonesian and Malaysian Affairs* 43, no. 1 (2009): 75–94.

Craig, Gordon. *Politics and Culture in Modern Germany: Essays from the New York Review of Books*. Palo Alto, Calif.: Society for the Promotion of Science and Scholarship, 1999.

Crampton, Richard. *A Concise History of Bulgaria*. Cambridge: Cambridge University Press, 2005.

Cribb, Robert. *Gangsters and Revolutionaries: The Jakarta People's Militia and the Indonesian Revolution, 1945–1949*. Sydney: Allen and Unwin, 1991.

Cropsey, Seth. "On the Pearl Harbor Anniversary, Japan Still Says 'Don't Blame Me.'" Heritage Lecture, no. 353. November 30, 1991. http://www.heritage.org/research/lecture/on-the-pearl-harbor-anniversary-japan-still-says-dont-blame-me.

Cumings, Bruce. *Korea's Place in the Sun: A Modern History*. New York: Norton, 1997.

Cwiek-Karpowicz, Jaroslaw. *Public Opinion on Fears and Hopes Related to Russia and Germany*. Warsaw: Institute of Public Affairs, 2005. http://www.isp.org.pl/files/16004582900515529001143205142.pdf. Accessed March 15, 2013.

Dahm, Bernhard. *Soekarno, en de strijd om Indonesiës onafhankelijkheid, 1901–1950*. Meppel, Netherlands: J. A. Boom en Zoon, 1964.

Dallin, Alexander. *German Rule in Russia, 1941–1945: A Study of Occupation Policies*. Boulder, Colo. Westview Press, 1981.

———. "Ostland and the Baltic States." In *The Politics of Illusion and Empire: German Occupation Policy in the Soviet Union, 1942–43*, edited by Timothy P. Mulligan. New York: Praeger, 1988.

Davies, Norman. *No Simple Victory: World War II in Europe, 1939–1945*. New York: Penguin, 2006.

Deák, István. "A Fatal Compromise? The Debate over Collaboration and Resistance in Hungary." In *The Politics of Retribution in Europe: World War II and Its Aftermath*, edited by István Deák, Jan Gross, and Tony Judt, 39–73. Princeton, N.J.: Princeton University Press, 2000.

———. Introduction to *The Politics of Retribution in Europe: World War II and Its Aftermath*, edited by István Deák, Jan Gross, and Tony Judt, 3–14. Princeton, N.J.: Princeton University Press, 2000.

Deák, István, Jan Gross, and Tony Judt, eds. *The Politics of Retribution in Europe: World War II and Its Aftermath*. Princeton, N.J.: Princeton University Press, 2000.

Dean, Carolyn J. "Against Grandiloquence." *History and Theory: Study in the Philosophy of History* 45, no. 2 (2006): 276–87.

De Gaulle, Charles. *The Complete War Memoirs of Charles de Gaulle*. Translated by Richard Howard. New York: Carroll and Graf Publishers, 1998.

De Haan, Ido. "Nederland deportatieland?" *NRC Handelsblad*, May 7, 2011.

De Jonge, B. C., and W. Röell. "Appendix, 'Brieven.'" In *Herinneringen van Jhr. Mr. B. C. de Jonge met brieven uit zijn nalatenschap*, edited by S. L. van der Wal. Groningen, Netherlands: Wolters-Noordhoff, 1968.

De Moor, Jaap. *Generaal Spoor: Triomf en tragiek van een legercommandant*. Amsterdam: Boom, 2011.

Dempsey, Judy. "Old Foes See Reasons to Get Along." *International Herald Tribune*, December 9, 2010.

Dershowitz, Alan. *Contrary to Popular Opinion*. New York: Pharos Books, 1992.

De Swaan, Abram. "In the Vicinity of Anne Frank." Presentation by Abram de Swaan, Anne Frank House, Amsterdam, April 28, 2010.

Deutschkron, Inge. *Israel und die Deutschen: Zwichen Ressentiment und Ratio*. Cologne: Wissenschaft und Politik, 1970.

Dewulf, Jeroen. "The Many Meanings of Freedom: The Debate on the Legitimacy of Colonialism in the Dutch Resistance, 1940–1949." *Journal of Colonialism and Colonial History* 12, no. 1 (Spring 2011). doi: 10.1353/cch.2011.0002.

———. "Zes kaarsen voor Indië: Indonesië in de Nederlandse clandestiene literatuur (1940–1945)." *Indische Letteren* 25, no. 1 (2010): 39–62.

Diamond, Hanna. *Fleeing Hitler: France 1940*. Oxford: Oxford University Press, 2007.

Dickie, Mure, and David Pilling. "Sino-Japanese Historians Battle to Find Consensus." *Financial Times*, February 16, 2007.

Dierkes, Julian. *Postwar History Education in Japan and the Germanys: Guilty Lessons*. Oxon: Routledge, 2010.

Dommering, E. J. "De Nederlandse publieke discussie en de politionele acties in Indonesië." *Nederlands Juristenblad*, no. 8 (March 4, 1994): 277–95.

Dong Xiaogrong, Wang Xialing, and Li Yungchun. "Hanguo gongzhong dui Zhongguo jueqi de renzhi yu taidu fenxi." *Xiandai Guoji Guanxi*, no. 10 (2010): 46.

Dong-A Ilbo. "Opinion Poll on Chinese and South Korean Attitudes toward Japan and Other Nations." April 26, 2005. http://mansfieldfdn.org/program/research-education-and-communication/asian-opinion-poll-database/listofpolls/2005-polls/march-2005-dong-a-ilbo-opinion-poll-on-chinese-attitudes-toward-japan-and-other-nations.

Don-Yehiya, Eliezer. "Memory and Political Culture: Israeli Society and the Holocaust." In *Studies in Contemporary Jewry* 9 (1993): 139–162.

Douzou, Laurent. *La résistance française: Une histoire périlleuse.* Paris: Seuil, 2005.

Dower, John W. *Embracing Defeat: Japan in the Wake of World War II.* New York: Norton, 1999.

Dudden, Alexis. "Dangerous Islands: Japan, Korea, and the United States." *Asia-Pacific Journal: Japan Focus*, August 11, 2008. http://www.japanfocus.org/-Alexis-Dudden/2852.

———. *Troubled Apologies among Japan, Korea, and the United States.* New York: Columbia University Press, 2008.

Dujarric, Robert. "Retour sur un Japon conquérant." *Le Monde*, December 25, 2007. http://www.lemonde.fr/.

Eckert, Carter J. *Offspring of Empire: The Koch'ang Kims and the Colonial Origins of Korean Capitalism, 1876–1945.* Seattle: University of Washington Press, 1991.

Economist. "The Ghost of Wartimes Past." November 5, 2008. http://www.economist.com/node/12544740.

Economist (Tokyo). "Back to the Future." January 5, 2013.

Eizenstat, Stuart E. *Imperfect Justice: Looted Assets, Slave Labor, and the Unfinished Business of World War II.* New York: Public Affairs, 2003.

Elon, Amos. *Journey through a Haunted Land: The New Germany.* New York: Holt, Rinehart and Winston, 1967.

———. *The Pity of It All: A Portrait of the German-Jewish Epoch, 1743–1933.* New York: Picador, 2003.

Elster, Jon. *Alchemies of the Mind: Rationality and the Emotions.* Cambridge: Cambridge University Press, 1997.

———. *Closing the Books: Transitional Justice in Historical Perspective.* New York: Cambridge University Press, 2004.

Engel, David. "On Continuity and Discontinuity in Polish-Jewish Relations: Observations on *Fear*." Review of *Fear: Anti-Semitism in Poland after Auschwitz—an Essay in Historical Interpretation*, by Jan Gross. *East European Politics and Societies* 21, no. 3 (Summer 2007): 534–48.

Esbenshade, Richard S. "Remembering to Forget: Memory, History, National Identity in Postwar East-Central Europe." *Representations*, no. 49 (Winter 1995): 72–96.

Etiévent, Michel. *Guy Môquet: "J'aurais voulu vivre."* Calles-Les Eaux: Editions GAP, 2007.

European Parliament, Justice and Home Affairs. "European Parliament Resolution on European Conscience and Totalitarianism." April 2, 2009. http://www.europarl.europa.eu/sides/getDoc.do?pubRef=-//EP//TEXT+IM-PRESS+20090401IPR53245+0+DOC+XML+V0//EN.

Eurozine. "European Histories: Toward a Grand Narrative." May 3, 2005. http://www.eurozine.com/articles/2005-05-03-eurozine-en.html.

Eurozine. "Eurozine Conference Held in Vilnius." May 20, 2009. http://www.eurozine.com/articles/2009-05-20-summary-en.html.

Evans, Richard J. *The New Nationalism and the Old History: Perspectives on the West German Historikerstreit.* Chicago: University of Chicago Press, 1987.

Evropa: Zhurnal Pol'skogo Instituta Mezhdunarodnykh Del. "Trudnoe nasledie proshlogo: Rossiia v poiskakh istoricheskoi pravdy." Special issue. Vol. 9, no. 2 (2009): 7–60.

Fackler, Martin. "Japanese Mayor's Comments about Massacre Anger Nanjing." *New York Times* (Tokyo), February 23, 2012.

Falkowski, Mateusz. *Meinungen der Polen über die deutsch-polnischen Beziehungen nach dem Regierungswechsel in beidern Länder.* Warsaw: Institute of Public Affairs, November 2005.

Falkowski, Mateusz, and Agnieszka Popko. *The Germans about Poland and the Poles, 2000–2006.* Warsaw: Institute of Public Affairs.

Farmer, Sarah. *Martyred Village: Commemorating the 1944 Massacre at Oradour-sur-Glane.* Berkeley: University of California Press, 2000.

Felman, Shoshana. "Film as Witness: Claude Lanzmann's Shoah." In *Holocaust Remembrance: The Shape of Memory*, edited by Geoffrey Hartman. Oxford: Blackwell, 1994.

Feng Zhaokui. "Zhongri liangguo lishi wenti de zhengjie." *Liaowang*, no. 6 (2010): 38–40.

Fennema, Meindert. "Laat de oorlog even rusten." *Trouw*, March 13, 2010.

"Ferrant, Anatole." Sénat: Un site au service des citoyens. Accessed February 3, 2010. http://www.senat.fr/senateur-4eme-republique/ferrant_anatole0401r4.html.

Ferretti, Maria. "'Obretennaya identichnost': Novaya 'ofitsial'naya istoriya' putinskoi Rossii." *Neprikosnovenny Zapas*, no. 4 (2004). http://magazines.russ.ru/nz/2004/4/fe11.html.

Filippov, Aleksandr. *Noveishaia istoriia Rossii, 1945–2006 gg.: Kniga dlia uchiteia.* Moscow: Prosveshchenie, 2007.

Fineman, Daniel. *A Special Relationship: The United States and Military Government in Thailand, 1947–1958.* Honolulu: University of Hawaii Press, 1997.

Finn, Richard B. *Winners in Peace: MacArthur, Yoshida, and Postwar Japan.* Berkeley: University of California Press, 1995.

Foner, Eric. *Who Owns History? Rethinking the Past in a Changing World.* New York: Hill and Wang, 2003.

Foray, Jennifer L. *Visions of Empire in the Nazi-Occupied Netherlands.* Cambridge: Cambridge University Press, 2011.

François, Etienne. "Le manuel franco-allemand d'histoire: Une enterprise inédite." *Vingtième Siècle: Revue d'Histoire*, no. 94 (April–June 2007): 73–86.

Frankel, Benjamin, and Brian D. Kux. "Recalling the Dark Past of Lithuanian Nationalism." *Los Angeles Times*, April 29, 1990.

Frankfurter Allgemeine Zeitung. "Europa sucht neue Wurzeln." June 24, 2007.

Frankfurter Allgemeine Zeitung. "Schwierige Verhandlungen in Brüssel." June 23, 2007.

Frederick, William H. "Weerspiegelingen in stromend water: Indonesische herinneringen aan de oorlog en de Japanners." In *Beelden van de Japanse bezetting van Indonesië*, edited by Remco Raben. Zwolle: Waanders; Amsterdam: NIOD, 1999.

Freedom House. *Nations in Transit 2013.* http://www.freedomhouse.org/report/nations-transit/nations-transit-2013. Accessed August 3, 2013.

Frei, Norbert. "Preodolennoe proshloe? Tretii reikh v sovremennom nemetskom soznanii." *Ab Imperio*, no. 4 (2004): 21-40.
Friedlander, Saul. *Nazi Germany and the Jews, 1939-1945: The Years of Extermination*. New York: Harper Collins, 2007.
Friedman, Jonathan. "The Past in the Future: History and the Politics of Identity." *American Anthropologist* 94, no. 4 (1992). doi:10.1525/aa.1992.94.4.02a00040.
Friedrich, Jorg. *Die kalte Amnestie: NS-Täter in der Bundesrepublik*. Berlin: List Taschenbuch Verlag, 2007.
Friend, Julian. *The Linchpin: French-German Relations, 1950-1990*. Washington Papers 154. Westport, Conn.: Praeger; Washington, D.C.: Center for Strategic and International Studies, 1991.
———. *Unequal Partners: French-German Relations, 1989-2000*. Washington Papers 180. Westport, Conn.: Praeger; Washington, D.C.: Center for Strategic and International Studies, 2001.
Friend, Theodore. *The Blue-Eyed Enemy: Japan against the West in Java and Luzon, 1942-1945*. Princeton, N.J.: Princeton University Press, 1988.
———. *Indonesian Destinies*. Cambridge, Mass.: Harvard University Press, 2003.
Frijda, Nico. *The Emotions*. Cambridge: Cambridge University Press, 1987.
Funabashi Yoichi, ed. *Reconciliation in the Asia-Pacific*. Washington, D.C.: United States Institute of Peace, 2003.
Fusayama Takao. *A Japanese Memoir of Sumatra, 1945-1946: Love and Hatred in the Liberation War*. Ithaca, N.Y.: Cornell Southeast Asia Program Publications, 1993.
Gans, Evelien. "Iedereen een beetje slachtoffer, iedereen een beetje dader: De Nederlandse Historikerstreit over de grijze oorlog." *De Groene Amsterdammer*, January 28, 2010.
Gao Lan. "Lishi jiaokeshu wenti: Zhongri moshi yu Fade moshi de bijiao." *Riben Xuekan*, no. 3 (2010): 3-15.
Gardner, Paul F. *Shared Hopes, Separate Fears: Fifty Years of U.S.-Indonesian Relations*. Boulder, Colo.: Westview Press, 1997.
Geertz, Clifford. *Negara: The Theater State in Nineteenth-Century Bali*. Princeton, N.J.: Princeton University Press, 1981.
Gehler, Michael. "'Eine grotesk überzogene Dämonisierung eines Mannes': Die Waldheim Affäre 1986-1992." In *Politische Affären und Skandale in Österreich: Von Mayerling bis Waldheim*, edited by Michael Gehler and Hubert Sickinger, 614-65. Thaur, Germany: Kultur Verlag, 1995.
———. "Kontraproduktive Intervention: Die 'EU 14' und der Fall Österreich oder vom Triumph des 'Primates Der Innenpolitik' 2000-2003." In *Österreich in der Europäischen Union: Bilanz einer Mitgliedschaft*, edited by Michael Gehler, Anton Pelinka, and Günter Bischof. Vienna: Böhlau Verlag, 2003.
Geismar, Alain. *Mon mai 1968*. Paris: Perrin, 2008.
Gelber, Yoav. *A New Homeland: The Immigration from Central Europe and Its Absorption in Eretz Israel, 1933-1948*. [In Hebrew.] Jerusalem: Leo Baeck Institute and Yad Izhak Ben-Zvi, 1990.

———. *Palestine 1948: War, Escape and the Emergence of the Palestinian Refugee Problem*, Brighton and Portland, U.K.: Sussex Academic Press, 2006.

George, Alexander, and Andrew Bennett. *Case Studies and Theory Development in the Social Sciences*. Cambridge, Mass.: MIT Press, 2005.

Gerbrandy, Pieter Sjoerds. *De scheuring van het rijk: Het drama van de Indonesische crisis*. Kampen: J. H. Kok N.V, 1951.

Gerstenfeld, Manfred. "Anti-Israelism and Anti-Semitism: Common Characteristics and Motifs." *Jewish Political Studies Review* 19, nos. 1–2 (2007): 83–108.

Geyer, Michael, and Sheila Fitzpatrick, eds. *Beyond Totalitarianism: Stalinism and Nazism Compared*. New York: Cambridge University Press, 2009.

Giebels, Lambert. *Soekarno*. Vol. 1, *Nederlandsch onderdaan: Biografie 1901–1949*. Amsterdam: Bert Bakker, 1999.

———. *Soekarno*. Vol. 2, *President: Biografie 1950–1970*. Amsterdam: Bakker, 2001.

Gilbert, Martin. *Exile and Return: The Struggle for a Jewish Homeland*. Philadelphia: Lippincott, 1978.

———. *Jewish History Atlas*. New York: Macmillan, 1969.

Giles, Frank. *The Locust Years: The Story of the Fourth French Republic, 1946–1958*. New York: Carroll and Graf, 1991.

Gledhill, John. "Integrating the Past: Regional Integration and Historical Reckoning in Central and Eastern Europe." *Nationalities Papers* 39, no. 4 (July 2011): 481–506.

Glenny, Misha. *The Balkans: Nationalism, War, and the Great Powers, 1804–1999*. London: Penguin, 2000.

Goldhagen, Daniel. *Hitler's Willing Executioners: Ordinary Germans and the Holocaust*. New York: Alfred A. Knopf, 1996.

Golsan, Richard, ed. *Memory, the Holocaust, and French Justice: The Bousquet and Touvier Affairs*. Hanover, N.H.: University Press of New England for Dartmouth College, 1996.

———. "Memory's *bombe à retardement*: Maurice Papon, Crimes against Humanity and 17 October 1961." *Journal of European Studies* 28 (1998): 153–72.

———, ed. *The Papon Affair: Memory and Justice on Trial*. London: Routledge, 2000.

Gordon, Peter. "The Guilty." Review of *The Eichmann Trial*, by Deborah Lipstadt. *New Republic*, September 29, 2011. http://www.newrepublic.com/book/review/the-guilty#.

Goss, Andrew. "From Tong-Tong to Tempo Doeloe: Eurasian Memory Work and the Bracketing of Dutch Colonial History, 1957–1961." *Indonesia* 70 (October 2000): 23–39.

Gouda, Frances. *Dutch Culture Overseas: Colonial Practice in the Netherlands Indies, 1900–1942*. 2nd ed. Jakarta: Equinox Publishers, 2008.

———. "Primitivity, Animism, and Psychoanalysis: European Visions of the Native 'Soul' in the Dutch East Indies, 1900–1949." In *The Transnational Unconscious: Essays in the History of Psychoanalysis and Transnationalism*, edited by Joy Damousi and Mariano Ben Plotkin, 73–97. Houndmills, Basingstoke, Hampshire: Palgrave Macmillan, 2009.

———. "The Unbearable Lightness of Memory: Fragmentations of Cultural Memory and Recycling the Dutch Colonial Past." *Groniek Historisch Tijdschrift*, no. 174 (April 2007): 9–27.

Gouda, Frances, and Thijs W. Brocades Zaalberg. *American Visions of the Netherlands East Indies / Indonesia: US Foreign Policy and Indonesian Nationalism, 1920-1949.* Amsterdam: Amsterdam University Press, 2002.

———. *Indonesia merdeka karena Amerika? Politik luar negeri AS dan nasionalisme Indonesia, 1920-1949.* Jakarta: Serambi Ilmu Semesta P.T., 2009.

Green, Michael. *Japan's Reluctant Realism: Foreign Policy Changes in a Era of Uncertain Power.* New York: St. Martin's Press, 2001.

Greene, Samuel A., ed. *Engaging History: The Problems and Politics of Memory in Russia and the Post-socialist Space.* Moscow: Carnegie Moscow Center, 2010.

Gries, Peter Hays. *China's New Nationalism: Pride, Politics, and Diplomacy.* Berkeley: University of California Press, 2004.

Groen, Koos. *Fout en niet goed: De vervolging van collaboratie en verraad na de Tweede Wereldoorlog.* Hilversum: Just Publishers, 2009.

Gross, Jan. *Fear: Anti-Semitism in Poland after Auschwitz.* New York: Random House, 2006.

———. *Neighbors: The Destruction of the Jewish Community in Jebwadne, Poland.* Princeton, N.J.: Princeton University Press, 2001.

———. *Polish Society under German Occupation: The Generalgouvernement, 1939-1944.* Princeton, N.J.: Princeton University Press, 1979.

———. "A Tangled Web: Confronting Stereotypes concerning Relations between Poles, Germans, Jews, and Communists." In *The Politics of Retribution in Europe: World War II and Its Aftermath*, edited by István Deák, Jan Gross, and Tony Judt, 74–129. Princeton, N.J.: Princeton University Press, 2000.

Grossman, David. *See Under: Love.* Translated by Betsy Rosenberg. New York: Picador, 2002.

Grove, Thomas. "Russia Must Exorcise Stalin's Legacy—Kremlin Aide." Reuters, December 7, 2010. http://in.reuters.com/article/2010/12/06/idINIndia-53388420101206.

Grunfeld, Frederic V. *Prophets without Honour: Background to Freud, Kafka, Einstein, and Their World.* New York: Holt, Rinehart and Winston, 1979.

Guo Rui and Ling Shengli. "Minzuzhuyi yu Hanguo waijiao zhengce." *Shijie Jingji yu Zhengzhi Luntan*, no. 3 (2010): 150–59.

Gutterman, Steve. "Dead Sixty Years, Stalin's Influence Lingers in Putin's Russia." Reuters, March 5, 2013. http://www.reuters.com/article/2013/03/05/us-russia-stalin-idUSBRE9240O120130305.

Hahm, Chaibong. "How the East Was Won: Orientalism and the New Confucian Discourse in East Asia." *Development and Society* 29, no. 1 (2000): 97–109.

Hallet, Theo. *Umstrittenen Versöhnung: Reagan und Kohl in Bitburg 1985.* Erfurt: Sutton, 1985.

Hamby, Alonzo L. "Endgame: How the Big Three Concluded the Good War." *Weekly Standard*, 16, no. 1 (2010). http://www.weeklystandard.com/articles/endgame.

Hampl, Patricia. "The Whole Anne Frank." *New York Times*, March 5, 1995.

Han Li. "Zhongguo jueqi yu Dongbeiya de anquan zhanlue xuanze." *Yanbian Dangxiao Xuebao*, no. 10 (2010): 67–69.

Hara, Kimie. *Cold War Frontiers in the Asia-Pacific: Divided Territories in the San Francisco System*. New York: Routledge, 2007.

———. "Cold War Frontiers in the Asia-Pacific: The Troubling Legacy of the San Francisco Treaty." *Asia-Pacific Journal: Japan Focus*, September 4, 2006.

Harbutt, Fraser J. *Yalta 1945: Europe and America at the Crossroads*. New York: Cambridge University Press, 2010.

Hasegawa Tsuyoshi and Kazuhiko Togo, eds. *East Asia's Haunted Present: Historical Memories and the Resurgence of Nationalism*. Westport, Conn.: Praeger, 2008.

He Yinan. *Overcoming Shadows of the Past: Post-conflict Interstate Reconciliation in East Asia and Europe*. Cambridge, Mass.: MIT Press, 1970.

———. "Remembering and Forgetting the War: Elite Mythmaking, Mass Reaction, and Sino-Japanese Relations, 1950–2006." *History and Memory* 19, no. 2 (Fall 2007): 43–74.

———. *The Search for Reconciliation: Sino-Japanese and German-Polish Relations since World War II*. Cambridge: Cambridge University Press, 2009.

Herf, Jeffrey. *Divided Memory: The Nazi Past in the Two Germanys*. Cambridge, Mass.: Harvard University Press, 1997.

Hering, Bob. *Soekarno: Founding Father of Indonesia*. Leiden: KITLV Press, 2002.

Herman, Steven. "Burning Memories: Tokyo Reflects on the Night Fifty Years ago That U.S. Bombers Set It Ablaze." *Far Eastern Economic Review* 158, no. 15 (April 1995): 40–41.

Hessel, Stéphane. *Indignez-vous!* Montpellier: Indigène éditions, 2010.

Hicks, George. *Japan's War Memories: Amnesia or Concealment?* Aldershot: Ashgate, 1997.

Higashinakano Shudo. "Top-Secret Chinese Nationalist Documents Reveal the Truth about the Nanking Incident." Tokyo: Society for the Dissemination of Historical Fact, 2008.

Hilberg, Raul. *Perpetrators Victims Bystanders: The Jewish Catastrophe, 1933–1945*. New York: HarperCollins, 1992.

Hill, Fiona, and Clifford Gaddy. "Putin and the Uses of History." *National Interest*, no. 1 (January/February 2012). http://nationalinterest.org/article/putin-the-uses-history-6276.

Hockenos, Paul. "The Fine Line of Blood." *Internationale Politik Global Online*, August 23, 2011. http://www.ip-global.org/2011/08/23/the-fine-line-of-blood.

Holborn, Hajo. *A History of Modern Germany, 1840–1945*. Princeton, N.J.: Princeton University Press, 1969.

Honda Katsuichi. *Chūgoku no Nihongun*. Tokyo: Sōjusha, 1972.

———. *Chūgoku no tabi*. Tokyo: Asahi Shimbunsha, 1972.

Horvat, Andrew. "A Strong State, Weak Civil Society, and Cold War Geopolitics: Why Japan Lags behind Europe in Confronting a Negative Past." In *Rethinking Historical Injustice and Reconciliation in Northeast Asia: The Korean Experience*, edited by Gi-Wook Shin, Soon-Won Park, and Daqing Yang, 216–34. New York: Routledge, 2007.

Hou Zhigong. "Guanyu Zhongri guanxi de shikong weidu tantao." *Dongyue Lunceng*, no. 7 (2010): 144–47.
Ienaga Saburō. *The Pacific War, 1931–1945: A Critical Perspective on Japan's Role in World War II*. New York: Pantheon Books, 1978.
Ikenberry, G. John. "Japan's History Problem." *Washington Post*, August 17, 2006.
Ioanid, Radu. *The Holocaust in Romania: The Destruction of Jews and Gypsies under the Antonescu Regime*. With a foreword by Elie Wiesel. Chicago: Ivan R. Dee, 2000.
International Crisis Group. *North East Asia's Undercurrents of Conflict*. Report no. 108. December 15, 2005. http://www.crisisgroup.org/en/regions/asia/north-east-asia/108-north-east-asias-undercurrents-of-conflict.aspx.
Irie Yoshimasa. "The History of the Textbook Controversy." *Japan Echo* 24, no. 3 (August 1997): 35–36.
Ishii Susumu, Itoo T., Kasahara Kazuo, et al. *Japanese History in Detail (Yamakawa Japanese History B Textbook)*. Tokyo: Yamakaway Shuppansha, 2002.
Israel Central Bureau of Statistics Report. 2010. [In Hebrew.] http://www.cbs.gov.il/reader/shnaton/shnatonh_new.htm?CYear=2010&Vol=61.
Istorychna pam'yat' yak pole zmahan' za identychnist': Materialy "kruhloho stolu." Kiev: Natsional'nyi Instytut Strategichnykh Doslidzhen', 2008.
Jackson, Julian. *France: The Dark Years, 1940–1944*. Oxford: Oxford University Press, 2001.
———. "La Rafle." *Film and Fiction for French Historians: A Cultural Bulletin*, no. 1 (December 2010). http://h-france.net/fffh/the-buzz/la-rafle.
———. "Les 18 juin de Pompidou à Sarkozy." In *Les 18 juin: Combats et commémorations*, edited by Philippe Oulmont, 208–35. Paris: André Versaille, 2011.
James, Clive. "Blaming the Germans." Review of *Hitler's Willing Executioners: Ordinary Germans and the Holocaust*, by Daniel Goldhagen. *New Yorker*, April 22, 1966, 44–50.
Japan Times. "Hirohito Visits to Yasukuni Stopped over War Criminals." July 21, 2006.
———. "Japan, S. Korea Researchers at Odds over Forced Labor, Comfort Women." March 24, 2010.
———. "Yasukuni, State in '69 OK'd War Criminal Inclusion." March 29, 2007.
Japanese Cabinet Office. "Gaikō ni kan suru yoronchōsa." October 2009. http://www8.cao.go.jp/survey/h21/h21-gaiko/index.html.
"Japanese War Crimes: Introduction." http://www.users.bigpond.com/battleforaustralia/WarCrimeIntro.html. Accessed in 2009.
Jardin, Alexandre. *Des gens trés bien*. Paris: Grasset, 2011.
Jeans, Roger B. "Victims or Victimizers? Museums, Textbooks, and the War Debate in Contemporary Japan." *Journal of Military History* 69, no. 1 (January 2005): 149–95.
Jewish World. "Anne Frank Tree Saplings Keep Symbol of Hope Alive." June 12, 2009.
Jilge, Wilfried. "Zmahannya shertv." *Krytyka*, no. 5 (2006). www.krytyka.com/.
Joffe, Josef. "Germany and Israel: Between Obligation, Taboo, and Resentment." In *European-Israeli Relations: Between Confusion and Change?*, edited by Manfred Gerstenfeld, 139–48. Jerusalem: Jerusalem Center for Public Affairs, 2006.
Joffrin, Laurent. "Oui il faut lire la lettre de Guy Môquet." *Libération*, May 27, 2007.

Jones, Gregg. *Honor in the Dust: Theodore Roosevelt, War in the Philippines, and the Rise and Fall of America's Imperial Dream*. New York: New American Library, 2012.

Judt, Tony. "From the House of the Dead: On Modern European Memory." *New York Review of Books* 52, no. 15 (October 6, 2005): 12–16. http://www.nybooks.com/articles/archives/2005/oct/06/from-the-house-of-the-dead-on-modern-european-memo/?pagination=false.

———. "Interview with Historian Tony Judt: 'Dreaming about Washington Is One of East Europe's Great Mistakes.'" Radio Free Europe / Radio Liberty, October 1, 2009.

———. "The Past Is Another Country: Myth and Memory in Postwar Europe." *Daedalus* 121, no. 4 (Fall 1992): 83–118.

———. "The Past Is Another Country: Myth and Memory in Postwar Europe." In *The Politics of Retribution in Europe: World War II and Its Aftermath*, edited by István Deák, Jan Gross, and Tony Judt, 293–323. Princeton, N.J.: Princeton University Press, 2000.

———. *Postwar: A History of Europe since 1945*. New York: Penguin, 2006.

Jun Yonaha. *Chugokuka suru Nihon (bunmei no shototsu) issennenshi*. Tokyo: Bungei Shunju, 2011.

Kabachiy, Roman. "Ukradennaya pamyat." Polit.ru, May 6, 2010. http://www.polit.ru/institutes/2010/05/06/memory_print.html.

Kamm, Henry. "Lithuania Halts the Reversal of War-Crimes Convictions." *New York Times*, October 17, 1991.

Kamo Takehiko. "Globalism, Regionalism, and Nationalism: Asia in Search of Its Role in the Twenty-First Century." In *Globalism, Regionalism, and Nationalism: Asia in Search of Its Role in the Twenty-First Century*, edited by Yoshinobu Yamamoto. London: Blackwell, 1999.

Kansteiner, Wulf. "Losing the War, Winning the Memory Battle: The Legacy of Nazism, World War II, and the Holocaust in the Federal Republic of Germany." In *The Politics of Memory in Postwar Europe*, edited by Richard Ned Lebow, Wulf Kansteiner, and Claudio Fogu, 102–76. Durham, N.C.: Duke University Press, 2006.

Kaplan, Vera. "The Vicissitudes of Socialism in Russian History Textbooks." *History and Memory* 21, no. 2 (2009): 83–109.

Kappeler, Andreas. "From an Ethnonational to a Multiethnic to a Transnational Ukrainian History." In *A Laboratory of Transnational History: Ukraine and Recent Ukrainian Historiography*, edited by Georgiy Kasianov and Philipp Ther, 51–81. Budapest: Central European University Press, 2009.

Karaganov, Sergei. "Drugaya nasha istoriya." *Rossiiskaya Gazeta*, March 19, 2010.

———. "Russkaya Katyn." *Rossiiskaya Gazeta*, July 22, 2010.

Karaganov, Sergei, and Arseny Roginsky. "Stenograficheskii otchet o zasedanii Soveta po razvitiyu grazhdanskogo obshchestva i pravam cheloveka." Kremlin.ru, February 1, 2011. http://news.kremlin.ru/transcripts/10194.

Karavayev, Aleksandra. "'Novy istoricheskii mif' i konflikty interpretatsii." Prognosis.ru, June 29, 2007. http://www.prognosis.ru/news/nacional/2007/6/29/histiry.html.

Karnow, Stanley. *Vietnam: A History*. New York: Viking Press, 1983.

Kasyanov, Georgiy. "Golodomor i stroitel'stvo natsii." *Pro et Contra* 13, nos. 3–4 (2009): 24–42.

———. "Natsionalizatsiya istorii ta obraz inshoho." *Krytyka*, nos. 1–2 (2006). www.krytyka.com/.

Katsuichi Honda. *Chūgoku no tabi*. Tokyo: Asahi Shimbunsha, 1972.

Kattago, Siobhan. "Agreeing to Disagree on the Legacies of Recent History: Memory, Pluralism, and Europe after 1989." *European Journal of Social Theory* 12, no. 3 (2009): 375–95.

Katz, Dovid. "Why Red Is Not Brown in the Baltics." *Guardian*, October 1, 2010.

Kawai Atushi. *Kyokasho kara kieta Nihonshi: Gakko de naratta (rekishi) wa machigaidarake*. Tokyo: Kabunsha, 2008.

Kershaw, Ian, and Moshe Lewin, eds. *Stalinism and Nazism: Dictatorships in Comparison*. Cambridge: Cambridge University Press, 1997.

Khazanov, Anatoly, and Stanley Payne. "How to Deal with the Past?" *Totalitarian Movements and Political Religions* 9, nos. 2–3 (2008): 411–31.

Kiernan, Ben. *Blood and Soil: A World History of Genocide and Extermination from Sparta to Darfur*. New Haven, Conn.: Yale University Press, 2007.

Kimmelman, Michael. "No Laughs, No Thrills, and Villains All Too Real." *New York Times* (Berlin), February 27, 2008.

Kingston, Jeff. "Nanjing's Massacre Memorial: Renovating War Memory in Nanjing and Tokyo." *Asia-Pacific Journal: Japan Focus*, April 2008.

Kinzer, Stephen. "Lithuania Starts to Wipe out Convictions for War Crimes." *New York Times*, September 5, 1991.

Kissinger, Henry. *Does America Need a Foreign Policy? Toward a Diplomacy for the Twenty-First Century*. New York: Simon and Schuster, 2001.

Köbben, Andre. *De tijdgeest en andere ongemakken*. Amsterdam: Mets en Schilt, 2008.

Kolthoff, Kees. *Veilige afstand: De geschiedenis van oorlogsherinneringen*. Soesterberg, Netherlands: Aspekt, 2010.

Koposov, Nikolai. *Pamiat' strogogo rezhima: Istoriya i politika v Rossii*. Moscow: NLO, 2011.

Koschmann, J. Victor., ed. *Authority and the Individual in Japan: Citizen Protest in Historical Perspective*. Tokyo: University of Tokyo Press, 1978.

Kozak, Warren. "LeMay and the Tragedy of War: When Basic Survival Trumps Civil Liberties." *Wall Street Journal*, May 18, 2009.

Kritzman, Lawrence D., and Pierre Nora, eds. *Realms of Memory: The Construction of the French Past*. Translated by Arthur Goldhammer. Vol. 3. New York: Columbia University Press, 1998.

Krzeminski, Adam. "As Many Wars as Nations: The Myths and Truths of World War II." *Sign and Sight*, April 6, 2005. http://www.signandsight.com/features/96.html.

Kuitenbrouwer, Marteen. *Tussen oriëntalisme en wetenschap: 150 jaar KITLV*. Leiden: KITLV Press, 2001.

Kundnani, Hans. *Utopia or Auschwitz? Germany's 1968 Generation and the Holocaust*. London: Hurst and Company, 2009.

Kuzio, Taras. "History, Memory, and Nation Building in the Post-Soviet Colonial Space." *Nationalities Papers* 30, no. 2 (2002): 241–64.

———. "Nation Building, History Writing, and Competition over the Legacy of Kyiv Rus in Ukraine." *Nationalities Papers* 33, no. 1 (2005): 29–58.

Laborie, Pierre. *Le chagrin et le venin: La France sous l'occupation, mémoire et idées reçues.* Montrouge: Bayard, 2011.

Lagrou, Pieter. *Mémoires patriotiques et Occupation nazie: Résistants, requis et déportés en Europe occidentale, 1945-1965.* Brussels: Complexe, 2003.

Le Bars, Stéphanie. "Le projet de parrainage d'enfants de la Shoah contesté." *Le Monde*, February 16, 2008. http://www.lemonde.fr/.

Lebow, Richard Ned, Wulf Kansteiner, and Claudio Fogu, eds. *The Politics of Memory in Postwar Europe.* Durham, N.C.: Duke University Press, 2006.

Le Dantec, Jean-Pierre. *Les dangers du soleil.* Paris: Presses d'aujourd'hui, 1978.

Lee, Carol Ann. *The Hidden Life of Otto Frank.* New York: Viking, 2000.

Lee, Chulwoo. "Modernity, Legality, and Power in Korea under Japanese Rule." In *Colonial Modernity in Korea*, edited by Gi-Wook Shin and Michael Robinson, 21–51. Cambridge, Mass.: Harvard University Asia Center, 1999.

Lee, Ivy. "In Search of Redress for Historical Injustice: The Slave Labor Lawsuits against Japanese Corporations." *East Asia* 19, no. 4 (Winter 2001): 143–54.

Leggewie, Claus. "Seven Circles of European Memory." *Eurozine*, December 20, 2010. http://www.eurozine.com/pdf/2010-12-20-leggewie-en.html.

Le Monde. "Une dette imprescriptible." April 4, 2003. http://www.lemonde.fr/.

Levkov, Ilya, ed. *Bitburg and Beyond: Encounters in American, German, and Jewish History.* New York: Shapolsky Publishers, 1987.

Levy, Robert I. *Tahitians: Mind and Experience in the Society Islands.* Chicago: University of Chicago Press, 1973.

Lewin, Christopher. *Le retour des prisonniers de guerre français: Naissance et development de la FNPGD, 1944-1952.* Paris: Publications de la Sorbonne, 1986.

Li Xing. "Yao jinji Sulian diyuan waijiao de jiaoxun." *Huanqiu Shibao*, April 12, 2011.

Lieven, Anatol. *The Baltic Revolution: Estonia, Latvia, Lithuania, and the Path to Independence.* New Haven, Conn.: Yale University Press, 1993.

———. "Reexamining Russian History." *National Interest*, September 15, 2010. http://nationalinterest.org/commentary/reexamining-russian-history-4081.

Lijphart, Arend. *The Trauma of Decolonization: The Dutch and West New Guinea.* New Haven, Conn.: Yale University Press, 1966.

Lind, Jennifer. The Limits on Nationalism in Japan." *New York Times*, July 24, 2013.

———. *Sorry States: Apologies in International Politics.* Ithaca, N.Y.: Cornell University Press, 2008.

Lindeperg, Sylvie. *"Nuit et Brouillard": Un film dans l'histoire.* Paris: Odile Jacob, 2007.

Lindsay, Jennifer, and Maya H. T. Liem. *Heirs to World Culture: Being Indonesian, 1950-1965.* Leiden: KITLV Press, 2011.

Lindsay-Hartz, Janice, Joseph de Rivera, and Michael Mascolo. "Differentiating Guilt and Shame and Their Effects on Motivation." In *Self-Conscious Emotions: The Psy-*

chology of Shame, Guilt, Embarrassment, and Pride, edited by June Price Tangney and Kurt W. Fischer, 274–300. New York: Guilford Press, 1995.

Lipman, Masha. "The Third Wave of Russian De-Stalinization." *Foreign Policy*, December 16, 2010. http://www.foreignpolicy.com/articles/2010/12/16/the_third_wave_of_russian_de_stalinization.

Logvinov, Mikhail. "Istoricheskaya politika na postsovetskom prostranstve, ili: Na vostochnom fronte bez peremen." *Forum Noveishei Vostochnoevropeiskoi Istorii i Kul'tury*, no. 1 (2009). http://www1.ku-eichstaett.de/ZIMOS/forum/inhaltruss11.html.

Lorey, David E., and William H. Beezley. Introduction to *Genocide, Collective Violence, and Popular Memory: The Politics of Remembrance in the Twentieth Century*, edited by David E. Lorey and William H. Beezley, xi–xxxiii. Wilmington, Del.: Scholarly Resources, 2002.

Luks, Leonid. "Predchuvstvie zakata Evropy i strakh pered Rossiei." *Forum Noveishei Vostochnoevropeiskoi Istorii i Kul'tury*, no. 1 (2005). http://www1.ku-eichstaett.de/ZIMOS/forum/inhaltruss3.html.

Ma, Sheng-mei. "Contrasting Two Survival Literatures: On the Jewish Holocaust and the Chinese Cultural Revolution." *Holocaust and Genocide Studies* 2, no. 1 (1987): 81–93.

Mackenzie, James. "Berlusconi Defends Mussolini, Draws Outrage from Political Left." Reuters, January 27, 2013. http://www.reuters.com/article/2013/01/27/us-italy-berlusconi-mussolini-idUSBRE90Q0B620130127.

MacMillan, Margaret. *Dangerous Games: The Uses and Abuses of History*. New York: Modern Library, 2009.

Maier, Charles. *The Unmasterable Past: History, Holocaust, and German National Identity*. Cambridge, Mass.: Harvard University Press, 1988.

Maier, Robert. "Learning about Europe and the World: Schools, Teachers, and Textbooks in Russia after 1991." In *The Nation, Europe, and the World: Textbooks and Curricula in Transition*, edited by Hanna Schissler and Yasemin Nuhoğlu Soysal, 138–62. New York: Berghahn Books, 2005.

Maksymiuk, Jan. "Ukraine: Parliament Recognizes Soviet-Era Famine as Genocide." Radio Free Europe / Radio Liberty, November 29, 2006.

Malaka, Tan. *From Jail to Jail*. Translated and introduced by Helen Jarvis. 3 vols. Athens: Ohio University Center for International Studies, 1991.

Mälksoo, Maria. "The Memory Political Horizons of Estonian Foreign Policy." *Diplomaatia*, no. 82 (June 2010). http://www.diplomaatia.ee/en/article/the-memory-political-horizons-of-estonian-foreign-policy.

———. "The Memory Politics of Becoming European: The East European Subalterns and the Collective Memory of Europe." *European Journal of International Relations* 15, no. 4 (2009): 653–80.

Marples, David R. *Heroes and Villains: Creating National History in Contemporary Ukraine*. Budapest: Central European University Press, 2007.

Marrus, Michael, and Robert O. Paxton. *Vichy et les Juifs*. Translated by Marguerite Delmotte. Paris: Calman-Lévy, 1981.

Maruyama Masao. "Chôkokkashugi no ronri to shinri." Reprinted in Maruyama, *Gendai seiji no shisô to kôdô*. Tokyo: Miraisha, 1974.

Maspero, François. *Les Abeilles et la guêpe*. Paris: Seuil, 2002.

Matsuo, Fumio. "Tokyo Needs Its Dresden Moment." *Wall Street Journal*, August 16, 2005.

Mayer, Arno J. *Why Did the Heavens Not Darken? The "Final Solution" in History*. New York: Pantheon Books, 1988.

Mazower, Mark. "The Cold War and the Appropriation of Memory: Greece after Liberation." In *The Politics of Retribution in Europe: World War II and Its Aftermath*, edited by István Deák, Jan Gross, and Tony Judt, 212–32. Princeton, N.J.: Princeton University Press, 2000.

———. *Inside Hitler's Greece: The Experience of Occupation, 1941–1944*. New Haven, Conn.: Yale University Press, 1993.

McCurry, Justin. "Far Right Closes Yasukuni Screening in Tokyo." *Guardian*, March 19, 2008. http://www.guardian.co.uk/world/2008/mar/19/japan.filmnews.

Meijer, Remco. "Den Haag-Jakarta." *Elseviers Weekblad*, January 1950, 177.

———. *Oostindisch doof: Het Nederlandse debat over de dekolonisatie van Indonesië*. Amsterdam: Bert Bakker, 1995.

Mendelsohn, Ezra. *The Jews of East Central Europe between the World Wars*. Bloomington: Indiana University Press, 1983.

Merlingen, Michael, Cas Mudde, and Ulrich Sedelmeier. "The Right and the Righteous? European Norms, Domestic Politics, and the Sanctions against Austria." *Journal of Common Market Studies* 39, no. 1 (March 2001): 59–77.

Michel, Gundega, and Valters Nollendorfs. "Das Lettische Okkupatsionsmuseum, Riga." In *Der Kommunismus im Museum Formen der Auseinandersetzung in Deutschland und Ostmitteleuropa*, edited by Daniela Ruge. Cologne: Böhlau Verlag, 2005.

Michener, James A. *The Voice of Asia*. New York: Random House, 1951.

Miller, Alexei. "Istoricheskaya politika: Update." Polit.ru, November 25, 2009. http://www.polit.ru/lectures/2009/11/05/istpolit_print.html.

———. "'Istoricheskaya politika' v Vostochnoi Evrope: Plody vovlechennogo nablyudeniya." Polit.ru, May 7, 2008. http://www.polit.ru/lectures/2008/05/07/miller_print.html.

———. "Istoriya imperii i politika pamyati." *Rossiya v Global'noi Politike* 6, no. 4 (2008). http://www.globalaffairs.ru/number/n_11151.

Mironov, Boris. "The Fruits of a Bourgeois Education." *Kritika: Explorations in Russian and Eurasian History* 10, no. 4 (2009): 847–60.

Miscamble, Wilson. *The Most Controversial Decision: Truman, the Atomic Bombs, and the Defeat of Japan*. New York: Cambridge University Press, 2011.

Misiunas, Romuald J., and Rein Taagepera. *The Baltic States: Years of Dependence, 1940–1980*. Berkeley: University of California Press, 1983.

Mitani Hiroshi. "Writing History Textbooks in Japan." In *History Textbooks and the Wars in Asia: Divided Memories*, edited by Gi-Wook Shin and Daniel Sneider, 193–207. London: Routledge, 2011.

Mitani Hiroshi, and Teruyuki Hirota. *Rekishi kyōkasho mondai*. Vol. 2. Tokyo: Nihon Tosho Sentā, 2007.
Mitchell, B. R. *European Historical Statistics, 1750–1970*. New York: Columbia University Press, 1978.
Mitten, Richard. *The Politics of Anti-Semitic Prejudice: The Waldheim Phenomenon in Austria*. Boulder, Colo.: Westview Press, 1992.
Mizokami, Kyle. "Sekai no Kansen: Japan's Strategy against the Senkaku Island Dispute." *Japan Security Watch*, September 5, 2012. http://jsw.newpacificinstitute.org/?p=10495.
Mommsen, Hans. "Changing Historical Perspectives on the Nazi Dictatorship." *European Review* 17, no. 1 (2009). doi:10.1017/S106279870900057X.
Monroe, Kristen R. Review of *Hitler's Willing Executioners: Ordinary Germans and the Holocaust*, by Daniel Goldhagen. *American Political Science Review* 91 (March 1997): 212–13.
Moore, Bob. *Survivors: Jewish Self-Help and Rescue in Nazi-Occupied Western Europe*. Oxford: Oxford University Press, 2010.
Morahg, Gilead. "Israel's New Literature of the Holocaust: The Case of David Grossman's *See Under: Love*." *Modern Fiction Studies* 45, no. 2 (1999): 457–79.
Morelli, Paula. *Trauma and Healing: The Construction of Meaning among Survivors of the Cambodian Holocaust*. Saarbrücken: Lambert Academic Publishing (VDM Verlag), 2010.
Morina, Christina. *Legacies of Stalingrad: Remembering the Eastern Front in Germany since 1945*. Cambridge: Cambridge University Press, 2011.
Mulder, Gerard, and Paul Koedijk. *H. M. van Randwijk: Een biografie*. Amsterdam: Nijgh En Van Ditmar, 1988.
Müller, Melissa. *Anne Frank: The Biography*. New York: Henry Holt, 1999.
Mulligan, Timothy P. "The OSS and the Nazi Occupation of the Baltic States, 1941–1945: A Note on Documentation." *Journal of Baltic Studies* 13, no. 1 (1982): 53–58.
Murakami Haruki. *Kafka on the Shore*. Translated by Philip Gabriel. New York: Vintage, 2005.
Mytsyk, Yuri. "Novoe ili podzabytoe staroe." *Zerkalo Nedeli*, February 7–13, 2009.
Nagamoto Tomohiro. "Who 'Owns' Okinawa?" Nippon.com, July 3, 2013. http://www.nippon.com/en/currents/d00086.
Naimark, Norman. *Fires of Hatred: Ethnic Cleansing in Twentieth-Century Europe*. Cambridge, Mass.: Harvard University Press, 2001.
——— . *Stalin's Genocides*. Princeton, N.J.: Princeton University Press, 2010.
Namer, Gérard. *Batailles pour la mémoire: La commémoration en France de 1945 à nos jours*. Paris: Papyrus, 1983.
New Republic. Untitled and unsigned editorial, October 29, 1945.
New York Times. "Indonesia: Dutch Apologize for 1947 Massacre of 430 Villagers." December 10, 2011.
Nils, Odette. *Guy Môquet mon amour de jeuenesse*. Paris: Editions de l'Archipel, 2007.
Niven, William, ed. *Germans as Victims: Remembering the Past in Contemporary Germany*. New York: Palgrave Macmillan, 2006.

The Nizkor Project. "The Trial of Adolf Eichmann: Session 68." June 7, 1961. Pt. 1 of 9. http://www.nizkor.org/hweb/people/e/eichmann-adolf/transcripts/Sessions/Session-068-01.html.

Nollendorfs, Valters. *Museum of the Occupation of Latvia*. Riga: Strelnieku Laukums, 2002.

Nora, Pierre. "Gaullistes et communistes." In *Les lieux de mémoire*, edited by Pierre Nora, 2:2489–532. Paris: Gallimard, 1997.

Novick, Peter. *The Holocaust in American Life*. Boston: Houghton Mifflin, 1999.

Oestreich, James. "Orchestra to Disclose Its Nazi Past." *New York Times*, March 1, 2013.

Oguma Eiji and Ueno Yoko. *Iyashi nashionarizumu: Kusa no ne Hoshu undō no jishō*. Tokyo: Keiō Gijuku Daigaku Shuppankai, 2003.

Oi, Mariko. "What Japanese History Lessons Leave Out." *BBC News*, March 13, 2013. http://www.bbc.co.uk/news/magazine-21226068.

Olszanski, Tadeusz. "Yushchenko's Historical Policy — a Tentative Assessment." *Eastweek CES*, January 27, 2010. http://www.osw.waw.pl/en/publikacje/eastweek/2010-01-27/yushchenkos-historical-policy-a-tentative-assessment.

Orr, James J. *The Victim as Hero: Ideologies of Peace and National Identity in Postwar Japan*. Honolulu: University of Hawai'i Press, 2001.

Ortony, Andrew, Gerald Clore, and Allan Collins. *The Cognitive Structure of Emotions*. Cambridge: Cambridge University Press, 1988.

OSCE Parliamentary Assembly. "Vilnius Declaration." June 29–July 3, 2009. http://www.oscepa.org/images/stories/documents/activities/1.Annual%20Session/2009_Vilnius/Final_Vilnius_Declaration_ENG.pdf.

Osveshchenie obshchei istorii Rossii i narodov postsovetskikh stran v shkol'nykh uchebnikakh istorii novykh nezavisimykh gosudarstv. Moscow: Natsional'naya Laboratoriya Vneshnei Politiki, 2009.

Overy, Richard. *The Dictators: Hitler's Germany, Stalin's Russia*. London: Penguin, 2005.

Oz-Salzberger, Fania. "Europe, Rivers, and Trams: Reflections of an Ex-European." In *Reflections on Europe: Defining a Political Order in Time and Space*, edited by Hans-Åke Persson and Bo Stråth, 203–10. Brussels: P.I.E. Peter Lang, 2007.

———. "Forty Years of Diplomatic Relations, Four Hundred Years of Cultural Ties." In *The Legacy of the German-Jewish Religious and Cultural Heritage: A Basis for German-Israeli Dialogue?*, edited by Benjamin Ollov. Berlin: Konrad Adenauer Foundation and Ramat-Gan: Bar-Ilan University, 2006.

———. *Israelis in Berlin (Yisraelim, Berlin)*. Translated into German from Hebrew by Ruth Achlama. Frankfurt am Main: Suhrkamp, Jüdischer Verlag, 2001.

———. "Israelis in Berlin: Ein neues Bücherregal." In *Rück-Blick auf Deutschland. Ansichten hebräisch-sprachiger Autoren*, edited by Anat Feinberg, 151–70. Munich: Edition Text + Kritik, 2009.

Oz-Salzberger, Fania, and Eli Salzberger. "The Secret German Sources of the Israeli Supreme Court." *Israel Studies* 3, no. 2 (1998): 159–92.

Pappé, Ilan. *The Making of the Arab-Israeli Conflict, 1947–1951*. London: I. B. Tauris, 1992.

Paver, Chloe E. M. "Exhibiting the National Socialist Past: An Overview of Recent German Exhibitions." *Journal of European Studies* 39, no. 2 (2009): 225–49.

Paxton, Robert O. *Europe in the Twentieth Century*. New York: Harcourt Brace Jovanovich, 1985.
——— . *La France de Vichy*. Translated by Claude Bertrand. Paris: Éditions du Seuil, 1973.
Payne, Stanley. *Franco and Hitler: Spain, Germany, and World War II*. New Haven, Conn.: Yale University Press, 2008.
Péan, Pierre. *Une jeunesse française: François Mitterrand, 1934–1947*. Paris: Fayard, 1994.
Peattie, Mark R., Edward J. Drea, and Hans van de Ven, eds. *The Battle for China: Essays on the Military History of the Sino-Japanese War of 1937–1945*. Stanford, Calif.: Stanford University Press, 2011.
People's Daily. "China-Japan Scholars' Report Completed," February 1, 2010.
Petersen, Roger. *Understanding Ethnic Violence: Fear, Hatred, and Resentment in Twentieth-Century Eastern Europe*. Cambridge: Cambridge University Press, 2002.
——— . *Western Intervention in the Balkans: The Strategic Use of Emotion in Conflict*. New York: Cambridge University Press, 2011.
Petersen, Roger, and Sarah Zukerman. "Anger, Violence, and Political Science." In *A Handbook of Anger: Constituent and Concomitant Biological, Psychological, and Social Processes*, edited by Michael Potegal, Gerhard Stemmler, and Charles Spielberger. New York: Springer, 2010.
Petrescu, Dragoş, and Christina Petrescu. "The Piteşti Syndrome: A Romanian Vergangenheitsbewältigung?" In *Postdiktatorische Geschichtskulturen im Süden unde Osten Europas*, edited by Susan Baumgartl. Göttingen: Wallstein Verlag, 2010.
Pick, Hella. *Guilty Victim: Austria from the Holocaust to Haidar*. London: I. B. Tauris, 2000.
Pipes, Richard. "A New Russian History That's Sensational for the Right Reasons." Radio Free Europe / Radio Liberty, December 5, 2009.
Pitts, Jennifer. *A Turn to Empire: The Rise of Imperial Liberalism in Britain and France*. Princeton, N.J.: Princeton University Press, 2005.
Plokhy, Serhii M. *Yalta: The Price of Peace*. New York: Viking, 2010.
Power, Samantha. *A Problem from Hell: America and the Age of Genocide*. New York: Basic Books, 2002.
Prins, J. "In Memoriam Victor Emanuel Korn." *Bijdragen tot de Taal-, Land- en Volkenkunde* 126, no. 2 (1970): 192–202.
Purcell, Sarah J. "War, Memory, and National Identity in the Twentieth Century." *National Identities* 2, no. 2 (2000): 187–95.
Pyongjik An. *The Economic Structure of Modern Korea*. [In Korean.] Seoul: Pibong Press, 1989.
Rachinsky, Ian. "Istoriia kak pole boya." *Evropa: Zhurnal Pol'skogo Instituta Mezhdunarodnykh* 9, no. 2 (2009): 47–59.
Rakotoarison, Sylvain. "Carnage de Maillé (1): Un des nombreux massacres nazis de 1944." Cent Papiers. September 13, 2008. http://www.centpapiers.com/carnage-de-maille-1-un-des-nombreux-massacres-nazis-de-1944/2784.
Raymond, Gina. "Sarkozy–de Gaulle: Recycling the Resistance Myth." *French Cultural Studies* 24, no. 3 (2013): 93–103.

Rayski, Adam. *Le cadavre était trop grand: Guy Môquet piétiné par le conformisme de gauche.* Paris: Denoël Impact, 2008.
Reilly, James E. *Strong Society, Smart State: The Rise of Public Opinion in China's Japan Policy.* New York: Columbia University Press, 2012.
Reinharz, Jehuda, and Yaacov Shavit. *Glorious, Accursed Europe: An Essay on Jewish Ambivalence.* Translated by M. Engel. Waltham, Mass.: Brandeis University Press and University Press of New England, 2010.
Reisner, Oliver, Zaur Gasimov, Sergey Minasyan, and Giorgi Maisuradze. "Writing National Histories: Coming to Terms with the Past." *Caucasus Analytical Digest*, no. 8 (July 2009). http://www.css.ethz.ch/publications/pdfs/CAD-8.pdf.
Reitlinger, Gerald. *The House Built on Sand: The Conflicts of German Policy in Russia, 1939–1945.* Westport, Conn.: Greenwood Press, 1960.
Renan, Ernest. *Qu'est-ce qu'une nation?* Paris: Calman Lévy, 1882.
Ribbens, Kees. "Anne Frank as Global Comic Book Hero: Visualizing a Holocaust Victim in Transnational Popular Culture." Presentation, ESSHA Conference, Ghent, Belgium, April 2010.
Rigney, Ann. "Plenitude, Scarcity, and the Circulation of Cultural Memory." *Journal of European Studies* 35, no. 1 (2005): 11–28.
Rodgers, Pierre W. "'Compliance or Contradiction?' Teaching History in the 'New' Ukraine: A View from Ukraine's Eastern Borderlands." *Europe-Asia Studies* 59, no. 3 (2007): 503–19.
Roginsky, Arseny. "Pamyat' o stalinizme: Doklad na konferentsii 'Istoriya stalinizma.'" Moscow, December 5, 2008. http://www.boell.ru/downloads/pamiat_o_stalinizme.pdf.
Rogov, Kirill. "Destalinizatsiya: Muzei na Lubyanke." *Vedomosti*, February 4, 2011.
Romein, Jan. "Een kinderstem." *Het Parool*, April 3, 1946.
Röling, B. V. A. Introduction to *The Tokyo War Crimes Trial: An International Symposium*, edited by C. Hosoya, N. Ando, Y. Onuma, and R. Minear, 15–27. Tokyo: Kodansha, 1986.
Romijn, Peter. "'Restoration of Confidence': The Purge of Local Government in the Netherlands as a Problem of Postwar Reconstruction." In *The Politics of Retribution in Europe: World War II and Its Aftermath*, edited by István Deák, Jan Gross, and Tony Judt, 173–93. Princeton, N.J.: Princeton University Press, 2000.
———. *Snel, streng en rechtvaardig: Politiek beleid inzake de bestraffing en reclassering van "foute" Nederlanders, 1945–1955.* Amsterdam: Olympus, 2002.
Rose, Caroline. *Sino-Japanese Relations: Facing the Past, Looking to the Future?* New York: RoutledgeCurzon, 2005.
Rose, Mavis. *Indonesia Free: A Political Biography of Mohammad Hatta.* Ithaca, N.Y.: Cornell Southeast Asia Program Publications, 1987.
Rosenthal, A. M. "Absolution for Killers." *New York Times*, September 10, 1991. http://www.nytimes.com/1991/09/10/opinion/on-my-mind-absolution-for-killers.html.
Rosoux, Valérie. *Les usages de la mémoire dans les relations internationales: Le recours au passé dans la politique étrangère de la France à l'égard de l'Allemagne et de l'Algérie de 1962 à nos jours.* Brussels: Complexe, 2001.

Rothschild, Joseph. *East Central Europe between the Two World Wars.* Seattle: University of Washington Press, 1974.
Rousso, Henry. *Vichy: Un passé qui ne passe pas.* Paris: Fayard, 1994.
———. *The Vichy Syndrome: History and Memory in France since 1944.* Translated by Arthur Goldhammer. Cambridge, Mass.: Harvard University Press, 1994. Original edition in French, 1987.
Rozman, Gilbert. "China's Changing Images of Japan, 1989–2001: The Struggle to Balance Partnership and Rivalry." *International Relations of the Asia-Pacific* 2, no. 1 (2002): 95–129.
———. "China's Concurrent Debate about the Gorbachev Era." In *China Learns from the Soviet Union, 1949–Present*, edited by Thomas P. Bernstein and Hua-Yu Li, 449–76. Lanham, Md.: Lexington Books, 2010.
———. *The Chinese Debate about Soviet Socialism, 1978–1985.* Princeton, N.J.: Princeton University Press, 1987.
———. "Chinese National Identity and East Asian National Identity Gaps." In *National Identities and Bilateral Relations: Widening Gaps in East Asia and Chinese Demonization of the United States*, edited by Gilbert Rozman, 203–32. Washington, D.C.: Woodrow Wilson Center Press; Stanford, Calif.: Stanford University Press, 2013.
———. "Chinese National Identity and Its Implications for International Relations in East Asia." *Asia-Pacific Review* 18, no. 1 (2011): 84–97.
———. "Chinese National Identity and the Sino-U.S. Civilizational Gap." In *National Identities and Bilateral Relations: Widening Gaps in East Asia and Chinese Demonization of the United States*, edited by Gilbert Rozman, 233–64. Washington, D.C.: Woodrow Wilson Center Press; Stanford, Calif.: Stanford University Press, 2013.
———. "Chinese Strategic Thinking on Multilateral Regional Security in Northeast Asia." *Orbis*, Spring 2011, 296–311.
———. "The Confucian Faces of Capitalism." In *Pacific Century: The Emergence of Modern Pacific Asia*, edited by Mark Borthwick, 310–22. Boulder, Colo. Westview Press, 1992.
———. "Cultural Prerequisites of East Asian Regionalism in an Age of Globalization." *Korean Observer* 37, no. 1 (2006): 149–79.
———, ed. *East Asian National Identities: Common Roots and Chinese Exceptionalism.* Washington, D.C.: Woodrow Wilson Center Press; Stanford, Calif.: Stanford University Press, 2012.
———. "History as an Arena of Sino-Korean Conflict and the Role of the United States." *Asian Perspective* 36, no. 2 (2012): 287–308.
———. "Invocations of Chinese Traditions in International Relations." *Journal of Chinese Political Science* 17, no. 2 (2012): 111–24.
———. "Japan and Korea: Should the U.S. Be Worried about Their New Spat in 2001?" *Pacific Review* 15, no. 1 (2002): 1–28.
———. "Narrowing the Values Gap in Sino-Japanese Relations: Lessons from 2006–2008." In *Reconceptualising the Divide: Identity, Memory, and Nationalism in Sino-Japanese Relations*, edited by Gerrit Gong and Victor Teo, 25–51. Newcastle upon Tyne, U.K.: Cambridge Scholars, 2010.

———, ed. *National Identities and Bilateral Relations: Widening Gaps in East Asia and Chinese Demonization of the United States*. Washington, D.C.: Woodrow Wilson Center Press; Stanford, Calif.: Stanford University Press, 2013.

———. *Northeast Asia's Stunted Regionalism: Bilateral Distrust in the Shadow of Globalization*. Cambridge: Cambridge University Press, 2004.

———, ed. *U.S. Leadership, History, and Bilateral Relations in Northeast Asia*. New York: Cambridge University Press, 2011.

Russian Analytical Digest. "History Writing and National Myth-Making in Russia." Special issue. No. 72 (February 9, 2010). http://www.css.ethz.ch/publications/pdfs/RAD-72.pdf.

Russian President's Decree no. 549. "O Komissii pri Prezidente Rossiiskoi Federatsii po protivodeistviiu popytkam fal'sifikatsii istorii v ushcherb interesam Rossii." Kremlin.ru, May 15, 2009. http://graph.document.kremlin.ru/page.aspx?1;1013526.

Saaler, Sven. *Politics, Memory, and Public Opinion: The History Textbook Controversy and Japanese Society*. 2nd ed. Munich: Iudicium Verlag, 2006.

Sachar, Howard M. *A History of Israel from the Rise of Zionism to Our Time*. New York: Alfred A. Knopf, 1998.

Sagi, Nana. *German Reparations: A History of the Negotiations*. London: Palgrave Macmillan, 1986.

Samarina, Aleksandra. "Istoriya umolchaniya." *Nezavisimaya Gazeta*, December 2, 2009.

Samsudin. Introduction to *Lukisan revolusi rakjat Indonesia, 1945–1949*. Edited by Sudarjwo Tjondonegoro. Yogyakarta: Menteri Penerangan Republik Indonesia, 1949.

Sanua, Marianne R. *Let Us Prove Strong: The American Jewish Committee, 1945–2006*. Waltham, Mass.: Brandeis University Press; Hanover, N.H.: University Press of New England, 2007.

Scagliola, Stefania Ingrid. *Last van de oorlog: De Nederlandse oorlogsmisdaden in Indonesië en hun verwerking*. Amsterdam: Uitgeverji Balans, 2002.

Schlögel, Karl. "Places and Strata of Memory: Approaches to Eastern Europe." *Eurozine*, December 19, 2008. http://www.eurozine.com/articles/2008-12-19-schlogel-en.html.

Schmale, Wolfgang. "'Osteuropa': Zwischen Ende und Neudefinition?" In *Europa im Ostblok: Vorstellungen und Diskurse (1945–1991)*, edited by Jose M. Faraldo, Raulina Gulinska-Jurgiel, and Christian Domnitz. Cologne: Bohlau, 2008.

Schöpflin, George. *Politics in Eastern Europe, 1945–1992*. Oxford: Blackwell, 1993.

Schulte Nordholt, Henk. *Een staat van geweld*. Rotterdam: Erasmus University Oratiereeks; Leiden: IIAS, 2000.

———. *The Spell of Power: A History of Balinese Politics*. Leiden: KITLV Press, 1996.

———. *Staat van geweld*. Rotterdam: Erasmus University Oratiereeks, 2000.

Seaton, Philip A. *Japan's Contested War Memories: The "Memory Rifts" in Historical Consciousness of World War II*. New York: Routledge, 2007.

Segev, Tom. *One Palestine, Complete: Jews and Arabs under the British Mandate*. Translated by Haim Watzman. New York: Owl Books, 2001. Original Hebrew edition 1999.

Selden, Mark. "Japanese and American War Atrocities, Historical Memory and Reconciliation: World War II to Today." *Asia-Pacific Journal: Japan Focus*, April 15, 2008.

Senyavskaya, Yelena, and Aleksandr Senyavsky. "'Vtoraia mirovaia voina i istoricheskaia pamiat': Obraz proshlogo v kontekste sovremennoi geopolitiki." Special issue. *Vestnik MGIMO—Universiteta*, 2009, 299–310.

Seraphim, Franziska. *War Memory and Social Politics in Japan, 1945–2005*. Cambridge, Mass.: Harvard University Press, 2006.

Shafir, Shlomo. *Ambiguous Relations: The American Jewish Community and Germany since 1945*. Detroit: Wayne State University Press, 1999.

Shain, Yossi. "Ethnic Diasporas and U.S. Foreign Policy." *Political Science Quarterly* 109, no. 5 (1994): 811–41.

Shapira, Anita. "The Holocaust: Private Memories, Public Memory." *Jewish Social Studies* 4, no. 2 (1998): 40–58.

Sheffi, Naama. *Vom Deutschen ins Hebräisch: Übersetzungen aus dem Deutschen in jüdischen Palästina 1882–1948*. Göttingen: Vanderhoeck und Ruprecht, 2011.

———. *The Ring of Myths: The Israelis, Wagner, and the Nazis*. Translated by Martha Grenzeback. Portland, Ore.: Sussex Academic Press, 2001. Original Hebrew edition 2001.

Sherlock, Thomas. *Historical Narratives in the Soviet Union and Post-Soviet Russia: Destroying the Settled Past, Creating an Uncertain Future*. New York: Palgrave Macmillan, 2007.

———. "History and Myth in the Soviet Empire and the Russian Republic." In *Teaching the Violent Past: History Education and Reconciliation*, edited by Elizabeth A. Cole. Lanham, Md.: Rowman and Littlefield, 2007.

Shevel, Oxana. "The Politics of Memory in a Divided Society: A Comparison of Post-Franco Spain and Post-Soviet Ukraine." *Slavic Review* 70, no. 1 (Spring 2011): 137–64.

Shimov, Yaroslav. "Vtoraia mirovaia: Konets eposa." Gazeta.ru, September 1, 2009. http://www.gazeta.ru/comments/2009/09/01_a_3254449.shtml.

Shin, Gi-Wook. "Beyond Apology, Moral Clarity." *Christian Science Monitor*, April 2, 2007.

———. "Historical Disputes and Reconciliation in Northeast Asia: The U.S. Role." *Pacific Affairs* 83, no. 4 (December 2010): 663–73.

———. "History Textbooks, Divided Memories, and Reconciliation." In *History Textbooks and the Wars in Asia: Divided Memories*, edited by Gi-Wook Shin and Daniel Sneider, 3–20. New York: Routledge, 2011.

Shin, Gi-Wook, and Michael Robinson, eds. *Colonial Modernity in Korea*. Cambridge, Mass.: Harvard University Asia Center, 1999.

Shin, Gi-Wook, and Daniel Sneider, eds. *History Textbooks and the Wars in Asia: Divided Memories*. New York: Routledge, 2011.

Shiraishi Takashi. "The Phantom World of Boven Digul." *Indonesia* 62 (April 1996): 93–118.

Shkil'na istoriya ochyma istorykiv-naukovtsiv: Materialy robochoi narady z monitoryngu shkil'nykh pidruchnykiv istorii Ukrainy / Uporyadkuvannya ta redaktsiya Natali Yakovenko. Kiev: Vydavnytstvo Imeni Oleny Telihy, 2008.

Shnirelman, Victor. "Rossiiskaya shkola i natsional'naya ideya." *Neprikosnovenny Zapas*, no. 6 (2006). http://magazines.russ.ru/nz/2006/50/sh21-pr.html.

———. *Shkil'na istoriya ochyma istorykiv-naukovtsiv: Materialy robochoi narady z monitoryngu shkil'nykh pidruchnykiv istorii Ukrainy / Uporyadkuvannya ta redaktsiya Natali Yakovenko*. Kiev: Vydavnytstvo Imeni Oleny Telihy, 2008.

———. "Stigmatized by History or by Historians? The Peoples of Russia in School History Textbooks." *History and Memory* 21, no. 2 (2009): 110–49.

Simon, Thomas W. *The Laws of Genocide: Prescriptions for a Just World*. Santa Barbara: Praeger Security International, ABC-CLIO, 2007.

Sjahrir, Sutan. *Indonesische overpeinzingen*. Amsterdam: De Bezige Bij, 1945.

———. *Out of Exile*. Translated by Charles Wolf. New York: John Day, 1949.

Slackman, Michael. "Hitler Exhibit Explores a Wider Circle of Guilt." *New York Times*, October 16, 2010.

Slezkine, Yuri. *The Jewish Century*. Princeton, N.J.: Princeton University Press, 2004.

Sneider, Daniel. "The War over Words: History Textbooks and International Relations in Northeast Asia." Paper presented at the conference "Divided Memories: History Textbooks and the Wars in Asia," Stanford University, February 2008.

———. "The War over Words: History Textbooks and International Relations in Northeast Asia." In *History Textbooks and the Wars in Asia: Divided Memories*, edited by Gi-Wook Shin and Daniel Sneider, 246–68. New York: Routledge, 2011.

Snel, Jan Dirk. "De grijze massa was goed." *Trouw*, April 30, 2011.

Snyder, Timothy. *Bloodlands: Europe between Hitler and Stalin*. New York: Basic Books, 2010.

———. "The Historical Reality of Eastern Europe." *East European Politics and Societies* 23, no. 1 (February 2009). doi:10.1177/0888325408328750.

———. Introduction. *East European Politics and Societies* 24, no. 1 (2010): 3–5.

———. "Neglecting the Lithuanian Holocaust." *NYR* (blog), *New York Review of Books*, July 25, 2011. http://www.nybooks.com/blogs/nyrblog/2011/jul/25/neglecting-lithuanian-holocaust.

Sociologie. "Beelden van (on)mannelijkheid in de koloniale cultuur van Nederlands-Indië, 1900–1949." Vol. 3, no. 1 (2007): 64–81.

Soeroto, Noto. "Aziatisch imperialisme." *Wederopbouw: Maandschrift Gewijd aan de Jong-Javanenbeweging en het Javaansche Geestesleven* 3, nos. 1–4 (January 20, 1920): 16–17.

Sokolov, Nikita. "Vek surka, ili Kratkaya istoriya kolovrashcheniya rossiiskikh uchebnikov istorii." Polit.ru, October 15, 2008. http://www.polit.ru/analytics/2008/10/15/history_print.html.

Solonari, Vladimir. "Normalizing Russia, Legitimizing Putin." *Kritika: Explorations in Russian and Eurasian History* 10, no. 4 (2009): 835–46.

———. *Purifying the Nation: Population Exchange and Ethnic Cleansing in Nazi-Allied Romania*. Baltimore: Johns Hopkins University Press, 2010.

Sommier, Isabelle. *La violence politique et son deuil: L'après 68 en France et en Italie*. Rennes: Presses Universitaires de Rennes, 1998.

Song Jihe and Luo Baocheng. "Lun kangmei yuanchao zhanzheng zhengyixing." *Dianzi Kezhi Daxue Xuebao*, no. 6 (2010): 70–74.
Soysal, Yasemin Nuhoğlu, Teresa Bertilotti, and Sabine Mannitz. "Projections of Identity in French and German History and Civics Textbooks." In *The Nation, Europe, and the World: Textbooks and Curricula in Transition*, edited by Hanna Schissler and Yasemin Nuhoğlu Soysal, 13–34. New York: Berghahn Books, 2005.
Speer, Albert. *Inside the Third Reich*. New York: Simon and Schuster, 1970.
"Stenograficheskii otchet o vstreche s delegatami Vserossiiskoi konferentsii prepodavatelei gumanitarnykh i obshchestvennykh nauk." Novo-Ogarevo, June 21, 2007. Kremlin.ru, http://archive.kremlin.ru/text/appears/2007/06/135323.shtml.
Stern, Fritz. "The Goldhagen Controversy: One Nation, One People, One Theory?" *Foreign Affairs*, November/December 1996, 128–38.
Stoddard, Lothrop. "Spice Islands: A Colonial Model." *Christian Science Monitor*, March 2, 1938.
Straub, David. "The United States and Reconciliation in East Asia." In *East Asia's Haunted Present: Historical Memories and the Resurgence of Nationalism*, edited by Tsuyoshi Hasegawa and Kazuhiko Togo, 207–19. Westport, Conn.: Praeger, 2008.
Streiff, Gérard. *Guy Môquet: Chateaubriant, le 22 Octobre 1941; Docu-fiction*. Paris: Temps Des Cerises, 2007.
Sukarno. *Sukarno: An Autobiography, as Told to Cindy Adams*. Indianapolis: Bobbs-Merrill, 1965.
Suziedelis, Saulius. "The Perception of the Holocaust: Public Challenges and Experience in Lithuania." *EES News: Woodrow Wilson International Center for Scholars, East European Studies Center*, January/February 2008, 7–10.
Takino Takahiro. "Visit to Hiroshima by President Bush Considered in Sixtieth Postwar Year." *Mainichi*, January 3, 2009.
Tanaka Akihiko. "The Yasukuni Issue and Japan's International Relations." In *East Asia's Haunted Present: Historical Memories and the Resurgence of Nationalism*, edited by Tsuyoshi Hasegawa and Kazuhiko Togo, 119–41. Westport, Conn.: Praeger, 2008.
Tao Wenjian. "Haiyuan lishi, zhaoyue lishi: Canjia Zhongri lishi gongtong yanjiu de ganxiang." *Xiandai Guoji Guanxi*, no. 10 (2010): 53–58.
Taratuta, Yulia, and Vladimir Vodo. "Rossiya popala v plokhuyu istoriyu." *Kommersant*, July 2, 2009. http://www.kommersant.ru/doc/1196402.
Tetsuya Takahashi. "Legacies of Empire: The Yasukuni Shrine Controversy." In *Yasukuni, the War Dead, and the Struggle for Japan's Past*, edited by John Breen, 105–24. New York: Columbia University Press, 2008.
Time. "Willy Brandt, Person of the Year." January 4, 1971. http://www.time.com/time/covers/0,16641,19710104,00.html.
Toby, Ronald A. *State and Diplomacy in Early Modern Japan: Asia in the Development of the Tokugawa Bakufu*. Stanford, Calif.: Stanford University Press, 1984.
Tokudome Kinue. "POW Forced Labor Lawsuits against Japanese Companies." Japanese Policy Research Institute, Working Paper no. 82. November 2001. http://www.jpri.org/publications/workingpapers/wp82.html.

Torpey, John. "Dynamics of Denial: Responses to Past Atrocities in Germany, Turkey, and Japan." In *Rethinking Historical Injustice and Reconciliation in Northeast Asia: The Korean Experience*, edited by Gi-Wook Shin, Soon-Won Park, and Daqing Yang, 173–91. New York: Routledge, 2007.

Trenin, Dmitry. "Rossiya i Pol'sha: Druzhba, kotoraya ne dolzhna provalit'sya; K vizitu Dmitriya Medvedeva v Varshavu." Polit.ru, December 6, 2010. http://www.polit.ru/institutes/2010/12/06/poland_print.html.

Trigano, Shmuel. "Que faire avec l'indemnisation des spoliations." *Le Monde*, March 2, 2000. http://www.lemonde.fr/.

Troebst, Stefan. "Jalta versus Stalingrad, Gulag versus Holocaust: Konfligierende Erinnerungskulturen im grosseren Europa." *Berliner Journal fur Soziologie*, 15, no. 3 (2005): 381–400.

———. "'Kakoi takoi kover?' Kul'tura pamiati v postkommunisticheskikh obshchestvakh Vostochnoi Evropy: Popytka obshchego opisaniya i kategorizatsii." *Ab Imperio*, no. 4 (2004): 41–78.

Tsuchiyama Jitsuo. "The End of the Alliance? Dilemmas in the U.S.-Japan Relationship." In *United States–Japan Relations and International Institutions after the Cold War*, edited by Peter Gourevitch, Takashi Inoguchi, and Courtney Purrington. San Diego: Graduate School of International Relations and Pacific Studies, University of California, San Diego, 1995.

Uhl, Heidemarie. "From Victim Myth to Co-responsibility Thesis: Nazi Rule, World War II, and the Holocaust in Austrian Memory." In *The Politics of Memory in Postwar Europe*, edited by Richard Ned Lebow, Wulf Kansteiner, and Claudio Fogu, 40–72. Durham, N.C.: Duke University Press, 2006.

Université Aix-Marseille (formerly Université de Provence). *Discours 2007: Les discours présidentiables*. http://sites.univ-provence.fr/veronis/Discours2007. Accessed August 1, 2013.

Valentino, Benjamin. *Final Solutions: Mass Killing and Genocide in the Twentieth Century*. Ithaca, N.Y.: Cornell University Press, 2004.

Van Buuren, Martin. *De afrekening: Ontmaskering van het gewapende verzet*. Rotterdam: Lemniscaat Uitgeverij, 2011.

Van den Doel, H. W. *Afscheid van Indië: De val van het Nederlandse imperium in Azië*. Amsterdam: Prometheus, 2002.

Van der Heijden, Chris. *Dat Nooit Meer: De Nasleep Van De Tweede Wereldoorlog in Nederland*. Amsterdam: Contact, 2011.

———. "De oorlog als mensenverhaal: Grijs verleden Revisited." *De Groene Amsterdammer*, April 28, 2010.

———. *Grijs verleden: Nederland en de Tweede Wereldoorlog*. 10th ed. Amsterdam: Atlas Contact, 2009.

———. "Het einde van historische correctheid." *Vrij Nederland*, May 5, 2003.

———. "Moordenaars onder ons: Een essay over de zaak-Demjanjuk." *De Groene Amsterdammer*, November 25, 2009.

Vanderweert, Susan J. "Seeking Justice for 'Comfort' Women: Without an International Criminal Court, Suits Brought by World War II Sex Slaves of the Japanese Army

May Find Their Best Hope of Success in United States Federal Courts." *North Carolina Journal of International Law and Commercial Regulation* 27, no. 1 (2001): 141–82.

Van der Zee, Sytze. *Vogelvrij: Wie verraadde Anne Frank?* Amsterdam: De Bezige Bij, 2010.

Van Doorn, J. A. A. *De laatste eeuw van Indië: Ontwikkeling en ondergang van een koloniaal project.* Amsterdam: Bakker, 1994.

Van Leeuwen, Lizzy. "De wreker van zijn Indische grootouders: De politieke roots van Geert Wilders." *De Groene Amsterdammer*, September 2, 2009.

———. *Ons Indisch erfgoed: Zestig jaar strijd om cultuur en identiteit.* Amsterdam: Bert Bakker, 2008.

Van Maurik, Justus. *Indrukken van een totok: Indische typen en schetsen.* Amsterdam: Van Holkema en Warendorf, 1899.

Van Oldenburgh, Wendelien. *A Well Respected Man, or Book of Echoes.* Utrecht: Casco and Sternberg Press, 2010.

Van Randwijk, Henk. "Tegen het opkomend onweer." *Vrij Nederland*, no. 2 (October 20, 1945).

Van Till, Margreet. "Batavia Bij Nacht: Bloei En Ondergang Van Het Indonesische Roverswezen in Batavia En Ommenlanden, 1869–1942." Ph.D. diss., University of Amsterdam, 2006.

Van Wulfften Palthe, P. M. *Psychological Aspects of the Indonesian Problem.* Leiden: Brill, 1949.

Vedomosti. "Boyazn' proshlogo." October 22, 2009.

Venclova, Tomas. "Jews and Lithuanians." *Cross Currents* 8 (1989): 55–73.

Vergès, Jacques, and Étienne Bloch. *La face cachée du procès Barbie: Compte-rendu.* Paris: Samuel Tastet, 1983.

Verzetsmuseum. "Koninkrijk der Nederlanden." Accessed November 9, 2011. http://www.verzetsmuseum.org/tweede-wereldoorlog.

Vigna, Xavier. "Le crible de la mémoire: Usage du passé dans les lutes ouvrières des années 68." In *Concurence des passés: Usage politique du passé dans la France contemporaine*, edited by Maryline Crivello, Patrick Garcia, and Nicolas Offenstadt, 147–56. Aix-en-Provence: Université de Provence, 2006.

Vonnegut, Kurt. *Bluebeard: A Novel.* New York: Dial Press / Random House, 2011. First edition 1987.

Wahl, Alfred, ed. *Mémoire de la seconde guerre mondiale.* Metz: Centre de Recherche Histoire et Civilisation de l'Université de Metz, 1984.

Wakamiya Yoshibumi. *The Postwar Conservative View of Asia: How the Political Right Has Delayed Japan's Coming to Terms with Its History of Aggression in Asia.* Tokyo: LTCB International Library Foundation, 1998.

———. *Sengo hoshu no Ajia kan.* Tokyo: Asahi Shimbunsha, 1995.

Wang Daowei and Tang Fuquan. "Kangmei yuanchao zhanzhengzhong dang de lingdao jiti zhanju kongzhi sixiang yanxi." *Junshi Lishi Yanjiu*, 2009 (special ed.).

Wang Hailong and Wang Jing. "Lun Meijunzheng yu Hanguo chinripai dezhuanxing." *Dangdai Hanguo*, Winter 2009, 70–75.

Wang Jisi. "China's Search for a Grand Strategy: A Rising Power Finds Its Way." *Foreign Affairs* 90, no. 2 (2011): 68–79.
Wang Sheng. "Shixi dangdai Hanguo minzuzhuyi." *Xiandai Guoji Guanxi*, no. 2 (2010): 36–41.
Wang Xianfeng. "Meiguo jueqi jinchengzhong de waijiao zhengce xuanze jidui Zhongguo heping fazhan de qishi." *Kexue Shehuizhuyi*, no. 4 (2010): 150–53.
Wang Zheng. "National Humiliation, History Education, and the Politics of Historical Memory: Patriotic Education Campaign in China." *International Studies Quarterly* 52, no. 4 (2008): 783–806.
Wang Zhensuo. "Luelun fujiaoqian daozhi Zhongri guanxi didui taishi de yinsu." *Riben Xuekan*, no. 2 (2010): 28–39.
Wassermann, Heinz P. *Naziland Österreich!? Studien zu Antisemitismus, Nation und Nationalsozialismus im öffentlichen Meinungsbild*. Vienna: Studien Verlag, 2002.
———. *"Zuviel Vergangenheit tut nicht gut!": Nationalsozialismus im Spiegel der Tagespresse der Zweiten Republik*. Vienna: Studien Verlag, 2000.
Watts, Larry. *Romanian Cassandra: Ion Antonescu and the Struggle for Reform, 1916–1941*. Boulder, Colo.: East European Monographs; New York: distributed by Columbia University Press, 1993.
Weinberg, Gerhard L. *A World at Arms: A Global History of World War II*. Cambridge: Cambridge University Press, 1994.
Weiner, Amir. *Making Sense of War: The Second World War and the Fate of the Bolshevik Revolution*. Princeton, N.J.: Princeton University Press, 2001.
Weinreb, Friedrich. *Collaboratie en verzet 1940–1945: Een poging tot ontmythologisering*. Vol. 1. Amsterdam: Meulenhoff, 1969.
Westad, Odd Arne. *The Global Cold War: Third World Interventions and the Making of Our Times*. Cambridge: Cambridge University Press, 2007.
Wieviorka, Annette. *Déportation et génocide: Entre la mémoire et l'oubli*. Paris: Plon, 1992.
———. "Vers une communauté? Les Juifs en France depuis la guerre des Six-Jours." In *Les Juifs de France: De la Révolution française à nos jours*, edited by Jacques Becker and Annette Wieviorka, 362–405. Paris: Liana Lévi, 1998.
Wieviorka, Olivier. *La mémoire désunie: Le souvenir politique des années sombres, de la Libération à nos jours*. Paris: Seuil, 2010.
———. "Les avatars du statut de résistant." *Vingtième Siècle: Revue d'histoire* 50 (April–June 1996): 55–66.
Wikipedia, "Bombing of Tokyo." http://en.wikipedia.org/wiki/Bombing_of_Tokyo. Accessed July 8, 2013.
Wilhelm, Maria. *The Other Italy: Italian Resistance in World War II*. New York: Norton, 1988.
Willems, Wim. *Tjalie Robinson: Biografie van een Indo-schrijver*. Amsterdam: Bert Bakker, 2008.
Wolczuk, Kataryna. "History, Europe, and the 'National Idea': The 'Official' Narrative of National Identity in Ukraine." *Nationalities Papers* 28, no. 4 (2000): 671–94.

Wolffson, Michael, and Thomas Brechenmacher. *Denkmalsturz? Brants Kniefall.* Munich: Olzog, 2005.

Wood, Nancy. *Vectors of Memory: Legacies of Trauma in Postwar Europe.* Oxford: Berg, 1999.

Xia Jiting and Qi Linayun. "Chaoxian zhanzheng yu Dongbeiya geju." *Taipingyang Xuebao,* October 2010, 34–42.

Yablonka, Hannah. *The State of Israel vs. Adolf Eichmann.* New York: Schocken, 2004.

Yakovenko, Natalya. "Kontseptsiya novogo uchebnika ukrainskoi istorii." Polit.ru, March 18, 2010. http://www.polit.ru/lectures/2010/03/18/uchebniki_print.html.

———. "Likbez dlya professora." *Zerkalo Nedeli,* March 7–13, 2009.

Yamazaki, Jane W. *Japanese Apologies for World War II: A Rhetorical Study.* London: Routledge, 2005.

Yang Jiazhen, Liu Shaozhou, and Gao Shuquan. *Riben baike cidian.* Changchun: Jilin Renmin Chubanshe, 1990.

Yomiuri Shimbun. Who Was Responsible: From Marco Polo Bridge to Pearl Harbor. Edited by James Auer. Tokyo: Yomiuri Shimbun, 2006.

Yoneyama, Lisa. "Traveling Memories, Contagious Justice: Americanization of Japanese War Crimes at the End of the Post–Cold War." *Journal of Asian American Studies* 6, no. 1 (February 2003): 57–93.

Yonnet, Paul. *Voyage au centre du malaise français: L'antiracisme et le roman national.* Paris: Gallimard, 1993.

Yoshida Takashi. "Revising the Past, Complicating the Future: The Yushukan War Museum in Modern Japanese History." *Asia-Pacific Journal: Japan Focus,* December 2, 2007. http://japanfocus.org/-Takashi-YOSHIDA/2594.

Yoshida Yutaka. *Nihonjin no sensōkan: Sengoshi no naka no hen'yō.* Tokyo: Iwanami Shoten, 1995.

Yoshimasa Irie. "The History of the Textbook Controversy." *Japan Echo* 24, no. 3 (August 1997): 34–38.

Young, James. *At Memory's Edge: After-Images of the Holocaust in Contemporary Art and Architecture.* New Haven, Conn.: Yale University Press, 2000.

Zehfuss, Maja. *Wounds of Memory: The Politics of War in Germany.* Cambridge: Cambridge University Press, 2007.

Zertal Idith. *From Catastrophe to Power: The Holocaust Survivors and the Emergence of Israel.* Berkeley: University of California Press, 1998.

———. *Israel's Holocaust and the Politics of Nationhood.* Cambridge: Cambridge University Press, 2005.

Zhang Chengjun and Liu Jianye. *An Illustrated History of China's War of Resistance against Japan.* Beijing: Foreign Languages Press, 1995.

Zhang Hongyi. "Meiguo shi ruhe cong yishixingtai yingxiang Heluxiaofu de?" *Gaoxiao Lilun Zhanxian,* no. 7 (2010): 58–62.

Zhao Yan. "Hexie linian yu Zhongguo heping jueqi." *Sheke Zongheng,* no. 4 (2009): 5–8.

Zheng Ruifeng and Peng Xuetao. "Kangmei yuanchao zhanzhengzhong Zhongsu kongjun hezuo shimuo." *Dangshi Zongheng,* no. 11 (2010): 27–30.

Zolotov, Andrei, Jr. "The Storm of History." *Russia Profile*, September 8, 2010.
Zubkova, Elena. "The Filippov Syndrome." *Kritika: Explorations in Russian and Eurasian History* 10, no. 4 (2009): 861–68.
Zubov, Andrei, ed. *Istoriya Rossii: XX vek*. Moscow: AST, 2009.
Zuroff, Efraim. "A Dangerous Nazi-Soviet Equivalence." *Guardian*, September 30, 2010.
Zuvintas, A. "An Open Letter to Tomas Venclova." *Cross Currents* 8 (1989): 62–67.

Contributors

THOMAS BERGER is Associate Professor of International Relations at Boston University. He is the author of *War, Guilt, and World Politics after World War II* (2012) and *Cultures of Antimilitarism: National Security in Germany and Japan* (1998) and the coeditor of *Japan in International Politics: The Foreign Policies of an Adaptive State* (2007).

DANIEL CHIROT is the Herbert J. Ellison Professor of Russian and Eurasian Studies at the University of Washington's Henry M. Jackson School. He has authored books about social change, ethnic conflict, Eastern Europe, and tyranny. He coauthored *Why Not Kill Them All?* (2nd edition, 2010) about political mass murder and has edited or coedited books on Leninism's decline, on entrepreneurial ethnic minorities, on ethnopolitical warfare, and on the economic history of Eastern Europe. He founded the journal *East European Politics and Societies*.

FRANCES GOUDA is Professor of Political Science at the University of Amsterdam. She is the author of *Poverty and Political Culture: The Rhetoric of Social Welfare in the Netherlands and France, 1815–1853* (1994), *Domesticating the Empire: Race, Gender and Family Life in French and Dutch Colonialism* (1998), *American Visions of the Netherlands East Indies / Indonesia: US Foreign Policy and Indonesian Nationalism, 1920–1949* (2002), and *Dutch Culture Overseas: Colonial Practice in the Netherlands Indies, 1900–1941* (2nd edition, 2009).

JULIAN JACKSON, Fellow of the British Academy, is Professor of History at Queen Mary, University of London. He is the author of many books about French and European history, including most prominently *The Politics of Depression in France, 1932–1936* (1985), *The Popular Front in France: Defending Democracy 1934–38* (1988), the prize-winning *France: The Dark Years, 1940–1944* (2001), and *The Fall of France: The Nazi Invasion of 1940*

(2003). He is also the author of *De Gaulle* (2003) and *Living in Arcadia: Homosexuality, Politics, and Morality in France from the Liberation to AIDS* (2009).

FANIA OZ-SALZBERGER is Professor of History at the University of Haifa Faculty of Law and the Center for German and European Studies. Her many publications include *Translating the Enlightenment: Scottish Civic Discourse in Eighteenth-Century Germany* (1995), *Israelis in Berlin* (2001), and *Jews and Words*, coauthored with Amos Oz (2012). She often writes for major newspapers including *Haaretz*, the *International Herald Tribune*, the *Wall Street Journal*, and *Frankfurter Allgemeine Zeitung*.

ROGER PETERSEN is the Arthur and Ruth Sloan Professor of Political Science at the Massachusetts Institute of Technology. He is the author of *Resistance and Rebellion: Lessons from Eastern Europe* (2001), *Understanding Ethnic Violence: Fear, Hatred, Resentment in Twentieth-Century Eastern Europe* (2002), and *Western Intervention in the Balkans: The Strategic Use of Emotion in Conflict* (2011), which has won three major book prizes.

GILBERT ROZMAN is the Emeritus Musgrave Professor of Sociology at Princeton University. He is the author of the classic *Population and Marketing Settlements in Ch'ing China* (1982). Among his very many authored, edited, and coedited books about Northeast Asia and Russia, the most recent are *Northeast Asia's Stunted Regionalism: Bilateral Distrust in the Shadow of Globalization* (2004), *Chinese Strategic Thoughts Toward Asia* (2010), and *Strategic Thinking about the Korean Nuclear Crisis: Four Parties Caught between the United States and North Korea* (2011). He is currently the editor of the Strategic Thought in Northeast Asia series.

GI-WOOK SHIN is the Director of the Walter H. Shorenstein Asia-Pacific Research Center and the Tong Yang, Korea Foundation, and Korea Stanford Alumni Chair of Korean Studies at Stanford University. He has authored and edited a dozen books. Among his most recent works are *Ethnic Nationalism in Korea: Genealogy, Politics, and Legacy* (2006), *Rethinking Historical Injustice and Reconciliation in Northeast Asia: The Korean Experience* (2006), *One Alliance, Two Lenses: U.S.-Korea Relations in a New Era* (2010), and *South Korean Social Movements: From Democracy to Civil Society* (2011).

DANIEL SNEIDER is the Associate Director for research at the Walter H. Shorenstein Asia-Pacific Research Center at Stanford University. He was a foreign correspondent, columnist, and editor in South Asia, Japan, Korea, and Moscow for the *San Jose Mercury News* and the Knight Ridder media company. He is the coeditor of *Cross Currents: Regionalism and Nationalism in Northeast Asia* (2007), *First Drafts of Korea: The U.S. Media and Perceptions of the Last Cold War Frontier* (2009), *Does South Asia Exist? Prospects for Regional Integration* (2010), *History Textbooks and the Wars in Asia: Divided Memories* (2011), and *Troubled Transition: North Korea's Politics, Economy, and External Relations* (2012).

IGOR TORBAKOV is a Senior Fellow at the Center for Russian and Eurasian Studies at Uppsala University. He is a historian of Russia and Eurasia as well as a specialist on current international relations. He has served at the Russian Academy of Sciences, the Kennan Institute at the Woodrow Wilson Center in Washington, D.C., and at Harvard, Columbia, and Stanford Universities as a Visiting Fellow. He has written a large number of articles on Russia's foreign policy, on energy and resources in the countries that were once part of the Soviet Union, and on politics in the Caucasus, Central Asia, Ukraine, and Eastern Europe, particularly with respect to their relations with Russia.

Index

Note: page numbers followed by "n" and "t" indicate endnotes and tables, respectively.

A

Abe, Shinzo: apologies and, 9, 164; China visit, 220; joint history project and, 168; platform of, 218; return as prime minister, 8, 226; revisionists and, 213; right-wing nationalists and, 8, 21; Senkaku Islands and, 3
"Absolution for Killers" (Rosenthal), 275–78
action tendencies, 260–62
adat circles, 119, 133n59
Adenauer, Konrad, 37, 86, 115, 136, 192, 195, 199
Algerian National Liberation Front (FLN), 140–41
Algeria War, 137, 140–41
Alien Tort Claims Act (U.S.), 166
Allied policies in occupied territories, 83–85
Alterman, Nathan, 191, 195
anti-Semitism. *See* Holocaust (Shoah)
anti-Semitism, secondary, 112
Antonescu, Ion, 30–31
apathy, 110, 221
apologies: Abe and, 9; "apology failure" in East Asia, 164–65; apology fatigue in Japan, 104n56, 164; determinants and metrics of apologetics, 80–83; Dutch, 13–14, 18; French, 35; Germany vs. Japan and, 5; Japan and, 5, 21, 95–96, 159t–160t, 161–65; questions surrounding, 17–19; trend toward, 79; U.S., 184n33; Vietnam and, 18–19
Appelfeld, Aharon, 201
Arab-Israeli conflict, 193, 194, 197
Arendt, Hannah, 197–98
Argentina, 3
Aristotle, 259, 263, 278, 279

Armenian genocide, 17, 19
Arnold, Magda B., 280n10
Ashes and Dust (Poliker and Gilad), 201
Asian American community, 185n62
Asian Women's Fund, 95, 170, 182n2
Asia-Pacific Economic Cooperation, 179
asymmetrical warfare, resistance movements and, 16
atomic bombs. *See* Hiroshima and Nagasaki atomic bombs
Auschwitz, 52, 135, 148–49, 188–89
Austria: awareness in, 34; collaboration and, 6; effects of war on, 85; as "first victim of Nazism," 84, 86–87; party politics, 88, 96; politics of history, early–Cold War, 83–88; politics of history, late–Cold War, 90–91, 93–94; politics of history, post–Cold War, 95, 96–97; pro-Nazism and Holocaust in, 25, 33–34; Waldheim and, 33–34, 90–91
Austrian People's Party, 88, 96
The Awakening Lion (sculpture), 50

B

backlash as emotional response, 262–65, 264t
Baltics. *See* Lithuanian-Jewish discourse and emotional dynamics
Barbie, Klaus, 141
Barisan Pelopor (Corps of Pioneers), 123
Bauer, Yehuda, 27
Because of That War (film), 201
Be'er, Chaim, 203
Bélâbre, France, 14–15, 42
Bell, Franklin, 16
Ben Dor-Niv, Orna, 201

Benedict, Ruth, 82
Ben-Gurion, David, 195, 199
Ben-Natan, Asher, 199
Berlin, 203, 204
Berlin Wall, 201
Berlusconi, Silvio, 21
Bezborodko, Aleksandr, 247
Bidault, Georges, 140
biological weapons testing, 179, 185n54
Bitburg, Germany, 89, 92
Bix, Herbert P., 76n30, 173
Blue Swallow (film), 62
Bohlen, Charles, 244
Bork, Robert, 180–81
Bourdet, Claude, 140
Bousquet, René, 138
Boven Digoel prison camp, 125–26
Brandt, Willy, 89
Breen, John, 67
Breman, Jan, 134n106
Britain (United Kingdom), 3, 193–94
Brizgys, Vincentas, 268, 273
Budi Utomo (Beautiful Endeavor), 118
Bulgaria, 24, 30
Bu Ping, 168, 183n22
Buruma, Ian, 22, 40, 111
Bush, George W., 179, 231

C

Carter, Jimmy, 184n34
Catherine the Great, 247
Catholic Church in Lithuania, 270, 273
Catholic People's Party (Katholike Volkspartij) (Netherlands), 116
Central Europe. *See* Eastern and Central Europe
Centre de documentation juive contemporaine (CDJC), 148
Chang, Iris, 52
"A Child's Voice" (Romein), 108
China: anti-Japanese protests in, 98; civil war, 38, 52–53; collaboration and, 39; Communist-National civil war narrative, 48–49, 52–53, 56–57; Diaoyu/Senkaku Islands and, 3, 75, 99; "harmonious world" concept, 216; Japan UN Security Council bid and, 58; joint history projects, 168–69, 214, 227–28; losses in Sino-Japanese War, 50; Marco Polo Bridge Incident, 50; Nanjing massacre, 40–41, 53, 183n8; Nanjing Memorial, 41, 51–52, 54; national-unity resistance narrative, 49, 54–55, 57–59; normalization of relations, 53, 157; public opinion in, 59, 164; Sinocentrism, 212, 215–16, 218, 228–29; textbooks, 56–58; "Twenty-One Demands" on (1915), 169, 183n22; War Resistance museum, 50–51, 54–55. *See also* national identity narratives and historical memory in East Asia; reconciliation in East Asia
Chinese Communist Party (CCP): historical narratives of, 48–49, 52–55, 229; nationalist vs. Marxist narratives of, 39, 221; regime legitimacy concerns, 59, 214, 220
Chirac, Jacques, 136, 137–38, 150
Chirot, Daniel, 48
Cho Gab Je, 62
Cho Jeong Rae, 62
Christian Democratic Party (Germany), 89
Christian groups and Franco-German reconciliation, 184n28
Chun Doo-Hwan, 49, 61
City of Life and Death (film), 40
civilian deaths in war, 15–17
Civil Liberties Act of 1988 (U.S.), 184n33
Civil War, American, 17
Clendinnen, Inga, 111
Clinton, Bill, 179
Clore, Gerald, 280n10
Cold War: East Asian national identity, revisionism, and, 221–26; East Asian reconciliation and, 171, 175; French-German reconciliation and, 37; Japanese war memory and, 48; politics of history, early–Cold War, 83–88; politics of history, late–Cold War, 88–94
collaboration: apathy and, 110; asymmetrical warfare and, 16; comparison of East Asia and Europe, 39; denial of, 5–6; in Eastern and Central Europe, 24–25, 30–34; France and, 14–15, 23–24, 149–50 (*see also* France, Vichy regime in); Holocaust and, 30–36; Indonesia and, 119–24; Korea and, 61–62; Netherlands and, 113–14. *See also* Holocaust (Shoah)
Collins, Allan, 280n10

colonialism: apology, question of, 18; French in Algeria, 140–41; genocides and, 17; Korean "colonial modernization" debate, 62–63; Korean narratives on, 60. *See also* Indonesia (Dutch East Indies)

"comfort women" and sex slavery: apology to, 95; Asian Women's Fund and, 95, 170, 182n2; Dokdo/Takeshima Islands and, 99; litigation by, 165–66; U.S. and, 177–78

Communism: blame assigned to Germany and, 25; Chinese narratives of KMT vs., 48–49, 52–53, 56–57; Chinese narratives on USSR and, 222; ethnonationalist conflict ignored by, 26–27; Greek civil war and, 25; Japan as bulwark against, 171; Jewish Communists, 31–32; "Jews" confounded with, 33. *See also* Cold War; Soviet Union (USSR)

Communism, collapse of. *See* Eastern and Central Europe; Lithuanian-Jewish discourse and emotional dynamics; Russia

Communist Party (France), 141–42, 151–52

Communist Party (Greece), 25

comparative context, 271–72

comparison of Japan and Germany: apologies and, 5; Buruma on, 22; Central and Eastern European evasion of responsibility and, 26–27, 30–34; collaboration, East Asian question of, 39; European interpretations blaming Germany, 23–26; guilt vs. shame and, 40–41; Holocaust, genocide, and morality, questions of, 27–36; international contexts and, 36–39, 48; political contexts and, 19–20; reconciliation and, 171–76; simple contrast, 20–22; territorial disputes and, 4–5; war crimes vs. genocide and, 18; Western European evasion of responsibility and, 23–24, 34–36

compensation: Austria and, 96–97; Germany and, 94; Japan and, 84, 95; litigation and, 165

concentration (death) camps: Auschwitz, 135, 148–49, 188–89; Dutch East Indian prison camps compared to, 125–26; Sobibor, 109. *See also* Holocaust (Shoah)

Confucianism, 215

contempt in emotional dynamics, 263

context and decontextualization, 269–73

contrition as emotional response, 262–65, 264t

co-responsibility (*Mitschuld*), 95, 96

court cases, 165–67, 180–81

cultural exchanges in East Asia, 169–71

culturalist perspective, 82, 100

Czechoslovakia/Czech Republic, 96, 97

D

Dallin, Alexander, 281n36

Darquier de Pellopoix, Louis, 149

decontextualization, 269–73

de Gaulle, Charles, 23–24, 136, 139, 141–42, 143, 146, 147

de Jong, Lou, 109–10

Demjanjuk, John (Ivan), 107

democracy: Baltic nations and, 281n39; China on South Korea and, 224; dissent, tolerance of, 252; "good" vs. "evil" and, 241–42; Japan and, 230; liberation of Europe and, 242–43

Democratic Party of Japan (DPJ), 220

Deng Xiaoping, 53, 221

Denmark, 140

deportee categories, French, 144–45, 148–49

de Swaan, Abram, 131n11

Dewulf, Jeroen, 125

Diaoyu/Senkaku Islands, 3, 75, 99

Dierkes, Julian, 8

Dinur, Yehiel (Katzetnik 135633), 188–89

Divided Memory (Herf), 131n1

Dokdo/Takeshima Islands, 4, 99, 175, 177, 228

Dower, John W., 76n30, 181, 185n53

Drumont, Édouard, 28

Dudden, Alexis, 177

Dutch East Indies. *See* Indonesia

E

East Asian national identity. *See* national identity narratives and historical memory in East Asia

Eastern and Central Europe: evasion of responsibility in, 26–27; Holocaust, collaboration with, 30–34; "liberation" vs. "occupation," 240–43; "national Holocausts" and victim status in, 255n36; new historical narratives, post-Soviet, 239–45; partisan resistance, overestimation of, 24–25; post-Soviet state emergence

and memory wars, 235–39; reconciliation prospects, 252–53; textbooks, 237–38. *See also specific countries*
East Germany (German Democratic Republic), 195
Éboué, Félix, 24
Eichmann, Adolf, 149, 186, 188, 192, 197–98, 205
Eichmann in Jerusalem (Arendt), 197–98
Elon, Amos, 200
Elster, Jon, 102n1, 280n17, 280n20
emotional dynamics. *See* guilt; Lithuanian-Jewish discourse and emotional dynamics; shame and shaming
Erhard, Ludwig, 199
Eshkol, Levi, 199
Estonia, 235, 258
ethnonationalist conflict, Eastern European denial of, 26–27
Europeanness, 241
European Parliament, 240–41, 244–45
European Union (EU): Austria and, 96; enlargement of, 244; German-Polish relations and, 97, 101; Russia and, 236
European unity, Franco-German relationship and, 37–38
"Everyone a Bit of a Victim, Everyone a Bit of a Perpetrator" (Gans), 111–12
Exode, 139

F
Falkland Islands, 3
fascism: Communist narratives of global struggle against, 49, 55, 58; Indonesia and, 120, 123; Lithuania and, 275–76; Marxist interpretation of, as class phenomenon, 26; in Romania and Hungary, 30; Wilders on Islam and, 134n102; Zionism and, 148. *See also* collaboration; Germany; Japan
Fear (Gross), 32–33
Federal Republic of Germany. *See* Germany
Fedotov, Mikhail, 250
Ferrant, Anatole, 15
Filippov, Aleksandr, 256n52
Fires on the Plain (Nobi; film), 69
Foner, Eric, 256n71
Foray, Jennifer, 125
Fox, Eytan, 203

France: Algerian War and, 137; associations and categories of deportees, 144–46; Bélâbre, village of, 14–15, 42; civilian massacres in, 15–16; collaboration and, 14–15, 23–24; extreme Left and move away from terrorism, 147–48; fragmentation of war experience in, 144; Gaullist myth, questioning of, 144–46; Gaullist narrative, 141–42, 150; Germany, postwar relationship with, 37–38, 135–36; Holocaust in, 34–35; Jewish memory in, 148–50; Leftists and Communist Party in, 141–42, 151–52; national identity and the occupation, post-Gaullist, 150–52; occupation, contemporary obsession with, 136–38; Oradour massacre, 15, 18, 144; postwar negotiations on Germany and, 36–37; radicals of 1968 and post-Gaullism, 142–44, 146–48; schoolbooks, 38; specificities of the French experience, 138–41; Touvier affair, 143–44. *See also* French Resistance
France, Vichy regime in: autonomy of, 139–40; domestic support for, 23; in Gaullist narrative, 141, 144, 150; initial legitimacy and, 139; Jewish memory and anti-Semitism of, 149–50, 151; Mitterand and, 138; national identity and, 150–51; National Revolution and, 140; Paxton's *Vichy France*, 142–43; relationship to Germany, 14; in *The Sorrow and the Pity* (film), 147
Franco-German Treaty (1963), 136
Frank, Anne, 35, 105–6, 108–9, 112–14, 130
Frankel, Benjamin, 267–75, 279n6, 281n40
Freedom Party (Austria), 88, 96
Free French movement, 24, 142, 143, 146
French Resistance: Algeria and, 140–41; in Bélâbre, 15; Gaullist narrative on, 141–42, 144; marginalization of, 146; memory and, 136, 138, 143, 146, 147, 151; Môquet as symbol of, 151–52; overestimation of, 23–24; resistance deportees, 145; rules defining former resisters, 144; Vichy regime and, 139, 149–50
Frijda, Nico, 260–61, 279n10
Fujio Masayuki, 93
Fukuda Yasuo, 215
Fumimaro, Konoe, 74
Funabashi, Yoichi, 158

G

Galbraith, John Kenneth, 244
Gans, Evelien, 111–12
Gaullist narrative, 141–42, 144–46, 150
genocide: Armenian, 17, 19; colonialism and, 17; defined, 18; guilt, apology, and reconciliation questions, 17–18; Japan and question of, 29, 39; Ukrainian Holomodor recognized as, 235–36; war crimes vs., 18. *See also* Holocaust (Shoah)
Georgia, Republic of, 235
German Democratic Republic (East Germany), 195
Germanic Lore, 191
German Slave Labor Foundation, 181
Germany: apologies and, 5; Bitburg military cemetery, 89, 92; compensation and, 94; Czech Republic, relations with, 96, 97; effects of war on, 85; European blame placed on, 23–26; extreme Left, evolution of, 147–48; France, postwar relationship with, 37–38, 135–36; *Historikerstreit* ("historians' conflict"), 22, 135, 187; Israeli travel to, 191, 200, 202; Jewish cultural influences on, 187–88; massacres and atrocities by, 15–16; memorial sites and museums, 95, 254n21; party politics, 88–89, 93; Poland, relations with, 96, 97; politics of history, early–Cold War, 83–88; politics of history, late–Cold War, 88–90, 93–94; politics of history, post–Cold War, 94–95, 96, 97–98; postwar negotiations on fate of, 36–37; right-wing extremists in, 21; schoolbooks, 8–9, 20; war crimes vs. genocide and, 18. *See also* comparison of Japan and Germany; Israel and Israeli-German relations
Germany Historical Museum, 254n21
Gilad, Ya'akov, 201
Ginsburg, Ruth Bader, 166
Giscard d'Estaing, Valéry, 136, 138
Goldhagen, Daniel, 265–66
Gomikawa, Junpei, 69
Goodrich, Frances, 108–9
Gorbachev, Mikhail, 222, 226, 258
Gray Past (*Grijs verleden*) (van der Heijden), 110–11
Greece, 25
grief as emotional response, 261

Gross, Jan, 32–33
Grossman, David, 200–201
guilt: blame, displacement of, 23, 25–26; Buruma's *The Wages of Guilt*, 22, 111; in emotional interplay, 262–65, 264t; Holocaust and, 29; Japanese progressive narrative and, 47; shame vs., 40–41, 259, 263

H

Hackett, Alfred, 108–9
Haider, Jörg, 96
Hanil Yondae 21 (Korea-Japan Solidarity 21), 170–71
Hara, Kimie, 175
"harmonious world" concept (China), 216
Harp of Burma (*Biruma no tategoto*; film), 69
Hatoyama Ichiro, 225
Hatta, Mohammed, 115, 116, 119, 123–24, 125
Hayden Bill (California), 167
Hebrew University of Jerusalem, 189–90
Heine, Heinrich, 191
Herf, Jeffrey, 131n1
Hessel, Stéphane, 138
Het Koninkrijk der Nederlanden in de Tweede Wereldoorlog (Kingdom of the Netherlands during the Second World War) (de Jong), 109–10
Heydrich, Reinhard, 197
Hicks, George, 102n4
Hier, Marvin, 258
Higashinakano Shudo, 183n8
Hirohito, Emperor, 65, 68, 74, 102n11, 173–74
Hiroshima and Nagasaki atomic bombs: justification and, 19; Left-Right agreement on, in Japan, 39; Peace Memorial Museum, 71–72; U.S. acknowledgment, need for, 179–80; U.S. visits to, 172, 179–80, 184n34; victimhood and, 17
Hiroshima Peace Memorial Museum, 71–72, 173
Hiroshima Peace Memorial Park, 172, 184n34
historical determinist position, 81
historical realism, 79–80
Historikerstreit ("historians' conflict"), 22, 135, 187
history, politics of. *See* policy and politics of history
A History That Opens to the Future, 170

Index 323

history writing: collaborative projects, 136, 167–69, 170, 214, 227–28; national identity and, 236. *See also* textbooks and schoolbooks
Hitler, Adolf, 24, 28, 241, 243
Hitler and the Germans: Nation and Crime exhibition (Germany Historical Museum), 254n21
Hitler's Willing Executioners (Goldhagen), 265–66
Hobbes, Thomas, 279n10
Holocaust (Shoah): American television, effects of, 29–30, 103n24, 103n33; apologies for, 35; borrowing of term, 187; collaboration and, 30–36; conspiracy myths and, 28; denial of, 30–31; Final Solution system and technology, 188–89, 197; in France, 137, 148–50; German extreme Left and, 148; in German schoolbooks, 21; Goldhagen's *Hitler's Willing Executioners*, 265–66; in Israeli writing, films, music, and art (1980s), 200–201; in Lithuania, 258; in Netherlands, 110–13; *rafle du Vél d'Hiver* roundup (July 16, 1942), 137, 138; rational realism, lack of, 27–28; secondary anti-Semitism, 112; "*Shoahisering*" (Shoahization), 110–11; singularity of, 186–90; Soviet Union and, 34; war crimes vs. genocide and, 18. *See also* collaboration; Lithuanian-Jewish discourse and emotional dynamics
Holocaust Museum (Washington, D.C.), 52
Honda, Mike, 177, 185n62
Horthy, Miklós, 30
House of Representatives, U.S., 177–78, 185n62
Howard, Michael, 252
Hu Jintao, 58–59, 215, 225
human rights discourse, 94
Hungary, 25, 28, 30, 260
Hu Yaobang, 92
Hwang Geum Joo, et al. v. Japan, 166

I
Ichikawa, Kon, 69
iconic memory, 106
identity politics. *See* national identity; *specific places*
Ikeda Hayato, 225
Ikenberry, G. John, 178

incentives and political leadership, 100–101
Independence Hall of Korea, 60–61
Indonesia (Dutch East Indies): divided memory and, 114–17; historical context of Asia-Pacific War and Japanese occupation, 117–24; historical imagination, postcolonial deficit, and, 127–31; postwar moral judgments and, 124–26; Sukarno and, 105–6, 115–17, 122–30; Zwaan apology in, 13–14, 18
Institute for Research in Collaborationist Activities (South Korea), 61–62
instrumentalist perspective, 81–82, 87, 100
International Women's Tribunal, 170
Israel and Israeli-German relations: absorption (stage one), 192–97, 205; Alterman's "The Liberation Lorelei" and, 190–91; Arab-Israeli conflict, 193, 194, 197; establishment of the Israeli state, 193; German cultural connections, 187–88, 188–89; heightened awareness and diplomatic rapprochement (stage two), 192, 197–200, 205; Holocaust identification and, 149; human encounters and intensification (stage four), 192, 202–4, 206; individual engagement (stage three), 192, 200–201, 205–6; lessons for other post-conflictual cultures, 205–6; Palestinian-Israeli conflict, 193, 203–4; party politics, Israeli, 190; "reparations," 195–96; singularity of Holocaust and, 186–90. *See also* Holocaust (Shoah)
Istoriya Rossii: XX vek (Zubov), 256n67
Italy, 21, 25

J
Jaeger, Karl, 268, 281n40
James, Clive, 266
Japan: apologies and, 5, 21, 95; apology fatigue in, 104n56, 164; biological weapons testing by, 179, 185n54; Chinese perceptions of, 59; civilians killed in, 172; Cold War and, 48; compensation policies, 84, 95; conservative narrative, 46–47, 67–68; defeat, outside narratives about, 55; delayed pressure to admit guilt, 38–39; effects of war on, 85; elite regime legitimacy concerns, 213; genocide question and, 29, 39; Indonesia, occupation of, 116–24;

Japan (continued)
joint history projects, 168–69, 170, 214, 227–28; losses in Sino-Japanese War, 50; military clique thesis, 174; museums, 65–67, 68, 69–70; Nanjing massacre, 40–41, 53, 183n8; normalization of relations, 53, 88, 157, 175–76; "orthodox" outside interpretation, 67–68; outside perceptions of, 46–47; pacifist narrative, 46, 47, 71–73; party politics, 47, 69, 213, 220; politics of history, early–Cold War, 83–88; politics of history, late–Cold War, 91–94; politics of history, post–Cold War, 95–96, 98–99; progressive narrative, 46, 47, 68–71; right-wing nationalism in, 8, 20–21, 161, 164, 174; Senkaku/Diaoyu Islands and, 3, 75, 99; shame vs. guilt and, 40–41; South Korea, relations with, 96; Soviet declaration of war on, 74; statements and language of, 161–63, 162t–163t; Takeshima/Dokdo Islands and, 4, 99, 175, 177, 228; textbooks and schoolbooks, 8–9, 20, 21–22, 47, 54, 58, 69, 92, 98, 164, 182n2; UN Security Council membership issue, 58; U.S. occupation of, 47–48, 68, 73; victimhood psychology in, 171–73; Yasukuni Shrine, 58, 63–65, 74, 86, 92, 98; *Yomiuri Shimbun* research project on responsibility, 73–74. *See also* comparison of Japan and Germany; Hiroshima and Nagasaki atomic bombs; national identity narratives and historical memory in East Asia; reconciliation in East Asia
Japan-ROK Joint History Research Committee, 168
Japan–South Korea Joint Study Group on History Textbooks, 170
Jardin, Alexandre, 138
Jardin, Jean, 138
Jaurès, Jean, 14
Jewish American community, 185n62
Jews: confounded with "Communists," 33; as "others," 7; as percent of population, 27–28; in postwar Communist cadres, 31–32. *See also* Holocaust (Shoah); Israel and Israeli-German relations; Lithuanian-Jewish discourse and emotional dynamics
Jilge, Wilfried, 255n36

joint history writing projects, 167–69, 214, 227–28
Josselin de Jong, J. P. B. de, 116
Judt, Tony, 247
Justes, 137
justification of war, 19

K
Kaczynski, Lech, 97
Kaniuk, Yoram, 203
Kappeler, Andreas, 253
Karaganov, Sergei, 249–50
Kästner, Erich, 196
Kasynov, Georgiy, 238
Katyn crime, 249
Katzetnik 135633 (Yehiel Dinur), 188–89
Kawamure, Takashi, 20
Kennan, George, 244
Khrushchev, Nikita, 222
Kim Dae Jung, 61, 96, 102, 168
Kishi Nobusuke, 225
Kissinger, Henry, 102n2
Kitaoka, Shin'ichi, 168
Klestil, Thomas, 96
Klimaitis, Algirdas, 267–68, 274
Koguryo, 215, 216
Kohl, Helmut, 89, 136
Koizumi, Junichiro, 58, 65, 98, 100, 163–64, 168
Korea, 38. *See also* North Korea; South Korea
Korean War, 17, 49, 222–24, 229
Kousbroek, Rudy, 130
Kreisky, Bruno, 88
Kundera, Milan, 243
Kuomintang (KMT; Chinese Nationalists), 48–49, 52–53, 56–57. *See also* Taiwan
Kurile Islands, 175
Kux, Brian D., 267–75, 279n6, 281n40

L
Labor Party (Partij van de Arbeid) (Netherlands), 115–16
Landsbergis, Vytautas, 276–77
Lanzmann, Claude, 149, 187
Latvia, 235, 258
Laval, Pierre, 138
Lee, Chul-woo, 63
Lee Myun Bak, 99

Index

Leggewie, Claus, 239
Levy, Robert I., 265
Liberal Democratic Party (LDP) (Japan), 47, 213
"The Liberation Lorelei" (Alterman), 190–91
Li Datong, 54
Lieven, Anatol, 278
Lind, Jennifer, 102n4, 174
Lithuania, 33, 236, 281n39
Lithuanian-Jewish discourse and emotional dynamics: backdoor shaming, perception and misperception of, 266–67, 274; background, 258–59; concerns and action tendencies, 260–62; definitions, 259–60; Frankel & Kux article and backdoor-shaming devices, 267–75; identity construction and, 278–79; interplay of emotions, 262–65, 264t; norms against shaming, 265–66; Rosenthal article as counterexample, 275–78
litigation, 165–67, 180–81
Lübbe, Hermann, 85–86
Lukisan revolusi rakjat Indonesia (Pictures of the Indonesian People's Revolution), 118–21
Luxembourg Agreement, 195

M

MacArthur, Douglas, 102n11
Malaka, Tan, 121, 124
Mälksoo, Maria, 235, 240–41, 256n46
Malraux, André, 142
Maoism, 216
Maoists of the Gauche prolétarienne, 147
Mao Zedong, 56, 222
Marco Polo Bridge Incident, 50
Maruyama Masao, 68–69
Maspero, François, 141
May, Karl, 196
Mayer, Arno J., 281n40
Medvedev, Dmitry, 245, 249, 250, 251
Mémorial de la déportation (France), 146
Mémorial de Mont Valérien (France), 146, 147
Memorial Hall of the Victims in Nanjing Massacre by Japanese Invaders (Nanjing Memorial), 51–52, 54
memorials. *See* museums, memorials, and monuments

memory: authoritarian conditions and, 252; contentiousness of, 235; foreign policy dimension of, 235; forgetting and, 106; iconic, 106; scarcity principle in cultural memory, 106. *See also specific places and topics, such as* apologies
"memory wars," 235
Mendelsohn, Ezra, 271
Merkel, Angela, 136
Michener, James, 114
military clique thesis (Japan), 174
minjok ("the nation"), 218
Mitterand, François, 136, 138, 150
Miyazawa, Kiichi, 161, 163
Mondale, Walter, 172, 184n34
Monnet, Jean, 37, 135
Monroe, Kristen R., 266
monuments. *See* museums, memorials, and monuments
Môquet, Guy, 136–37, 151–52
Môquet, Prosper, 151
Moulin, Jean, 138, 141–42
Murakami, Haruki, 186
Murayama Tomiichi, 100, 161, 182n2
Museum of the War of Chinese People's Resistance against Japanese Aggression, 50–51, 54–55
museums, memorials, and monuments: Austrian, 95; in Eastern Europe and Baltics, 235–36; in France, 35, 146, 147, 148–49; in Germany, 29–30, 95; Hiroshima, Japan, 71–72, 172, 173; Holocaust Museum (Washington, D.C.), 52; Nanjing Memorial, China, 41, 51–52, 54; Okinawa Peace Memorial Museum, 69–70; War Resistance museum, China, 50–51, 54–55; Yad Vashem (Israel), 7, 22, 52, 112; Yasukuni Shrine, Japan, 58, 63–65, 74; Yushukan war museum, Japan, 65–67, 68
Mussolini, Benito, 21, 25

N

Naimark, Norman, 243
Nakasone Yasuhiro, 65, 92–93
Nanjing massacre, 40–41, 53, 183n8
Nanjing Memorial, 41, 51–52, 54
National Federation of Labor Deportees (FNDT), 145

National Federation of Victims and Survivors of the Nazis' Forced Labor Camps, 145
national identity: constant construction and reconstruction of, 234–35; French, 150–52; historical memory and, 45–46; history writing and, 236; othering and, 237; post-Soviet, 238; Soviet Union and the "national question," 236–37. *See also* specific places
national identity narratives and historical memory in East Asia: China-Japan joint history projects and, 214, 227–28; Cold War era and, 221–26; dominant historical memories, 212; early modern era and, 218–21; Japanese historical memory, 68; premodern era and, 215–18; regime legitimacy, elite concerns with, 213–14; Sino-Japanese comparisons and international relations, 227–29
nationalism: China and, 59, 221, 224; Germany and, 21, 37, 41; identity construction and, 237; Indonesian, 116; Italian, 21; Japanese, 8, 20–21, 161, 164, 172, 174, 177; Korean, 61, 62–63; Lithuanian, 267–68; Russian, 9, 257n67; Soviet Union and the "national question," 236–37; ultranationalism, 26, 30, 41, 69
nationalization of history, 237
National Revolution (France), 140
National-Socialist Alliance (NSB) (Netherlands), 114
NATO (North Atlantic Treaty Organization), 244
Nazis. *See* Germany; Holocaust (Shoah)
Neighbors (Gross), 32
Nengen no joken (*The Human Condition;* film trilogy), 69
Netherlands: Anne Frank as icon of memory, 105–6, 108–9, 112–14, 130; black and white vs. shades of gray and, 107, 109–14; civil servant ancestry registration in, 113; contemporary identities and postcolonial deficits, 127–31; Holocaust and collaboration in, 35; immigrants in, 128, 130–31; memory work and, 106; party politics in, 115–16; postwar moral judgments and, 124–26; Sukarno as icon of memory and "trauma of decolonization," 105–6, 115–17, 122–30. *See also* Indonesia (Dutch East Indies)
New Popular Resistance (NRP) (France), 147
Nietzsche, Friedrich, 196
Night and Fog (film), 149
Nihonjinron (theory of Japaneseness), 217–18
Nolte, Ernst, 112
Nora, Pierre, 150–51
normalization of relations in East Asia, 53, 88, 157, 175–76
North Korea, 223, 224–25, 229. *See also* Korean War
Noto Soeroto, 119
Nuremberg trials, 83–85

O

Obama, Barack, 179–80, 226, 231
Obuchi Keizo, 102
occupation. *See specific places*
Oi, Mariko, 8
Okinawa, Battle of, 71
Okinawa Peace Memorial Museum, 69–70
Olympics (Munich, 1972), 148
Omura Masujiro, 64
"On the Perpetuation of the Memory of the Victims of the Totalitarian Regime and on National Reconciliation" project (Russia), 250
Ophüls, Marcel, 142
Oradour massacre (France), 15, 18, 144
Ortony, Andrew, 280n10
Orwell, George, 246, 256n46
Ota, Masahide, 70–71
Oz, Amos, 203

P

Pal, Radhabinod, 67, 172
Palestine under British Mandate, 193–94
Palestinians, 193–94, 203–4
Papon, Maurice, 137, 141, 149–50
Park Chung Hee, 39, 49, 61, 214
Park Geun-hye, 214
Park Kyung-won, 62
Patriotic Education Campaign (China), 54, 56, 57, 59
Paulauskas, Artusas, 276
Pauley Commission, 84
Pauls, Rolf, 199

Paxton, Robert O., 142–43
Peace Treaty of San Francisco (1951), 86, 87, 165, 166, 174–75, 177, 180–81
Pelosi, Nancy, 172, 184n34
People's Party for Freedom and Democracy (Volkspartij voor Vrijheid en Democratie; VVD) (Netherlands), 115–16
People's Republic of China (PRC). *See* China
Pétain, Philippe, 23, 139–40. *See also* France, Vichy regime in
Peters, Friedrich, 88
Philippine-American War, 16–17
Poland: anti-Semitism and Holocaust in, 32–33; Germany, relations with, 96, 97; resistance in, 26; Russian acknowledgment of Katyn crime, 248–49
policy and politics of history: apologetics, determinants and metrics of, 80–83; capacity for political consensus and, 100; early Cold War, Allied policies, and war crimes trials and, 83–88; historical determinist, instrumentalist, and cultural perspectives on, 81–82, 100; historical realism and, 79–80; incentives and, 100–101; late-Cold War, 88–94; objectives of politics of history, 234; post–Cold War, 94–99; prospects for, 101–2; trend toward apology, 79
Poliker, Yehuda, 201
"political deportees" (France), 145, 148–49
politics of history. *See* policy and politics of history; *specific places*
Polyakov, Leonid, 246
Pompidou, Georges, 138, 143–44
Portisch, Hugo, 91
postcolonialism. *See* Indonesia (Dutch East Indies)
post-conflict management and individuals, 205–6
process tracing, 102n7
Protocols of the Elders of Zion, 28
public opinion: Austrian, 90–91; Chinese, 59, 98, 164; German, 89–90, 97, 103n24; Indonesian, 128; Israeli, 199; Japanese, 20–21, 92, 164; Korean, 98, 164; Polish, 97; Russian, 251, 252–53
Putin, Vladimir, 9, 245–46

R

rafle du Vél d'Hiver roundup (July 16, 1942), 137, 138
The Rape of Nanking (Chang), 52
Reading the Holocaust (Clendinnen), 111
Reagan, Ronald, 89
realism, historical, 79–80
reconciliation in East Asia: apologies and, 5, 21, 95–96, 159t–160t, 161–65; Germany compared to Japan, 171–76; the "history problem," recognition of, 158; history writing, collaborative, 167–69; Japanese efforts (overview), 95; language and statement from Japan, 162t–163t; litigation, 165–67, 180–81; need for, 157; regional exchanges and activism, 169–71; San Francisco Peace Treaty and, 165, 166, 174–75, 180–81; South Korean Truth and Reconciliation Commission, 49; "thin" vs "thick," 157–58; U.S. role in, 176–81
reconciliation in Europe: Christian groups, role of, 184n28; French-German, 37; Germany and, 94–95; Germany compared to Japan, 171–76; Russia and post-Soviet states and, 248–49, 250, 252–53
remembrance. *See* memory
remorse as emotional response, 262–65, 264t
Renan, Ernest, 150
"reparations," 195–96
reproach, emotion of, 261
Republic of Korea (ROK). *See* South Korea
resistance: asymmetrical warfare and, 16; Dutch, 110, 111, 113, 124–25; in Eastern and Central Europe, 24–25; Italian, 25; Korean, 60; overestimation of, 23–27; Polish, 26; Yugoslav, 26–27. *See also* French Resistance
"resistance deportees" (France), 145
Resnais, Alain, 149
revisionism. *See specific places and topics*
Rhee, Syngman, 49, 224
Rhetoric (Aristotle), 259
right-wing nationalists: German, 21; Italian, 21; Japanese, 8, 20–21, 161, 164, 174. *See also* nationalism
Robinson, Tjalie, 128
Roginsky, Arseny, 250
Rogov, Kirill, 251

Roh Moo Hyun, 168
Roh Tae Woo, 161
Röling, B. V. A., 185n54
Romania, 25, 28, 30–31
Romein, Jan, 108
Roosevelt, Franklin D., 173
Rose, Caroline, 161
Rosenthal, A. M., 260, 275–78
Rothschild, Joseph, 271
Rousso, Henry, 141, 146, 150
Rozman, Gil, 177
Rum, Mohammad, 121
Russia: de-Stalinization agenda, 250–51; great power status and memory wars, 242; Hilter-Stalin equivalence thesis, reaction to, 241; independent scholarly expertise, need for, 256n61; public attitudes in, 251, 252–53; reconciliation with Eastern Europe, prospects for, 252–53; rivalry with EU, 236; Stalin as nationalist hero and, 9; symbolic politics, Soviet past, and national identity, 245–51; textbooks, 254n16, 256n67. *See also* Soviet Union (USSR)

S

San Francisco Peace Treaty (1951), 86, 87, 165, 166, 174–75, 177, 180–81
Sarkozy, Nicolas, 35, 136–37, 151, 152
Sato Eisaku, 225
scarcity principle in cultural memory, 106
Schlögel, Karl, 252
Schmidt, Helmut, 136
Schneersohn, Isaac, 148
schoolbooks. *See* textbooks and schoolbooks
Schröder, Gerhard, 136
Schuman, Maurice, 37
Schuman, Robert, 135
See Under: Love (Grossman), 200–201
Selden, Mark, 184n33
Senkaku/Diaoyu Islands, 3, 75, 99
Senyavsky, Aleksandr, 247
Senyavsky, Yelena, 247
Seraphim, Franziska, 47
Sereda, Viktoria, 238
Service du travail obligatoire (STO), 139, 145
sex slavery. *See* "comfort women" and sex slavery
shame and shaming: action tendencies and, 261–62; backdoor shaming, 259–60, 266–75; defined, 259; guilt vs., 40–41, 259, 263; norms against, 265–66; perception of, 264–65; pridefulness vs., 274; as social emotion, 263. *See also* guilt; Lithuanian-Jewish discourse and emotional dynamics
Sharet, Moshe, 195
Shazar, Zalman, 199
Sherman, William Tecumseh, 17
Shimov, Yaroslav, 241
Shintoism, 64
Shoah. *See* Holocaust
Shoah (film), 149, 187
Shoahisering (Shoahization), 110–11
Sinocentrism, 212, 215–16, 218, 228–29
Sjahrir, Sutan, 115, 125
Slamet, Mas, 123
"slave mentality" (*slavengeest* or *jiwa budak*), 122
Sneider, Daniel, 182
Snyder, Timothy, 15–16, 243, 271–72
Sobibor death camp, 109
Social Democratic Party (Germany), 88–89, 93
Social Democrats (Austria), 88
Society for Creating New Textbooks (Atarashii Kyokasho Tsukurukai), 164
Soewardi Soerjaningrat, 126
The Sorrow and the Pity (film), 142, 146–47
South Korea (Republic of Korea): Chinese criticism of, 224–25; collaboration and, 39; "colonial modernization" debate, 62–63; comfort women issue and, 99; democratization of, 61; Dokdo/Takeshima Islands and, 4, 99, 175, 177, 228; elite regime legitimacy concerns, 213–14; Independence Hall of Korea, 60–61; Japan, relations with, 96; joint history projects, 168, 170; normalization of relations, 88, 157, 175–76; progressive vs. conservative narratives, 49, 60–62; public opinion in, 164; Supreme Court of, 167; Truth and Reconciliation Commission, 49. *See also* national identity narratives and historical memory in East Asia; reconciliation in East Asia
Soviet Union (USSR): anti-Semitism in, 34; Chinese narratives on, 222, 226, 229–30; Hitler's invasion of, 28; Japan, declaration of war on, 74; Jewish Communists in, 32;

Index

Korean War and, 223; Kurile Islands and, 175; "liberation" vs. "occupation" in Eastern Europe, 240–43; Lithuania and, 258, 270–71; "national question" in, 236–37; Nazism-Stalinism comparison and, 242–45; postwar negotiations on Germany and, 36–37. *See also* Eastern and Central Europe; Russia; Stalin, Joseph

SS (*Schutzstaffel*), 15, 89, 270

Stahlecker, Franz, 281n40

Stalin, Joseph: anti-Semitism and, 34; Catherine the Great compared to, 247; China on, 222; extermination policies, 187; Hitler, broken treaty with, 24; Hitler-Stalin equivalence thesis, 241, 243; Jewish Communists and, 32; as nationalist hero again, 9; postwar negotiations and, 36–37; in Russian public opinion, 251; Yalta and, 243–44

Stauffenberg, Claus von, 147

Stern, Fritz, 266

Stikker, Dirk, 116

strategic context, 270–71

Sukarno, 105–6, 115–17, 122–30

T

Taiwan, 59, 225–26

Takeshima/Dokdo Islands, 4, 99, 175, 177, 228

Tel Aviv, 203

textbooks and schoolbooks: Austrian, 95; Chinese, 56–58; Eastern European, 237–38; French, 38; Japanese, 47, 54, 58, 69, 92, 98, 164, 182n2; Japanese and German, compared, 8–9, 20, 21–22; jointly written, 136, 167–69, 170, 214, 227–28; Korean, 61; Russian, 254n16, 256n67; Yugoslav, 27

Thailand, 38

Thorez, Maurice, 151

Tito, 26–27

Tojo Hideki, 64

Tokugawa Japan, 217–18

Tokyo War Crimes Tribunal, 67, 74, 83–85, 172, 178–79, 185nn53–54

Tomb of the Unknown Jewish Martyr (Tombeau du martyr juif inconnu), 148

Tomita Tomohiko, 65

totalitarianism, Eastern European narratives on, 242, 243

Touvier, Paul, 138, 143–44

"transnational" or "transcultural" history, 253

Transylvania, 30

trials. *See* war crimes and trials

Turkey, 17, 19

"Twenty-One Demands" on China (1915), 169, 183n22

U

Uchovsky, Gal, 203

Ukraine, 235–36

United Kingdom (Britain), 3, 193–94

United Nations (UN) Security Council, 116, 121, 126

United States: acknowledgment of responsibility by, 172, 178–80; Chinese narratives on, 218; East Asian litigation in, 166–67; East Asian reconciliation and, 176–81; Indonesia and, 118; Japan, occupation of, 47–48, 68, 73; Japanese American internment by, 184n33; Japanese civilians killed by, 172; Jewish American and Asian American communities, 185n62; Lithuania and, 267–68; Philippine-American War, 16–17. *See also* Cold War; Hiroshima and Nagasaki atomic bombs

V

Valdai Discussion Club, 256n60

Vallat, Xavier, 149

van der Heijden, Chris, 110–11

van Maurik, Justuk, 131n8

van Randwijk, Henk, 126

van Vollenhoven, Cornelis, 133n59

Venclova, Tomas, 279n3

Vergès, Jacques, 141

Vichy France (Paxton), 142–43. *See also* France, Vichy regime in

Vietnamese Communist Party, 18–19

Vietnam War, 17, 18–19

Vives, Juan Luis, 279n10

Vonnegut, Kurt, 280n18

Vos, Marijke, 114

Vranitzsky, Franz, 91

W

Waffen SS, 89, 270

The Wages of Guilt (Buruma), 22, 111

Wagner, Richard, 196
Wajda, Andrzej, 249
Waldheim, Kurt, 33–34, 90–91
Wałęsa, Lech, 32
Walk on Water (film), 203
war: civilian deaths in, 15–17; as "glorious" in Japan's Yushukan museum, 66–67; justification of, 19
war crimes and trials: delay of, 109; Eichmann trial, 186, 192, 197–98, 205; genocide vs., 18; German juridical system and Nazis, 200; Japanese enshrinement of war criminals, 64–65; Nuremberg trials, 83–85; Papon trial, 149–50; Tokyo War Crimes Tribunal, 67, 74, 83–85, 172, 178–79, 185nn53–54; victims redefined in Hayden Bill (CA), 167
Watanabe, Tsuneo, 73–74
Watts, Larry, 31
Weisel, Elie, 30, 31
Weizsäcker, Richard von, 90
Western Europe. *See* European Union (EU); *specific countries*
Western imperialism, narratives on, 219–20, 230
West Germany. *See* Germany
Wieviorka, Olivier, 141
Wilders, Geert, 130, 134n102, 134n109
World War II. *See specific places and topics, such as* French Resistance

X
xenophobia, 130

Y
Yad Vashem, 7, 22, 52, 112
Yakovenko, Natalya, 238
Yalta order, 243–44
Yamazaki, Jane W., 102n4
Yasukuni Shrine: about, 63–65; political leaders' visits to, 58, 65, 92, 98, 163–64; war criminals enshrined at, 64–65, 74, 86
Yehoshua, A. B., 203
the Yishuv, 193–94
Yomiuri Shimbun research project, 73–74
Yonnet, Paul, 151
Yoshida Shigeru, 225
Yugoslavia, 26–27
Yushukan war museum, 65–67, 68, 172–73

Z
Zhu Cheng Shan, 52, 53, 54
Zubov, Andrei, 256n67
Zwaan, Tjeerd de, 13
Zykon B, 188

www.ingramcontent.com/pod-product-compliance
Lightning Source LLC
Chambersburg PA
CBHW030521230426
43665CB00010B/707